Photographers' Guide to Web Publishing

Photographers' Guide to
Web Publishing

Charles Saunders

photographers'
pip
institute press

First published 2004 by
Photographers' Institute Press,
166 High Street, Lewes, East Sussex BN7 1XU

ISBN 1 86108 352 1
A catalogue record of this book is available from the British Library.

Publisher: Paul Richardson
Art Director: Ian Smith
Production Manager: Stuart Poole
Managing Editor: Gerrie Purcell
Commissioning Editor: April McCroskie
Editor: James Evans

Cover and book design: Francis & Partners
Typeface: RotisSemiSans

Colour origination: Icon Reproduction
Printed and bound: Kyodo Printing Co

For Helen, Amy and Tom

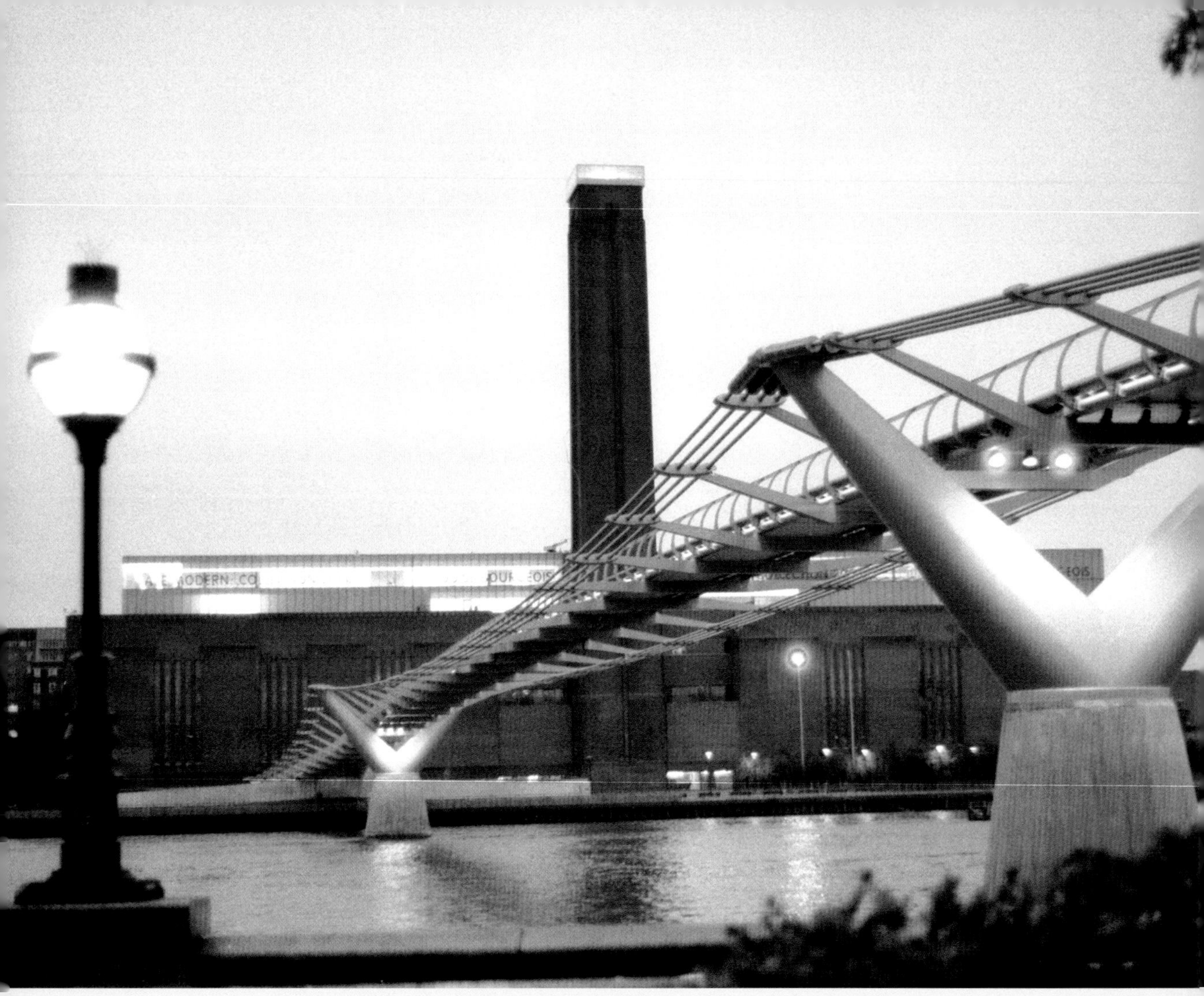

Contents

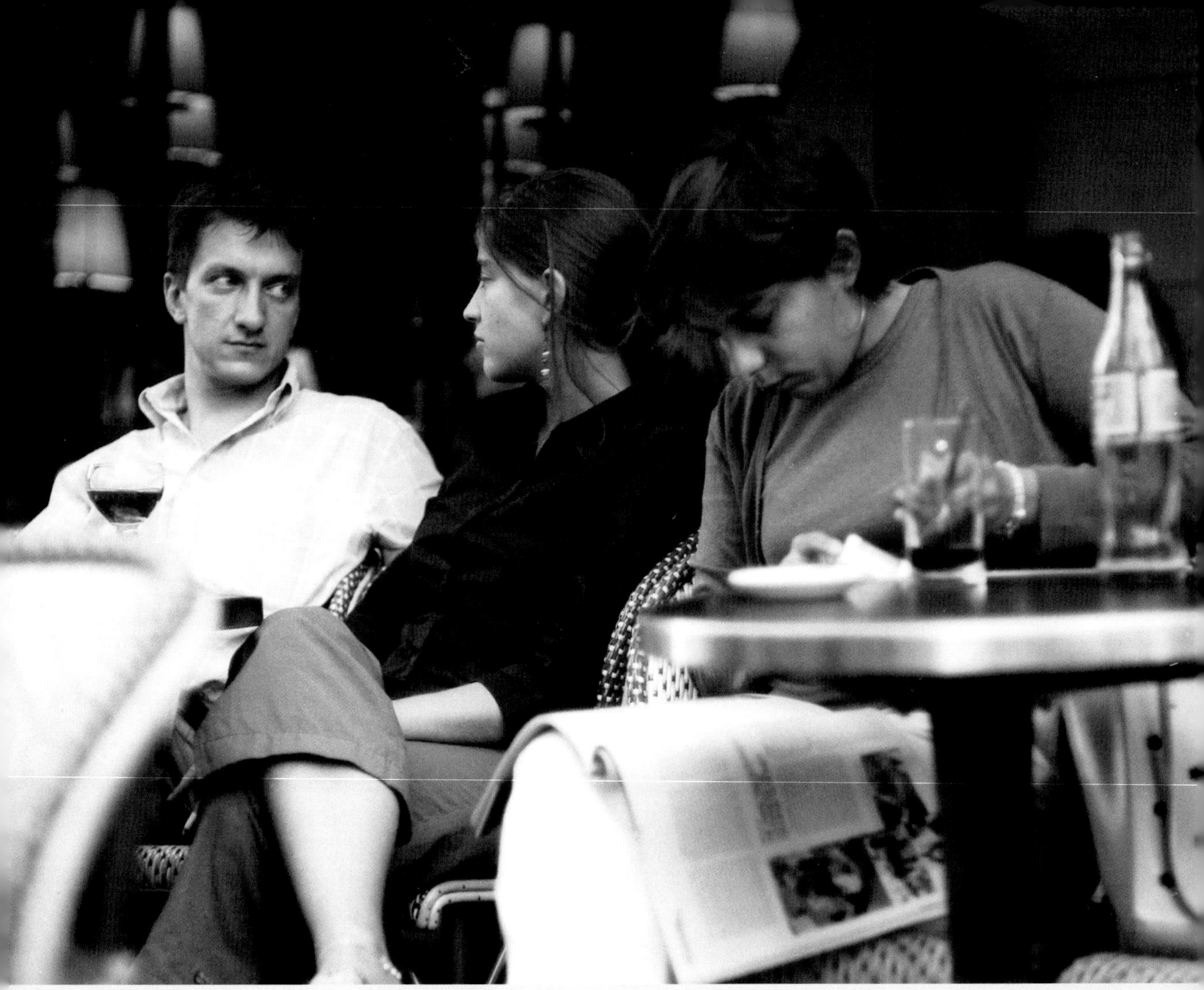

Introduction to Web Publishing

All the world is a gallery

I don't know many photographers who like to hide their work away. Even if they show it only to friends and family (who can normally be relied upon for largely uncritical comments) there still remains a great desire to display their photographic endeavours to a wider public.

Within a few days of publishing my first photographic website dedicated to black-and-white photography, I started receiving comments from around the world. I was hooked. The idea that my images could be developed and printed in a converted garage in the South of England one day, and viewed in New England the next, astonished me. At around the same time, I was invited to join my local photographic society. Don't get me wrong – I love talking about photography while sharing a beer and discussing 'the one that got away', but my interests are fairly eccentric. Using 30-year-old medium-format rangefinder cameras for monochrome photojournalism simply doesn't have mass appeal, especially at the club's highlight of the year, a small display in the town-centre library. Oh, and they wanted money as well. So instead I found myself favouring the 'virtual world' where I could find kindred spirits, and it wasn't long before I was a photographic web-publishing addict. I was soon receiving constructive reviews from expert photographers around the globe and a wealth of ideas for new photographic projects. I saw stunning examples of other photographers' work that I would otherwise never have seen, and I gained tremendous technical support on the eclectic range of cameras I liked to use. These are just some of the benefits of being part of an online community.

As I soon discovered, it is remarkably easy to build a good photographic website; but it is even easier to build a bad one. Surf the Internet for a few hours and you'll soon notice a huge disparity in the quality of different photographic sites.

The purpose of this book is to help you think about the creative process behind web design and to give you specific examples that you might like to apply to your own site. There are plenty of books on the market that can teach you how to write the program code to create a website. Similarly, you can buy any number of books on good web design. However, there are fewer books available that discuss good web design, give solid examples in plain English for the non-technical reader, and do so in the context of photographic web publishing. This is the rationale behind this book. At a later date the reader may elect to study more technical texts, but my hope is that the material contained here will make that particular experience a little less painful.

Assuming this is your first foray into creating a website, your expectations of what you might like to build should change after reading the first half of the book – at least that's the idea.
The book is divided into two main parts. Part One is about understanding the Internet's capabilities and, importantly, its limitations. Good designs recognize and overcome these restrictions, and though it is indeed theory, after reading this section you should have a much better appreciation of how your site might be engineered to be both effective and efficient. As in all aspects of design, there is no 'right way', and, inevitably, some of the content boils down to personal belief. Nevertheless, I have attempted present many opinions in as balanced a manner as possible.

Part Two, on the other hand, is about rolling up your sleeves and writing the code necessary to create and publish a simple photographic website. There's less room for debate; it either works or it doesn't. The temptation for most people must surely be to flick ahead to

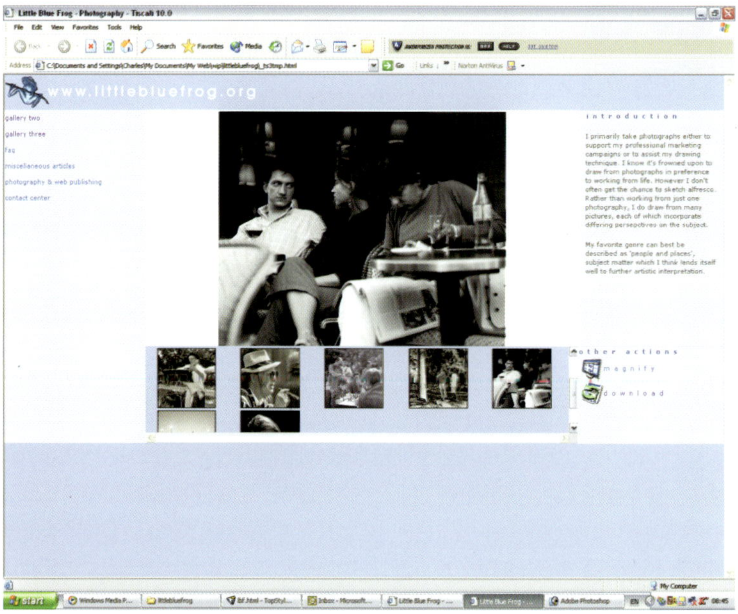

[0.1] Various considerations must be taken into account when creating clean website design

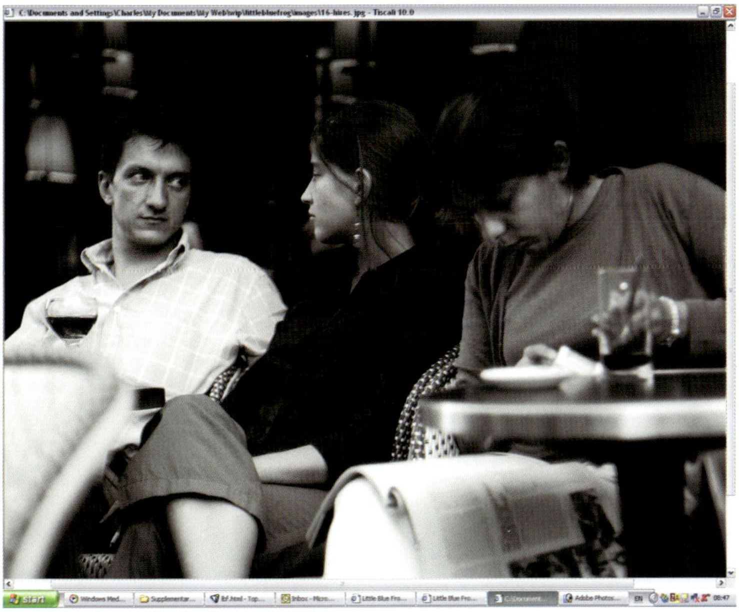

[0.2] Efficient picture compression is an important part of successful web publishing (see page 102)

Part Two and start tinkering with your images and favoured web-authoring tool. I put myself into this category, and so my suggestion is that if you feel you really must start coding, do so using the samples provided and resist the temptation to upload anything to the web until you have read Part One.

If all this 'focus on design' sounds a little academic, let me illustrate my point with an example. My father recently gave me a vintage German rangefinder camera – why can't all fathers be like that I hear you say. Naturally, I wanted to get more information, perhaps even an instruction book on this famously classic camera. Which was the first site to surf? The obvious choice had to be the manufacturer's own site, or so you might think. And yet, it seemed as if the manufacturer was in denial that this historic camera ever existed and was still used today by thousands of camera aficionados. At the time I found nothing other than a brief sentence in the manufacturer's product history. My previously high expectations for an online instruction manual, user club, forum and gallery were sorely disappointed. In stark contrast, I discovered www.photo.net. Suffice to say that there was more information there than I could read in a week of surfing. The manufacturer's site became nothing more than a one-hit wonder, yet photo.net got bookmarked.

Basic computer skills

- Power up a computer and log on.
- Open documents, understand the difference between files and directories, and be comfortable with manipulating both (e.g. create, edit and delete).
- Read and send emails.
- Surf the web and find a website of any given name (or 'URL').

Basic equipment requirements

With regards to what you need from an equipment perspective, there are some important prerequisites:

- A computer, screen, keyboard, mouse and modem.
- An Internet browser.
- An HTML editor, although Notepad or any similar basic text-editing tools are more than sufficient and are normally included as part of the computer's operating system.
- Image-editing software.
- A digital camera, or a conventional camera plus an image capture device such as a film scanner (scanning is not entirely necessary if you elect for this to be done at the development stage).
- An Internet connection.

A website's success is generally assessed by the amount of traffic a site generates, and it may seem like this manufacturer was missing out on a great opportunity to take advantage of their web presence. However, many organizations have not yet grasped that good websites need to be so much more than online brochures or retail outlets.

This book also attempts to help you appreciate the dynamics of website creation and to think in terms that will have users coming back to your site time and again. You never know – you might also break even in the process.

What do you need to have and know?

This is a book for photographers who are not programmers by nature. It is not a deeply technical book, though tasks considered by some to be technical, such as writing code, are introduced steadily. That said, there are some basic computing skills that the reader should already possess before they embark on this journey (as shown top left). If any of these prerequisites seem complicated, I urge you to read one of the many books on personal computing.

An Internet connection is actually optional insofar as you can build your website locally on your computer. No one else can see it of course, but there is nothing stopping you from gleaning much of the theory of this book and applying it, only to publish your site at a much later date. Suggestions for web hosting are discussed in Part One (see page 22).

As you can see, these are fairly straightforward prerequisites and, perhaps surprisingly, there is no great need for sophisticated and expensive software. If you don't already have a particular software component and are unsure where to look, see the online reference guide at www.photowebpublish.com. However, I should emphasize that I do not endorse any particular software or hardware product and I am in no way affiliated to any manufacturer of these items.

I look forward to discovering your own sites online soon, and please email me with the results of your labours.

Charles Saunders
Web: www.photowebpublish.com
Email: charles@photowebpublish.com

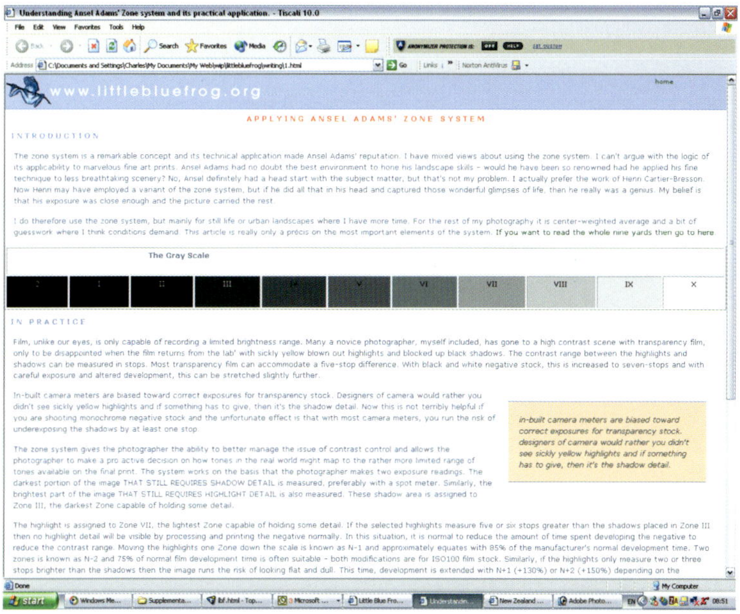

[0.3] Create effective typographic styles and layouts for your own site (see page 42)

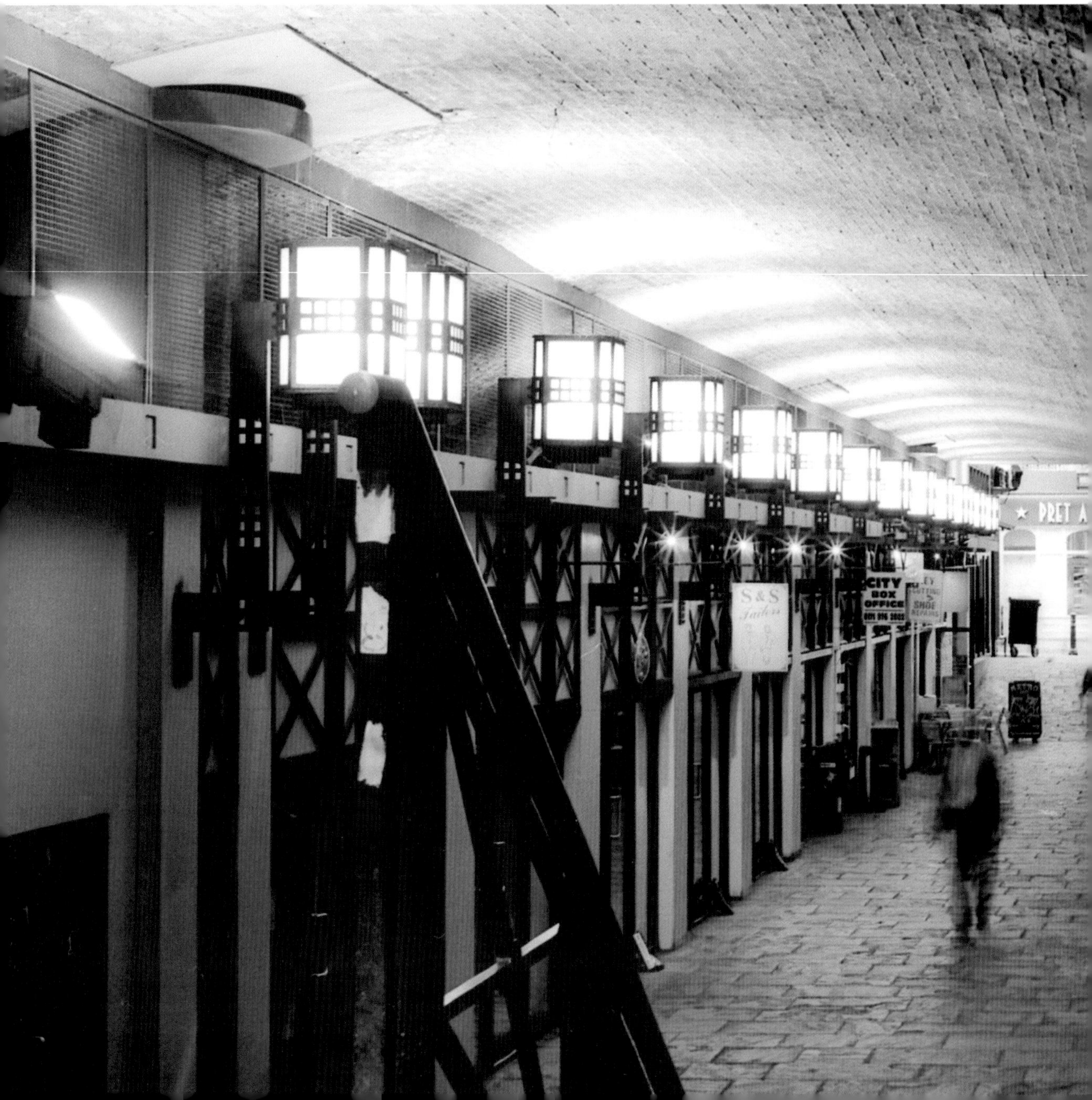
S&S
Tailors
CITY
BOX
OFFICE
SHOE
PRET A

Part One

Getting the most from the medium

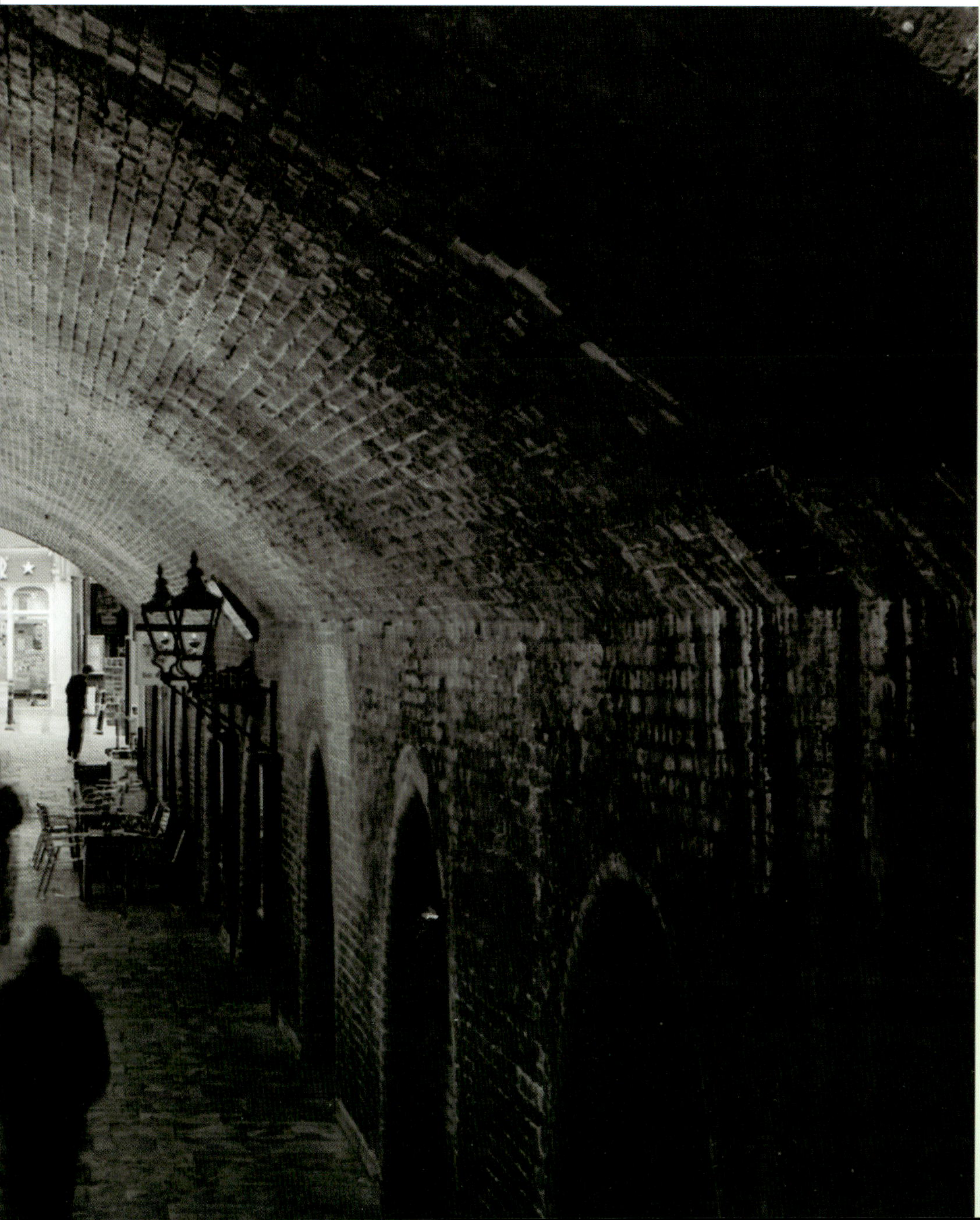

1 How the Internet Functions

The Internet is nothing more than a series of interconnected computers that know how to find each other and can provide information to each other in a format that all can understand. It grew out of a military information and intelligence project called ARPANET, which was created for the US Department of Defense in the 1960s. Originally conceived as a tool for the Cold War, it has since become the most accessible and comprehensive library of information that civilization as ever known. Despite its military origins, the scientific community was soon using the network to share research information and, more importantly, send emails to one another. It was only later, in 1974, that the term Internet was first coined.

During the early 1980s, two eminent technologists, Bob Kahn and Vint Cerf, led a team of programmers to build TCP/IP: the common language of Internet computers. That was when things really began to take off, and it wasn't long before connections to the Internet began to grow at an exponential rate.

Worldwide Internet Population 2002:	580 million
Projection for 2004:	709.1 million

Nation	Population	Internet Users	ISPs
Australia	19.5 million	10.63 million	571
Canada	31.9 million	16.84 million	760
United Kingdom	59.8 million	34.3 million	<400
United States	280.5 million	165.7 million	7,000

Source: http://cyberatlas.internet.com/

The technical subculture loves 'cool' terminology. The term 'network' quickly reached the point at which it was considered too passé for such cutting-edge work, and it was not long before the phrase 'World Wide Web' (www), or simply 'web', was coined to describe the network of communication channels that exist between the computers.

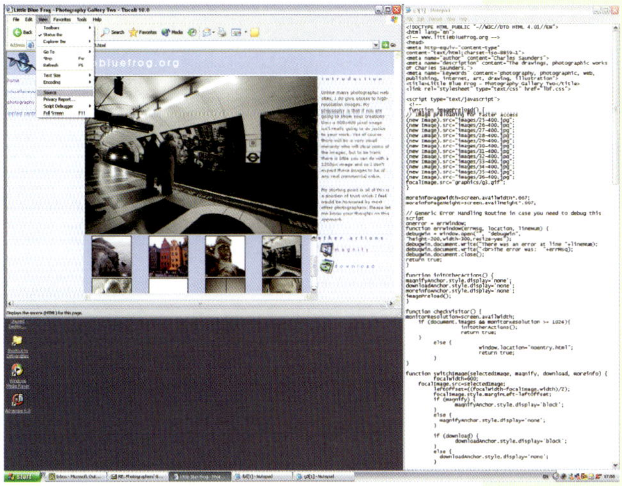

[1.1] The view/source menu option on most browsers allows you see how the web page has been created

The World Wide Web is a collection of pages of information stored on a multitude of computers around the globe, and because it was designed to withstand a nuclear strike, the web can send data across the network by a number of different routes. This means that if one communication route becomes blocked or busy, an alternative route is found. Amazingly, all of these pages of information are individually identifiable by a unique reference. Also, these pages may cross-reference each other by means of links, thereby helping the reader to move effortlessly from one document to another. The Internet acts as the mechanism by which information can be exchanged from an information provider (the server computer) to an information consumer (the client computer). Using the address mechanisms mentioned above, pages of information are 'served' to clients as they request them. The pages are written is a standard format called HyperText Mark-up Language (HTML) that can be read and interpreted by software programs collectively known as Internet browsers. Of course, HTML pages are not the only file types that can be exchanged. Literally any digital file may be moved throughout the Internet, and we are now seeing new media types such as video and sound to complement the visual experience of graphics and images. However, HTML acts as the foundation that brings these disparate data sources together in a unified document.

1

Shortcut

Domain Name System (DNS)

Get a name for yourself

Before you can do anything on the Internet, you need an address. The Internet Protocol (the IP of TCP/IP) uses this address to deliver email and other data from one computer to another. IP addresses are really a series of four numbers separated by periods (for example, 207.171.166.19).

Domain Name System (DNS)

How many phone numbers can you remember by heart? Not many, I suspect; and it's even harder if the numbers change from time to time. It's far easier to remember names, so Sun Microsystems developed a textual representation of numeric IP addresses, called the Domain Name System (DNS). This is why websites have the names with which we are so familiar today.

The DNS establishes groups of computers on the Internet. These groupings are further organized into hierarchies. Using letters and words in place of numbers, the DNS system gives each computer on the Internet an address. Reading from right to left, the domain names reflect their hierarchical structure and become more and more specific. Take for example the email address cinjun.sanders@ntlworld.com .com signifies a grouping of commercial organizations of which my telecommunications company NTL (who use ntlworld to describe their domain) is but one. Within ntlworld you'll find the user Cinjun Sanders.

Thousands of powerful computers are linked on the Internet and provide the invaluable service of not only understanding the hierarchy of domains, but also the ability to 'resolve' the names into the IP numeric addresses. This ensures that telecommunications equipment can route your information request to the correct computer on the network. The hardest part about getting your own domain name is choosing one that hasn't already been registered by someone else. The registration process itself is remarkably simple. There are hundreds of companies who want to sell you domain names that you then attach to your website. Having an enormous ego, I went to one of these companies and discovered that www.charlessaunders.net was available. Within hours, I had bought the domain and was able to point it to a location on the web where I had some space.

At its simplest, a remote machine 'hosts' the files you create in a directory, much like your own computer. Your domain name points to where that directory is physically located on the network. When a user types your domain name into their browser, the browser sends a

Creating an entry point

When you create a website, it is common to call your first page index.html. This will automatically be the default entry point into your site.

Shortcut

Creating an entry point

request for the information to the remote computer. In the absence of any specific file name, your computer receives a file called 'index', which is then displayed by your browser.

To publish your site, you merely copy the files from your computer to the remote computer using a process called FTP (File Transfer Protocol). The process looks just the same as copying files from one directory to another on your own computer. The only difference is that to access the remote computer, you have to provide your username and password.

Website creation

At the risk of repeating myself in Chapter 2 (see page 26), the most important step in the process of creating a website is the design. An old army saying states that 'time spent in reconnaissance is never wasted', and this is equally true in the field of web publishing. Reconnaissance and planning before you start writing a single line of HTML will make an enormous difference to the effectiveness of your site. Human nature being what it is, you want to be cutting code, uploading images and telling search engines about your site – it feels like your making progress. However, design decisions that you make in haste are difficult to change radically at a later stage, and it is wiser to plan carefully beforehand. Based on bitter experience, there are two steps that I would recommend before building your site. First, surf the net. Look at as many photographic sites as possible and see how they work. Make a note of what you admire and similarly what you hate. Print off those pages, mark them up with your impressions and put them in a design file. The next step involves no computer at all. Instead, with only a pen and paper, start making notes on the following (see overleaf).

Setting up a website

At this point I should try to dispel a few myths about setting up a website. If you thought it was a complex and arcane task that could only be undertaken by the most technically adept, prepare to be surprised. If you have ever copied files from one directory on your computer to another, there is no more mystery. The process is exactly like that, except in the website example the directory you are copying to is on another machine.

Shortcut

Setting up a website

Planning website content

- Who is this website intended for? List the age, sex, language, culture, interests, and likely attitudes to technology of your target audience.
- Pretend you are a visitor. Ask yourself the question, what do I want to get from this site?
- Consider how often you expect the content to change on the site and whether or not you expect your visitors to return on a regular basis. Ask yourself why would they do so.
- Consider the extent to which you expect or want your visitors to participate on the site.

All visitors and, importantly, all browsers are not created equal. Attitudes to technology are going to dictate whether you will include more recent browser innovations. For example, a 'non-corporate younger audience' is statistically more likely to have the latest browser versions, and you could probably use cutting-edge technology such as JavaScript, Java, Frames, Shockwave and Flash in your design.

Similarly, a website dedicated to fashion photography and viewed by corporate buyers is going to have focus on high-quality images with accurate colour rendition. These users might reasonably be expected to have a faster than average connection to the web and will therefore be less concerned about file download times.

Sites that succeed are often not the prettiest or the ones with the best graphics. Many sites suffer from what I call the online corporate-brochure fixation. I am sure you know what I mean. These sites have lots of fancy graphics, multimedia animation and irritatingly high download times.

Great sites have one thing in common: excellent content that changes on a regular basis. They also have a sense of community in that visitors can contribute content to the core site. Let me build on the camera manufacturer example I introduced earlier. If I had been asked to design the site, opposite are my ideas to maximize traffic.

To be fair, some camera sites are moving in this direction. Yet many, because of the influence of their design agencies, are still locked into the graphic-bound online-brochure mentality.

For your site to be successful you should include 'community interaction', which in itself is a great content provider. You might write articles on technique, put other people's images on your site, host discussions, and offer advice and experience on equipment. If you are a professional photographer looking for wedding business, don't just put up your portfolio. You might try offering tips to the novice photographer on how they might also get the best from the big day, including film options, development choices, tips on composition and style, and so on. You're more likely to get the business if you do.

An ideal camera-manufacturer website

- Two versions of the site to accommodate those photographers who may not have upgraded their browsers to the latest version.
- Online documentation for every camera manual manufactured by the company.
- A bulletin board for camera users to post questions, moderated by manufacturer staff.
- A gallery of images from professional users with links back to their sites.
- A gallery of images from non-professional users (these pictures could be rated by the community and the highest-rated pictures each week would win a prize).
- The ability to act as a stock library and sell user-submitted images (while taking a small percentage).
- Brochures on the latest camera models with online buying facilities that don't undercut existing distribution mechanisms.
- Articles on photographic techniques covering every conceivable genre.
- Information on after-sale service, especially for older models.
- Serial numbers of stolen cameras, submitted by the users.
- The ability for users to tell the manufacturer what correspondence they would like to receive and how often.
- Online film-development facilities.

1

Hosting a website

To host a website you need two things: an Internet Service Provider (ISP), and a provider of web-hosting services. Many ISPs offer hosting services as part of their proposition – a sort of two-for-one deal. However, you can buy these functions separately. The ISP provides you with access to the Internet and in effect helps you get connected and surfing. A web-hosting company provides the web space and infrastructure for you to run your newly created site.

With regard to ISP choice, there are a number of payment models. You can choose pay-as-you-go, off-peak subscription, unmetered subscription and broadband. Pay-as-you-go is a great service when you are just getting accustomed to using the web, especially if you are only surfing for just a few hours a month. As the name suggests, you just have to pay for your minutes online, usually at local telephone-call rates. If you do find that the phone bill is becoming a little alarming, you could try off-peak subscription. Here you pay a flat fee to get free off-peak calls. Telecommunication companies have huge spare capacity during the evenings and weekends when the majority of businesses are closed, so it makes sense to offer this at a flat rate to Internet surfers, many of whom will be accessing

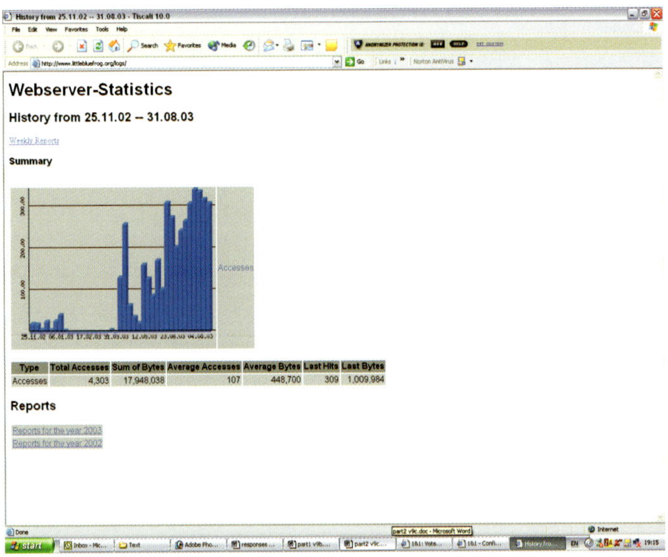

[1.2] Your ISP should offer web server usage statistics

the web during these times. Of course, if you anticipate heavy Internet access during peak times as well, you could take the next step and go for an unmetered subscription. The last and fastest way to connect to the Internet is via broadband. Rather than having to wait for your modem to dial up a connection to the Internet, with a broadband connection you are online permanently and have access to much-higher speeds of connection. Broadband offers instant gratification when surfing the most content-laden sites, but it wouldn't be my first choice for listening to music or watching video. Televisions and radios still have little to fear, despite the marketing hype.

Choosing an ISP

It's impossible to suggest an ISP. It all depends on your budget and requirements. The best advice I can offer is to buy an Internet magazine from your local newsagent. Much like wedding magazines that always seem to provide 'to-do' lists for the newly engaged, Internet magazines nearly always run league tables of ISPs showing how they rank. They use comparators such as connection costs, numbers of email accounts and free web-space volumes, as well as judging how fast and reliable these ISPs are at moving data.

Shortcut

Choosing an ISP

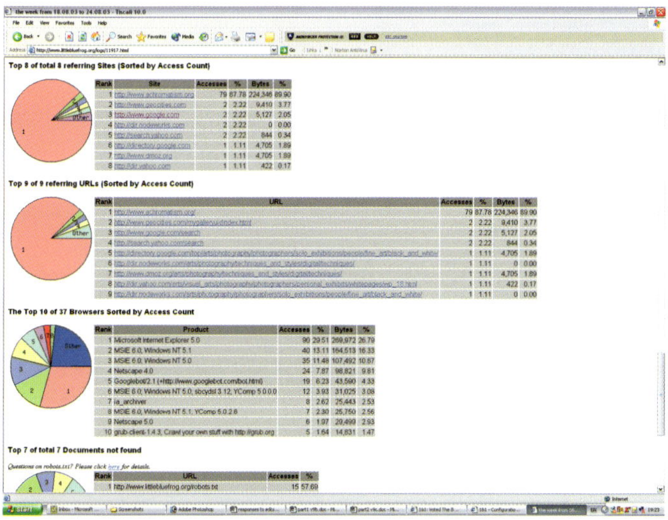

[1.3] Usage statistics can reveal a wealth of information about who is looking at your site

1

Nearly all ISPs offer free web space of some form and it is not a bad idea to use this space, even if it is only a test bed for you to become acquainted with the technology. The ISP makes very little revenue from the free web space, so you shouldn't expect too much in the way of dedicated customer service, sophisticated user tracking facilities or high data performance. Again, Internet magazines run league tables on hosting companies and it's fair to say that if you are a commercial business, in need of high-bandwidth serving capabilities, you probably should forego free web space and buy into a premium service.

Shortcut

Free web space

Free web space

If you are a commercial photography operation it is highly unlikely that the free web space will be suitable for your business. Firstly, the amounts available are normally quite small (10–50MB), and you would be surprised how quickly you can exhaust this limitation. Secondly, the free space rarely comes with any programming capability, so running a bulletin board, guest book or just a simple feedback form is always going to require some form of compromise.

In addition to the ISPs, you can also get free web space from companies who will host your site in return for placing banner advertisements around it. This was how I first got started. I registered with one of these companies and soon began building my first website with the host's own online tools. No knowledge of HTML was required and I was surprised by how quickly everything was up and running. The downsides were that I ended up with a remarkably long URL for the site, and, of course, I had to put up with a constant stream of peripheral advertising selling everything from impotency pills to school reunions. I fixed the problem unwittingly by buying a shorter domain name, which I then attached to the free web space. The domain provider included a function called a URL gripper that meant regardless of where I went on the site, the new URL would stay in the browser window. It seemed to kill the advertising as well as an added benefit.

The website ran for several months with this hosting provider and became quite popular due to the fact that I was filling it with numerous articles on monochrome photography. Then, in 2001, the majority of these free web-hosting companies realized that the advertising-based revenue model wasn't working for them, and they decided to push premium hosting services instead.

They also decided to switch off temporarily any sites that exceeded a certain number of hits and downloads in any given period. The site owner would be told that their site was suspended for an hour or so because excessive demand had pushed them over their allotted bandwidth allowance. The change in service made me re-evaluate hosting packages and I eventually moved my site to a different, premium provider.

You can still sign up for these free hosting companies, and the advertising-based revenue model still exists. It seems ironic that a model based on advertising would switch off sites that are getting too many views, but it does highlight an important consideration: web hosting is never entirely free. You pay for it somehow either in cheap services, telecommunication costs or intrusive advertising. Equally, there are costs for the hosting company, and they do have a right to expect some form of recompense. If you want a good-quality service, you are better off paying for it up front.

There are so many web-hosting companies, choosing one can seem like a bewildering decision. In general, I would make a shortlist of vendors based on an up-to-date assessment of the factors listed in the following panel.

Assessing web-hosting companies

- How do they rank in the magazine league tables?
- How much space is available, how much traffic is allowed and for how much?
- Are facilities such as email accounts and virus scanning included?
- What support is available? Can you speak to a real person without having to call a premium-rate line?
- What site statistics will they give you to track usage and help you tune your site to the community of users?
- What domain-name support is included in the price?
- What security features are included, such as firewalls and secure socket layers for e-commerce transactions?
- What server-side programming facilities are available?

Don't worry if you don't fully understand what some of these terms mean; you will by the end of this book.

You also want to get some idea of the sophistication of their data centre. If it's any good they will almost certainly boast about it. If your site is being hosted from a chicken shack in the middle of Afghanistan, they probably won't. Last but not least, it is not a bad idea to ask your photographic peer group what they use. Personal experience is nearly always more reliable than marketing material.

2 Website Planning and General Design Principles

Technical design considerations

It's important to remember that very few users 'surf' into your site as their first-ever Internet experience. The chances are much higher that users will have had some prior experience with well-known retail sites such as Amazon or search engines like Yahoo. It follows that by the time your site is reached, users will have accumulated a mental image of how good sites should look and operate, based on this prior experience.

Shortcut

Simplifying user interaction

Simplifying user interaction

Successful sites do exhibit some common traits and you ignore these at your peril. You probably have about ten seconds to sell your site to the user, and at the same time give them enough visual clues about how it operates. If you start to invent new ways of interacting, it might all become 'too hard' and the user will simply move on. This docs not mean that all websites should look the same, any more than the layout of magazines do, but it does mean being aware of common methods of interaction and communication.

Download time

The first barrier the photographic web designer has to overcome is download time. Get this wrong and it is highly unlikely your site will be successful. I am often asked how long it should take to download a page. My rule of thumb has always been around ten seconds as a maximum, although you have to take into account likely modem speeds for your user community. For example, the penetration of high-speed Internet access is currently much higher in North America than elsewhere. If your site addresses a primarily North-American audience, you may decide that your web pages can hold more graphical content than a site designed for dial-up modem access at 56kbps.

I have to say, though, that this is a risky strategy and your site could still be damaged by slow download times aggravated by factors beyond your control, such as network congestion. It is therefore wise to concentrate on minimum download times at the expense of fancy graphics, and if you achieve sub-second download access for high-speed users with a cable modem or DSL connection, so much the better.

In Part Two, I will highlight some technical tricks that can help speed up download times, such as providing size options for images or pre-loading images in JavaScript. Suffice to say that you should keep graphical components to a minimum in order to save that bandwidth for the photographs you want to display.

Reducing download time

I tend to shun background images, complex graphical headers and icons merely because their inclusion is an unnecessary overhead and you can still achieve good, clean, elegant design without them. Conversely, there are plenty of sites that would be lost without a graphical component to spice them up, and for some of them careful graphical usage is important for branding purposes. You'll have to balance these considerations for your own website. It is possible to compress images to minimize download times (see page 102). This is another area where you should spend some time and effort to experiment and understand what works best for your circumstances.

Browser compatibility

As a web designer, one of the most bewildering and annoying facts is that you have little influence over how your site will look. Inevitably, you are going to be at the mercy of the software and hardware configuration of every single user. A page that looks great on your computer may look very different on many others. Browser version, size of screen, available fonts, colour capabilities – the list of permutations simply gets longer and it is a wonder that websites are viewed at all by large communities. There really are no hard-and-fast rules here, except know your community and track your usage statistics. These should be available from any good web-hosting service. As an example, take a look at www.thecounter.com/stats for a free way to see browser usage globally.

Shortcut

Reducing download time

The last time I checked my own photographic site, I unearthed the following browser statistics:

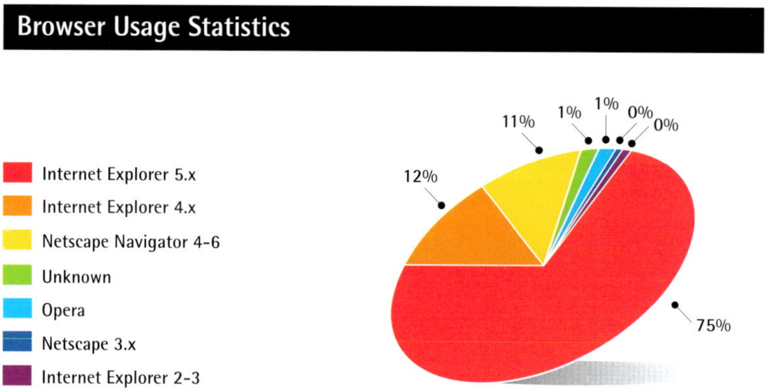

[2.1] Browser usage statistics

From this research I could infer that it is safe to include advanced browser functionality such as JavaScript, Style Sheets and Frames, topics that are addressed later in this book. It is also a fairly safe assumption that anyone with an interest in photography and owning a computer will have a medium- or high-resolution screen capable of displaying a full range of colours. My design technique is to play a risk-limitation strategy, whereby I apply a modest 'lowest common denominator' approach but use more advanced functionality if I think the usage statistics are better than 80%.

For example, I will use JavaScript because I think it can significantly add to the user experience and because the volume of browsers supporting this feature is in my 80% zone.

Other designers adopt differing perspectives. Some I know adhere to the latest standards and functionality on the basis that, because the pace of technological change is so fast, why build on legacy systems? Also, upgrades are free, so tell users to upgrade their browser. This does, however, ignore the fact that many corporate users may be unable to upgrade their browsers and most home users may not see the need to upgrade their browser – and all that it entails – at that precise moment. Yet another approach is to let the user choose which of your site 'experiences' they would like to enter. In effect, you then have something for everyone, although I would argue that it is hard enough to maintain the content for one site, let alone two or more.

Having painted a picture of Internet chaos, it seems only fair to make some solid recommendations to help you mitigate the problems of unknown viewing environments. These are not hard-and-fast rules, and you should feel at liberty to adapt your design to suit your own community.

Adhering to Internet standards and international conventions

As the name World Wide Web suggests, your web pages will be accessible from any Internet browser, anywhere in the world. For this to work, there have to be clearly defined standards for both HTML coding and the presentation of content. Though it is quite possible to create web pages that make no reference to the HTML standard that they have been written against or the alphabet used, it is good practice to define these parameters in your web pages. The issue of alphabet, or 'character sets' as they are known, may not seem wholly relevant to the majority of Western, English-speaking website designers. Yet for photographers who want to create web pages in Arabic, Chinese, Hebrew, French and so on, it is very important that you make this fact explicit for the Internet browser.

HTML standards

HTML has come a long way down a difficult path, and thanks to the World Wide Web Consortium (W3C) we now have standard specifications for this language. Even better news is that software vendors generally try to stick to the HTML standards, and this means that the code you write should work for the latest versions of all popular browsers. For an industry not well known for compatibility, this is a remarkable feat. At the time of press, the latest HTML standard is HTML 4.01 and the examples in the book are based on this standard. However, as a web designer, you should keep abreast of the latest standard developments and visiting the W3C website (www.w3.org) is a great place to start.

Shortcut

HTML standards

Over the next few years, we shall see greater use of XHTML 1.0. This standard is very similar to HTML 4.01, but it does have some important improvements, such as separating what a page says from how it says it. Another description for this function is separating content

2

from presentation. As an example, W3C would rather that you don't litter your code with the 'font tag' to tell the browser what fonts to use, but instead keep this instruction separate in a style sheet. We examine the benefits of this seemingly minor point in Part Two (see page 74). Though many modern development environments will automatically change your HTML 4.01 code to XHTML 1.0, if you follow the coding conventions in this book you will have little difficulty in producing pages that are readable by Internet browsers for some considerable time to come.

To complicate things further, there are three types of HTML 4.01, which can be thought of as different dialects. These exist to help with backward compatibility to older browsers – of which plenty are still in use. These are described by Document Type Definitions (DTD), a sort of dictionary of the language. These are Strict, Transitional and Frameset.

Shortcut
Strict DTD

Strict DTD

The HTML 4.01 Strict DTD excludes the presentation attributes and elements that W3C expects to phase out as support for style sheets matures, like the font tag. It is good practice to use this DTD for your web pages.

HTML 4.01 Transitional DTD lets you include presentation attributes and elements that W3C expects to phase out. You will often hear these attributes and elements referred to as being 'deprecated'. Examples include such things as <u></u> for underlining text, <menu></menu> for creating menus, and <center> which centres elements on a page. Don't worry if you don't understand what these strange things in brackets are, I am essentially saying that as far as the 'strict' variation of the language is concerned, these deprecated terms are not to be used any more. Using the transitional variation will still let you get away with it, which is important because there are still some browser manufacturers who have not fully implemented the improvements in the language to allow you to drop these deprecated items.

The last DTD is Frameset, which is identical to Transitional, except it also allows you to use the <frameset> element. HTML frames allow designers to subdivide browser windows into smaller sub-windows, each of which displays a different HTML page. As a concept they have an infamous reputation, but we'll try and have a more balanced view on their usage in Part Two (see page 69).

The document-type definition is only a single line of text that sits in the top of your HTML code. You won't even have to type this in as a sample blank page with the code examples can be found at www.photowebpublish.com. The examples in this book all comply with the Strict DTD, and I have avoided using deprecated elements and attributes.

Character sets

As I mentioned earlier, it is good practice to define the character set that the web page relies upon for accurate presentation. You also need to consider writing systems in which reading and writing from left to right is only one variation. I don't want to bog you down in too much detail because, as I said before, you can create a web page with no reference to these aspects and most browsers can default to the correct settings for Western, Latin-based writing. If you do plan to create a web page that utilizes different international characters and writing styles, you should refer to www.w3c.org/international, which contains a wealth of information on the topic.

For everyone else, you should just include a statement that specifies the character encoding and language. The character sets – remember these are definitions of the alphabets, ideographs and punctuation symbols – are defined

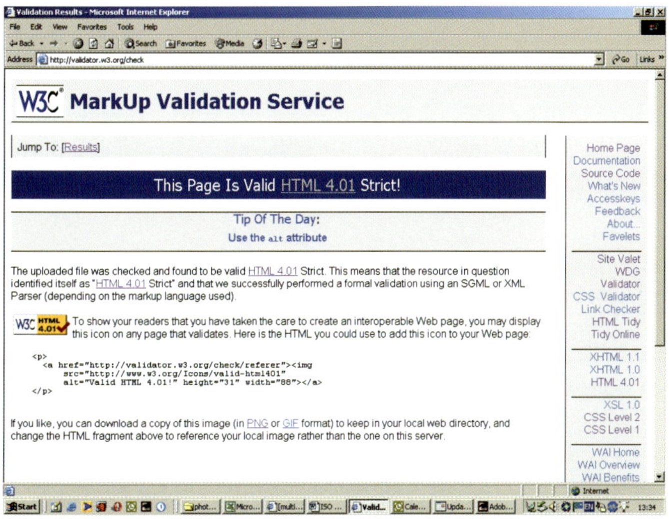

[2.2] The W3C HTML validation service is invaluable and very easy to use

by referring to an ISO standard. For example, 'charset=iso-8859-1' is used for Western languages, whereas 'charset=iso-8859-6' is used for Arabic.

Shortcut

Two-character language codes

Two-character language codes

Language is a little simpler with the use of a two-character code. For example, to specify the document's language as English you use the code 'en'. Other examples include Scots Gaelic (gd), Welsh (cy), German (de), Swahili (sw), Inuktitut (iu) and there are many more. Again, I have included both of these in the sample blank page and in my worked examples so you don't have to do anything other than include their definitions in your own pages.

If you do include DTD and character-set definitions in your HTML pages, you will be able to use the W3C HTML validating service. This checks your page for standards compliance and lets you know if there are any potential problems. This service is free and available at http://validator.w3.org/ (fig 2.2, previous page). If your pages pass the validation test, you may also use the relevant W3C logo on your page to show what a great web designer you are. The W3C standards logos are a great deal more helpful than the equivalent 'this page should be viewed in XYZ browser' statements that appear at the bottom of some pages and are ignored by all.

Common monitor resolutions

- 640x480
- 800x600
- 1024x768
- 1280x1024
- 1600x1200

Monitor resolution and page design

This issue provokes endless debate. Your computer screen creates images in a mosaic-like manner using tiny squares of colour called pixels. The word pixel is a contraction of the term 'picture element', which I think is a much clearer definition. The monitor resolution is the maximum number of pixels that can be displayed on the screen, normally expressed as a numeric value of width x height.

Currently, the majority of PC users operate with a monitor resolution of 800x600, and this is still the size most photographic web designers work to. This is despite the fact that an increasing number of monitors are capable of displaying 1024x768 or greater. If you are serious about computing and photography, you really ought to use 1024x800 as a minimum resolution. It makes the whole process a great deal more enjoyable and less like keyhole surgery. By the time this book is published, a greater percentage of photographic users will have upgraded their systems to the higher resolution, so it is worth considering whether you want your site to accommodate this change. A by-product of designing a photographic website for 800x600 is that the pictures on display will look physically smaller on screens with a higher monitor resolution, unless the screen itself is physically bigger. This can lessen the impact of the image, and you may elect to let the user view a version that at a higher resolution, thereby giving the chance for you to display your pictures in all their glory.

Monitor resolution is one consideration, but you have to be aware that your browser window uses up some of these pixels for itself. Scroll bars, navigation buttons and so on all take up valuable 'real estate' (as it is known), so you are left with much less working space for your web pages. Take the page width, for example. Assuming you are designing for an 800x600 PC, you actually have about 780 pixels to play with once scroll bars are taken into consideration. The figure is even less, about 750 pixels, if you are using a Mac. The situation is much the same with

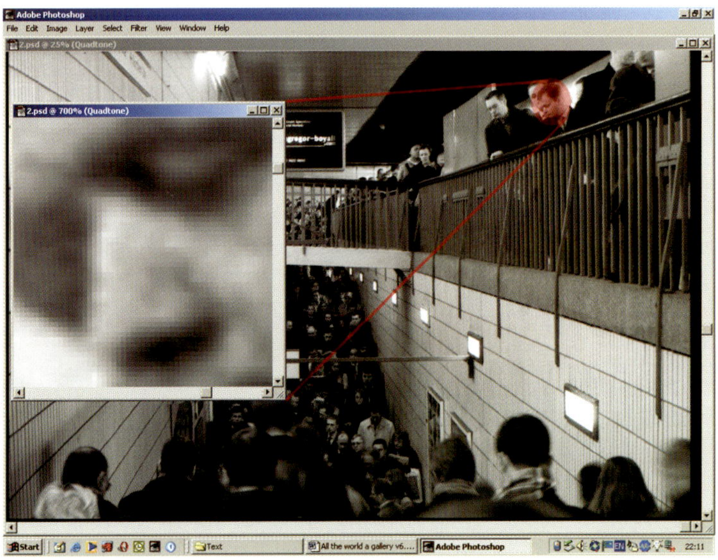

[2.3] Pixels, the building blocks of all digital images

2

Shortcut
Scrolling

page length except that you have even more space eroded because of the browser's buttons and menu-bar functionality. In the 800x600 PC example, you probably have around 420 pixels of working space before the user has to scroll down the page, making the upper portion of space on the page particularly important. Taking a term from newspaper design, this space is often referred to as 'above the fold' and has greater significance than the space immediately beneath that can only be reached by scrolling. Most websites I have seen do place content below the fold, but page length is limited to around two screens.

Scrolling

Users quickly get tired of scrolling and it is probably better to move extra content to supplementary pages rather than rely wholly on the scrolling mechanism. If you are going to place content below the fold, give the user a strong visual clue that content exists there. For example, a paragraph of text broken by the base of the browser.

Those of you who have visited www.photowebpublish.com will have realized that the site has been designed for users with a monitor resolution in excess of 800x600. I'm not being hypocritical here. My first responsibility

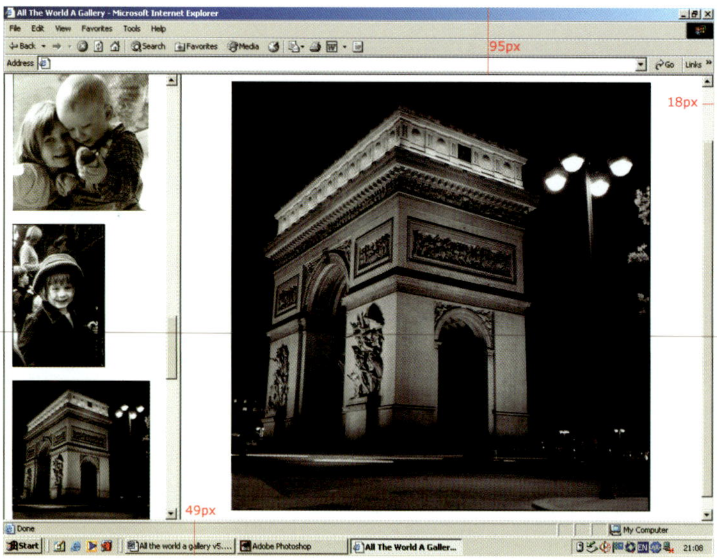

[2.4] How browsers can consume screen 'real estate'

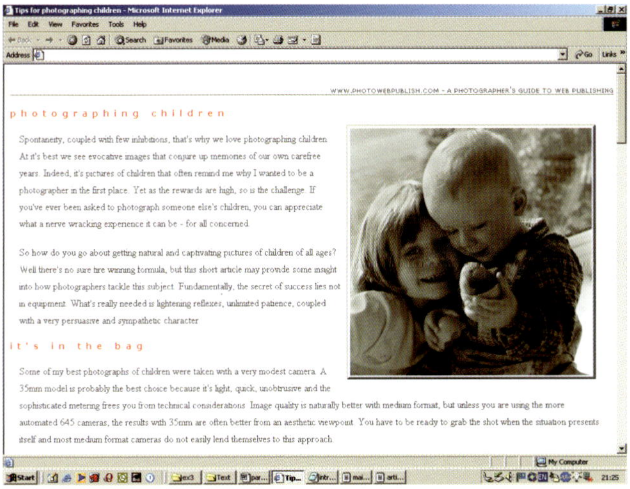

[2.5] A sample screen shot from www.photowebpublish.com

was to provide the publishers of this book with sizeable screen shots that would reproduce well. I chose to use this higher resolution, simply because it gave me larger, more detailed screen shot files. I did, however, utilize a liquid layout (see below) so you can at least view the site at 800x600 or lower resolutions. It merely illustrates my point that trade-offs such as these are an inevitable aspect of web publishing.

Liquid layouts

Related to monitor resolution is the design decision to either let the page adapt itself to the size of the user's browser window or to stick with a 'frozen layout' that remains the same size regardless. The term 'liquid layout' is used because as you change the size of the browser window – perhaps by dragging one of the corners – the text and other objects move as the amount of available space alters and, most noticeably, you see text 'flow' around other objects.

Web-page design is not at all like print, and there is no better illustration of this than the frozen vs. liquid design debate. The vast majority of sites you will visit have a frozen, unchanging layout. My personal preference, however, is for a liquid design. It's more in keeping with the original spirit of the web as a presentation tool and liquid designs do free you from concerns of monitor resolution. That said, on large screens related elements might begin to float around and lose some of their cohesiveness, making the design look untidy. The length of lines of text may also become uncomfortable to read at higher resolutions, but I think it is

2

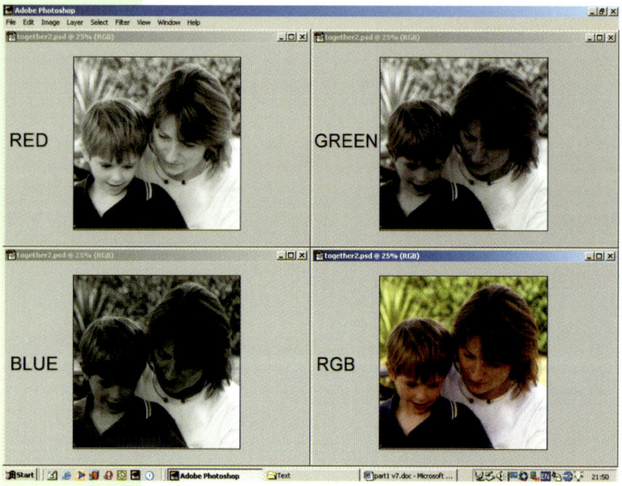

[2.6] The picture is made up of three colour components that are mixed to produce the final image

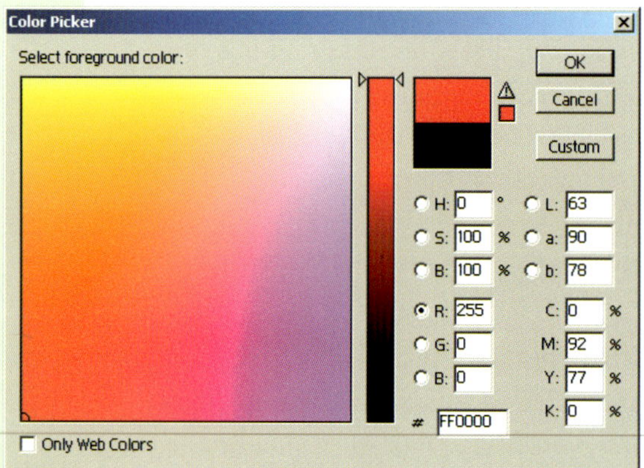

[2.7] Maximum red intensity

preferable to the alternative where large portions of screen space are potentially wasted and left blank when viewed on higher resolution monitors. Frozen designs are much easier to envisage and design, not least because they are so similar to what we are already used to in the print world. Liquid designs are more of a challenge, but exhibit the greatest usability for all concerned.

Understanding colour on the web

At first I was quite surprised when I discovered that not all computers display the same colour information consistently. I shouldn't have been. Anyone who has walked into a television showroom will recall seeing the same broadcast displayed in a subtle variety of hues, and the same principle applies to computer screens.

The simplest unit of information a computer can hold is the 'bit'. A 'bit' is a singular unit of information that can hold one of two values: 0 or 1. Using a combination of 8-bits and the binary counting system, a computer can represent 256 values. For the mathematically inclined, that's two to the power of eight. For a red component, that means we can display 256 shades of colour from black (0) to the maximum intensity of red capable of being displayed (255).

RGB colour

Computer monitors create colours by mixing varying proportions of red, green and blue light. This colour system is known as RGB colour. RGB is a 24-bit system with 8-bits of data for each colour component. If 8-bits can describe 256 colours it follows that the total possible combination of colours with 24-bits is 16,777,216 (256x256x256). Almost 17 million colours are enough to display vibrant pictures, and this is often referred to as the true colour space.

There are plenty of older monitors that cannot display a true colour space. 16-bit colour systems can display approximately 65,000 colours and, as we have seen, 8-bit colour systems can only display 256 colours. When colours from a 24-bit system are displayed in browsers running on 8-bit or 16-bit monitors, something has to give. The colours that cannot be represented are merely approximated or 'shifted', and an effect known as 'dithering' occurs (shown right).

Shortcut

RGB colour

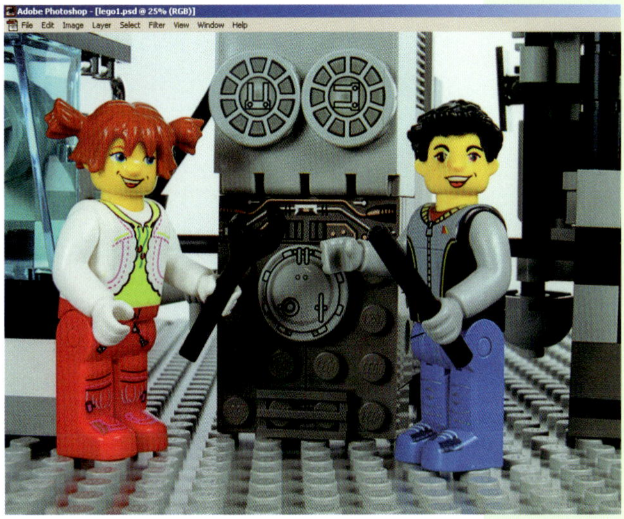

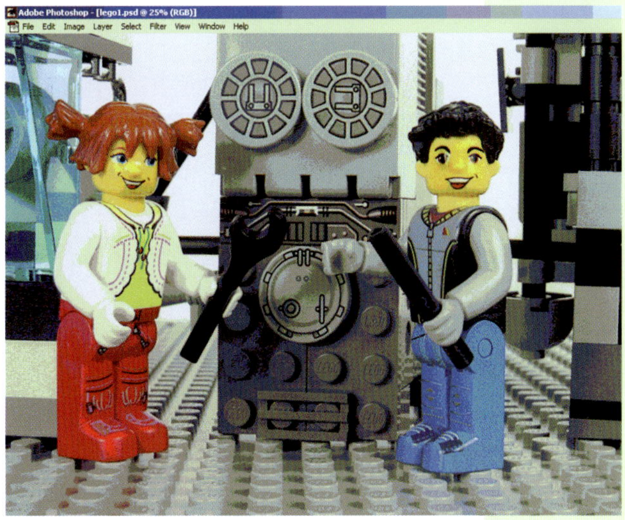

[2.8/2.9] The 'dithering' effect of a 24-bit image (top) shown on an 8-bit monitor (bottom)

Shortcut

Web-safe colours

Web-safe colours

With colour photographs, the designer doesn't have a great deal of control over what colours to choose. However, with graphical objects, there are 216 colours that do not dither on 8-bit displays across both PC and Mac platforms and these colours are known as the web palette. It is good practice to limit the colour of web-page elements to these web-safe colours to avoid unsightly dithering problems.

One of the effects you often see on photographic websites is an image that is blended into the background colour of a page. I don't want to suggest that this trick is hackneyed, but search for web pages on portraiture and you'll find an example soon enough. It's invariably something like a close up of an eye, often with a strong colour cast to match the underlying page.

The problem is that most photographers who use this trick try to match the colours of the image and page background visually. This often leads to a noticeable seam, especially if they match a 24-bit colour by eye and their site is viewed through a 16-bit colour system, leading to pronounced shifting.

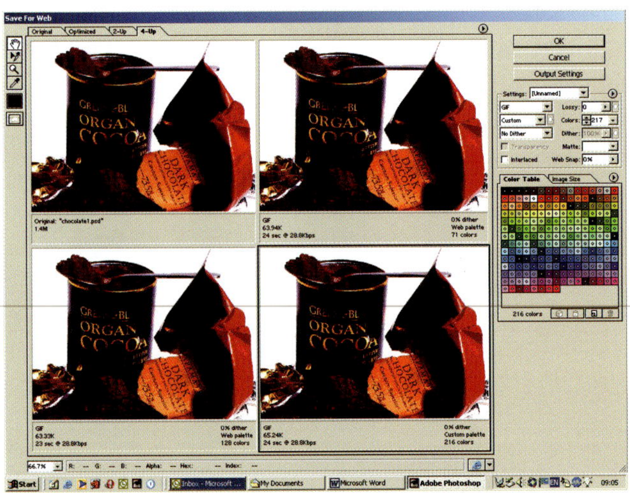

[2.10] The 216 web-safe colours can be selected to recolour a photographic image with variable results

RGB numbering

If you have a graphic image that you want to blend seamlessly into the background colour of a page, it is better to match the colour mathematically. The usual way to define colour in HTML is by using the RGB numbering system. Looking at your image in an image-editing program like Adobe PhotoShop allows you to determine the RGB value of the border colour. In the two 'hearts' example (below), the outer blue heart is Red 51 Green 51 Blue 153 and I want to blend this into the background colour of the page, showing only one heart.

Hexadecimal numbering

Humans like to count in tens and the decimal numbering system is, in no small part, derived from the number of fingers we have. Computers, on the other hand, are designed to count in twos or multiples thereof, while colours in HTML are defined using the hexadecimal numbering system, which uses a base of 16. Counting to 16 is as follows: 0,1,2,3,4,5,6,7,8,9,A,B,C,D,E,F. Colour is defined in HTML as three numbers in hexadecimal to represent the red, green and blue proportions. Thinking in 'hex' may seem complex, but

Shortcut

RGB numbering

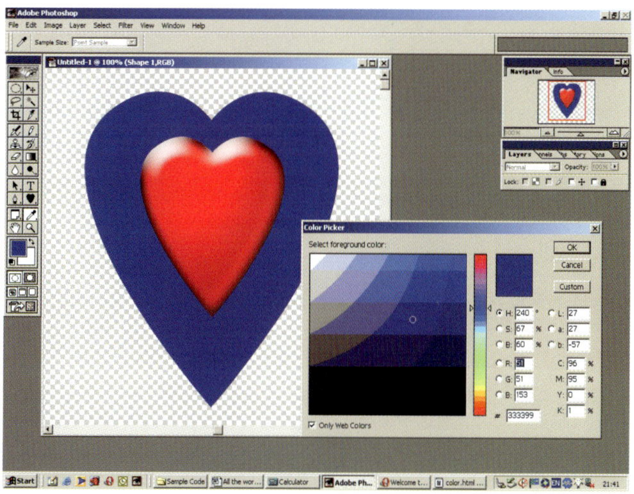

[2.11] Two coloured hearts

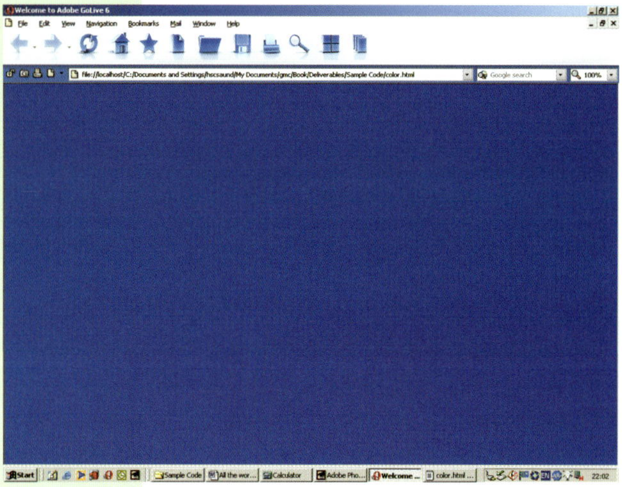

[2.12] Background page set to "#333399"

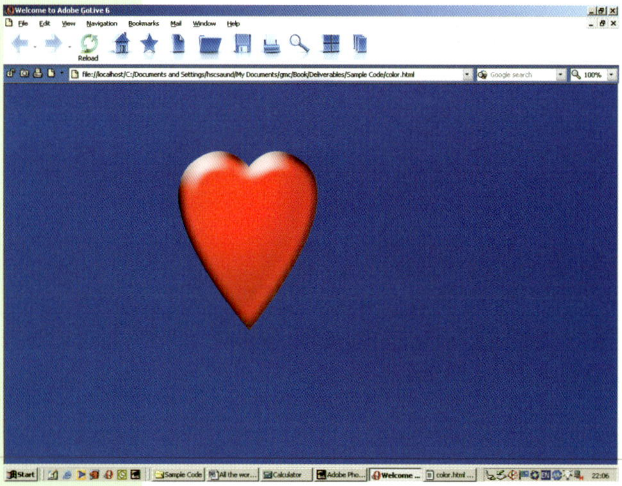

[2.13] Background and image blended together

thankfully you can easily switch from decimal to hexadecimal using the 'scientific notation' view on the standard Windows calculator. (If you use a Mac, a search using the string 'RGB to Hexadecimal conversion' will produce countless web pages that offer this facility.) This enables you to convert the individual numeric components of RGB to their hex values. For example, the equivalent of R51 G51 B153 in hexadecimal is 33 33 99. Many image-manipulation programs go further by showing you the RGB and hexadecimal values of any given colour, this makes the process of matching a colour to its numeric equivalent even easier. Within HTML the colour is described in the following format "#RRGGBB", and so in my example I would set the background page colour to be "#333399" (top left). You will see how exactly to do this in Part Two (see page 69).

When I insert the heart image (from the previous page) into the web page, the two blend almost invisibly together (bottom left). You would be hard pressed to make a closer match by eye.

2

Ensuring accurate colour definition

In addition to 'hex' definitions, there are almost 150 colours defined by textual names, some of which sound quite exotic (e.g. blanchedalmond, papayawhip, mistyrose). These do map to numeric values, yet the names themselves are not universally supported across all browsers. The vast majority of these colours are not web safe and will shift somewhat unpredictably on 8-bit displays. Hex may be a pain to use, but it is by far the best option for accurate colour definition. Interestingly, all the colours in the web-safe palette are made up of combinations of the following six hexadecimal values: 00, 33, 66, 99, CC and FF. If your Red, Green and Blue components only use one of these numbers, the resulting mixed colour is considered safe from dithering.

Gamma settings

Another term used in colour management is 'Gamma'. Think of it as the brightness of the monitor. Again, different platforms have different default Gamma settings. In effect this means that images created on one platform will look markedly different on another. The Mac platform has a Gamma setting of 1.8, while a PC platform typically has a Gamma setting of 2.2. If you view an image on a Mac that was originally created using a PC, it will usually look washed out. Similarly, Mac-originated images look unusually dark on a PC platform. If you have a sophisticated image-manipulation package such as Adobe ImageReady, you can simulate this effect and design for a middle ground so that your pictures can be viewed on both platforms.

Shortcut

Ensuring accurate colour definition

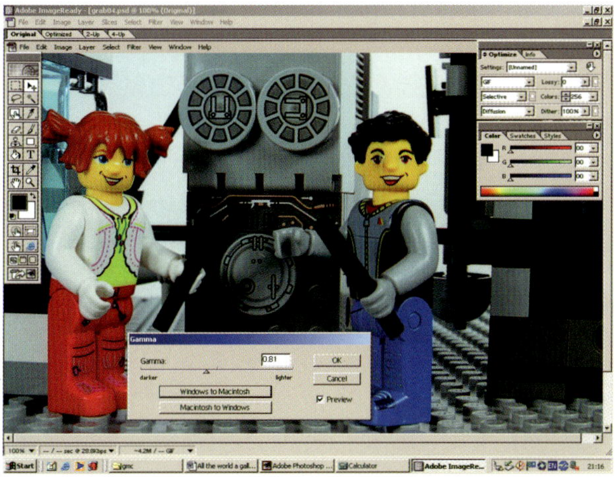

[2.14] Gamma manipulation in Adobe ImageReady

Monitor calibration

One of the first steps towards consistent colour representation is monitor calibration. Monitor calibration enables you to set the brightness, contrast and colour balance to a 'standardized display'. Once you have created a calibrated monitor profile, this can be saved to your operating system folder (System/ColourSync Profiles on a Mac and Windows/System/Colour for a PC). The state of your monitor will vary over time so it is a good idea to recalibrate at regular intervals. You should build a date into the filename of your monitor profile and then you'll easily be able to tell which profile to use when you manipulate your images.

Type the phrase 'monitor calibration' in a search engine and you will be presented with a variety of space-age systems that can attach to the front of your monitor and automatically create an accurate profile for you. Alternatively, you may find that your image-manipulation software comes with a monitor calibration program built in. Adobe PhotoShop does, and although it relies on your eyes for part of the process, it is remarkably effective nonetheless. Though there is more to colour management than monitor calibration, undertaking this initial step will at least improve the chances that what you see on your screen approximates to what someone else may see on a properly calibrated display.

Shortcut

Basic design priniciples: text

Web typography

If you don't have a strong design background, you may be surprised to learn just how powerful typography is in terms of its ability to invoke a psychological response in a reader. We don't just read text; we really do experience it. So how do you get the most from type? The concept of design suggests you have the ability to exert control and the fact remains that on the web at least, any control is illusory. This is perfectly illustrated in the world of web typography.

When you look at your browser's Internet options, you can see that typeface (font) control is handed over to the end user. For those used to print design this is a major cause of angst, because you really can't predict how your site will look if the user has elected

Basic design priniciples: text

Your brain looks for order, patterns and a rhythm when your eyes begin scanning pages of any sort, and good design is often about creating contrast between adjacent entities. These could be blocks of text, headlines, pull quotes or just white space between the objects.

to override your default typeface settings. At first glance this may seem an unusual thing to allow, yet there are plenty of visually impaired people who are only too pleased that they can still access the power of the Internet by being able to read enlarged content.

Typography on the web is not like print. To begin with, the resolution of type in its printed form is considerably higher than its on-screen equivalent, often by a factor of at least ten. This is just one reason why on-screen reading is more uncomfortable than print. Moreover, typefaces that have been designed for the world of print don't necessarily work well on the web, partly because of this resolution issue. Further problems arise when you elect to use a typeface that you believe suits your design, when there is no guarantee that the same typeface exists on your users' machines. Careful planning and forethought are required if your site is going to succeed from a typographical perspective.

The theory of typography is outside the scope of this book, but the following list contains a few guidelines that should enable you to make your web pages more legible. I'd like to stress the term 'guidelines'. This is not a list of irreducible laws, and you should feel free to ignore them if the circumstances dictate an alternative approach.

Basic typography guidelines

- Left-justified text is generally considered to be more legible than either centred or right-justified text. Similarly, the legibility of headlines is improved if they are left justified.
- The longer the line of text, the harder it is to read. This is a problem with liquid layouts (see page 35), which can easily flow to the full length of a very high-resolution monitor. One solution to is to increase the 'leading' or line spacing. This helps to allow a long line length and flexible layout, without sacrificing too much legibility.
- Insert a single space only (not a double space) after all punctuation.
- Use a smaller point size when type is all upper case.
- Use boldface or italicized text sparingly. Never use both together.
- Avoid using underlined text as this has a special meaning on the web, indicating a hyperlink. The same is true of colouring your text.
- Try to stick to one type family. Provide emphasis by varying type size or spacing, rather than by introducing new typefaces.

TrueType fonts

Microsoft has developed a range of 'TrueType' fonts (listed below) for both PC and Mac platforms that are easy to read online. I would suggest that you limit your typeface selection to these, in the knowledge that they should appear as expected on most users' machines.

- Andale Mono
- Arial
- Comic Sans
- Courier New
- Georgia
- Impact
- Times New Roman
- Trebuchet MS
- Verdana

Typefaces

We read by recognizing the shapes of words, not by looking at each letter. Words written in capitals only have a reduced shape and are therefore difficult to read. You should capitalize only the first word and any proper nouns if you want to maintain highly legible word forms.

Vary typefaces relative to the base typeface size – i.e. increase to 110% or decrease to 85%, rather than use specific point sizes. The latter will vary considerably in physical size depending on the user's environment and it is safer to adjust typeface sizes relative to the user's default parameters.

Having started by asserting that your web users maintain ultimate control over typefaces, it is interesting to note that the majority of users don't realize this. In which case, the likelihood is that for proportional typefaces (where each character subtly varies in size) you might expect to see default fonts such as Times or Helvetica. Likewise, with fixed-width typefaces (where the characters occupy space of exactly the same size) you are likely to see Monaco and Courier fonts. Chapter 5 (page 78) introduces a technique known as 'cascading style sheets', which can be used to suggest a list of suitable typefaces for your web pages, thereby increasing your chance of getting one that suits your design.

The exact appearance of some of the TrueType fonts can be seen in Fig 2.15 (above right). My personal favourite is Verdana, which I believe works remarkably well on screen. Incidentally, the 'handgloves' sample word is merely there to allow you to compare and contrast the typefaces against the same word form.

2

Arial - Handgloves

Courier New - Handgloves

Georgia - Handgloves

Times New Roman - Handgloves

Trebuchet - Handgloves

Verdana - Handgloves

[2.15] The most useful web-design fonts

If you want to use a specific typeface, perhaps as part of a logo or brand, the convention is to produce an image file that contains the appropriate text. This eliminates the need for the user to possess the typeface on their machine, but it does impose a download overhead. The GIF-file format (see page 54) is often used to encapsulate these text objects as graphics, and if used sparingly can help create quite attractive typographical effects within your design.

Testing your site

Ultimately, there is only one sure-fire way to know what your site is going to look like 'elsewhere', and that is to test it on a variety of platforms. Naturally, your mental picture of the types of users viewing your site should guide your testing, but you should take the opportunity to view your site on as much hardware as possible. That may mean using the computers of friends and family, or perhaps taking a few moments to look at your site from an Internet café. Some of the more sophisticated web-development environments will also run simple tests of your site against their understanding of different browser versions and HTML coding standards. This is another useful tool to help you anticipate potential problems for people viewing your site.

Choosing software for testing sites

In the absence of extra hardware, there are a few software recommendations I can make to help give you some assurance that your users will see something that approximates to your own impression. First, you might consider testing your site on different Internet browsers. To do this you will need to download browser programs onto your machine such as Internet Explorer (www.microsoft.com), Mozilla (www.mozilla.org) and Opera (www.opera.com). Opera is a neat little piece of browser technology, which at around 2MB in size is much more compact than most of its competitors. Opera's appeal is in the rigorous way it complies with Internet standards. It will tolerate no sloppy coding and will show your site 'warts and all', which is why so many professional web designers use this version as their primary test bed.

Shortcut

Choosing software for testing sites

2

Shortcut

Making web pages stand alone

Aesthetic design considerations

As I mentioned earlier, sticking to some established design practices need not necessarily stifle your creativity, and it certainly will help users understand how to interact with your site. Like the technical guidelines above, you obviously need to pick and choose from this list to suit your own audience. These guidelines have come from hours of surfing and from trying to quantify what it was that attracted me to any given photographic website.

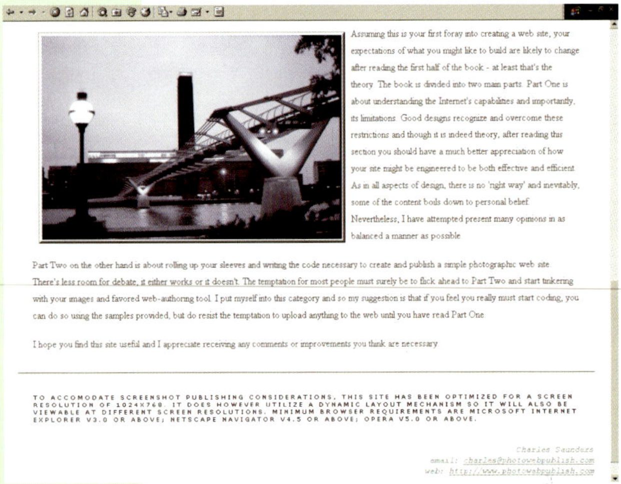

[2.16] Each page on photowebpublish.com contains navigation and contact information in the footer

Making web pages stand alone

There is one golden rule in web design: make all your web pages work independently of each other. The reason for this is that most surfers will probably not reach your site through the main page. Search engines have an annoying habit of finding the content that the user was looking for – which invariably lies buried deep within your site – and then leading them straight to it. The user then spends the next few moments trying to figure out where they are and where they really want to be. This is why each and every page on your site should stand by itself. It should also have an easily identifiable link to the main page of the site, giving the user to chance to start from the 'beginning'. In addition to making your pages independent, each page should also have an informative title. Not only does this title become the bookmark in your user's browser, it also contains very important information for search engines. In addition, I tend to include the author's identity and contact details at the foot of each page, as shown in Fig 2.16 (left).

Effective communication

The next design consideration is to ensure the effective communication of a site's purpose. If you are a professional photographer specializing in reportage or wedding photography, say so. If your time is mostly devoted to large-format food photography, don't be afraid to make this clear on the first page. If you are a generalist photographer who takes on just about anything and has a pretty mixed portfolio, then at the very least highlighting your location could be a way of differentiating your site. Users also want to understand fairly quickly how the site operates. Is it private and not for profit, or are you selling a service? Users are naturally suspicious of a site that does not declare how it is funded or what it is there for.

Include information about yourself or your company. If you have a company logo or brand, it is often a good idea to place this in the top left of the page. Nearly every good website should include both 'About us' and 'Contact us' sections. Professional photographers should also include a list of current clients – subject to the clients' written approval. While feedback should be encouraged, professional photographers should not offer a guest book – it will make the site look really amateurish.

If you are collecting information from your users, such as email addresses, it is helpful to have a clearly defined privacy policy. This will encourage users to part with such sensitive information. Search the web and you will see plenty of examples of privacy policies that could act as the starting point for your own.

If you try to coax the email address in return for receiving an online newsletter, break convention and provide an example of the publication before you ask for an email address.

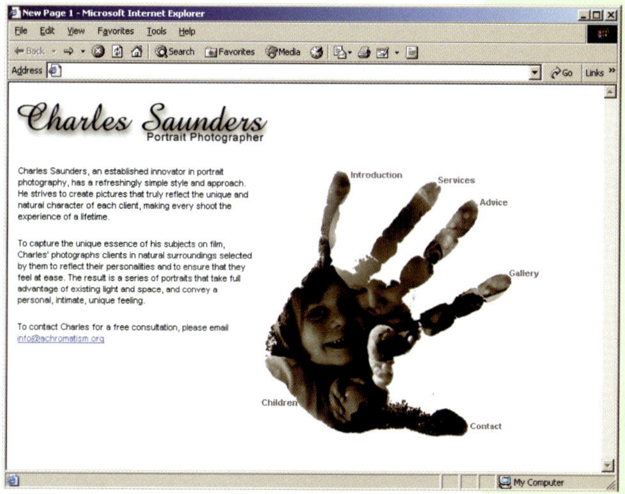

[2.17] Charles Saunders, the fictitious portrait photographer, might have a simple home page such as the one shown here

Shortcut

Keeping navigation simple

Navigation

It is very important to make the navigation of your site clear and simple. Many web designers put major navigation choices at the top of the page in a menu bar-type format. This 'macro-level' navigation typically takes you to new areas of the site or enables you to execute stand-alone tasks such as a site search. Navigation that is context sensitive is normally placed to one side of the page, often the left. This 'micro-level' navigation typically relates to the immediate content, such as moving within a gallery of images or perhaps looking at more detail of a given photograph.

It is also important to be consistent about where you place navigation objects and how they appear. For example, some designers use sans-serif fonts such as Verdana or Arial for navigation objects, and serif fonts such as Times New Roman or Georgia for the body content. The rationale behind this is that it is easier to read large quantities of text online when they are in a serif font. Sans-serif fonts, on the other hand, are used for their striking, clean appearance, which is well suited to the role of indicating where to go next. My preference is to use varying sizes of Verdana throughout.

Keeping navigation simple

The graphics-laden sites of most design agencies normally flout simple navigation rules in favour of something far more radical. Notice, when you visit one of these sites, how disconcerting it feels when you first begin to try to figure out how to use them.

Site maps

If you are going to succeed in producing clear and well-designed navigation structures, you must begin by creating a site map. Initially, this can be done on paper using a pen or pencil to produce a simple map showing the different pages and how they interrelate. This can then be annotated with the pages, their function and the type of content they will hold. You also need to be thinking about how the site information could be organized. For example, your pictures may fall into a natural hierarchy (portraits, sport, street, urban architecture, landscape, and so on) with a gallery of low-resolution thumbnails for each section allowing users to examine any particular image in greater detail. Alternatively, you may decide to create collections of images that are linked by a theme. This gives users a mental image of how the site is organized and makes the process of navigation much easier.

On the other hand, articles of text often need to be broken up into linked sequential chunks. These sections of text need to be divided logically, and this often means adopting a much more concise writing style and arranging the material in such a way that facilitates this subdivision of content. Tests have proven that embracing this approach helps considerably with online reading as it reduces the amount of scrolling users need to perform and assists the rapid scanning of content. I am afraid it is very unlikely that users will read your copy word for word. Online reading is not very easy, or indeed comfortable, due to screen size and resolution considerations. The logical division of text, supported by good heading construction, significantly assists in the rapid scanning of content and will make your website much more accessible.

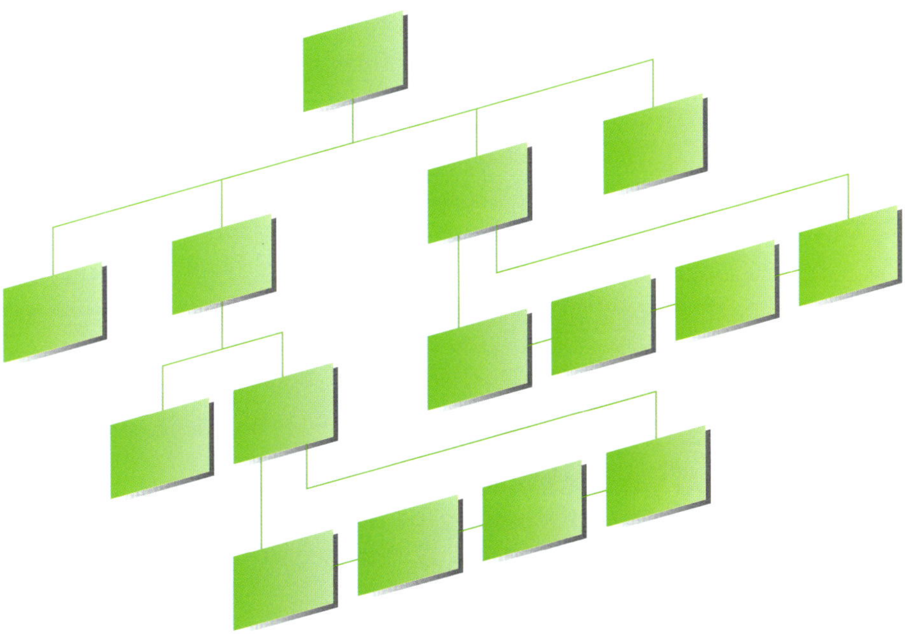

[2.18] Drawing a site map helps you conceptualize the site's form and function

A by-product of producing a site map should be an appreciation of the different types of pages that you want to create – gallery pages, picture-display pages, pages containing text, and so on. Creating a consistent look and feel to these different types of pages will not only make your site a great deal more user-friendly, it can also make your site considerably easier to build and, more importantly, maintain.

Page-design considerations

There are numerous books written solely on the subject of page design, so the following pages should only be seen as an outline. Design can be a repetitive process, with many ideas abandoned on the way to your finished site.

From a slightly abstract perspective, you should aim to create pages that offer an easy balance between visual stimulation and textual communication. The eye should be drawn into the page and follow a path that is clear and well ordered. Important elements must be emphasized within a strong visual hierarchy, but you must be selective; you cannot accentuate everything. No single object should shout for attention and content should be organized logically and, above all, predictably. If this sounds a little academic, go back to some of your favourite sites and try to see how they have arranged their branding, navigation and content. You will soon see patterns emerge that will help you build your own pages.

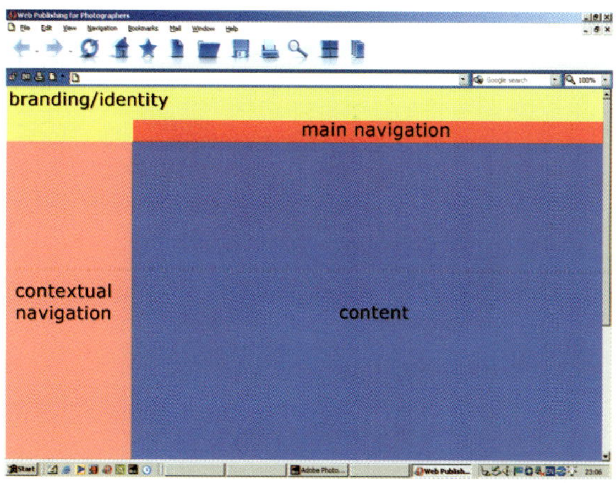

[2.19] A typical page design from which to base your own pages

Block designs

Another time for using a pen and paper comes when you begin sketching 'block designs' for your web pages. Remember: one of the most important elements is consistency. Certain block designs will suit a certain type of page, and you shouldn't be afraid to repeat the design on pages of similar function. Design consistency not only makes your site much easier to navigate and use, it also makes the site considerably easier to maintain after it has gone live.

As photographers, we need to be mindful of how we are going to exhibit our endeavours. The web is not like print; you cannot simply put up a sequence of glorious pictures that someone can browse at their leisure.

Since download burdens restrict how much any user can request at any one time, the convention is to show thumbnail-sized proxies of your photographs. The user then selects a thumbnail and is shown a larger version of the picture. In this way, the user does not waste time waiting for pictures they have little interest in to download.

Three-column layouts

The typical web-page design is the three-column layout, as shown in Fig 2.20 (below). The high-contrast colours are merely there to delineate regions within the page. Grids such as these bring order, familiarity and, as a result, ease of use to a design, and it is frequently the preferred choice for a site's entry point or 'home page'.

Shortcut

Three-column layouts

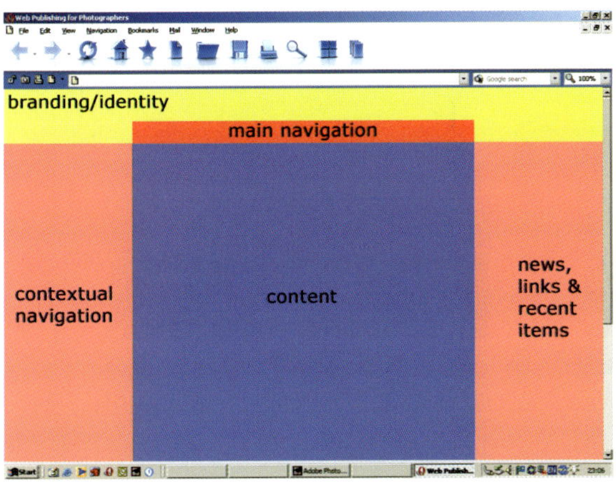

[2.20] The three-column design is the most popular and well-understood design on the web

2

Why provide multiple image sizes?

- There is a gradual yet steady shift in personal computer usage where 1024x768 monitor resolution is seen as standard, but many users will still have monitors set at 800x600.
- Photographers in particular are likely to view websites on a higher resolution monitor.
- Your pictures will be seen at their best, which is after all what we are trying to achieve.

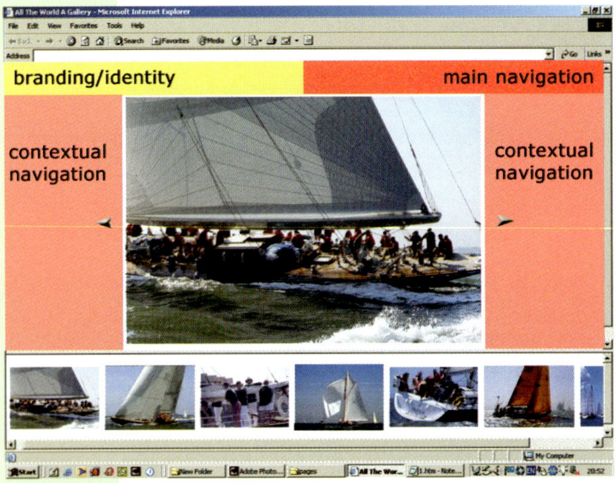

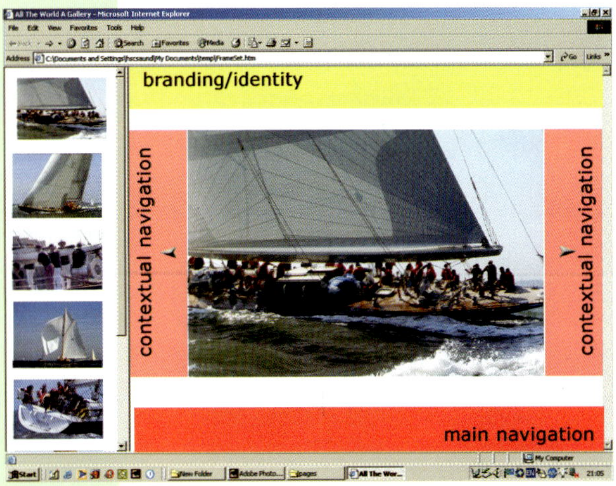

[2.21/2.22] Two simple approaches to organizing thumbnail images and a larger rendition

Most photographic websites allow you to view a larger picture that fits within an 800x600 monitor resolution. I suggest that you give your users the optional opportunity of viewing at least two further large versions of your pictures, which should fit within monitor resolutions such as 1024x768 and 1280x1024. While I concede this creates more work for the author of the website, it recognizes the issues listed above. It is then up to you as to how you might organize your collection of thumbnail images, and I have included two simple block designs to illustrate my point (see Figs 2.21 and 2.22, left).

General design points

Once you have your collection of block diagrams, you can begin comparing them to see if they work consistently. Good page design is simply about balance, composition, and sequences of patterns and contrast. If you follow these general design considerations, you won't go far wrong:

- Limit the numbers of graphics, colours and typefaces on each page. Simple, clean designs look better.
- Try to use web-safe pastel shades of colour for background or negligible components. Highly saturated bold colours should be used sparingly.
- Don't be afraid to use white space to add a sense of balance to your site. Many sites don't give the page elements space to 'breathe', and a cramped design is easy to spot.
- Avoid the use of animation – it slows down the site and draws the eye to a single area.
- The other great design flaw is 'splash screens' that pop up initially before a home page begins loading. Unless they are there to warn users of inappropriate content, such as nudity, they really serve no purpose other than to keep users away from the content they are after.

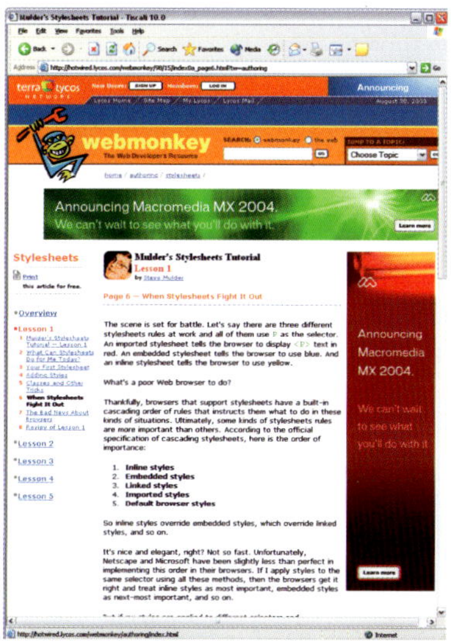

[2.23] Webmonkey is just one of the many great online sources of additional material to teach you web technologies. © Lycos Inc.

3 Preparing your Images for Publication

Understanding images on the web

Anyone building a website faces a dilemma. On the one hand, you want to give the greatest, most exciting multimedia experience possible and show off your creative endeavours. On the other hand, most users only have a relatively slow connection to the Internet and very little patience when it comes to waiting for web pages to load. While text is rarely the problem in terms of download time, other information such as graphics and photographs can really slow your site down. The more exciting imagery you pile into any given page, the longer it takes to load and the user experience degenerates dramatically.

In response to this situation, an awful lot of effort has been expended in finding ways to transmit picture information without incurring the high transmission cost. Image compression is a complex subject requiring an excellent grasp of mathematics. Thankfully for us photographers, this knowledge is encapsulated in numerous image-manipulation programs such as Adobe PhotoShop and Macromedia Fireworks. There are three graphic formats in common use on the web, and your chosen tool should support all of them. These file formats are GIF, JPEG and PNG. Different sorts of image respond to different compression algorithms and you need to match the right file format to the right type of image.

The GIF format

The latest GIF (Graphic Interchange Format) standard – GIF89a – is the de facto format for exchanging graphics on the web. GIF files use an 8-bit colour model, which means they can display up to a maximum of 256 colours (see Fig 3.1, below). The 'maximum' qualifier is significant – GIF files may hold fewer than 256 colours with a corresponding reduction in file size.

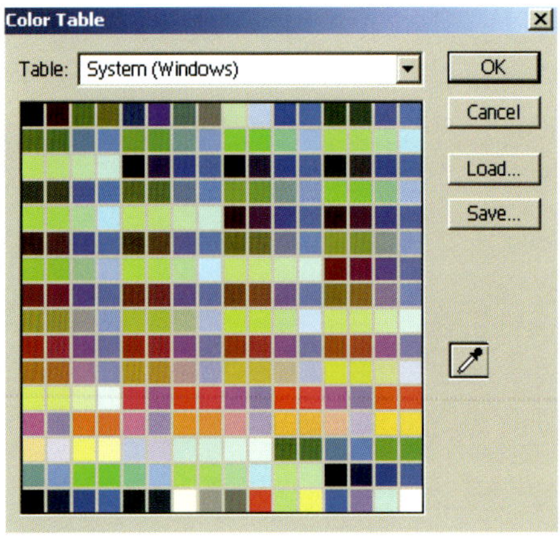

[3.1] A colour table for a Windows GIF file showing 256 colours

GIF files are sometimes referred to as 'indexed' colour, and this is because a palette of colours for the image file is held in a colour table. Every pixel in the image references or 'indexes' this table to get its correct colour. It is commonly thought that GIF files are best used for graphics such as logos, buttons, icons and so on. This is true, but they are more specifically ideal for graphic objects that contain large areas of flat colour. The reason for this lies in the compression algorithm used by GIFs, called LZW (Lempel-Zev-Welch), which is very effective at compressing rows of identical pixels. As a simplified example, imagine a row of 32 pixels that are all red in colour. It might be represented as 'rrrrrrrrrrrrrrrrrrrrrrrrrrrrrrrr' or as '32r'; the latter form is considerably more compact and hence smaller. By contrast, if the image is made up of patterns of constantly changing colour – as in most photographs – this type of compression algorithm is not as efficient.

Page-header graphic

I tend to shun graphic elements in favour of a more minimalist approach on my own websites. There are of course many websites that do use these elements successfully, and I have created a sample page-header graphic to illustrate the power of GIF compression (see Fig 3.2, below). It satisfies the compression algorithm criteria with regard to possessing large areas of repeating colour.

Photographs as GIF files

You should not exhibit your colour photographs as GIFs, merely because they can't represent the true colour space. By comparison, monochrome photographs fair slightly better as GIFs because 256 shades of grey are often sufficient for accurate reproduction. However, unless your monochrome image mixes text and graphic objects alongside photography, there are more efficient algorithms for compressing this type of picture (see page 57).

Shortcut

Photographs as GIF files

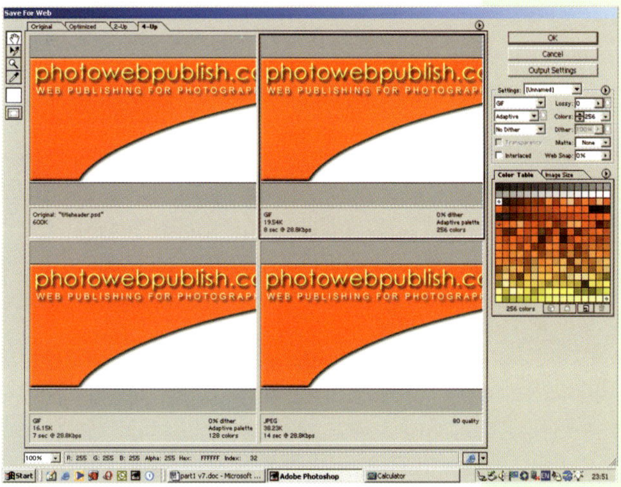

[3.2] A sample banner graphic is saved as a GIF file

3

Shortcut
Image compression and file size

Image compression and file size

Notice from Fig 3.2 (previous page) that the original image is 600k. That's far too big to be used in its uncompressed form. However, thanks to the LZW compression algorithm, we have managed to squeeze this file down to 19.54k at 256 colours and 16.15k at 128 colours. Nevertheless, that still could take somewhere between four and eight seconds to download, depending on your modem. In my view, that's valuable time that could have been saved for downloading photographs. Interestingly, the JPEG file format performs badly at compressing this image to only 38.23k. I could have pushed the JPEG compression algorithm harder than the 80% you see in the screen shot, but to make it a fair comparison, this compression level produced results that were visually equivalent to the GIFs. However, the JPEG format has strengths in different areas (see opposite).

Shortcut
GIF animation

GIFs are also useful if you want portions of your image to be transparent, thereby allowing the background to show through. While PNG files do support more sophisticated methods of transparency, GIF files still currently have the upper hand when it comes to universal browser compatibility. Be aware that transparency in GIF files may provide some unexpected results should your graphic contain anti-aliased edges.

Anti-aliasing is an artificially generated slight blur on curved edges that is used to create a smoother transition between edge colours. As you place your graphic on its background, you may witness a coloured 'halo effect' around your graphic where the anti-aliased pixels have not been properly blended into their surroundings. There are various strategies for fixing this situation, although fixing the edge pixel by pixel seems to be the most reliable. You should refer to your graphic program's help files for specific advice.

A dubious feature available with GIFs is 'interlacing'. For large images, an interlaced GIF builds up gradually on the screen from an initial, fuzzy full-sized proxy to the final sharp image once all the image data has been received. Some people think that this fuzzy preview is somehow visually attractive and psychologically helps the waiting user. However, after staring at your fuzzy picture for some time, the

GIF animation

You can also use GIFs for animation, but my advice is to avoid this. GIFs have no play controls and so a GIF animation just keeps looping forever. The average web page is simply the wrong place for animation of this kind, as it is too distracting and can soon overpower your page design.

3

user will then move on to view your next image having seen the sharp version for comparatively less time. As a result, you will have lost some of the visual impact of a sharp picture, and also increased download time, as an interlaced GIF has a larger file size than a plain one.

The JPEG format

The next and arguably most important file format for photographers is the JPEG format. JPEG stands for Joint Photographic Experts Group, and in contrast to GIFs, JPEGs are true-colour images. JPEGs use a different compression algorithm, based on a mathematical system called discrete cosine transformation. The important difference with JPEGs is that you are able to vary the amount of compression, although the amount you apply ultimately affects not only file size but also image quality.

Download times for graphics

The key to success with graphics is to keep the file size small. Your graphic-manipulation program should give you a hint for estimated download times for each image. Failing that, most designers I know use the one-second per kilobyte average download time for any object on your page. While this is only an average ballpark figure, it really is a good rule of thumb. Remember: you should be aiming for a maximum download time of ten seconds per page.

Shortcut

Download times for graphics

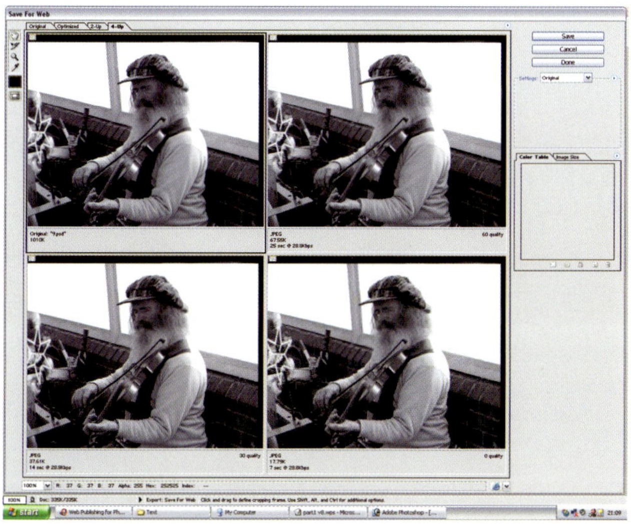

[3.3] JPEG compression in action

The JPEG compression algorithm samples the image in 8x8 pixel blocks and then translates the brightness and colour information into an arithmetical interpretation. These sampling squares become quite noticeable when you push the compression algorithm to its limits, as I have done in the screen shot in Fig 3.4 (below). The greater the compression, the more pronounced the image degradation.

One of the important facts to remember about JPEGs is that they utilize a 'lossy' method of compression. This means that unnecessary image data is discarded in order to achieve the reduction in file size. This loss is permanent and you cannot recover lost data from a JPEG file once the compression algorithm has been applied. One of the mistakes photographers often make is to keep their digital images in a JPEG format. It's an understandable error to make; after all, a JPEG is the file format that many digital cameras produce as their output. However, you should be aware that every time you open and resave a JPEG image, the compression algorithm is reapplied. The result over time is a cumulative loss of data and image degradation. It therefore makes good sense to keep your original files in a 'non-lossy' format, such as the native file format of your image-manipulation program. For example, I keep my images as PSD files, which is the native file format for Adobe PhotoShop, and only

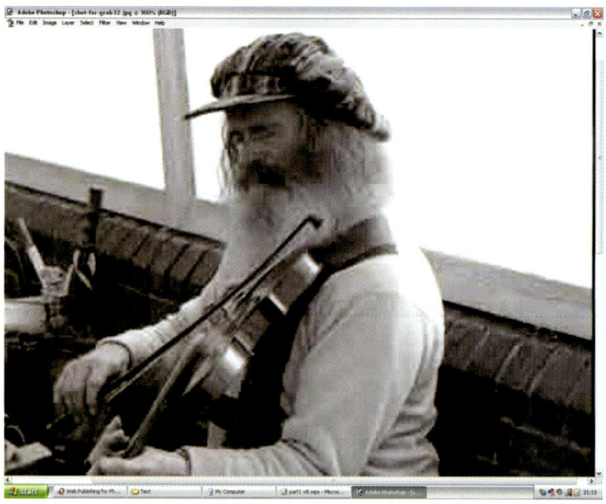

[3.4] 'Street performer' with excessive image compression applied to show sampling squares

Shortcut

Photographs as JPEG files

Photographs as JPEG files

From their name you can probably surmise that JPEGs are well suited for the compression of photographic images. They perform far better than GIFs in this regard. Equally, JPEGs are not good at compressing graphic objects with solid colour and strong colour boundaries. Over-compressed JPEG images often contain distortions and spurious features that are described collectively as 'artefacts'. Experiment with JPEG compression on these sorts of objects and you will see how easy it is to produce image artefacts as a result of the image compression algorithm, as shown in Fig 3.5 (right).

ever produce JPEGs when I want an image for the web. Furthermore, if I ever need to edit one of my pictures on the web, perhaps to resize it or apply some toning, I always go back to the original file and then reproduce the required JPEG.

As you can see from Fig 3.6 (right), JPEGs come into a field of their own with photographic compression, far outstripping the capabilities of the GIF format. Before you create JPEG files, you should consult the technical documentation of your favoured image-manipulation program. You should normally start with an RGB or greyscale image, as most programs work better

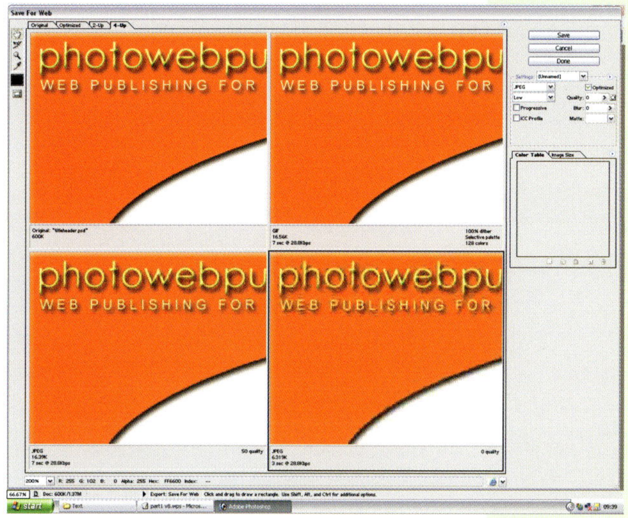

[3.5] JPEG compression is not well suited to graphic objects and easily produces image artefacts

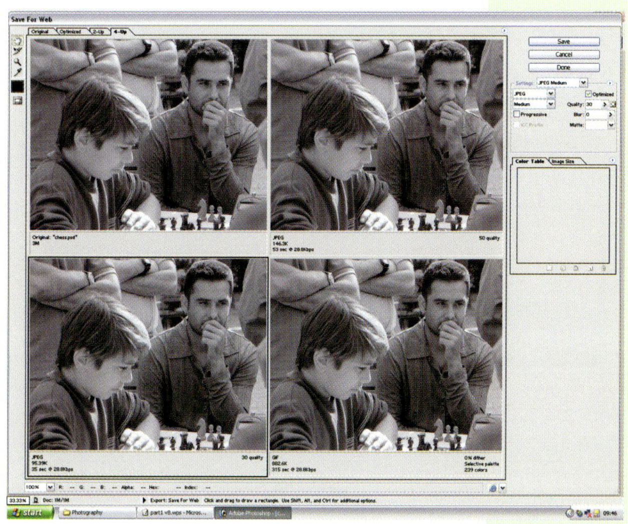

[3.6] JPEG files excel over GIFs when used for photographic compression

with these two modes. Most programs allow you to preview the image as you adjust the compression amount. It's then up to you to judge visually the acceptable trade-off between file size and image quality.

As we have seen from the graphics example in Fig 3.5, the JPEG compression algorithm doesn't work well against strong colour boundaries. You can play to this weakness by adding a slight blur to those parts of the image that are not required to be sharp. This will make a tremendous difference to the effectiveness of the compression algorithm. Often, photographers who have a selective-focus portrait take advantage of this situation by increasing the blur on the non-face portions of the image, producing a picture that the JPEG compression algorithm can really work well on.

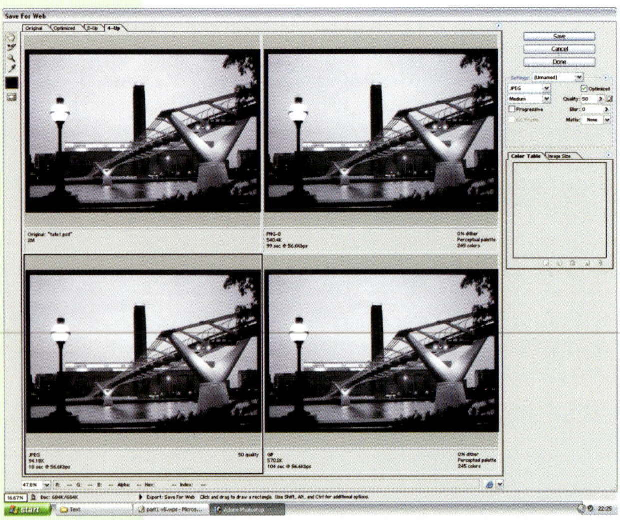

[3.7] How the three formats compare: (clockwise from top right) PNG, GIF and JPEG

Another compression feature supported by the more sophisticated image-manipulation programs is weighted optimization. This allows you to define the degree of compression selectively on different portions of the image. Using this technique, you can squeeze another few bytes out of your image with no discernible loss of detail. Also, much like GIFs, JPEGs are capable of being displayed gradually. In the case of JPEGs, this is not called interlacing. Instead, the term 'progressive JPEG' is used. Needless to say, I hold similar views on the doubtful benefits of this feature, as I do for interlaced GIFs (see pages 56–7).

The PNG format

The Portable Network Graphic (PNG) format, referred to as 'ping', is the latest development in web graphics technology. The PNG format was specifically designed for the web. It was intended to replace the older, simpler GIF format, and the much more complex TIFF format. PNG has also been adopted by the World Wide Web Consortium, which is no mean achievement and should ensure that the format becomes increasingly well supported over the coming few years.

If this sounds too good to be true, there are also some drawbacks to the PNG format. The biggest one is that browser compatibility is limited, so you can't guarantee that your user community will be able to see the images you post to the web. Equally, image-manipulation programs are varied in how well they support the full PNG specification. However, both these situations should improve with time.

Though the format outperforms GIFs in many areas, the JPEG's 'lossy' compression algorithm still wins the day for pure photographic images. For the time being therefore, it is better to stick with GIFs and JPEGs for maximum compatibility with the broadest

Main advantages of the PNG format

- Automatic gamma correction between PC and Macintosh platforms – something of key importance to fine-art photographers.
- Loss-less compression algorithm that outperforms the GIF file format on many images.
- 16-bit greyscale support enabling 65,536 shades of grey, which will be of particular interest to black-and-white photographers. This range of shades will enable a tremendous degree of subtlety in images that even Ansel Adams would be proud of.
- 24-bit and 48-bit colour support, which, while of questionable value today, lays a rich foundation for future website developments.
- More sophisticated transparency features allowing up to 65,000 shades of transparency, rather than the Boolean on/off pixel transparency supported by GIF files.
- For those that want to use it, this format also offers more sophisticated and faster interlacing for progressive display of images.

audience, while PNGs are a format to watch and be aware of. Until the majority of your community are using browsers that fully support the PNG specification, you should avoid using PNG files for the web. For more information on the latest PNG developments, go to the World Wide Web Consortium home page (www.w3.org).

The theory of scanning

To understand how to get the most from your compressed images, you need to appreciate the concept of resolution and the various terms used in computing. Resolution does two things. First, it describes how many pixels should be captured as a scan is made. Second, when you print it describes how large those pixels need to be. Alongside resolution, the three most confused phrases are: SPI, PPI and DPI.

SPI (Samples Per Inch)

When you scan an image, the SPI resolution setting determines the size of the image in pixels. The scanner looks at little portions (or samples) of your image and records what they look like. The more samples taken, the greater the detail recorded and the larger the image. Scan a 2x2in negative at 800SPI and you end up with an image that is 1800x1800 pixels, and the image has 3.2 million pixels in total.

PPI (Pixels Per Inch)

You may end up capturing a number of samples per inch, yet there is no reason why, when you print them, they need to occupy the same physical space. In other words, you can vary the size of the pixels and hence the number per inch. If you reproduce your image at 100% then the SPI and PPI values are indeed the same. However, what if you want to scale your image to twice its original size? In that case, you might take 800 samples per inch when the image is scanned, and then print at 400 pixels per inch. To understand this, think of our example of the 2x2in negative with 1800x1800 pixels at 800SPI. If you print them off at 400PPI then the printed image must be 4x4in (1800 divided by 400 = size in inches).

DPI (Dots Per Inch)

Most of us use inkjet printers. These printers construct colours or shades of grey from much smaller dots of ink. The dots are too small for your eye to focus on and so your brain is fooled into thinking that it is looking at solid tone of a certain hue, intensity and saturation. It follows, therefore, that you need a certain number of dots to reconstruct any given pixel, and the DPI setting literally translates to the number of ink dots per inch. The rule of thumb for this is simple – the PPI value should be lower that the DPI, and the general recommendation is that this should be by a factor of three. Therefore, if your inkjet printer prints at 720DPI, your PPI value should be around 240 for any given file size. There are exceptions, such as if you are using a dye sub printer, in which case the PPI and DPI should equate to each other.

Having gone to the trouble of defining the terminology that you might meet, you may be surprised to learn that the term DPI (dpi) is often used interchangeably for all three. My own scanner driver talks in terms of dpi, so for convenience I will adopt the same convention. As long as you appreciate the context of usage and that multiple definitions for the same word exist, the rest is much easier to understand.

Scanner and film types

This book does not seek to suggest hardware for web publishing. The rate of technological change is such that a book of this type can never hope to remain current. However, a choice does present itself to the photographer who wishes to scan their own photographic material, namely: should one scan prints or film, and if the latter, does one need a dedicated film scanner? The short answer, which will be explained in more detail later in this chapter (see pages 65–7), is that you should scan film in preference to prints and use a film scanner, as opposed to a flatbed scanner with a transparency hood.

There are always exceptions to these guidelines. For example, I predominantly shoot medium-format film, and the appropriate film scanners are beyond the scope of my budget. Therefore out of necessity I use a flatbed scanner with a transparency hood. My situation is aided by the fact that a medium-format frame contains much more visual information than a 35mm frame of the same subject, and the advantages offered by a dedicated film scanner are marginal at this size, at least for web-publishing purposes. Smaller-format film does, however, benefit from the increased optical performance of a dedicated film scanner.

Shortcut

Darkroom vs. digital manipulation

Darkroom vs. digital manipulation

Film stock is preferable to prints in much the same way that a musical CD is generally of better quality than an analogue tape. The film original can hold much more information than the print, and this poses an interesting dilemma for photographers who wish to exhibit their darkroom skills. Should these photographers scan in their prints or work in the 'digital darkroom' to achieve the same end? In the final analysis it's very much a personal choice. I should point out that what computer monitors lack in resolution, they make up for in contrast range. The contrast range in the print is condensed to, at best, 100:1. Scan a print and you cannot hope to exceed this limit; scan the film original and you may be able to approach the theoretical limits of 256:1. At this level, images will seem leap out from your screen – subject to the capabilities of your monitor.

Choosing the correct resolution

Once you have a scanner attached to your computer, the next decision is what resolution to scan at. There are two schools of thought on this topic. The first suggests that you scan at the highest resolution you are likely to need; if you intend to produce a 10x8in print and put the image on the web, scan at a higher resolution and scale the picture down for web use. In theory, you should only have to scan an image once, and if you add this to a high-resolution image library, you can return to it time and again without ever going back to the original film.

While it seems logical, I have two doubts about this approach. My first concern is that it makes the assumption that image-manipulation software will do a better job of producing a massively scaled-down image than your scanner could have achieved by sampling at the correct resolution. Small reductions in size generally produce no discernible problems, but you do need to be careful about substantial changes in image size through this kind of digital re-sampling. Secondly, unless you have a very powerful computer, working on unnecessarily large image files consumes too much time and computing resource. Your throughput will be much higher if you scan at a lower resolution in the first place. On occasion you may have to go back to the original film to re-scan it if a particularly high-resolution version is required – perhaps for publication in a book or magazine. However, on balance this will probably be less of an inconvenience than having constantly to deal with large image files. I have a ludicrously powerful computer and I still follow this scheme, simply because it saves on disk space and CDs.

Scanning for the Internet

There is an oft-quoted myth that images for the Internet should be scanned at 72dpi. This is erroneous advice, as you will soon find out if you try scanning a 35mm negative frame at this resolution – the result will be a very small, low-resolution image. The size of video screens is defined primarily in terms of pixels, not inches. However many pixels an image is made up of, it will vary in size (in inches) from one monitor to another. For example, I have a 21in monitor that would normally display an image of 1280x1024 pixels in a physical space of 16x12in. That's an apparent resolution of 80dpi (1280 divided by 16). However, if I increase my monitor resolution to 1600x1200, the apparent resolution rises to 100dpi and the 1280x1024 image shrinks to around 12.8x10.24in. As this suggests, inches are not a very helpful basis for defining images sizes on the web.

Video boards display pixels one-for-one; there is no concept of pixels per inch to control the size of the screen image. (By contrast, images for print use the pixels-per-inch concept to control the size of output.) When scanning an image for the web, you need to be aware of how big you want that image to be in pixels. Depending on the size of your original photograph or film frame, the dpi value is used to calculate how many pixels will be produced in the image. If you are scanning an 8x10in photograph, you will no doubt need a much lower dpi than if you were scanning a 35mm film frame. A given number of pixels are captured, and these are displayed at a one-to-one basis on your video board.

An approach to scanning for the web

When I scan for the web, I usually want to produce at least four images. First I need a small thumbnail, usually in the order of 150x100 pixels for a landscape picture. I would then produce three other images to fit monitor resolutions of 800x600, 1024x768 and 1280x1024. I generally scan at a resolution that gives me a picture in excess of 1280x1024. This gives me some flexibility to manipulate the image, if I feel it improves the composition.

Shortcut

An approach to scanning for the web

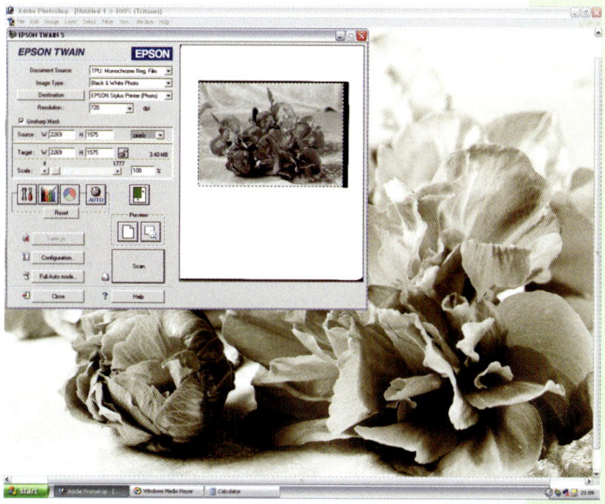

[3.8] Scanning and defining image size

3

Shortcut

Scanning at above 300dpi

In the scanning example, you can see how working in pixels is really quite straightforward. The black-and-white negative shown in Fig 3.8 (previous page) has a highlighted scan selection, the physical dimensions of which are 3.15x2.18in on the medium-format film itself. The scanning dialog box shows that I am working in pixels, and that by scanning at 720dpi I will end up with an image that is 2269x1575 pixels (3.15 multiplied by 720 x 2.18 multiplied by 720). I would typically then work on the picture in my 'digital darkroom', performing such functions as burn, dodge, sharpen, tone and so on. When the manipulation is complete, I would then go on to produce my largest master copy at around 1280x1024 pixels (depending on aspect ratio), from which all the other images are derived. As you can see, the parameter of 72dpi never figures in the equation.

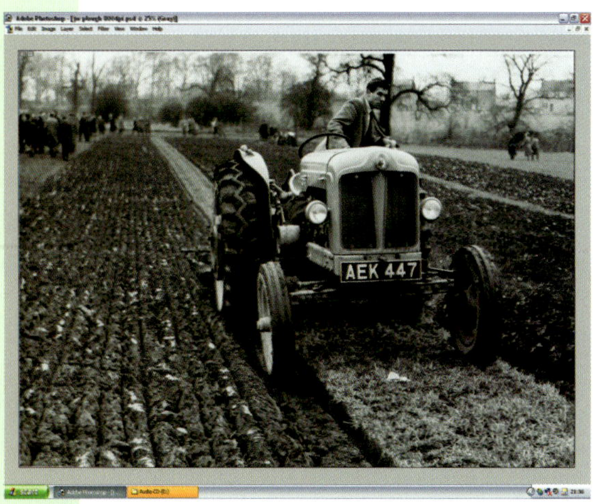

[3.9] A scanned print from a bygone era

Scanning at above 300dpi

Then there is the other extreme: those people who like to scan at the highest dpi possible to ensure they have a digital image that holds the greatest amount of information possible. In reality, there is no benefit in scanning at a resolution higher than 300dpi, as the information simply is not present in the print. To demonstrate this, I scanned a print of approximately 7x5in (see Fig 3.9, below left). As shown in Fig 3.10 (opposite), at 800dpi, the image on the left is twice the dpi resolution as the image on the right, which was scanned at 400dpi, although the later is viewed at twice the magnification to make a fair comparison. The interesting thing to note is that there is very little discernible difference in quality when you compare the fine details in the two pictures. The only reason for scanning a print in excess of 300dpi is if you want a bigger image from which to produce a bigger print.

Film is designed so that it can be enlarged, and responds well to scanning at higher resolution. For print purposes, it would not be uncommon to scan medium-format film at 1600dpi.

However, I do so because I want to produce a large, sharp, high-quality print, not because I intend to use it on the web.

Scanned images and computer memory

It is fairly easy to work out the resolution you need once you understand the mathematics; in fact, most scanner drivers do this for you. Imagine I have a $2\frac{1}{4}$x$2\frac{1}{4}$in piece of film and want an image that fits within a screen that is 1280x1024 pixels. I may choose 400dpi and end up with an image that is 900x900 pixels. How big this is in terms of memory depends on the image type. For a 24-bit true-colour image, you require 900x900x3 (i.e. 2,430,000) bytes of memory, as the RGB colour scheme requires 3 bytes per pixel to describe a colour image. By contrast, a 16-bit greyscale requires only 2 bytes per pixel (so the example image requires 1,620,000 bytes of memory), while an 8-bit greyscale image needs only 810,000 bytes of memory.

When people complain that their computer is running too slowly, it is invariably a shortage of memory that is at fault. When you start scanning prints at very high resolutions, you need to take into account how much memory you have in the computer. Bearing in mind that you need memory for the operating system, image-manipulation program and scanner software, that may not leave you much left for the image. If the computer can't hold the image in memory, it will have to swap out part of this memory to the hard disk. That is a slow process in itself, which progressively worsens. If you see the hard-drive disk light glow permanently as you manipulate your images, either contemplate buying more memory or scan at a lower resolution or bit depth. If you scan at a resolution that suits your web-publishing requirements, it's unlikely that memory shortage should present a problem.

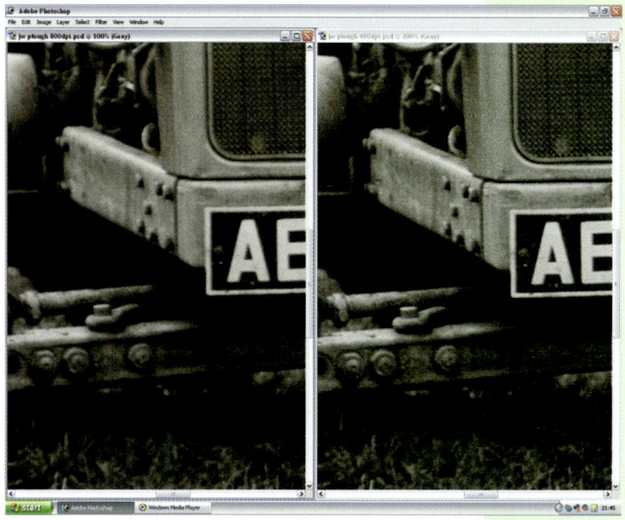

[3.10] 800dpi and 400dpi details compared on screen

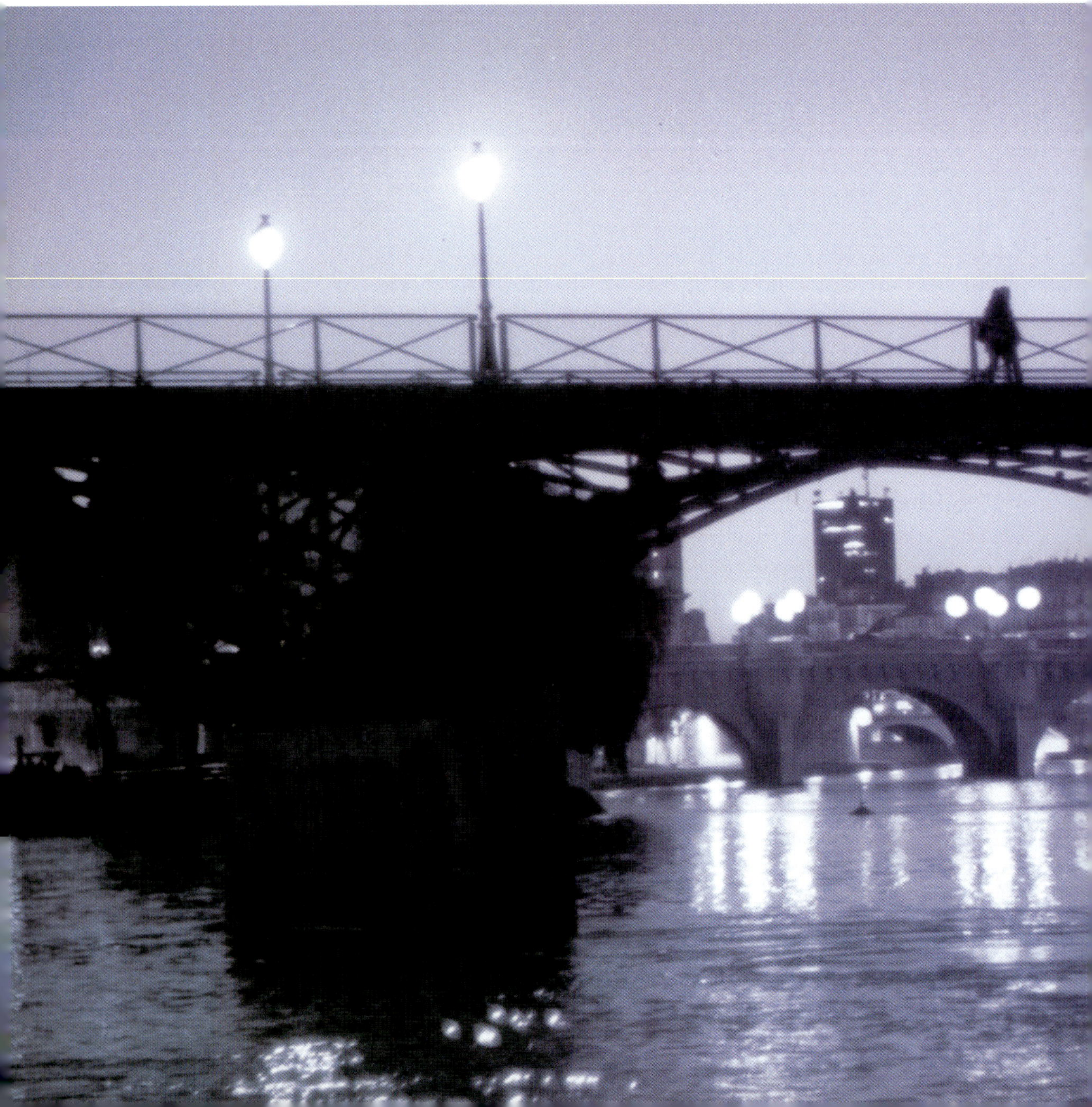

Part Two

How to construct your own site

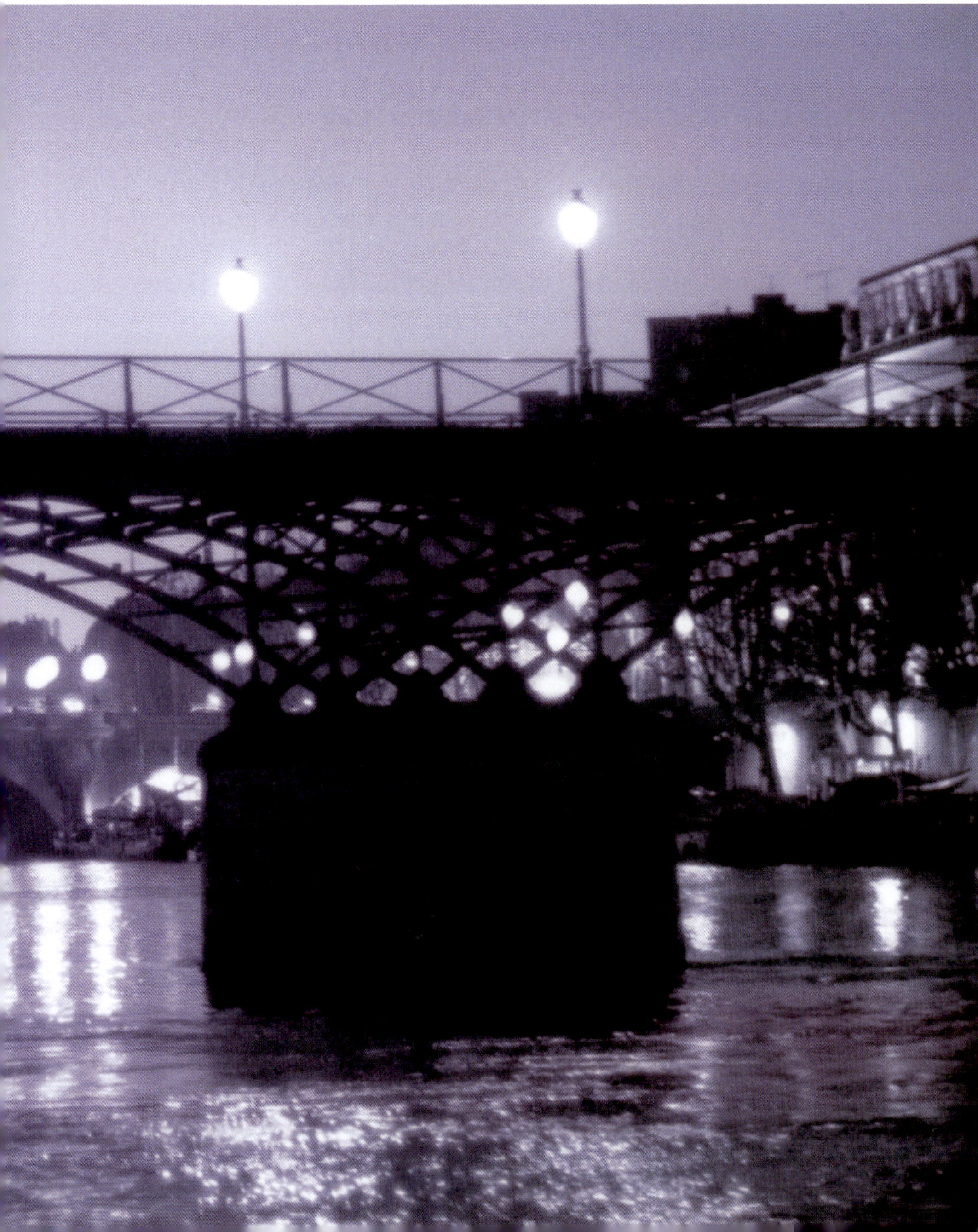

4 HTML: The Language of the Web

On the face of it, HTML may look quite intimidating. In fact, it is deceptively easy to learn and master. This section of the book will give a sufficient grounding in HTML for creating a professional-looking site. Armed with this experience, you should feel confident to address a more technical reference work.

HTML stands for Hypertext Mark-up Language, and put simply it is the language used to create web documents. Those of you who have already dabbled with web-authoring tools, where the underlying HTML code is hidden in favour of a graphical WYSIWYG (pronounced 'whizzywig', this is an acronym of 'what you see is what you get') editor, may wonder if there is any need to learn HTML at all.

It is certainly possible to create web pages without seeing a single line of HTML. However, some knowledge of the language will enable you to create far more suitably tuned pages. For example, some web-authoring tools have very limited page design facilities, in order to reduce their complexity. Additionally, the HTML they generate might not be wholly compliant with the latest standard specification, and some authoring tools are notorious for producing lengthy, inefficient code.

You might also see a very elegant design technique on a page you visit. By choosing the VIEW/SOURCE menu option on your browser, you can see precisely how this HTML was implemented and perhaps adopt a similar approach in your own pages by taking that code and modifying it to suit your circumstances. Learning by example – as long as you avoid wholesale plagiarism – is a good way of developing your HTML expertise. In the traditional software world, on the other hand, you simply don't have the opportunity to do this because the original source code is not present.

4

It is true that many web designers prefer not to see raw HTML and so opt for a graphical web-authoring tool. With 'point-and-click' user interface design, automatic browser-compatibility checks, site-management tools and other time-saving devices, you may be persuaded to buy one of these tools. Some of the better web-authoring tools also let you get the best from both worlds – they allow you to manipulate the components of a web page quickly and in an interactive way, yet still allow you to tweak the generated HTML by hand. However, at the price of a mid-range SLR, they represent a significant investment. By all means use a specialist tool if you prefer, but, as this book aims to show, a simple text editor is really all you need to get started.

Web-editing software

There are a number of dedicated editors (e.g. TopStyle from www.bradsoft.com) that allow you to write HTML and style sheets in a structured environment. Typically they include features such as syntax checking, textual formatting and design validation. This is my preferred way of working.

Shortcut
Web-editing software

Spelling HTML correctly

An important point to be aware of when writing HTML is that, as it was developed in the US, it uses American or 'International English' spelling throughout the language definition. For example, 'color', 'center' and so on.

Shortcut
Spelling HTML correctly

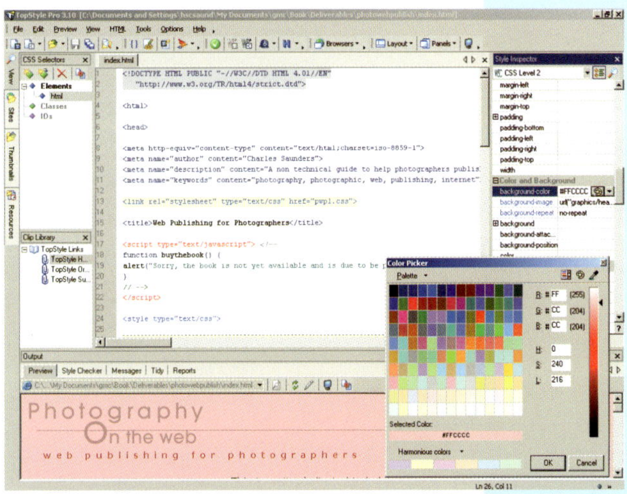

[4.1] TopStyle Pro in action

4

Creating your first HTML document

Rather than expect you to retype the sample HTML scripts included here (an inherently error-prone process) all the worked examples may be found on the web at: www.photowebpublish.com. Download instructions are also available on the site.

As shown in Fig 4.2 (below), a standard HTML document is comprised of three parts: a document-type section, a header section and a body section. These are identified using tags, which help the Internet browser make sense of the information as it reads and displays the HTML document. Most HTML tags have an opening and closing form. The closing form has a / symbol within it. It is important to remember that the tags do not appear in the browser window.

For example, the header section has the tag <head> to open it and </head> to close the section. Similarly, the body section tags are <body> and </body> to describe this region of the document. In our first example, we are going to publish a paragraph of text. We'll use the 'sunny 16 rule', as described by Roger Hicks and Frances Schultz in their book *Perfect Exposure*. The panel opposite shows a very simple HTML document that publishes this rule and its reference.

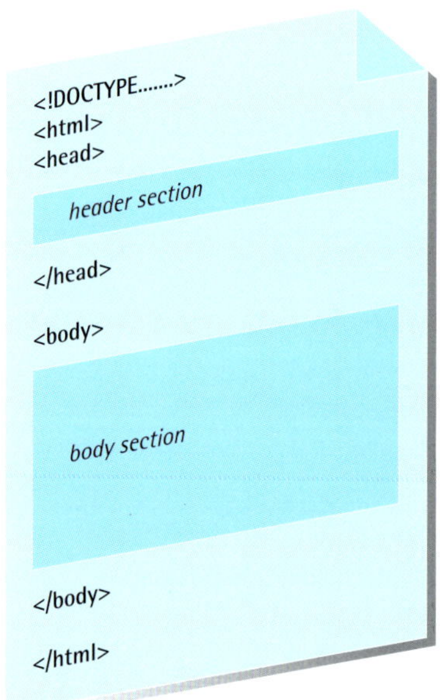

[4.2] An outline of the structure of an HTML document

```
<!DOCTYPE HTML PUBLIC "-//W3C//DTD HTML 4.01//EN"
    "http://www.w3.org/TR/html4/strict.dtd">
<html lang="en">
<!-- www.photowebpublish.com -->
<head>
<meta http-equiv="content-type" content="text/html;charset=iso-8859-1">
<title>Exposure Tricks</title>
</head>
<body>
<h1>Sunny 16 rule</h1>
<p>In full sun, with the sun behind you, the correct exposure is 1/ISO (arithmetic) at
f/16. Thus ISO 125 film demands 1/125 second at f/16, while ISO 1000 film demands
1/1000 second at f/16. If you need to round off exposures, give extra exposure for
negatives and less exposure for transparencies: ISO 400 should work well at 1/250 for
negatives, 1/500 for transparencies. For side-lit subjects, give up to 1 stop more; for
back-lit subjects, up to 2 stops more.</p>
<p><cite> Taken from Perfect Exposure, copyright &copy; Roger Hicks and Frances
Schultz</cite><br />
<small>ISBN 0 7153 0814 9</small></p>
</body>
</html>
```

Fig 4.3 (right) shows how this simple HTML document is displayed on my computer. There is a chance that if you try this on your machine, there may be some subtle differences, as described in Part One. The headings on pages 74–7 take a look at each section of the HTML file in turn.

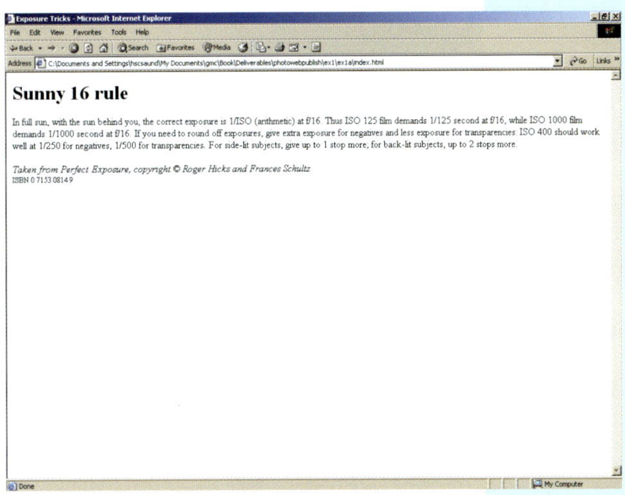

[4.3] The sunny 16 rule with default styling

Document-type section

```
<!DOCTYPE HTML PUBLIC "-//W3C//DTD
HTML 4.01//EN"
    "http://www.w3.org/TR/html4/
    strict.dtd">
```

The document-type (doctype) tag tells the browser what HTML standard is being used. In effect it says 'I speak this language' to the browser. Here we are using the strict version of HTML 4.01, where deprecated tags and non-standard browser behaviour are not tolerated (see page 30). Very often you will see HTML files without a doctype, but it is good practice to keep one in at the top of your file rather than let the Internet browser try and guess.

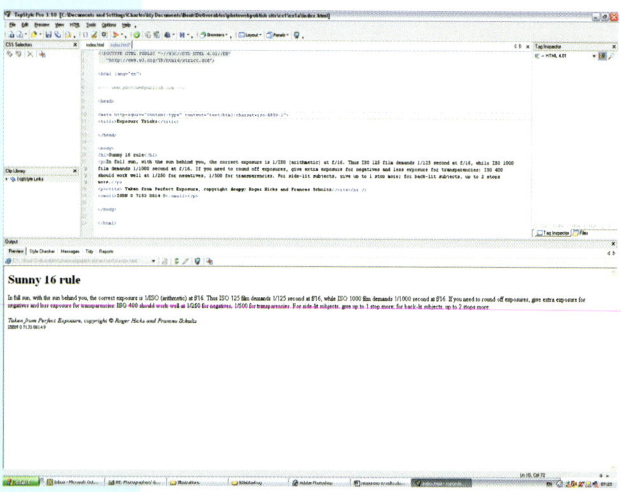

[4.4] The sunny 16 rule as defined in my HTML editor

Next we see the HTML tag definitions <html lang="en"></html>, which are placed at each end of the document. This tag informs the Internet browser that the document is written in HTML and English (en). Everything that follows sits within the HTML tags. After the opening HTML tag, we see an example of an HTML comment. Internet browsers ignore the text that exists between the special elements of <!– and -->, which means whatever is placed between these elements is not displayed or acted upon. I've inserted a reference to my site merely as an illustration. It is good practice to comment liberally within your HTML code so that later on, when you come to maintain your site, you can recall the train of thought that helped create the page in the first instance.

Header section

The document is then further subdivided into two parts: the header <head></head> and the body <body></body>. The header contains information about the document itself, the body the content to be published.

```
<head>
<meta http-equiv="content-type"
content="text/html;charset=iso-8859-1">
<title>Exposure Tricks</title>
</head>
```

Here we have a very small header part described within the <head></head> tags, but there is a great deal we can do in this section. The web needs to display all the languages of the world with all their alphabets or character sets (see pages 31–2). The first line of the header merely states, in a rather complex-looking way, that we shall be using the 8-bit character set for Western languages. If you were writing a web page in Hebrew you would declare the use of the iso-8859-8 character set. The next line is where we give the document its title. Any text that is typed between the <title></title> tags will appear at the top of the browser window. The title is also very important as this text is used both as the bookmark name and by search engines to index your page. It is good practice to give every page on your site a unique and meaningful title.

Body section

Next comes the body section, which is delineated by the tags <body> and </body> between them both, the bulk of the document definition resides, such as our main heading:

```
<h1>Sunny 16 rule</h1>
```

There then follows the tag <p></p>, which denotes the beginning and end of a paragraph. The paragraph tag is

The <h> tag

The <h1> tag means the following text is to be treated as a heading of type 1, until the closing tag </h1>. There are six different types of heading from <h1> to <h6>, the largest text definition begins at <h1>, and with each increase in number the text gets progressively smaller.

probably the tag you will use the most in writing HTML. Like the <h> heading tag before it, the <p> paragraph tag is an example of a 'block-level element'. In effect, this means that line breaks are normally inserted before and after the tag's occurrence. In this case, we insert the definition of the sunny 16 rule (which, incidentally, does work if you have ever found yourself without an exposure meter) between these tags, as shown below.

```
<p>In full sun, with the sun behind you,
the correct exposure is 1/ISO (arithmetic)
at f/16. Thus ISO 125 film demands 1/125
second at f/16, while ISO 1000 film
demands 1/1000 second at f/16. If you
need to round off exposures, give extra
exposure for negatives and less
exposure for transparencies: ISO 400
should work well at 1/250 for negatives,
1/500 for transparencies. For side-lit
subjects, give up to 1 stop more; for
back-lit subjects, up to 2 stops more.</p>
```

Shortcut

The <h> tag

Shortcut

HTML and text formatting

HTML and text formatting

The most important thing to remember about entering text as code is that the browser takes no notice of the formatting in the source document or how it is laid out. It simply sees a string of characters. Multiple spaces, carriage return and line-feed characters are simply ignored, which means that, when published, the code above looks exactly the same no matter how it is written. Those familiar with modern word processors may find this disconcerting, but text has to be capable of flowing into a wide variety of environments and it therefore makes sense for you to concentrate on content and let the browser worry about presentation.

After opening a new paragraph, I went on to insert the publication name and authors from which this definition was derived. In this instance, I used the 'inline' <cite></cite> tag, which can be used in cases like this, where the text requires an acknowledgement. Inline elements affect styling characteristics 'within the line', and unlike block-level elements do not force formatting characteristics such as a line break. The appearance of this citation will vary depending on your browser's in-built style sheet, but most browsers show citations as italicized text. To be extra cautious, I've also declared that Roger Hicks and Frances Schultz have copyright on this extracted text, and went a step further by using the copyright symbol (©). Such characters are not part of the normal alphanumeric character set and must be declared using what are called character entities. They can be described using the convention [&name;] or [&#nnn;] where n is a number. For example, the copyright character entity is © or ©. A list of valid character entities can be found on the W3C web page.

```
<cite> Taken from Perfect Exposure,
copyright &copy; Roger Hicks and
Frances Schultz</cite><br />
```

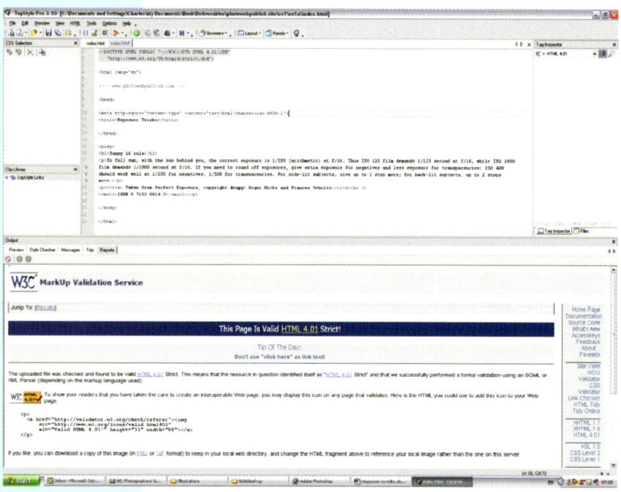

[4.5] You can validate your HTML on the fly with many HTML editors, although the service is also directly available from the W3C

4

After the citation text we create some space by adding a line break using the tag <br>. This tag is unusual in that it does not have a tag terminator </br>, and is an example of one of the empty or 'standalone' tags. The latest HTML standard suggests that line breaks should be written as <br /> with an explicit built in terminator, but the older format still works in all browsers.

Finally, I have inserted the ISBN number for the referenced book. My intention was to make this text smaller than the default size, so I used the <small></small> tags. I can't claim that it really shows in my version of Internet Explorer, but the difference seems more pronounced in my version of Opera. This merely serves to underline my earlier point about testing your web pages on different software platforms.

```
<small>ISBN 0 7153 0814 9</small>
```

The document is finally closed with the tags </body></html>, and that is really all there is to creating a simple text-based web page.

You should try this first example either by retyping the HTML code or by visiting www.photowebpublish.com to download the prepared HTML file onto your computer. Open the HTML file in your chosen browser and compare it to the screen grab in this chapter. You should now edit the HTML file (available under the VIEW/SOURCE menu option on most browsers) and change the ISO 400 illustration to ISO 100. Save the file and then go back to your browser and press the 'Reload page' or 'Refresh page' button. You should see the document changes you have made appear in the browser window. This cycle of edit, save and reload is one you will learn to do countless times as you build and develop web pages.

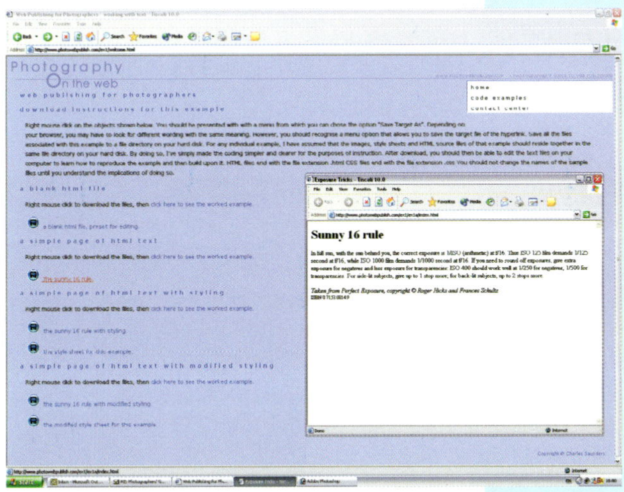

[4.6] All the worked examples are available on www.photowebpublish.com, so no retyping is necessary

5 Cascading Style Sheets

Shortcut

What is a style sheet?

The key to consistent design

In the last chapter we created a simple page of text using HTML alone (see pages 72–7), yet no one could claim that this looked anything other than bland. To improve this, we need to introduce the concept of style sheets. Cascading style sheets (CSS) are becoming an increasingly important element in web design, and offer significant benefits over traditional methods of styling pages with HTML.

The overwhelming majority of browsers are capable of reading and understanding the style-sheet

What is a style sheet?

A style sheet is a sequence of formatting instructions that can control the appearance and behaviour of many pages of HTML, and the use of cascading style sheets separates issues of presentation from content. The style sheet will control how a page looks, yet the HTML page defines what that page actually says. The advantage of this is clear: once we have settled on a design, which may incorporate more than one style sheet, it becomes considerably simpler to write the website. Furthermore, it will also be easier to maintain.

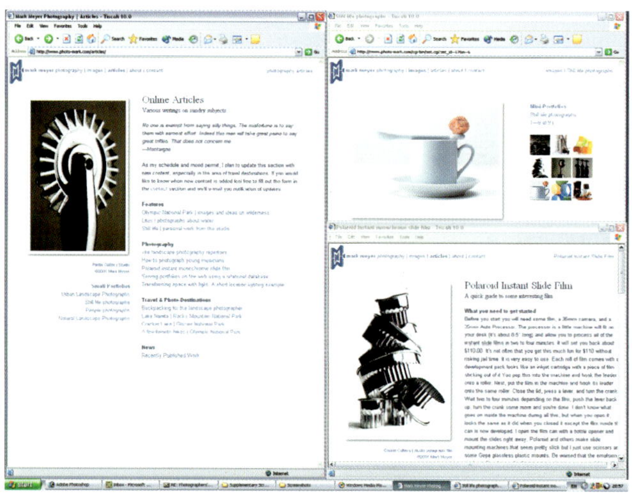

[5.1] Mark Meyer's website (www.photo-mark.com) has it all: fantastic content, branding, images and superb use of web technology. © Mark Meyer

declarations included here, so you can feel confident in embracing this approach to web design. The information presented here should provide a gentle introduction to cascading style-sheet principles and enough material to produce an effective website. It is not intended to be a comprehensive reference guide for CSS specification. Although you can buy many excellent reference books on CSS, information is also freely available on the web at www.w3.org/style/css. If you are more technically inclined and want to find out what else is possible, you should look at the full-blown specification at www.w3.org/TR/REC-CSS1 and www.w3.org/TR/REC-CSS2.

CSS in theory

Some theory is needed to take full advantage of cascading style sheets. The first is rule syntax. Style sheets are lists of one or more rules for describing how a page element is to be displayed. The format for the rule is as follows:

```
selector , selector {property: value;
property: value;}
```

This looks more complex than it actually is. The selector or list of selectors identifies the elements that are affected by the styling rule or rules. There then follows a sequence of one or more stylistic declarations, such as colour, length, fonts and so on, which act upon the selectors. An example might be:

```
h1 {color: red;}
```

This makes the typeface of all type1 headings <h1> appear in red.

Multiple selectors are separated by commas – for example, h1, h2, h3, h4, h4 {color: red;}. Multiple-property value pairs are separated by semicolons, as in h1 {color: red; background-color: black}. If you are writing style sheets and something doesn't appear to work properly, it's invariably because some of this crucial punctuation is missing.

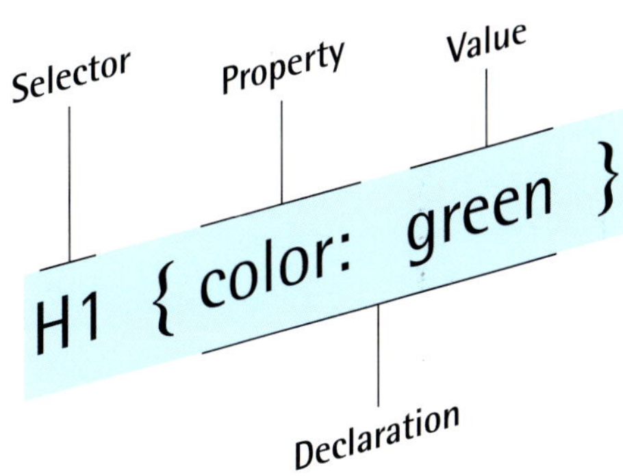

[5.2] The structure of a CSS rule

Shortcut
The box model

Referencing style information

There are three ways to reference style information. First, you can link your HTML file to an external style sheet. Second, you can embed the style sheet declaration within the <head> section of your HTML file. Third, you can include style information 'inline' within the tags themselves. As style information can come from three potential sources, there are rules of precedence. For example, linked style commands can be overruled by embedded style information, which can in turn be overruled by inline style commands. These precedence rules can be used to good effect to create generic style sheets that satisfy the bulk of your requirements, with local overriding styles in the HTML document as circumstances dictate.

The box model

Style sheets work on the basis that each selector on a web page is contained within a theoretical box (see Fig 5.3, below). Furthermore, this box can exhibit certain physical properties that can be altered by style commands. At the core of each selector, there exists the content. For example, this could be a piece of text, such as a heading, or an image. Around the content, there exists a further layer called the padding. Around the padding, there then exists a border and the last layer around the border is a margin, which is transparent and used to create separation between other objects on the web page. It is important to understand the box model, as it forms the basis of all presentation on the web page.

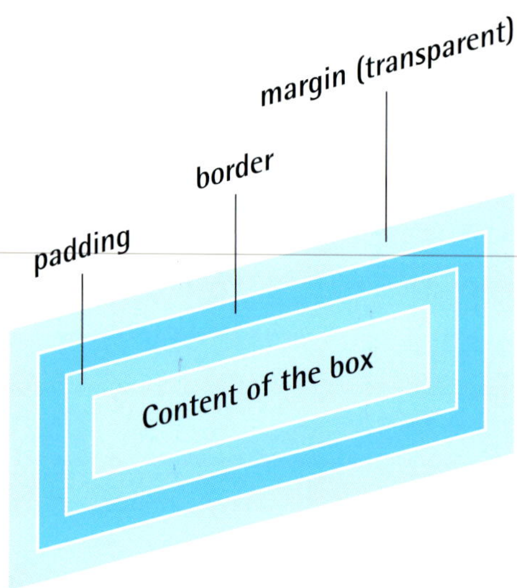

[5.3] The style-sheet box model

CSS in practice

Returning to our sunny 16 example (see page 73), I've now linked the HTML file to an external style sheet. The declaration to this style sheet is made within the <head> section thus:

```
<head>
...
<link rel="stylesheet" type="text/css"
href="ex1b.css">
...
</head>
```

The important thing to note is the name of the style sheet: ex1b.css. Style sheets by convention use a .css file extension. They are, however, just simple text files and this particular example resides in the same file directory as the HTML document that references it. When you open the style sheet, you can view the following commands:

```
html    {margin: 0px; padding: 0px;
        background-color: #ffffcc;
}
body    {margin: 5px 40px 20px 40px;
        font-family: Verdana, "Trebuchet
        MS", san-serif;
        text-align: left;
}
```

In our simple style-sheet example, I have defined style information for both the <html> and <body> elements. It is interesting to note that in the web page, the <body> element exists within the <html> element, so the former may also 'inherit' style properties from its 'parent', the <html> element. As we shall see, the concept of inheritance is very important in style sheets and is one of the reasons why the word 'cascading' is used.

In this example, the <html> element initially has its margin and padding properties set to 0 pixels. In theory all the content should abut against the walls of the browser window. In addition, the background colour property of the <html> element is set to a light shade of yellow.

The <body> section now has its margins reset to 5px, 40px, 20px and 40px. In a clockwise fashion, the four values specify the margin amounts for the top, right, bottom and left margins of the <body> section. With these new margins, it should appear as if the objects placed in the <body> have a little more 'space to breathe'. The next property is a definition of the typefaces to be used within the <body> section. Written in priority order, your browser will try to match its list of installed fonts to the list requested. If your

5

Shortcut

Using quotes for font names

Using quotes for font names

Font names that are made up of more than one word appear in quotes – e.g. "Times New Roman". These have to be in quotes or the browser will not be able to distinguish when a font name has ended and the CCS definition continues.

computer has Verdana installed, it will use this font. If not, it will then try "Trebuchet MS", and if all else fails your computer will resort to its default installed sans-serif font. Finally, the last statement in the <body> style definition is to make the <body> text aligned to the left of the page. Using this style sheet with our previous HTML document, you should see a screen that looks like the one shown in Fig 5.4.

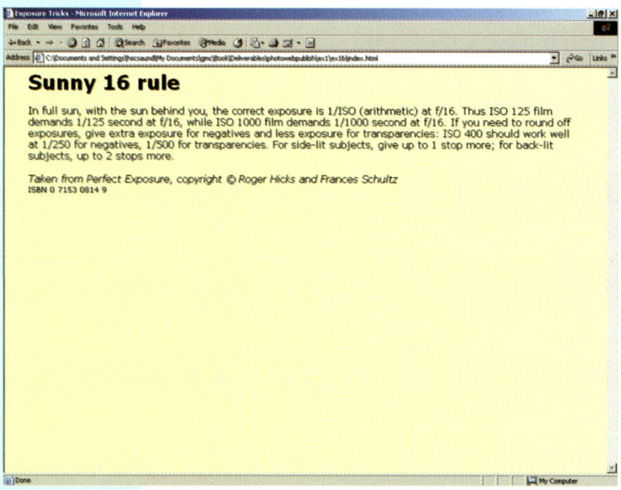

[5.4] Sunny 16 rule with a simple cascading style sheet applied

Using style sheets from multiple sources

Building on our last example, this next exercise illustrates how you can incorporate style information from a variety of sources. The revised style sheet for this example now contains the following:

```
html  {margin: 0px; padding: 0px;
       background-color: #ffffcc;
}
body  {margin: 5px 40px 20px 40px;
       font-family: Verdana, "Trebuchet
       MS", san-serif;
       text-align: left;
}
h1    {margin: 5px 40px 20px -20px;}
cite  {font-size: 0.75em;
       text-transform: lowercase;
}
```

I have now included a specific style for the <h1> heading, where I have altered the left-hand margin so that it is indented –20 pixels from its parent <body> element. If you want to see just where the <body> element lies in relation to the <h1> and <html> elements, try this example and temporarily change the background colour of the <body> element to #ffffff and the background colour of the <h1> element to #999999. On refreshing the page, you will clearly see where the elements reside within the context of the overall page.

Returning to our example, I have inserted some styling information for the <cite> tag. I have also reduced the font size and transformed the text to all lower case. The term 'em' hails from traditional typesetting where it refers to the width of the letter "M". To understand how this works, you need to appreciate that font sizes are set relative to the font size of the parent element. In this case, the parent element is a <p>, which in turn inherits its font size from the <body> element. The size 0.75em is equivalent to saying the font size should be 75% of the parent font. In other words, the <cite> font size is 25% smaller than the text you see in the <p> paragraphs. You could also write:

```
cite      {font-size: 75%;
          text-transform: lowercase;
}
```

You can also resize fonts using pixels or points as absolute units of measure, but the safest method is to use relative sizes as you cannot predict how these other units of measure will be rendered on differing monitor resolutions. A less sophisticated alternative to the use of 'em' is the use of font-size keywords for pre-set typeface dimensions. Within the CSS specification, there are seven sizes to choose from and their names are: xx-small, x-small, small, medium, large, x-large and xx-large. Irritatingly, differing browsers do not always set the default browser font size to the medium keyword, which can create some anomalies across different technical platforms. Finally, the text-transform rule was included to illustrate how you can manipulate the appearance of the text. Other values include: none, capitalize, (each word) and uppercase.

Looking at the screen grab for this example, you will notice that something strange has happened to the heading. The <h1> styling we have seen made no

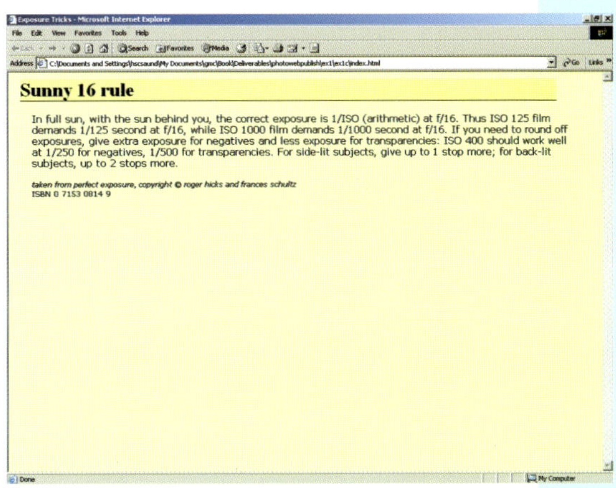

[5.5] The sunny 16 rule with multiple styling applied

5

reference to a dark yellow background or a serif font, so how did this happen? The answer can be found by looking at the source HTML document. Additional style information has been included in the <head> section of the web page, as shown here:

```
<head>
...
...
<style type="text/css">
h1 {background-color: #ffff99;font-family:
"Times New Roman", serif; border-
bottom: 1px solid black}
</style>
...
...
</head>
```

Though we link to an external style sheet, we have also included styling information between two <style></style> tags in the <head> section. Where applicable, this overrides the style information from the externally linked sheet. The <h1> element now has a darker background colour. Without this, its default styling would have been transparent, thereby showing the colour of its grandparent, the <html> element. The font-family declaration equally overrides the inherited value that would have been one of the available sans-serif fonts declared for the <body> element. Additionally, I have included a border at the bottom of the 'box', one pixel wide and in solid black. There will be more on border manipulation later when we examine the use of images (see Chapter Seven, page 102).

Inline style information is the most specific level of style definition you can achieve when applying styling rules; its use overrides all other style definitions. I tend to use them sparingly to override the default behaviour defined elsewhere. For example, if we wanted the citation and ISBN reference on this page only to appear in red, I could have applied the following inline style to the surrounding paragraph:

```
<p style="color: red;"><cite> Taken from
Perfect Exposure, copyright &copy;
Roger Hicks and Frances
Schultz</cite><br />
<small>ISBN 0 7153 0814 9</small></p>
```

The style information is declared in the opening tag of the element it pertains to. In this example, it is the paragraph containing both the citation and ISBN reference. They both inherit the red colour from their parent element <p>. You might try this for yourself and experiment with inline styles to see what you can achieve. For example, you could try turning the background colour of the <cite> element to something other than its transparent state. Inline styles are a great idea, but you should use them with caution as peppering your HTML with inline styles can make your overall site harder to maintain.

Finally, if there are rules that you never want to be overridden, you should declare them using the keyword !important after the value and before the semicolon:

```
body {color: black !important;}
```

In summary

Cascading style sheets offer great advantages to the web designer. Consistency between pages is significantly easier since many pages can share the same style sheet. Maintenance is much easier since a change in one style sheet can update the appearance of many hundreds of pages. Prior to this approach, style changes would be included with the HTML documents and this posed a significant maintenance burden if a differing look and feel was required.

By using style sheets, your web pages can become much more structured and you can avoid pollution with presentational mark-up tags. Take a look behind the scenes at any web page that is not using CSS and you will see what an awful mess it really is. Not only is it more bloated than its CSS-styled equivalent, it is also far less efficient when loaded into a browser. CSS already enables a much richer capability for styling than HTML alone ever allowed. In short, if you already have books on writing HTML, you should completely ignore any of the tags reserved for presentation mark-up such as bold <b> or italic <i>, and embrace CSS as the preferred mechanism for achieving design consistency.

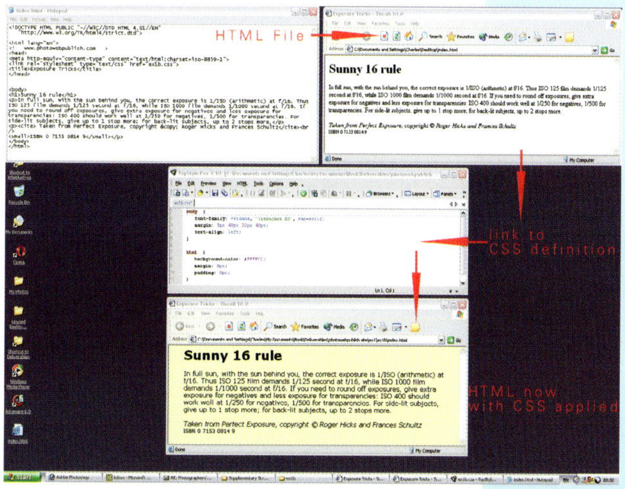

[5.6] A simple example to show how HTML and CSS definitions work together

6 Manipulating Blocks of Text with CSS

Styling text

Cascading style sheets can be used to manipulate and style blocks of text within a page, allowing you to create a much more dynamic-looking website.

Figs 6.1 and 6.2 show the next worked example. It seems remarkable to me that all that separates these two radically different web pages is a short cascading style sheet that contains the rules shown in the panel opposite.

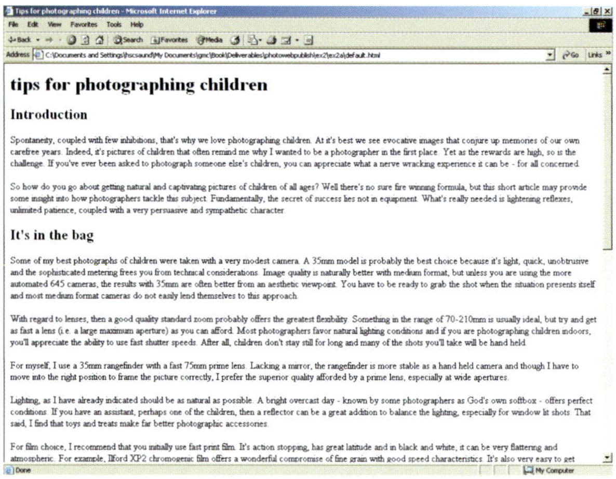

[6.1] The sample article with no styling applied

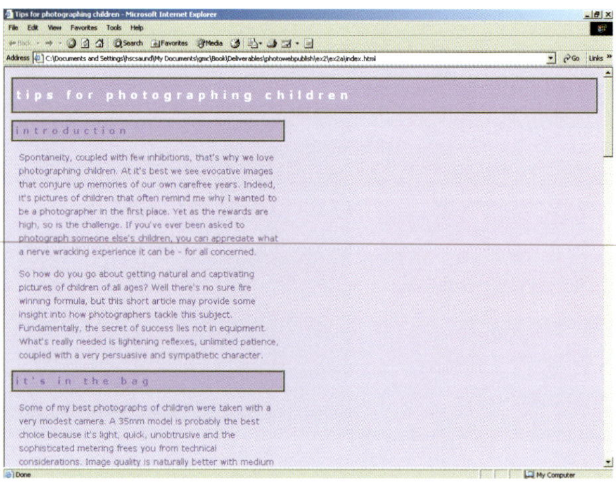

[6.2] The sample article with styling applied

```
html {
        margin: 0px;
        padding: 0px;
        background-color: #ffccff;
}
body {
        background-color: transparent;
        font-family: Verdana, "Trebuchet
        MS", Arial, sans-serif;
        text-align: left;
}
h1 {
        margin: 0px;
        padding: 15px 15px 15px 5px;
        background-color: #cc99cc;
        color: #ffffff;
        text-transform: lowercase;
        letter-spacing: 0.5em;
        text-align: left;
        font-size: 1.10em;
        border: ridge;
}
p {
        background-color: transparent;
        margin: 1em;
        padding: 0px;
        line-height: 1.6em;
        color: #660066;
        width: 45%;
        font-size: 0.85em;
}
h2, h3, h4, h5, h6 {
        margin: 10px 0px 0px 0px;
        padding: 5px;
        background-color: #cc99cc;
        border-style: ridge;
        text-transform: lowercase;
        color: #990099;
        letter-spacing: 0.5em;
        text-align: left;
        font-size: 0.95em;
        width: 45%;
}
```

The HTML for these two files is virtually identical, save for the missing style-sheet declaration in the non-styled version. The HTML document mark-up is shown overleaf. To keep things short, I have omitted reproducing the text for the entire article.

```
<!DOCTYPE HTML PUBLIC "-//W3C//DTD HTML 4.01//EN"
    "http://www.w3.org/TR/html4/strict.dtd">
<html lang="en">
<!-- www.photowebpublish.com -->
<head>
<meta http-equiv="content-type" content="text/html;charset=iso-8859-1">
<title>Tips for photographing children</title>
<link rel="stylesheet" type="text/css" href="ex2a.css">
</head>
<body>
<h1>tips for photographing children</h1>
<h2>Introduction</h2>
<p>Spontaneity, coupled with few inhibitions, that's why we love photographing
children. At its best we see evocative images that conjure up memories of our own
carefree years. Indeed, it's pictures of children that often remind me why I wanted to
be a photographer in the first place. Yet as the rewards are high, so is the challenge.
If you've ever been asked to photograph someone else's children, you can appreciate
what a nerve wracking experience it can be - for all concerned.</p>
<p>So how do you go about getting natural and captivating pictures of children of all
ages? Well there's no sure fire winning formula, but this short article may provide
some insight into how photographers tackle this subject. Fundamentally, the secret of
success lies not in equipment. What's really needed is lightning reflexes, unlimited
patience, coupled with a very persuasive and sympathetic character.</p>
<h2>It's in the bag</h2>
<p>Some of my best photographs of children were taken with a very modest camera.
A 35mm model is probably the best choice because it's light, quick, unobtrusive and
the sophisticated metering frees you from technical considerations. Image quality is
naturally better with medium format, but unless you are using the more automated
645 cameras, the results with 35mm are often better from an aesthetic viewpoint. You
have to be ready to grab the shot when the situation presents itself and most
medium format cameras do not easily lend themselves to this approach.</p>
...
...
...
</body>
</html>
```

The HTML section

Let's begin by taking apart the HTML document. This contains the title *Tips for Photographing Children*, and this text, as you would expect, appears in the title bar of the browser window. The HTML document links to a style sheet, of type CSS, called 'ex2a.css'. We can assume that this style sheet resides in the same file directory as the HTML document itself.

The <body></body> section is fairly straightforward. It contains a <h1></h1> heading, followed by a series of paragraphs demarcated by the <p></p> tags. Interspersed throughout the article are a series of level two heading tags denoted by the <h2></h2> tag, which break up the article into logical chunks.

Breaking down the style sheet

To understand why the page looks the way it does, we need to dissect the style sheet carefully. Its textual representation can be reproduced graphically in my favoured CSS editing program. It is included here to assist with the visualization of the style sheet's behaviour.

The <html> element

To begin with, the <html> element has its margins and padding set to 0 pixels. It also has its background colour set to a shade of purple (#FFCCFF). The next definition is that of the <body> element. Here the background colour is specifically set to transparent. You could argue that the inclusion of this rule is redundant, since 'transparent' is the default value of any element's background colour. However, specifically declaring this setting ensures that it overrides any end-user declared styles that may exist on the users' browser configuration. Finally, the preferred fonts for this page are declared and the text is left aligned.

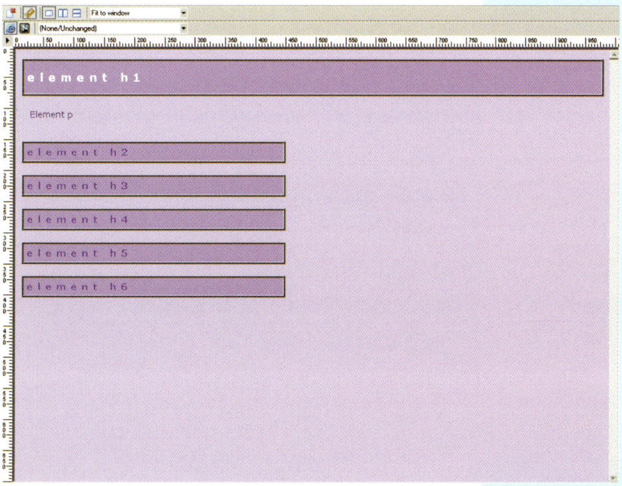

[6.3] The example style sheet with visual representation

The <h1> element

There then comes a series of formatting rules for the <h1> element. The margin of this element is set to 0 pixels, but padding values are set. (Remember: padding surrounds the heading content and takes on background characteristics.) In this case, the background characteristic is a darker purple colour (#CC99CC), and the padding value ensures that the dark purple container is greater in appearance than just the default space around the heading. The colour of the heading typeface is declared as white (#FFFFFF) and the text, irrespective of what is typed in the HTML document, is transformed to lowercase.

To emphasize the heading, I have increased the letter-spacing value from its default of 0 to 0.5em. An alternative to letter spacing would have been to increase the word spacing and this would have achieved a similar degree of emphasis. When using letter or word spacing, it is good practice to stick to either left- or right-aligned text. The text-align value 'justify' can, as you might expect, produce some unpredictable results.

The textual definitions are complete when the font size is set to 1.10em, and the <h1> declaration is finished by defining a border to surround the content.

Borders

You will recall from the box model that a border surrounds the content and padding of an element. A border has three properties: width, style and colour. In a border declaration, not all three need to be defined explicitly. For example, the default value of the width is 'medium', which is to be about 2–3 pixels. Other width keywords include 'thin' and 'thick'. Alternatively, you may elect to use pixel units for borders since they can be easier to envision. The border style defines the visual appearance of the border boundary and can take the values of dotted, dashed, solid, double, groove, ridge, inset and outset. There is also the style 'none', which means there is no border at all.

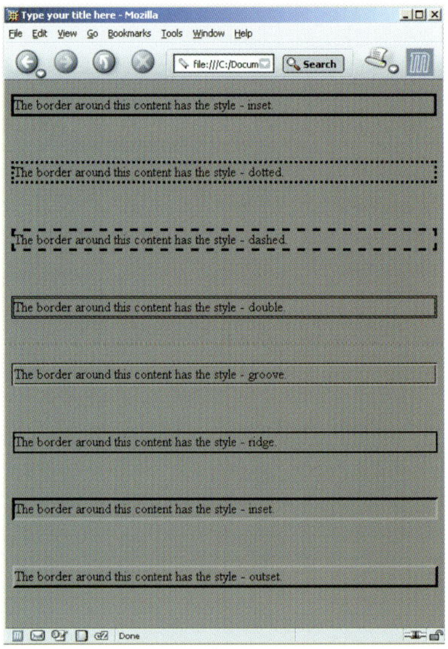

[6.4] Styles of borders

By default, the colour of the border is the same as that of the surrounded content, unless otherwise specified. The border declaration takes the syntax of:

```
selector {border: [width] [border-style] [color];}
```

Additionally, you can also declare rules for each side of the border using: border-top, border-right, border-bottom and border-left. This gives you greater flexibility when manipulating the individual border characteristics of all your elements on a page.

The <p> element

Following the <h1> declaration, we see the set of rules for the paragraph <p> element. Here we can see two new rules are introduced: line height and width. By increasing the line height you can increase the readability of long lines of text. Like font size, it is safest to use relative measurements such as 'em' or percentages, though absolute values like pixels or points can be used. The width property refers to the size of the paragraph content across the browser window. Absolute values such as pixels or relative percentage values are the most commonly applied. The main advantage of using percentage values is that they will adjust themselves to the size of the browser window and thereby allow fluid layouts. By setting the width value to 45%, I have left a block of space on the right-hand side of the browser window for some images to accompany this article in a later example (see overleaf).

The last style rule contains no new properties, yet it does illustrate how a series of styling declarations may apply to multiple elements. In this example, headings <h2> to <h6> have been grouped together and will all therefore exhibit the same stylistic behaviour. Notice how commas separate all the individual selectors. If you were to omit them accidentally, you would change the meaning entirely.

Styling text with class and id selectors

So far we have applied styles to HTML elements, but what if you want to change the style of some elements of a given type, but not all? For example, in the screen shot for advanced textual styling, I have changed the style of the leading paragraph. I can't create a style to turn the text of the <p> element orange, since this would affect all paragraph blocks in the document. Similarly, how is it possible to affect the style of a single word within a line (or 'inline')?

The answer lies in the use of 'class' and 'id' selectors. In effect, we create our own style selectors and associate them to the tags in our HTML document. Working hand in hand with class and id selectors are two new tags: <div> and <span>. The <div> and <span> tags are extremely useful and have been designed for use specifically with styles, since they contain no style formatting of their own. This means that areas of text or images that lie within these tags may take on the style characteristics of these 'parent' elements. The two elements differ in that <div> is a block-level element, whereas <span> is inline. Consider the HTML for our reformatted article (as shown opposite).

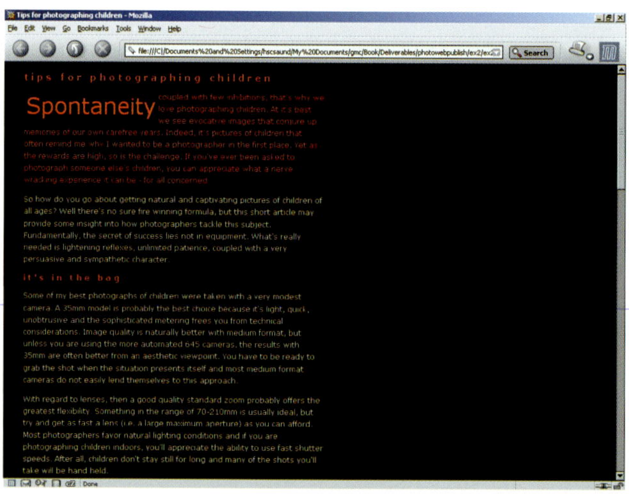

[6.5] The sample article with advanced textual styling applied

```
<!DOCTYPE HTML PUBLIC "-//W3C//DTD HTML 4.01//EN">
<html lang="en">
<!-- www.photowebpublish.com -->
<head>
<meta http-equiv="content-type" content="text/html;charset=iso-8859-1">
<title>Tips for photographing children</title>
<link rel="stylesheet" type="text/css" href="ex2d.css">
</head>
<body>
<div class="bodycopy">
<h1>tips for photographing children</h1>

<p id="firstpara"><span id="intro">Spontaneity</span>coupled with few inhibitions,
that's why we love photographing children. At its best we see evocative images that
conjure up memories of our own carefree years. Indeed, it's pictures of children that
often remind me why I wanted to be a photographer in the first place. Yet as the
rewards are high, so is the challenge. If you've ever been asked to photograph
someone else's children, you can appreciate what a nerve wracking experience it can
be – for all concerned.</p>

<p>So how do you go about getting natural and captivating pictures of children of all
ages? Well there's no sure fire winning formula, but this short article may provide
some insight into how photographers tackle this subject. Fundamentally, the secret of
success lies not in equipment. What's really needed is lightning reflexes, unlimited
patience, coupled with a very persuasive and sympathetic character.</p>
...
...
...
<p>Last but not least, good luck.</p>

<p>Copyright &copy; Charles Saunders</p>
</div>
</body>
</html>
```

Element 1

The first line to note is the tag <div class="bodycopy">, which is finally closed at the end of the <body> section with the corresponding </div> tag. Put simply, the opening tag declares that everything from this point on will be based on a style called 'bodycopy'. (We shall see what this style looks like when we examine the style sheet.) Setting the class attribute of the <div> tag is only one way to set a style. Another is to set the id of the opening paragraph tag <p id='firstpara'> to the style definition 'firstpara', which creates the leading orange paragraph. Naturally, the linked style sheet contains a style definition of this name that sets the typeface colour to orange.

There is very little to differentiate between class and id, and the differences that do exist are extremely subtle. The selectors in the style sheet are declared somewhat differently, but instead of creating an id I could have created a class called 'firstpara' and written <p class="firstpara"> to achieve the same effect. The key distinction is that id styles must be used only once in a document. In our example, it would not be possible to use 'firstpara' anywhere else in the document as it is declared as an id style. In contrast, class styles may be used a number of times in a document. Also, when resolving a contradiction of competing style definitions, id styles have higher precedence than class styles, which means you can use them to override default style behaviour.

Element 2

The next interesting style example is the use of the span element either side of the word 'Spontaneity'. The span element has been assigned to the id 'intro', which has been declared to create this highly emphasized textual style. Since the <span> declaration is closed immediately after the leading word, it can by definition only effect the first word in the paragraph. Moreover, since <span> is an inline element, it does not throw a line break into the text.

6

Style-sheet declarations

To further understand the use of class and id selectors, let's now take a look at the style sheet declarations.

```
body {
        background-color: #000000;
        color: #FFFFFF;
}
html    {
        margin: 0px;
        padding: 0px;
}
.bodycopy {
        background-color: #000000;
        color: #FFFFFF;
        font-family: verdana, "Trebuchet
        MS", heltetiva, arial, sans-serif;
        font-size: 0.75em;
        margin: 15px 25px 25px 25px;
        padding: 0;
        text-align: left;
        width: 50%;
}
.bodycopy h1 {
        background-color: #000000;
        color: #FF6600;
        font-family: verdana, heltetiva,
        arial, sans-serif;
        font-size: 125%;
        letter-spacing: 0.35em;
        text-align: left;
        text-transform: lowercase;
}
.bodycopy h2 {
        background-color: #000000;
        color: #FF6600;
        font-family: verdana, heltetiva,
        arial, sans-serif;
        font-size: 105%;
        letter-spacing: 0.35em;
        text-align: left;
        text-transform: lowercase;
}
.bodycopy p {
        line-height: 1.6em;
}
#firstpara {
        background-color: #000000;
        color: #FF6600;
}
#intro  {
        background-color: #000000;
        color: #FF6600;
        float: left;
        font-size: 3.0em;
        line-height: 1.1em;
        margin: 2px;
        padding: 2px;
}
```

Class selectors are declared using the following format: [.ClassSelectorName]. (Notice the use of the leading period.) In contrast, id selectors use a different leading character, the hash sign: [#IdSelectorName]. However, the rule declarations for both methods of styling are exactly as we have seen before.

As you can see, I have declared a class style called '.bodycopy', which should be familiar from previous examples. An interesting point to note, however, is the introduction of our first contextual declaration: '.bodycopy h1'. In effect this says that any <h1> elements within a '.bodycopy' class must take on the following style rules. The same contextual approach is used for <h2> elements and <p> elements within the same '.bodycopy' class.

Next, we see our first id declaration. Apart from the leading symbol variation, this is much the same as a class declaration. The '#firstpara' declaration simply sets the colour of its content to a shade of orange.

The second id declaration – '#intro' – is more interesting. This is the id that changes the leading word in the first paragraph. Apart from making the text considerably larger, this also introduces a new attribute: 'float'. This attribute enables an element to hover relative to following elements, which flow around the floating element. In this example, our leading word will float to the left and the following text will flow around to the right. The float property is used extensively with images as we shall see later, but interesting text effects are also possible. Valid values for the float attribute are left, right and none.

The eagle-eyed among you will have noticed that I did not really need to introduce the <div> element. I could have just used <body class="bodycopy">, as this would have resulted in exactly the same effect. However, had I only wanted to modify a subsection of my <body> mark-up, I would have needed to use the <div> element for whichever portion needed stylizing. (Also, this example has really only been constructed to help communicate a method of operation.)

A last word on fonts

There are just a handful of additional properties relating to fonts that you may want to employ within your own page designs: font-weight, font-style and font-variant. Advice for each property is shown opposite. They are straightforward to use, but I would encourage you to experiment with them to understand their behaviour.

Font-weight

This property can take on the keyword values: normal, bold, bolder and lighter. Alternatively, you may use keyword numbers: 100, 200, 300, 400, 500, 600, 700, 800 and 900. How this property affects a font depends on the individual typeface, and the best way to settle on a weight is through trial and error.

Font-style

The valid values for this property are italic, oblique and normal, and they are used to determine whether or not a font 'tilts' and, if so, by how much. Typeface designers sometimes create italic text by producing individual characters that have been optimized for the incline. This optimization is an implicit character of the particular font. Oblique text, however, is generally just normal text that has been slanted, and uses no character optimization. Again, this varies depending on typeface.

Font-variant

The last property is even simpler, and can take on only two values: normal and small-caps. Although all the letters appear as upper case text when the small-caps value is employed, those that were capitals before the transformation remain slightly larger. Given that capitals are harder to read than their lower-case counterparts, I suggest you avoid over-using this stylistic approach.

Creating textual lists

Lists are tremendously versatile objects on web pages. You may want to create a list of links to other pages, a list of your favourite film types, or even a list of your most impressive customer names. For this example (see fig. 6.6) I chose to produce a list of camera equipment. After studying this example you should be capable of producing quite complex list hierarchies, and also appreciate how to style these structures.

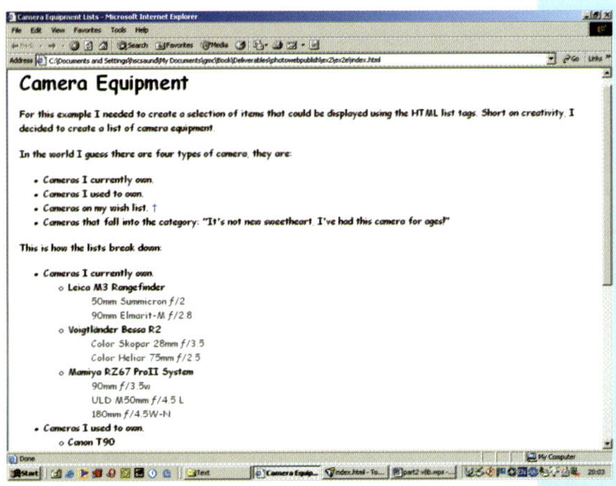

[6.6] The camera-equipment list example, as it appears in a web browser

To understand how we create lists, let's first take a look at the salient HTML.

```
<!-- A simple list -->
<ul>
<li>Cameras I currently own.</li>
<li>Cameras I used to own.</li>
<li>Cameras on my wish list. <span
class="note">&#134;</span></li>
<li>Cameras that fall into the category:
"It's not new sweetheart, I've had this
camera for ages!"</li>
</ul>
```

Here we see a simple example of an unordered list using the HTML tag pair <ul></ul>. The items within the list appear between the list item tags <li></li>. Within an unordered list, the list items appear with bullet points preceding the list-item text. Which bullet point is used depends upon the default properties of the browser, although this can be manipulated using style sheets. To create a numbered list, for example, simply use the 'ordered list' tags <ol></ol> rather than the unordered list tag, as I have done in my 'wish list' of camera equipment. The penultimate list item – 'Cameras on my wish list. †' – has a footnote using a character entity at the end of the line. The character entity is non-standard, so may not appear correctly in older browsers, though hopefully you will see this †, in preference to '†'.

Nested lists

Once you have created your first list, you will soon want to create a list within a list, or 'nested list' as it is known. You have to be careful about using the correct tag sequence, but a simple nested list would take the format shown opposite.

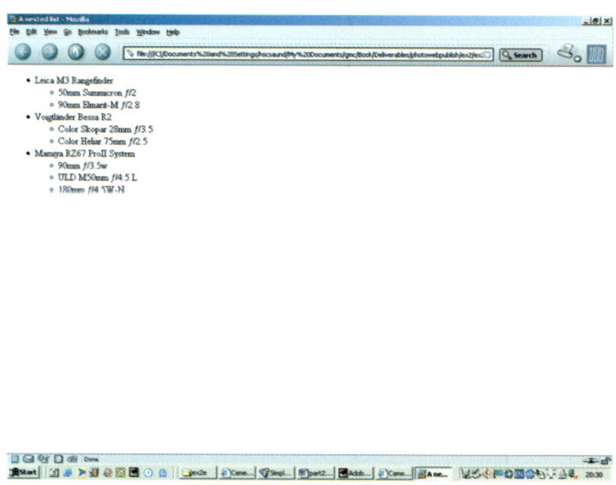

[6.7] A simple nested list

```
<!-- A simple nested list -->
<ul>
    <li>Leica M3 Rangefinder
        <ul>
        <li>50mm Summicron
        &fnof;/2</li>
        <li>90mm Elmarit-M
        &fnof;/2.8</li>
        </ul></li>
    <li>Voigtl&#228;nder Bessa R2
        <ul>
        <li>Color Skopar 28mm
        &fnof;/3.5</li>
        <li>Color Heliar 75mm
        &fnof;/2.5</li>
        </ul></li>
    <li>Mamiya RZ67 ProII System
        <ul>
        <li>90mm &fnof;/3.5w</li>
        <li>ULD M50mm &fnof;/4.5
        L</li>
        <li>180mm &fnof;/4.5W-N</li>
        </ul></li>
</ul>
```

The important thing to note is that you don't close the list-item tag of the item that is the 'immediate parent' of the nested list, until the nested list is itself complete. Specifically, see how the </li> tag does not appear at the end of the list item 'Leica M3 Rangefinder'. Rather, it appears after the subsequent nested list is complete and closed. Building on our earlier examples, I've also included two special character entities. They are '&#228', for the correct spelling of Voigtländer, and 'ƒ', which is a small f with pronounced hook that, although a non-standard character, seemed to better represent the typical character used to denote *f*-stop values.

6

The ordered 'wish list' at the end of the example is also a nested list and was written thus:

```
<!-- An ordered list -->
<ul>
<li>Cameras on the wish list – none of
which will make me a better
photographer.
        <ol>
        <li>Mamiya 645AF
        Autofocus</li>
        <li>Hasselblad Xpan</li>
        <li>Mamiya 7 II Rangefinder</li>
        <li>Leica M6 TTL</li>
        <li>Canon EOS-1DS</li>
        </ol></li>
</ul>
```

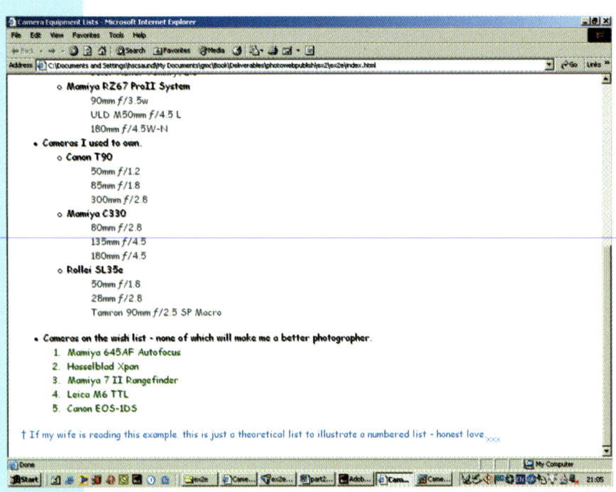

[6.8] An ordered list example

Styling lists

Having seen the various screen grabs, you'll have noticed that some simple styling must have been applied to this example. For instance, the typeface looks different from the Verdana definition I usually use. This is because I declared that the font-family for the <body> element should be 'cursive'. In my browser, the font "Comic Sans" is interpreted as the most appropriate typeface for this casual style of writing. In your browser, it may well appear as something quite different. The complete style sheet for this example is as follows:

```
html    {margin: 0px; padding: 0px;
        background-color: White;
        color: Black;
}
body    {margin: 20px;
        font-family: cursive;
        text-align: left;
}
ol li {
        background-color: White;
        color: #006600;
}
ul ul ul {
        color: #666666;
        background-color: White;
        list-style-type: none;
}
.note {
        background-color: White;
        color: #0066FF;
}
```

Other items of note include the use of contextual selectors. The ordered 'wish list' is a great example, whereby the list items of the ordered list appear in a shade of green. This is declared using 'ol li' selector which in effect is saying, apply the following style rules to list elements <li> that are preceded by a single ordered list element <ol>. The same use of contextual selectors is shown again for the styling that is applied to the list of lenses, nested within the cameras and camera categories. Thus 'ul ul ul' only displays the lenses with the grey colour if they appear within three levels of nested unordered lists.

Bullet styles

In addition to the usual margin and padding properties that you can manipulate lists with, there are other properties I would urge you to experiment with. The first property may be used for controlling either the bullet style or numbering system, depending on the type of list. The list-style-type property can be used to define bullet styles using the predefined keywords disc, circle, square and none. You can go further and create your own bullets as GIF or JPEG image files. To use these files you should apply the property list-style-image, which takes the format:

```
Selector {list-style-image:
URL(ImageFileName.gif);}
```

For ordered lists, you may use the list-style-type property to declare the numbering system, thus:

Value	Result
decimal	1,2,3,4,5, etc.
lower-roman	i,ii.iii,iv,v, etc.
upper-roman	I,II,III,IV,V, etc.
lower-alpha	a,b,c,d,e, etc.
upper-alpha	A,B,C,D,E, etc.
none	numbering omitted

List-style-position

One last property worth trying is the list-style-position, which can take the values 'inside' or 'outside'. The property declares the position of the bullet character, in relation to the list item block. To see the difference, you will need relatively long list items whose text wraps around the page. With the 'inside' attribute set, the text will wrap around the page and become level with the bullet. With the property set to the 'outside' value set, the bullet will protrude to the left as normal.

Shortcut

List-style-position

7 Adding Images to your Website

Shortcut

The image tag

Inserting a picture into a page

Web pages are made up of HTML documents and image files that are brought together and displayed on the user's browser. Unlike some desktop-publishing applications you may have seen, you do not actually insert an image into an HTML document, rather a link to it. To simplify the examples in this book, I have tended to keep the image files in the same file directory as the HTML document. This is not obligatory, and you can link an HTML document to image files in any file directory, or indeed web location, assuming you have system authorization to do so.

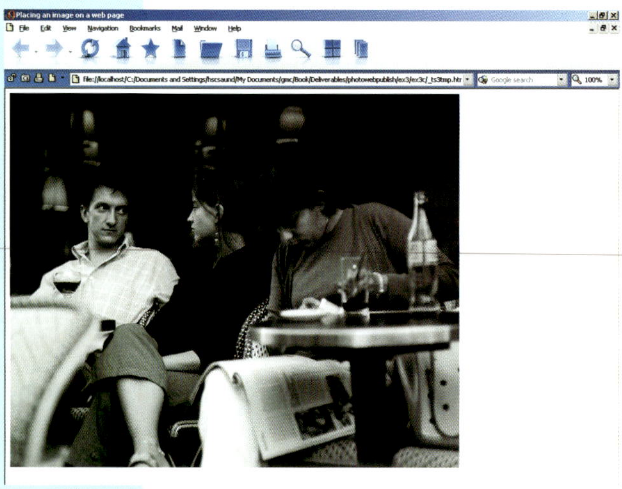

[7.1] Inserting a picture into a page

The image tag

To place an image on a web page you need to use the image tag: <img [parameter list]>. This is an example of an empty tag, which does not have a closing form – i.e. </img>. If you want to keep to the latest standards, you could use <img [parameter list] /> where a / is inserted after a space and before the closing angle bracket.

The picture of the Parisian café image was remarkably easy to insert. Consider the following statement:

```
<body>
<img src="ParisianCafe.jpg" alt="Parisian
Cafe" width="750" height="600">
</body>
```

The src parameter

The first parameter in the list is 'src', which stands for source. This statement tells the browser to look in the current file directory and locate the JPEG image, "ParisianCafe.jpg". On my own site, I often keep all the photographs in one directory and all the graphics in a separate location. Doing so makes the management of files considerably simpler. Assuming I had put all the photographs for this page in a file directory called images and this file directory resided in the same directory as the HTML file, I could have used relative addressing to reference the file.

In this case the source parameter would have taken the form src="./images/ParisianCafe.jpg". The leading period is shorthand for 'the current directory'. Another useful shorthand notation is ../ which means the parent directory. Thus src="../images/ParisianCafe.jpg" means the browser must move up a level from the current directory and in there it should find a file directory called 'images' containing the image 'ParisianCafe.jpg'. Relative addressing such as this can be a very powerful way to cross-reference files within your website, yet keep the individual files together within a logical structure.

The alt parameter

The next parameter shown is 'alt', which stands for alternate text. This parameter declares that the text should be displayed alongside the mouse pointer when the mouse hovers over the image location. The alternate text is very useful for the visually impaired or people who have switched images off while browsing, yet it has a number of other functions. For example, it gives users on slow Internet connections some indication of what is coming, and if the image also happens to be a hyperlink, the user can see the context and click on the link without having to wait for the full image to download. Additionally, some search engines, especially those that allow users to search for images, pick up on the alternate text. Suffice to say that it is good practice to attach alternate text to all your images.

The width and height parameters

The last two parameters in this example declare the width and height of the image in pixels. These parameters are not entirely necessary, but when armed with this information the browser can layout the surrounding text and other objects without having to wait for the image to download fully. In effect, their inclusion speeds up the rendering of the page and will give the appearance of better performance. You can also use the height and width parameters to resize an image, although image resizing is best done using your image-manipulation program and not left to the browser, which will at best produce a below-par result.

Intelligent web designers use this resizing ability to help speed up the performance of some of their pages. Images can consume remarkable amounts of bandwidth. Internet browsers cache images to disk and if they think that the image is required again, they will go to the cache rather than try to download it again. The trick is to anticipate which images are likely to be viewed and in what sequence.

Shortcut
Pre-loading hidden images

Pre-loading hidden images

You might attempt to pre-load the next image into cache, while you think the user is reading another page. Assuming you have used the width and height properties set for all your images on a page, the text should flow as you anticipate. Hidden at the bottom of your page, you can insert the image for pre-loading, but at a width and height of one pixel. With luck, this image proxy should never be noticed, especially if you omit the alternate text. However, when the user goes to the page with the properly sized picture, no download is required and the display is almost instantaneous. For this trick to work, you must use exactly the same source parameter in both images.

Mixing text and images on a page

An earlier advanced textual-styling example (Fig 6.5, see page 91), which was based around an article about photographing children, left some space on the page for the inclusion of images. The maximum allowed space for the 'bodycopy' was 50% of the browser window, leaving the remaining 50% for images to accompany the article. The reason why I decided to split the page in half like this was merely to limit the maximum line length and thereby improve the readability of the page.

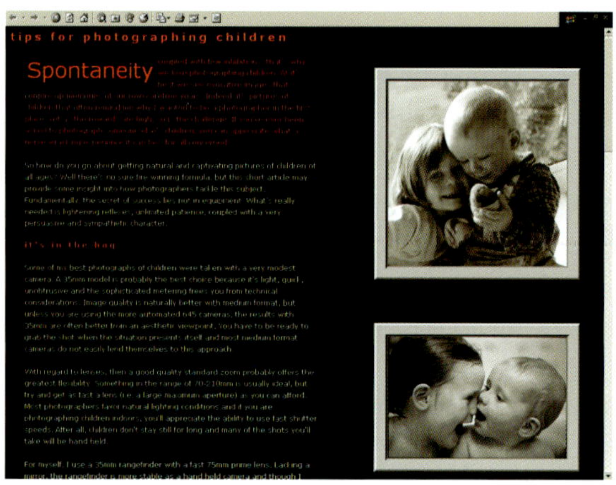

[7.2] Adding images alongside the photographic article

Before we take a look at page positioning, let's consider the borders around the pictures. Until recently, I had always created a border for a picture within my image-editing program. While this is an easy task to undertake for one picture, it really becomes a chore when working on many hundreds of images. When I finally got to grips with CSS, I discovered that there was no need to create picture borders, as the styling commands could do a very respectable job for me. My challenge was to create a realistic-looking border that approximated the real thing. After experimenting with a number of styles, I found that the answer lay in nesting a border within a border. Consider the following HTML fragment that inserts the first picture in the sequence:

```
<div class="bodyimageright"><img
src="6.jpg" class="pictureborder"
alt="Photographing Children"
height="303" width="300"></div>
```

Focus on the <img> tag first. I have inserted an image imaginatively named 6.jpg. Its height and width are declared for faster loading and it carries with it alternative text of 'Photographing Children'. If you think I have been somewhat vague with the naming, I make no apologies, as the Internet is not the place to identify these children by name. The interesting thing to note is that this picture has the class 'pictureborder' which is a style in the associated style sheet thus:

```
.pictureborder    {
      border: inset medium #CCCCCC;
      margin: 0px;
      padding: 0px;
}
```

This by itself gives the picture a light-grey, medium-thickness inset border right next to the image content. By itself and with no other styling the pictures on the page would appear quite differently.

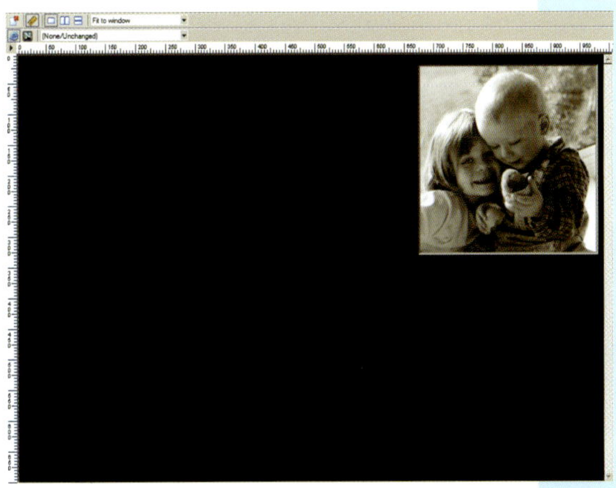

7.3] The picture with 'pictureborder' styling only

To complete the effect, I merely have to wrap the <img> tag in a <div> element with the class of 'bodyimageright'. This CSS fragment positions the picture on the page and also creates a second light-grey border to create the frame-like 3D effect.

```
.bodyimageright {
        background-color: #CCCCCC;
        border-style: outset;
        clear: both;
        float: right;
        margin: 20px 15px 50px 10px;
        padding: 15px;
}
```

Apart from the border style itself, the interesting properties are positional. The 'float: right' property ensures that the image appears on the right side of the browser window. Working in conjunction with the float property, the clear property causes a following element to clear the floating element, rather than wrap around the element. The cleared element is moved down until the 'left', 'right' or 'both' margins are clear. This simple statement ensures that the sequence of six pictures appear in a column, as opposed to a vertical line. The margin values then allow greater separation between the individual images.

```
<h1 id='mainheader'>tips for photographing children</h1>
<div class="bodyimageright"><img src="6.jpg" class="pictureborder"
alt="Photographing Children" height="303" width="300"></div>
<div class="bodyimageright"><img src="1.jpg" class="pictureborder"
alt="Photographing Children" height="199" width="300"></div>
<div class="bodyimageright"><img src="5.jpg" class="pictureborder"
alt="Photographing Children" height="300" width="300"></div>
<div class="bodyimageright"><img src="2.jpg" class="pictureborder"
alt="Photographing Children" height="401" width="300"></div>
<div class="bodyimageright"><img src="4.jpg" class="pictureborder"
alt="Photographing Children" height="417" width="300"></div>
<div class="bodyimageright"><img src="3.jpg" class="pictureborder"
alt="Photographing Children" height="446" width="300"></div>
<div class="bodycopy">
<p id="firstpara"><span id="intro">Spontaneity</span>coupled with few inhibitions,
that's why we love photographing children. At its best we see evocative images that
conjure up memories of our own carefree years. Indeed, it's pictures of children that
often remind me why I wanted to be a photographer in the first place. Yet as the
rewards are high, so is the challenge. If you've ever been asked to photograph
someone else's children, you can appreciate what a nerve wracking experience it can
be – for all concerned.</p>
...
...
...
</html>
```

Although the images are a mixture of square, landscape and portrait formats, the fact that they share the same width value creates a sense of balance and predictability in the design. This is also a good example of a dynamic design that tries to make a reasonable attempt at accommodating different monitor resolutions. On my development computer, the default resolution is 1280x1024. That is higher than most of the users that might typically be expected to surf my site. To check the integrity of my design I have created an image on the Windows XP desktop that demarks different monitor resolutions.

I can then quickly resize a browser window to check the design, without having to go to the trouble of changing the monitor resolution. Of course, while swift, this approach can only give an approximation of your page layout, as slight differences must occur in font sizes at any given resolution. However, this approach is close enough for general purposes.

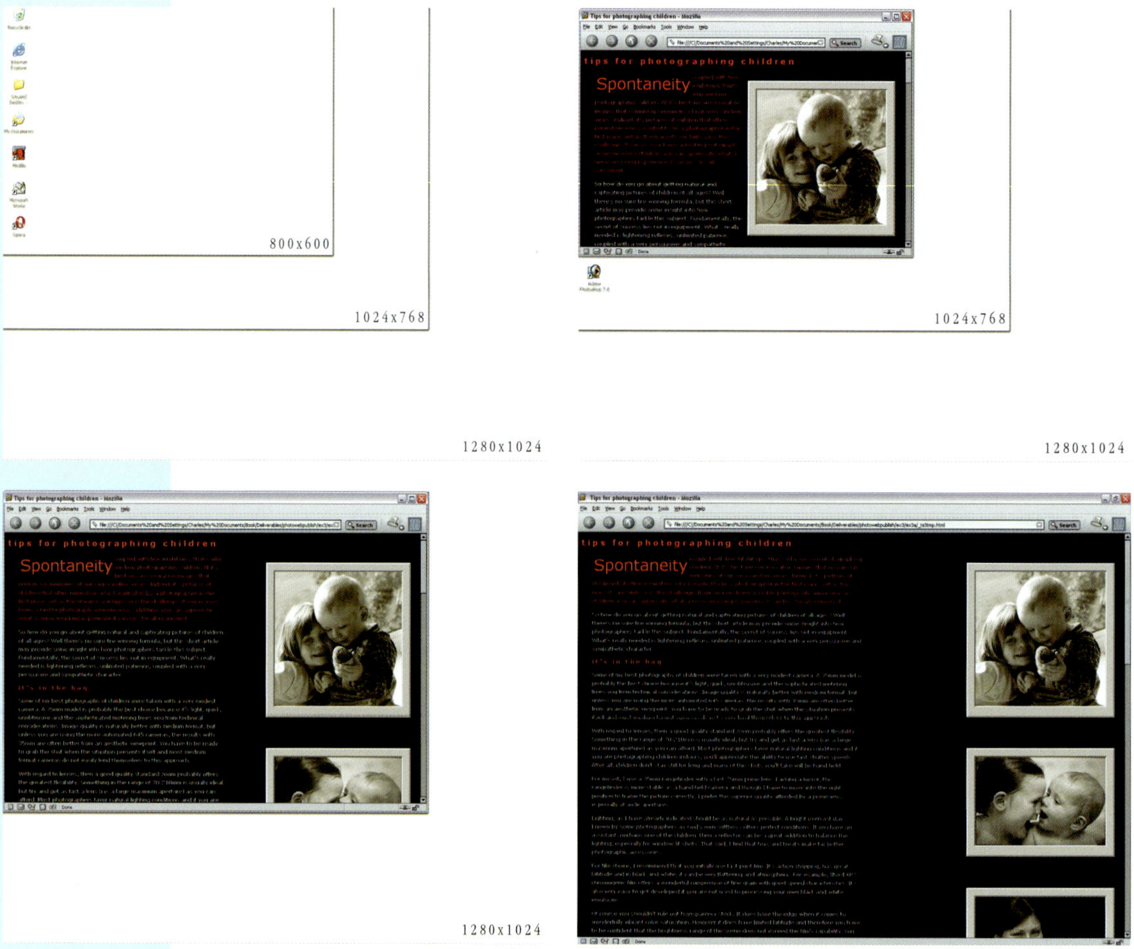

[7.4–7] Checking a page layout against different monitor resolutions

Notice at the higher resolutions how the page components can become more separated as the relative proportions increase. To mitigate this to a degree, instead of setting a fixed width percentage, you can declare upper and lower values for the 'bodycopy' elemental width using the properties 'min-width' and 'max-width'. Both of these CSS properties may take values in either percentages or length units, such as pixels or ems in the latter case. As a useful exercise, you could try setting the 'bodycopy' width to 90% and then try to insert the images within the article, with the text flowing around the images as appropriate.

Inserting an image into the background

So far we have looked at inserting an image into a document's foreground. Images inserted in this way will have any adjacent text flowed around them. However, there is another method for inserting images into a document, and that is inserting an image into a document element's background. Most of the time, designers insert images into the background of the body element, but even more creative effects may be obtained by inserting background images into other elements such as tables, headings and even your own class and ID selectors. The key difference between foreground and background images is that text can flow over background images.

Choosing the right background image

At this point I should stress that a consistent feature of poorly designed pages is misuse of the background-image feature. If you are going to flow text over a background image, you should select an image that can help maintain a strong contrast against the text. Otherwise the document can become extremely tiring to read. Another common mistake is to use an image that is simply too large and takes too much time to download. Again, if you elect to use a background image of sizeable proportions, it should be a well-compressed GIF or JPEG file that takes only a couple of seconds to download.

Shortcut

Choosing the right background image

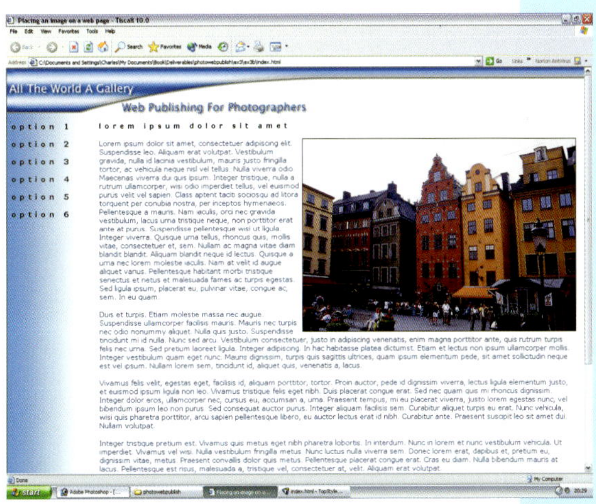

[7.8] A background image used to denote the document header and menu bar

Background images are often used to spruce up a document's opening section and reinforce site branding. In our sample document, I have created a fictitious website called 'All the world a gallery – web publishing for photographers'. The code for inserting this header is quite straightforward:

```
body {
        margin: 0px;
        padding: 100px 10px 10px 0px;
        background-color: white;
        background-image:
        url('header.gif');
        background-repeat: no-repeat;
}
```

To insert a background image in an element, you simply use the formatting rule background-image, and then provide a document reference such as the filename or an entire URL to an image file. If the image is smaller than the elemental space in which it is located, the image may optionally repeat. Images can repeat along the element's x-axis using the value 'repeat-x'. Similarly, they may repeat along the y-axis using the value 'repeat-y', or both using the value 'repeat'. In this example I have suppressed any image repeating for the header by using the value 'no-repeat'. It is good practice to include a suitable background colour with a background-image declaration. In the event that the background image does not download onto the user's computer successfully, a carefully chosen background colour can help to maintain the required contrast with surrounding text. For example, a dark image background over which white text is displayed should also have a background colour of black, just in case the dark background image fails to load, which may otherwise result in white text on a white background.

You will also note from the padding declaration in the above example that the text of the body section only starts 100 pixels from the top of the element. The 'header.gif' image is coincidentally 100 pixels high and this rule declaration merely serves to ensure that the content of the page begins below the page-header image.

Our current example also has a menu bar on the left of the document. Although it is not important at this stage to understand how the menu bar was created, it is interesting to note that this element has its own background image.

The CSS definition for the background image is simply:

```
...
        background-image:
        url("border.gif");
        background-repeat: repeat-y;
        background-color: White;
...
```

As you can see from the screen shot of the individual images, the effect of the repeat-y parameter is to create a vertical strip of colour over which the menu options for this page are placed. Repeating a small image in this manner is far more efficient than simply using a large block of colour to cover the entire length of the page, and using this repeating background trick will assist download times considerably.

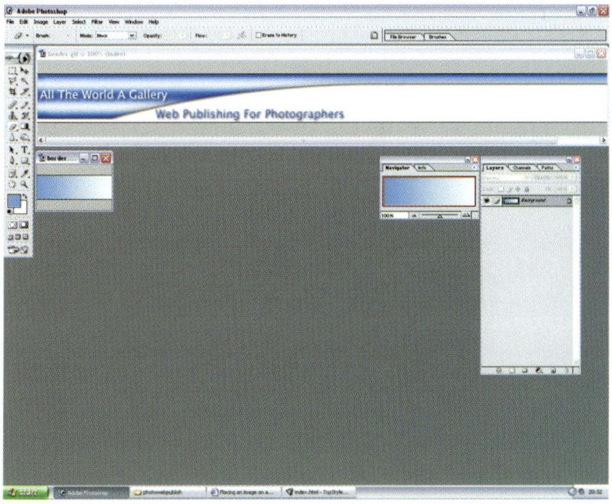

[7.9] A repeating background image provides a visual reference for the menu bar

Positioning an image on an element's background

Well-designed web pages make good use of background images to reinforce their branding. Aware of how to get the very best from the compression algorithms, designers of these pages often push their creative abilities to the limit and rely heavily on the use of background images. If you are ever in need of some design inspiration, go to www.coolhomepages.com – a remarkable site that is packed with examples of cutting-edge designs that get the very best from the web. One feature you will observe that is consistently applied across many of the 'cool homepages' is background image positioning; demonstrating that this is a very powerful addition to your creative repertoire. With this capability, you can declare an image position within the appropriate element displayed by your browser window.

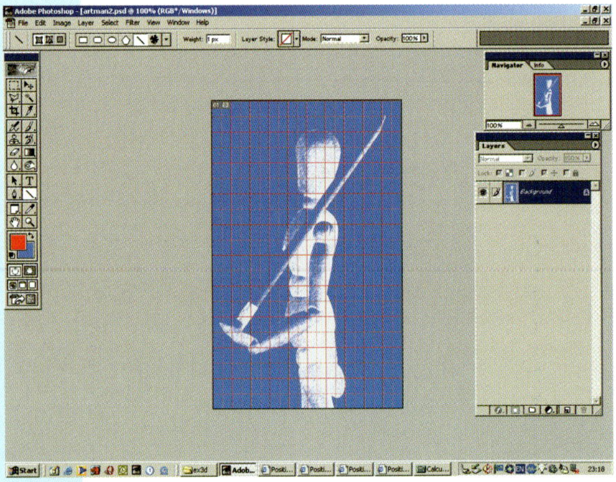

[7.10] The background image of the mannequin, shown in Adobe PhotoShop

To understand the theory behind background-image positioning, consider the image of an artist's mannequin (see Fig 7.10, below), which I want to place on a web page that has the same background colour.

The CSS attribute we use for background-image positioning is, unsurprisingly, background-position. There are a number of ways in which you can describe the exact position of a background image. You can use percentages, absolute units such as pixels or ems, or you can use keywords. The keyword approach is the least flexible, but does have the advantage of being the easiest to understand. Accurate positioning needs two dimensions and these are page width and page height. Measurements for positioning are taken from the top left-hand point of origin, as displayed by the browser window. Width keywords include 'left', 'center' and 'right'. Height keywords include 'top', 'center' and 'bottom'. To position an image at the bottom right of a page element, the keywords are simply:

```
Background-position: right bottom;
```

Alternatively, in order to centre a background image:

```
Background-position: center center;
```

Keywords are an effective way of maintaining relative positioning proportions, but greater control can be achieved using percentage values. Consider the following percentage declaration, which is equivalent to the centring statement seen above:

```
body {
        background-color: #6666FF;
        background-image:
        url('artman.gif');
        background-position: 50% 50%;
        background-repeat: no-repeat;
        color: #FFFFFF;
        margin: 0px;
        padding: 0px;
}
```

The accompanying screen shot shows the mannequin image, called 'artman.gif' centred on the browser window within the body element (see Fig 7.11, below). In this example, however, we use percentage values of 50% 50%, rather than the center keyword declaration seen previously.

The great thing about using percentage values is that they modify their exact positioning relative to the size of the browser window, and this approach is in keeping with a dynamic style of page management. The 50% 50% declaration in effect says, take a position that intersects the image halfway across and halfway down, and place this point

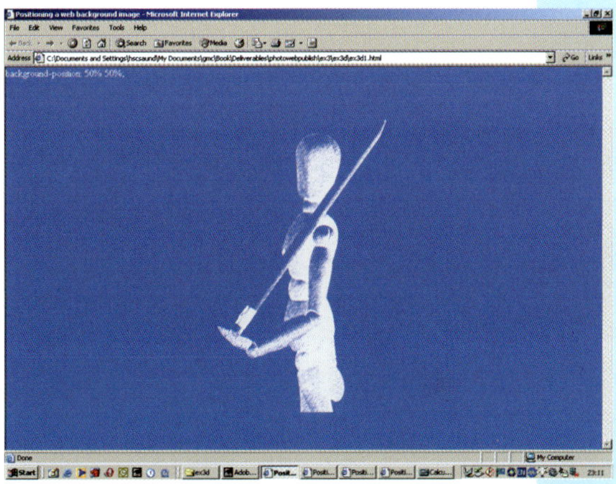

[7.11] Background image centred on screen using percentage values

within the browser windows halfway across and halfway down. This may seem like I am labouring a point, but things get slightly more complex when the following declaration is used:

```
body {
        background-color: #6666FF;
        background-image:
        url('artman.gif');
        background-position: 20% 80%;
        background-repeat: no-repeat;
        color: #FFFFFF;
        margin: 0px;
        padding: 0px;
}
```

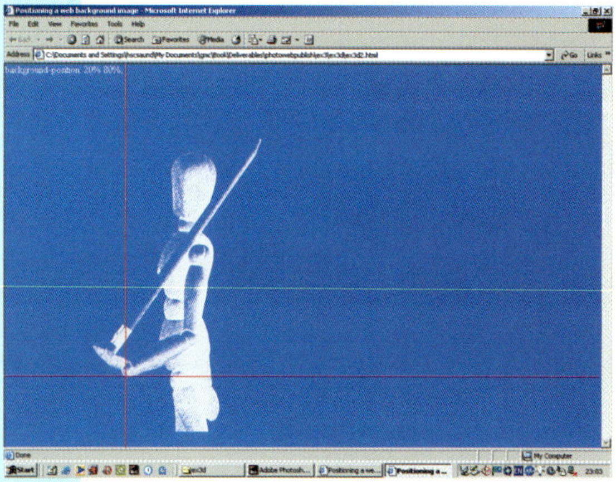

[7.12] 20% 80% positioning of the background image

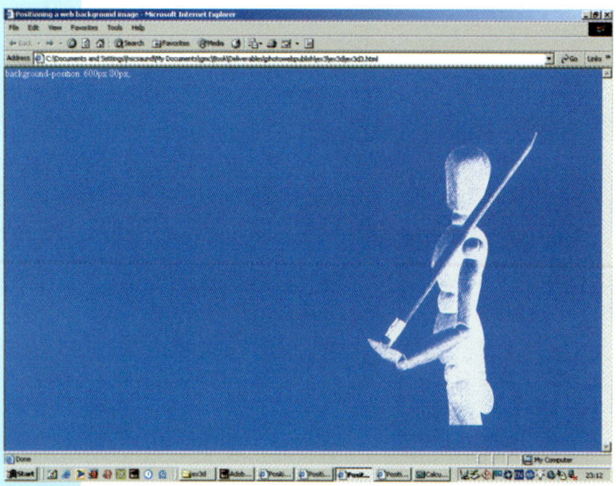

[7.13] Absolute positioning of the background image using pixel coordinates

Again, take a position that intersects the image 20% across and 80% down and place this point within the browser window that similarly is 20% across and 80% down. Notice, however, that by using percentages, you not only have to think about the position in the browser window, but also the positional point of origin within the image. As you can see, this approach is a great deal more flexible than using keywords.

Needless to say, you can also position the image using absolute coordinates. In this case, the top-left corner of the background image is positioned 600 pixels across and 80 pixels down from the point of origin of the containing element. The use of pixel coordinates does have its advantages, not least that you know exactly where the image will reside for any browser window. However, you don't always know the size of your user's screen, so this approach is best reserved for small pixel measurements relative to a containing element that you let float dynamically on a web page.

Finally, you can combine both absolute and relative positioning specifications in the same rule, as I have done in the following example:

```
body  {
        background-color: #6666FF;
        background-image:
        url('artman.gif');
        background-position: 100% 300px;
        background-repeat: no-repeat;
        color: #FFFFFF;
        margin: 0px;
        padding: 0px;
}
```

Though you cannot combine keywords with any other unit of measure, this approach offers great flexibility to control one dimension relatively, yet allow another to be static and precise.

For simplicity, all the above examples inserted a background image into the body element. However, you can employ this feature in more creative ways when you apply background images to other elements on the page, tables being the most common.

Scrolling background images

The last background manipulation parameter is a little hard to demonstrate in a book. It is the background attachment. In effect, this declaration states whether the background image should move as a user scrolls up or down the page, or remain fixed solidly in position. The rule is simply background-attachment: with keyword values of either 'scroll' or 'fixed'. The value 'scroll' is the initial default value.

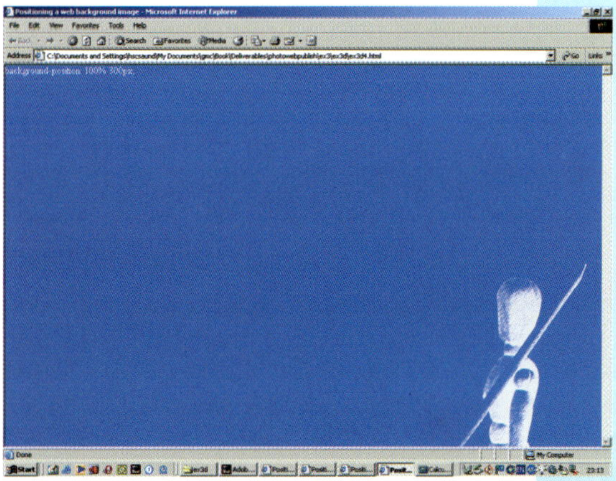

[7.14] Background image positioning using both absolute and relative units of measure

Shortcut

Scrolling background images

8 Organizing Content through Hypertext Links

Introducing the anchor tag for creating links

It's possibly the most influential HTML tag in this book; the <a> or 'anchor' tag provides the mechanism by which users may move easily from one piece of information to another. The anchor tag is the very essence of the 'hypertext' in Hypertext Mark-up Language (HTML). The tag can be applied in a number of contexts, but the most frequently encountered are shown in Fig 8.1 (below).

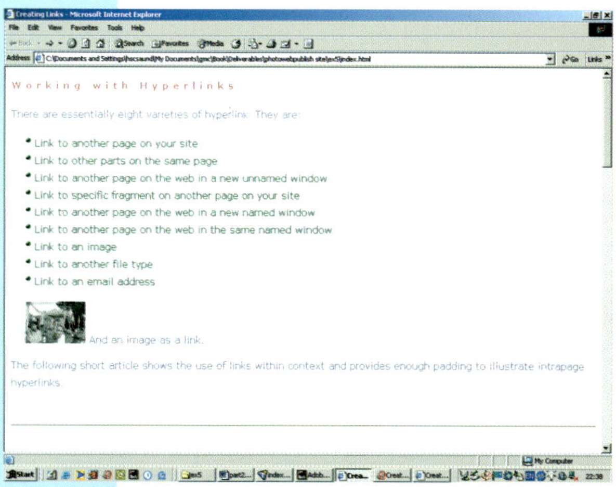

[8.1] A sample page of example links

Once you have mastered the subtleties of each link variant, you can easily apply these basic constructs to quite sophisticated page designs. This chapter examines each in turn. In Fig 8.1, I chose to list the different links within an unordered list object. As the list tag has been explained previously (see pages 97–100), we shall concentrate our attention solely on the anchor <a> tag declarations. In our simplest example, the purpose is merely to link to another page on the site. For our worked example, the HTML code is:

```
<a target="_self" href="page2.html">Link
to another page on your site</a>
```

Between the <a> and </a> tags you will find the text that appears as the hyperlink. This text will take on text formatting properties either defined automatically by your browser or per

The most common uses of links

- Link to another page on your site
- Link to other parts on the same page
- Link to another page on the web in a new unnamed window
- Link to another page on the web in a new named window
- Link to an image
- Link to another file type
- Link to an email address

the declarations on a CSS styling definition. Appropriately inserted HTML tags can also modify the link text between the tags. The anchor tag in this example also has two parameters. The attribute 'href' defines where the page should link. In this case it is an HTML document called 'page2.html'. As no relative or absolute addressing is included, we can assume that this file resides in the same directory as the current document.

The target attribute

The target attribute is a particularly interesting one. It may take on the values of '_blank', '_self', '_parent' and '_top'. The values of '_parent' and '_top' are only relevant in the context of frames, which we will cover in a later chapter (see page 140).

Opening a link in the same window

The value '_self' means that the link will open a document in the current window. This is the default condition. The value '_blank', on the other hand, opens the link in another new window. This is extremely useful inasmuch as you may not want someone to follow a link off your site, and the convention is that all links that traverse to pages off your site are opened using the '_blank' value. This ensures that a browser window displaying your site remains on your user's computer desktop.

Opening a link in a new window

Sometimes the '_self' option isn't necessarily the correct option. For example, imagine you have a page that lists your favourite black-and-white photography sites. By using the '_blank' approach, a new window would be opened every time the user clicked on a link to visit one of these sites. Annoyingly, the user would have to close down windows if they wanted to limit the number of open browser sessions. A better solution would be to open just one additional browser window for the 'foreign sites', which would be used to display a new page every time a link leading off your site was clicked. This is simply done by creating a named target value such as:

```
<a target="offsite"
href="http://www.bbc.com">Link to
another page on the web in a new
named window</a>
```

Assuming a window called 'offsite' declared in the target parameter does not exist already, a new window will be opened and given the name 'offsite'.

However, should another link be selected which references the 'offsite' window, the new page is opened within this window. The benefits to this approach are twofold. First, you avoid cluttering up your user's desktop with

Shortcut

Opening a link in the same window

unnecessary browser windows. Second, and perhaps more importantly, the named window is already in the computer memory, so subsequent links targeted to that window open in a fraction of the time required. Accordingly, this also means that you use less of the user's computer memory.

Creating links within your site

Linking inside the same page

Not only is it possible to link from page to page, you can also link within pages using intra-page links. This feature is very helpful with long documents in which you want to help the user by reducing the amount of scrolling necessary to locate the appropriate section. The process is essentially achieved in two steps. In step one, you insert an anchor point with a specific and unique id and name. Why use both id and name? While id is the preferred method for identifying an anchor, the name attribute has greater browser support and ensures compatibility with older browsers. In this code, I have declared a fragment at the bottom of my page, underneath a rather long article on Ansel Adams's zone system:

```
<a name="bottom" id="bottom"></a>
```

This is not a link; it doesn't go anywhere since it has no href parameter. There is also no link text between the tags, so this statement is effectively invisible to the user. Having defined the fragment, it is simply a matter of linking to this otherwise-empty anchor from the top of my document, thus:

```
<a href="#bottom">Link to other parts on the same page</a>
```

Note the use of the hash (#) symbol as part of the href attribute. This indicates that the browser should seek out a fragment anchor. Building on this example, you can also link to a specific portion on another page. In our previous example, we linked to a file of dummy text called page2.html. In this next example, we merely link to a fragment called 'Curabitur' within this page, thus:

```
<a target="_self"
href="page2.html#Curabitur">Link to
specific fragment on another page on
your site</a>
```

This simply ensures that not only do we open the document, we do so at precisely the right position in the text for the user.

Linking to an image

The next most useful link is to link to an image. The format is much the same as we have seen previously and you may elect to vary your target parameter as previously discussed. An example of linking to an image might be:

```
<a target="_self" href="r1.jpg" title="Eiffel Tower, Paris">Link to an image</a>
```

In Fig 8.2, this opens an image of the Eiffel Tower in the browser window. The additional attribute of title adds a mouse-activated tool tip of 'Eiffel Tower, Paris' as it moves over the link (in much the same manner as 'alt' does for image alternate text). In our example, this link opens a JPEG photograph in the same browser window.

Unfortunately, using this particular method you have no control over the size or position of the window, and can end up with a rather unbalanced large picture, displayed in the top left-hand corner of the browser. Though this approach has the important merit of being simple, much greater degrees of image control and presentation can be achieved through the use of JavaScript (see page 148).

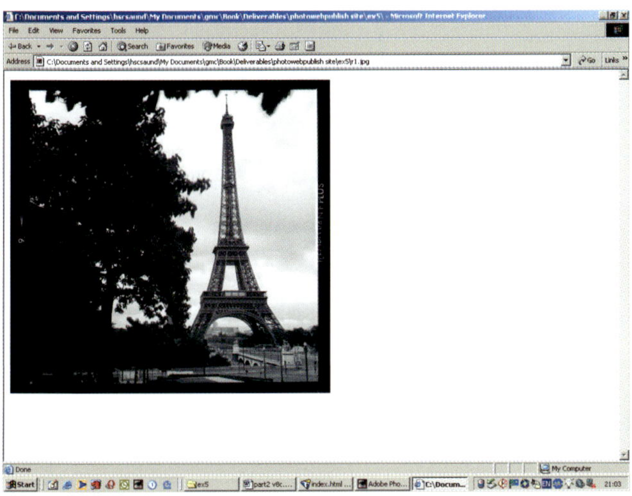

[8.2] The image of the Eiffel Tower as a link target

8

Shortcut

.pdf files

The picture of the Eiffel Tower loads in the browser window because browsers know how to handle JPEG image files. It is equally possible to link to other file types, assuming the browser software understands the file type or has a specific 'plug in' or additional software component loaded to enable it to interpret the given file type. For example, .pdf files are often used to promote such items as camera brochures and technical documentation. Thanks to the .pdf format, anyone can read these files, irrespective of which program they were originally created in. For example, although I don't know which program Hasselblad used to create the online brochure for their panoramic camera (the Hasselblad

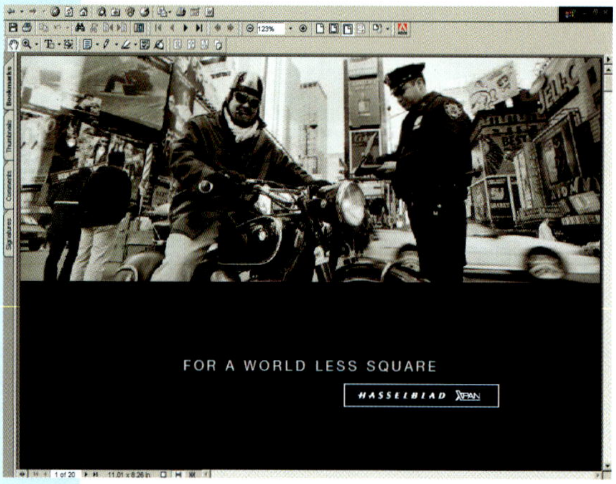

[8.3] The .pdf file of the Hasselblad Xpan loads easily into my version of Internet Explorer

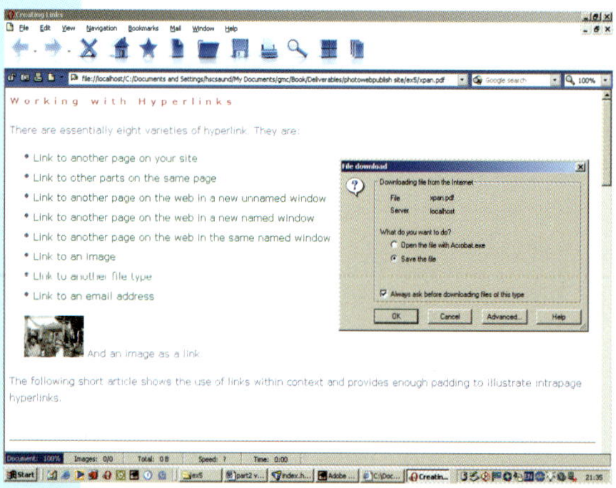

[8.4] My version of Opera is set up to ask me what to do with files of type .pdf

.pdf files

You often see that pages link to .pdf files. The .pdf format stands for Portable Document Format and is the creation of Adobe, who provide the .pdf reader for free. The advantage of .pdf files is that they offer a way of sharing complex document types that may otherwise require specific software. To illustrate this concept, you may elect to create a photography price list in Microsoft Publisher – a simple yet easy to use desktop-publishing environment. There is no guarantee, however, that your community of users may be capable of reading this native file type. By creating a .pdf file from the original document, you thereby create a portable version of the document that can be read by anyone who has access to the Adobe .pdf reader.

Xpan), thanks to the .pdf format I can open the file and also link to it after I have downloaded it to my computer (as shown in Fig 9.3). My browser, like most, is aware how to handle .pdf files, and so easily loads the document. If your browser comes across a linked file that it does not know how to manipulate, it will automatically prompt you with a download dialog sequence for copying the file to your local computer.

The HTML for this type of link is merely a variant of what we have already seen with images:

```
<a target="_self" href="xpan.pdf">Link to
another file type</a>
```

Linking to an email address

Another important link action is linking to an email address. This has the action of 'firing up' the user's email program with the pre-programmed recipient email address already programmed into the dialog sequence. Linking to an email address is one of the most powerful ways of eliciting user feedback and certainly helps users quickly post messages to you with minimal effort. The format is quite simply:

```
<a href="mailto:charles@photowebpubli
sh.com">Link to an email address</a>
```

If you want to be slightly more sophisticated, you could use additional parameters for the mailto URL, such as subject, cc, bcc and even some text for the email body. Unfortunately this level of complexity is supported only in later versions of most browsers. However, if you want to try out this augmented mailto link, an example might be:

```
<a href="mailto:charles@photowebpubl
ish.com?subject=Site%20Improvements
&cc=webmaster@photowebpublish.com
">Link to an email address</a>
```

This might look complicated, but the format is simple enough. After the first email address, the first parameter is preceded by a question mark. In this case, it is the subject line. As the subject-line content contains a space character, the hexadecimal character %20 has to be used. Subsequent parameters such as cc or bcc are appended to the sequence by using the ampersand symbol, and in this case the email is additionally copied to webmaster@photowebpublish.com.
A word of warning: I try not to provide my email address in this manner simply because there are people out there using software to collect every type email address on the web, which they sell to all manner of businesses. If you

8

publish your email address in this way, I guarantee you will begin receiving junk mail – some of it quite disgusting and illegal – within a few weeks. There is a simple solution to this problem, which we will examine in a later chapter (see page 174).

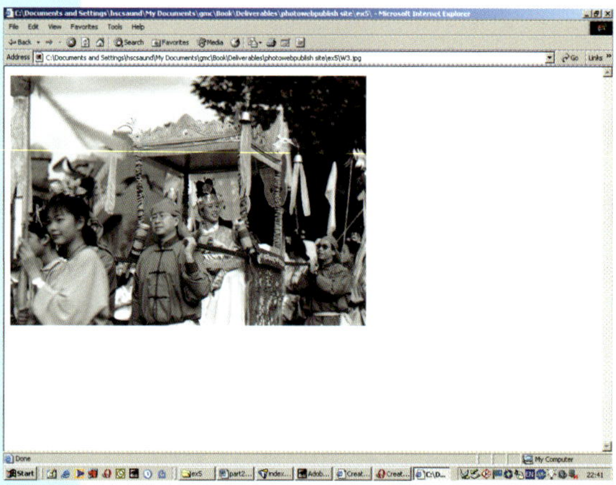

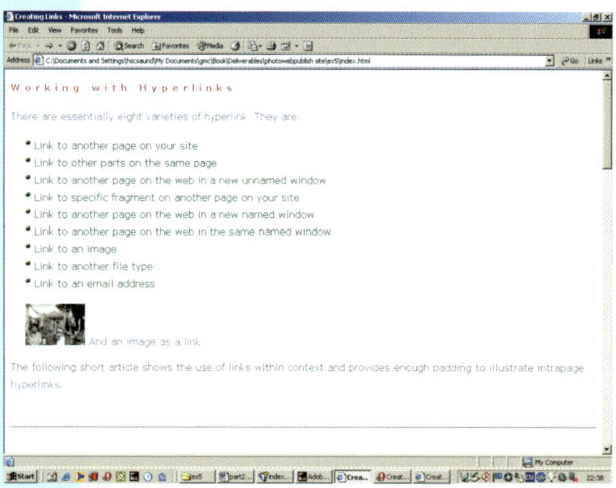

[8.5–6] Using an image as a link

Linking from thumbnails

In our last example on links, we shall link from an image thumbnail to a larger version. Using images rather than text as links is an extremely expressive addition to our design armoury. For example, images are often used in this way to control content delivery and limit excessive download times. Some sites additionally use images as buttons, but as I have indicated, you have to be very careful about weighing up the relative cost (in time) of downloading these additional components as opposed to using more mundane yet faster textual links.

The format of this type of linkage is quite simple – replacing the link text with an <img> image tag will create an image-based link. For example:

```
<a href="W3.jpg"><img alt="image"
border="0" src="W3_small.jpg"
width="100" height="67"></a>
```

When the user clicks on the image thumbnail w3_small.jpg, the browser automatically opens the larger image file w3.jpg. One item of note is the use of the border="0" attribute, which removes the default formatting of the image to indicate that it is a link. Without this parameter set, the image might otherwise take on an unpleasant-looking blue border.

Styling links with CSS

It should come as no surprise that it is necessary for Internet browsers to indicate which text or image is a link. They do this by either applying their own default formatting parameters or by adopting relevant CSS style definitions. As you can see from the Internet Explorer dialog in Fig 8.7, there are three states a link can be in. These are: 'unvisited', 'visited' and 'hover'. 'Unvisited' simply means that you have never traversed this link before and that therefore the link represents new content to you. 'Visited', on the other hand, indicates that you have visited the document at the end of this link before. This is quite a handy feature for more complex sites, as you may not be able to recall where you have been before. The last variation, 'hover', simply requests that the current link colour changes to the colour defined by the hover statement as the user's mouse 'hovers' over the link. This provides a simple visual clue that the link is ready to be selected.

Replicating the browser-defined parameters in CSS is easy enough by using what are called pseudo-classes. To reproduce the action of the browser settings shown in the screen grab, you merely have to define three rules for the anchor <a> element:

```
a:link {color: blue;}
a:visited {color: purple;}
a:hover {color: red;}
```

There is also an additional pseudo-class that defines the styling that should be applied at the precise moment when the mouse button is pressed down on the link. This is:

```
a:active {color: yellow;}
```

Some of the older browsers do not support the hover pseudo-class so you may decide to additionally use this active declaration.

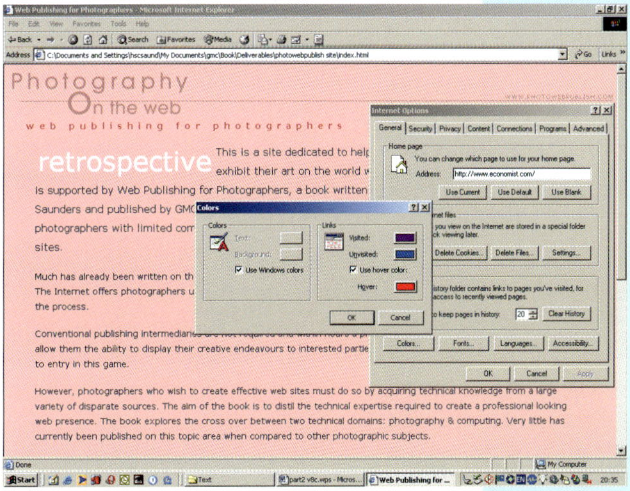

[8.7] Setting link formatting colours in Internet Explorer

8

Shortcut

Emphasizing hyperlinks on a page

The default setting shows links with their text underlined to help emphasize that they are capable of this special action. However, you may decide that your links do not need this additional formatting. To remove it is simply a matter of using:

```
a {text-decoration: none;}
```

The underline decoration can be turned back on as the mouse hovers over the link. This styling approach is used frequently on web pages, and can be achieved with the following code:

```
a {color: blue; text-decoration: none;}
a:hover {color: red; text-decoration:
underline;}
```

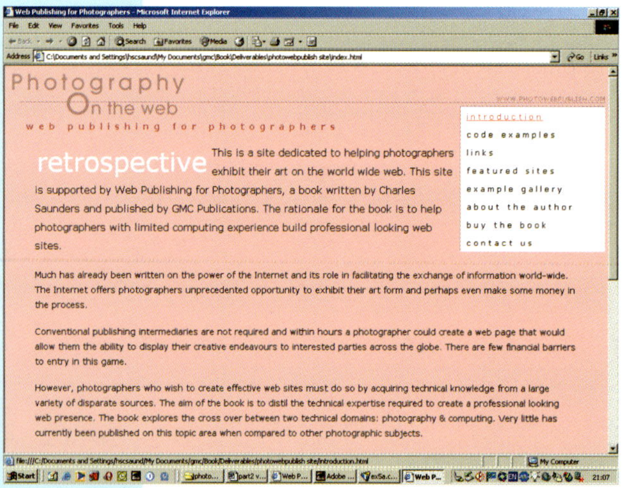

[8.8] The menus of www.photowebpublish.com

Emphasizing hyperlinks on a page

It is important to note that if you turn off the default underlining setting of hyperlinks, you must think of an effective way to draw attention to them in the absence of this styling condition, such as creating floating menus and side panels.

I use this stylistic mechanism for the floating menus that sit in the top right-hand corner of most of the pages on my own site. The HTML for these links is simple enough:

```
<div class="sidebarsmall">
<a href="introduction.html">introduction
</a>
<a href="codeexamples.html">code
examples</a>
<a href="links.html">links</a>
<a href="uc.html">featured sites</a>
<a href="gallery.html">example
gallery</a>
<a href="about.html">about the
author</a>
<a href="javascript:buythebook()">buy
the book</a>
<a href="mailto:charles@photowebpub
lish.com">contact us</a>
</div>
```

The CSS for sidebarsmall is composed of three declarations: the textual area itself, the <a> anchor elements within this area, and the pseudo-class for the hover state on the anchor tags.

```
.sidebarsmall     {
        margin: 0 -20px 25px 0;
        padding: 0;
        float: right;
        width: 25%;
        text-transform: lowercase;
        font-family: verdana, "Trebuchet
MS", heltetiva, arial, sans-serif;
        color: #333333;
        letter-spacing: 0.3em;
        text-align: left;
        font-size: 0.85em;
        border-top: 1px solid #cc9999;
        border-bottom: 1px solid #ffffff;
        background-color: #FFFFFF;
        }
.sidebarsmall a   {
        display: block;
        padding: 8px 0 5px 10px;
        color: #333333;
        text-decoration: none;
        border-left: 1px solid #cc9999;
        border-right: 1px solid #ffffff;
        }
.sidebarsmall a:hover {
        color: #ff6666;
        text-decoration: underline;
        }
```

On careful examination, much of this CSS should be understandable based on the areas covered in chapter 5 (see page 78). It is interesting to note that one can float text as well as images, which we have seen previously. The other new parameter can be found in the anchor declaration. The parameter 'display: block' makes the anchor elements block level rather than inline, in effect, forcing them to behave as if they were nested in paragraph tags. Remove this declaration and all the links will revert to their default condition and try and fit on just one line.

Using this simple sequence of declarations allows me to produce a very flexible menu structure that holds a relative position and behaves in a dynamic manner on window resizing.

9 Organizing Content on the Screen

Introduction to tables

Like many photographers, I find tables invaluable devices for holding thumbnail images that can then be selected for magnified viewing. Although the W3C discourages the use of tables for positioning content on the screen in favour of CSS, they remain common.

Shortcut

Using tables

The reason is this: though CSS positioning capabilities are superior to tables, they are inconsistently supported across even the latest browser implementations. For instance, I spent a frustrating evening trying to figure out why my CSS layout examples for this book didn't work, only to discover it was a bug in the browser software. I decided that the safest bet was to emphasize the use of tables for content positioning and pay lip service to the CSS method. No doubt the situation will improve with time as the browser manufacturers catch up with the W3C standards.

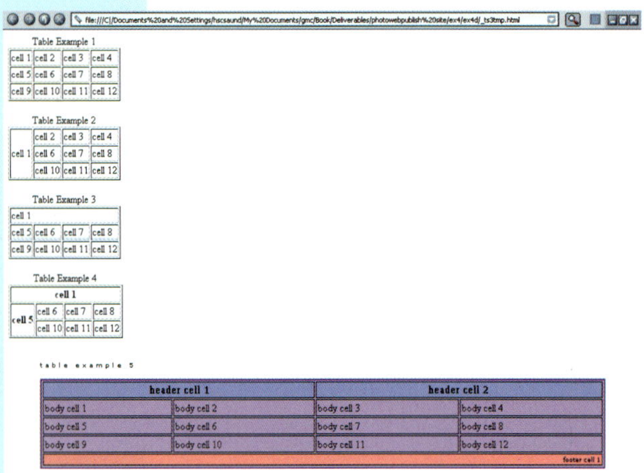

[9.1] Sample table configurations

Using tables

Tables of information, created using the <table> tag, offer a very powerful design construct in HTML. They are employed on a number of different levels. First, they can be used to represent tabular information (information organized in rows and columns). More often, you see them being used to arrange content on a web page and designers employ all manner of <table> gymnastics to ensure that they may position content accurately and effectively. Lastly, you may see them being used to slice up an image in order to facilitate animation and hyperlink effects.

Basic table construction

Tables are containers made up of rows and cells (rather than columns). Tables in HTML are biased towards rows, and there are few commands that can be used to manipulate entire columns of information. The maximum number of cells in any given row dictates the number of columns appearing in a table. Fig 9.1 (left) shows five example tables, which will be explained in turn.

Table example 1

The tags that are used to create tables include <table></table> for the overall table object, <caption></caption> for a caption associated with the table, <tr></tr> for the table's rows and <td></td> for the table cells that actually hold the content. Consider table example 1:

```
<table border=1>
<caption>Table Example 1</caption>
<tr>
<td>cell 1</td>
<td>cell 2</td>
<td>cell 3</td>
<td>cell 4</td>
</tr>
<tr>
<td>cell 5</td>
<td>cell 6</td>
<td>cell 7</td>
<td>cell 8</td>
</tr>
<tr>
<td>cell 9</td>
<td>cell 10</td>
<td>cell 11</td>
<td>cell 12</td>
</tr>
</table>
```

The table declaration begins unsurprisingly with the <table> tag. Next follows an optional tag sequence <caption></caption>, which allows the designer to name the table. The caption tag sequence is not often used.

The first row, delineated by <tr></tr>, contains four cells of data, defined by the four instances of the <td></td> tag sequence. Once all the data cells have been defined, the table row is closed using the </tr> tag and the next row may begin.

When all the rows are complete, the table definition is closed using the </table> tag. More sophisticated structures can be created by spanning by rows and columns. The benefit of this is apparent when you consider that tables may be scaled up to occupy an entire page and therefore used to arrange content on the screen.

9

Table example 2

In example 2, the first cell in the first row is set to span the remaining two cells down. Including itself, this makes a row span count of three and this is precisely what is defined in the definition of cell 1:

```
<table border=1>
<caption>Table Example 2</caption>
<tr>
<td rowspan=3>cell 1</td>
<td>cell 2</td>
<td>cell 3</td>
<td>cell 4</td>
</tr>
<tr>
<td>cell 6</td>
<td>cell 7</td>
<td>cell 8</td>
</tr>
<tr>
<td>cell 10</td>
<td>cell 11</td>
<td>cell 12</td>
</tr>
</table>
```

The cell command <td rowspan=3>cell 1</td> ensures that cell 1 spans the height of the table. To ensure that the table retains its original structure, I have also removed the declarations for cell 5 and cell 9.

Table example 3

Similarly, columns can be spanned in exactly the same manner as shown in example 3:

```
<table border=1>
<caption>Table Example 3</caption>
<tr>
<td colspan=4>cell 1</td>
</tr>
<tr>
<td>cell 5</td>
<td>cell 6</td>
<td>cell 7</td>
<td>cell 8</td>
</tr>
<tr>
<td>cell 9</td>
<td>cell 10</td>
<td>cell 11</td>
<td>cell 12</td>
</tr>
</table>
```

As you can see, cell 1 of the table now spans all four columns due to the command <td colspan=4>cell 1</td>. Again, to retain the original structure of the table, I had to additionally delete cells 2, 3 and 4.

Table example 4

This example merely serves to show row and cell span declarations in operation. One point to note is that I have used the <th></th> tags rather than <td> for this example. The tag <th> stands for table header and though logically equivalent to the <td> tag, is often used to denote a header cell which may require special formatting. As you can see, the Mozilla browser used in the screen grab treats the data in a header cell as centred and bold, but this may vary between browsers and may certainly be overruled in appropriate CSS definitions.

Row and column groups

Due in part to the fact that table construction in HTML had been focused on rows, the HTML 4.01 specification for tables introduced the concept of row and column groupings, allowing the definition of styling commands to larger structural elements within the table.

Table example 5

In table example number 5, I have incorporated row and column groups, as well as linking the table to CSS styling definitions. Though the table's design is not visually attractive, the purpose of this example is to illustrate how the differing elements of the table may be manipulated. Consider the HTML and CSS definitions, first the HTML:

```
<table id=ex5>
<caption>Table Example 5</caption>
<colgroup>
<col span="2" id="leftgroup">
<col span="2" id="rightgroup">
</colgroup>
<thead>
<tr>
<th colspan="2">header cell 1</th>
<th colspan="2">header cell 2</th>
</tr>
</thead>
<tfoot>
<tr>
<td colspan="4">footer cell 1</td>
</tr>
</tfoot>
<tbody>
<tr>
<td>body cell 1</td>
<td>body cell 2</td>
<td>body cell 3</td>
<td>body cell 4</td>
</tr>
<tr>
<td>body cell 5</td>
<td>body cell 6</td>
<td>body cell 7</td>
<td>body cell 8</td>
</tr>
<tr>
<td>body cell 9</td>
<td>body cell 10</td>
<td>body cell 11</td>
<td>body cell 12</td>
</tr>
</tbody>
</table>
```

Shortcut

Row and column groups

The linked CSS commands:

```
table#ex5 {
    background: #FF99FF;
    color: black;
    border: 3px ridge #CC33CC;
    margin-left: auto;
    margin-right: auto;
    width: 90%;
}
#ex5 caption {
    background-color: #FFFFFF;
    caption-side: top;
    color: #333333;
    font-family: verdana, heltetiva, arial,
    sans-serif;
    font-size: 0.65em;
    letter-spacing: 0.4em;
    margin-left: auto;
    margin-right: auto;
    padding-bottom: 1.5em;
    padding-top: 1.5em;
    text-align: left;
    text-transform: lowercase;
}
```

```
#ex5 col#leftgroup {
    font-family: cursive;
}
#ex5 col#rightgroup {
    background-color: #FF9900;
    color: Black;
}
#ex5 tfoot {
    background-color: #FF9999;
    color: #000000;
    font-family: Verdana, Geneva, Arial,
    Helvetica, sans-serif;
    font-size: xx-small;
    text-align: right;
}
#ex5 th, #ex5 td {
    border: 1px solid #000000;
    padding: 2px;
}
#ex5 thead {
    background-color: #CB99FF;
    color: #000000;
    font-family: "MS Serif", "New York",
    serif;
    text-align: center;
}
```

Don't be overawed by this example, there really isn't much here that you haven't already seen in other contexts. First, I wanted the styling commands to apply only to my last example, rather than affect all the tables defined in the HTML document. This was easily achieved by defining contextual styles linked to the table's id. It was given an id of 'ex5' and I began my definitions by declaring some characteristics for the entire table using the selector table#ex5. There is nothing too remarkable here. The table is given a width of 90% with automatic margins, thereby ensuring that it is dynamically sized and positioned horizontally on the centre of the page. The border definition allows us to see the outline of the table.

Applying id styles

Remember: id styles should only apply to one structural element in the HTML document, unlike class definitions (see page 92 for more details).

The table is divided structurally into three row-oriented regions. They are a header, body and footer. In this example, the cell data for each region is appropriately named to help you identify their occurrence. The header section is defined by the tag pair <thead></head>. Likewise the body and footer sections are outlined by <tbody></tbody> and <tfoot></tfoot> respectively. It is now possible to apply CSS styles to these regions with ease. For example, #ex5 thead and #ex5 tfoot are contextual selectors that allow styling commands to alter the appearance of the top and bottom rows of the table #ex5. Note that in the HTML, it is not necessary to define the <thead>, <tbody> and <tfoot> sections in this logical sequence; the browser is intelligent enough to construct the table correctly, irrespective of which region is declared first.

In order to control the size and characteristics of the individual cells, we need to operate at the <td> and <th> level. In our example, I have been able to define border and cell padding characteristics using the selector #ex5 td, #ex5 th, which in effect modifies the appearance of any data cell in the table.

Shortcut

Applying id styles

While <thead><tbody> and <tfoot> act on rows, the <colgroup></colgroup> construct that appears at the beginning of our table declaration enables the definition and manipulation of columns within the table. The <colgroup> structure is made up of a number of <col> elements that are used to identify (by using: id) columns or groups of columns in the table's structure. In this example there are four columns, which are divided into two groupings of two columns, called 'leftgroup' and 'rightgroup'. I was then able to apply different styling commands to each seperate group. For instance, the left group of columns displays a cursive font, while the right group of columns displays an orange background colour.

The last item of note is that I have been able to manipulate the caption of the table using the selector #ex5 caption. Again, there is nothing too surprising here and the only new parameter is caption-side, which may take the values top; bottom; left and right.

There is quite a lot to absorb in this last section and you would do well to experiment with your own table designs to get a feel of how you can manipulate these structures. A more complex example of a series of tables can be found at www.photowebpublish.com.

Using tables to organize thumbnail images

Although the previous section on tables may have seemed a little intimidating, you are probably only likely to construct the simplest of tables to hold thumbnail images of your pictures. Remember, this is a mechanism by which your users can see a selection of your available photographs quickly and without having to download a vast amount of information, enabling them to be far more efficient in choosing the images they wish to view in more detail. The thumbnail is a link to a larger picture,

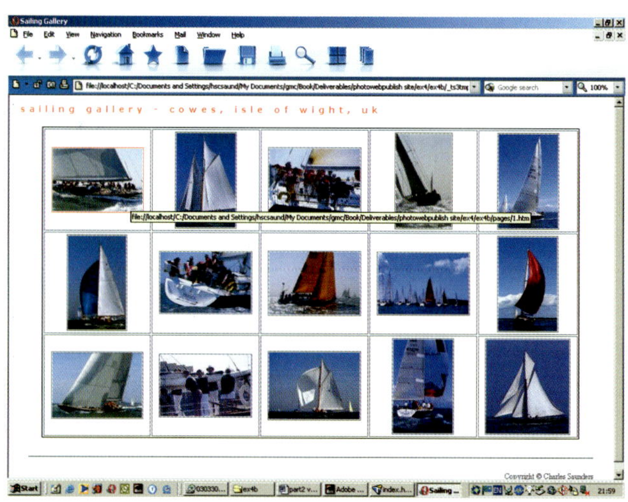

[9.2] A simple gallery of thumbnail-size sailing images

either on a new page or in isolation. For example, consider the gallery of thumbnails in Fig 9.2 (below left).

Thankfully, the HTML for this method of arranging thumbnail images is a great deal more straightforward than some of the examples used earlier:

```
<table>
<tr>
<td><a href="pages/1.htm"><img
src="thumbnails/1.jpg" alt="1"
height="100" width="150"></a></td>
<td><a href="pages/2.htm"><img
src="thumbnails/2.jpg" alt="2"
height="150" width="98"></a></td>
<td><a href="pages/3.htm"><img
src="thumbnails/3.jpg" alt="3"
height="101" width="150"></a></td>
<td><a href="pages/4.htm"><img
src="thumbnails/4.jpg" alt="4"
height="150" width="92"></a></td>
<td><a href="pages/5.htm"><img
src="thumbnails/5.jpg" alt="5"
height="150" width="99"></a></td>
</tr>
<tr>
<td><a href="pages/6.htm"><img
src="thumbnails/6.jpg" alt="6"
height="150" width="97"></a></td>
<td><a href="pages/7.htm"><img
src="thumbnails/7.jpg" alt="7"
height="97" width="150"></a></td>
<td><a href="pages/8.htm"><img
src="thumbnails/8.jpg" alt="8"
height="100" width="150"></a></td>
<td><a href="pages/9.htm"><img
src="thumbnails/9.jpg" alt="9"
height="98" width="150"></a></td>
<td><a href="pages/10.htm"><img
src="thumbnails/10.jpg" alt="10"
height="150" width="98"></a></td>
</tr>
<tr>
<td><a href="pages/11.htm"><img
src="thumbnails/11.jpg" alt="11"
height="104" width="150"></a></td>
<td><a href="pages/12.htm"><img
src="thumbnails/12.jpg" alt="12"
height="98" width="150"></a></td>
<td><a href="pages/13.htm"><img
src="thumbnails/13.jpg" alt="13"
height="107" width="150"></a></td>
<td><a href="pages/14.htm"><img
src="thumbnails/14.jpg" alt="14"
height="150" width="99"></a></td>
<td><a href="pages/15.htm"><img
src="thumbnails/15.jpg" alt="15"
height="150" width="138"></a></td>
</tr>
</table>
```

9

Shortcut

Minimum viewing resolution

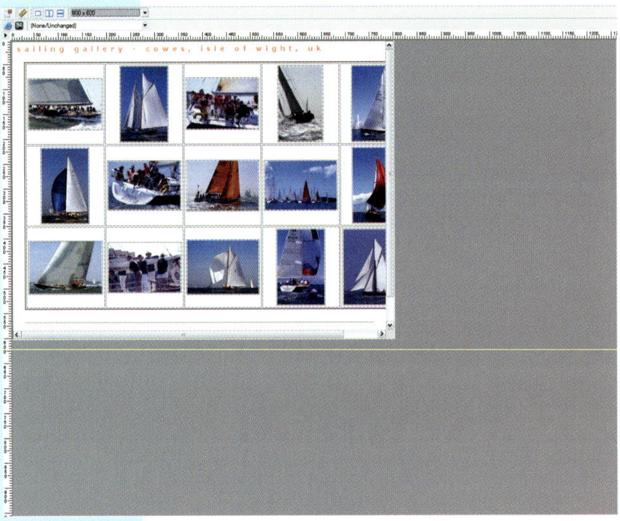

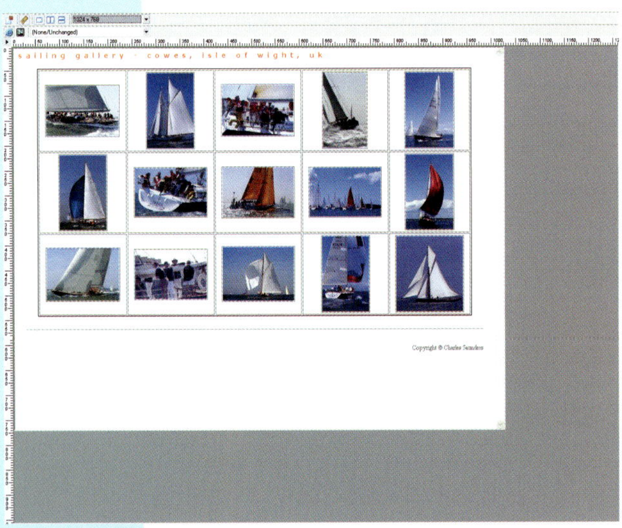

[9.3–4] Tables of thumbnail images must be designed with a minimum resolution in mind. In this case we see two examples of viewing at 800x600 and 1024x768

Minimum viewing resolution

Although tables size themselves automatically to the content they contain, images do not lend themselves to dynamic sizing without writing considerable amounts of programming code. Therefore, when you design your thumbnail table, you will need to consider the minimum viewing resolution and then design a table of images that suites these constraints, that is if you want to avoid the user scrolling in both axes. In Fig 9.4 (bottom left), I opted for 1024x768 pixels because I wanted to create a screen grab that would stand a better chance of clear reproduction in a book. You may elect to choose 800x600 pixels as your baseline, as shown in Fig 9.3 (top left). Any sophisticated development environment should be able to display pages at different resolutions, so that you can instantly see what is in and out of the frame.

The table is made up of three rows and, implicitly, five columns. The data within each cell is a thumbnail image that links to a separate page on which is arranged a larger rendition of the picture. It's easy to forget the image dimension parameters and they are indeed optional, yet their inclusion will speed up the overall rendering of your page in the user's browser window.

The CSS styling definitions are similarly fairly straightforward. The table has a width set to 95%, allowing the size to be controlled dynamically. The margins both left and right are set to auto, enabling the table to sit squarely in the centre of the document's flow. Each anchor-based image has a grey border that turns to orange as the mouse hovers over the link.

```
table {
        border: 1px solid #000000;
        border-spacing: 2px;
        margin-left: auto;
        margin-right: auto;
        padding: 2px;
        width: 95%;
}
td      {
        border: 1px solid #808080;
        text-align: center;
        vertical-align: middle;
}
td a img {
        border: 1px solid #808080;
        margin: 2px;
        padding: 1px;
}
td a:hover img {
        border: 1px solid #FF6600;
}
```

On clicking any of the thumbnail images, the user would be presented with a new page that displays a larger version of the thumbnail image.

A simple piece of navigation is also included on each 'detail' page, which allows the user to move onto the next image in the sequence, go back to prior image, or return to the thumbnail main menu. Overall, this design approach has a great deal going for it. It is relatively easy to implement, it works on most

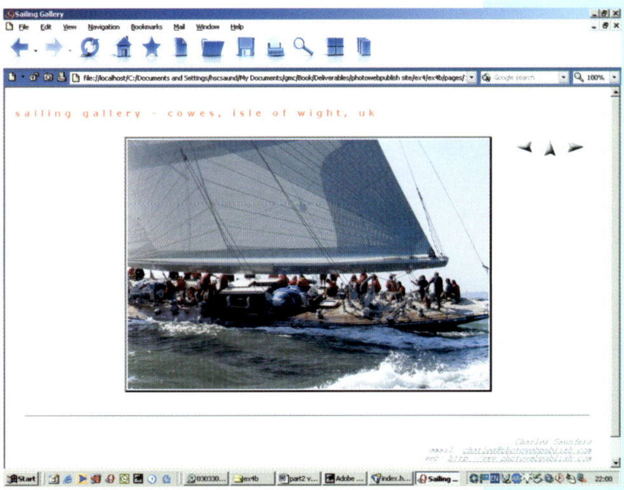

[9.5] An enlarged view of the first selected thumbnail image

browsers and the thumbnail images can all be viewed together and in context. That said, linking to fifteen pages from fifteen thumbnail images is remarkably wasteful in terms of program code. Producing fifteen almost identical sub-pages merely to change the current image on view is a particular problem if you ever need to make a slight change to the HTML document that describes this enlarged view, as you would have to make the change fifteen times. This would quickly become a tiresome exercise, as I found out for myself. A different and more efficient approach would be to use JavaScript.

Using Javascript to display images

In this modified design, which uses JavaScript (see page 148), the table of thumbnail images has been removed and instead we see a single column of thumbnail images, as shown in Fig 9.6 (below). When each thumbnail is clicked on, a larger version of the thumbnail image is displayed in the adjacent data cell. There is only one row for this table and the HTML is shown below. To keep things short, I have not listed every single thumbnail image reference within the first data cell.

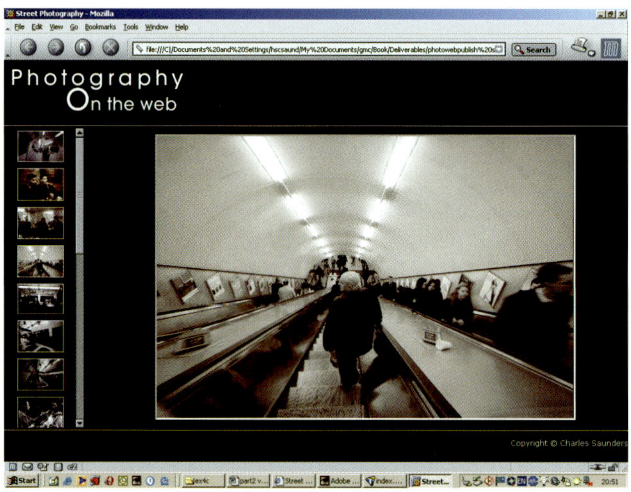

[9.6] Using JavaScript to switch images on display is far more efficient in terms of coding

```
<table>
<tr>
<td>
<div id="thumbnailribbon">
<a
href="javascript:switchImage('images/1.j
pg')"><img alt="image"
src="images/thumbnails/1.jpg"
height="48" width="75"></a>
<a
href="javascript:switchImage('images/2.j
pg')"><img alt="image"
src="images/thumbnails/2.jpg"
height="50" width="75"></a>
...
...
...
</div></td>
<td id="selectedimagezone">
<img src="images/1.jpg"
name="mainImage">
</td>
</tr>
</table>
```

To appreciate how this example works, you actually need to look initially at the second data cell. Within the cell there is a simple image link that initially references, through the use of the src parameter, the image file 1.jpg within a subdirectory called 'images'. This image element has the name 'mainImage', which you can think of as a unique identifier. Coincidentally, the initial thumbnail image that appears in the first data cell is a smaller rendition of this mainImage.

Now take a look at the first data cell in the table. It holds a list of image links and you should imagine that we have clicked on the second thumbnail image in the list of links. However, instead of invoking an HTML link as we have previously seen, when the thumbnail image is clicked it calls a JavaScript function called switchImage(). This takes a single parameter 'images/2.jpg', which is the name of the relevant image file for the thumbnail that was just clicked.

```
<a href="javascript:switchImage('images
/2.jpg')"><img alt="image"
src="images/thumbnails/2.jpg"
height="50" width="75"></a>
```

The switchImage() function couldn't be much simpler. JavaScript functions are often written in the head section of the document between the <script></script> tags. The parameters within the opening <script> tag merely tell the browser what sort of scripting language are we using and should be reproduced in your examples exactly as you see here. We'll come back to the <!-- and // --> marks in a moment. The function is then declared as shown and the processing that needs to be undertaken for this function is bounded by { } characters. The function itself merely says, receive the parameter from the function-calling link and name it selectedImage. The incoming parameter of selectedImage is called a variable and contains the value of 'images/2.jpg'. The one and only line of the function essentially takes the src parameter of our original image in cell 2 (named mainImage within our document) and gives it the new src value of 'images/2.jpg', causing the picture to change as the link is activated.

The <!-- and // --> marks alongside the <script></script> tags are, as you may have guessed, HTML comment marks. They are used to hide the script from older browsers that don't understand JavaScript. This trick is pretty much standard practice to avoid unsightly problems with browsers which pre-date scripting capabilities.

As you can see, this approach is a great deal more efficient than creating countless pages for each thumbnail image. However, this produces its own set of problems. As I have already indicated, the user's browser may not recognize JavaScript or, more likely, the user may have switched off this feature because of wider security concerns. We'll look briefly at how to mitigate against this problem later in the book (see page 150). All that remains is to understand the CSS (shown opposite) that accompanies this example.

```
<script language="javascript" type="text/javascript"> <!--
function switchImage(selectedImage) {
document.mainImage.src=selectedImage
}
// -->
</script>
```

```
body {
        font-family: Verdana, "Trebuchet
        MS", san-serif;
        margin: 0px;
        padding: 0px;
        text-align: left;
}
html {
        background-color: #000000;
        color: #FFFFFF;
        margin: 0px;
        padding: 0px;
}
table {
        background-color: #000000;
        border-bottom: 1px solid #FFFFFF;
        border-left: 0px;
        border-right: 0px;
        border-top: 1px solid #FFFFFF;
        height: 480px;
        margin-top: 0px;
        width: 100%;
}
td#selectedimagezone {
        background-color: #000000;
        color: #FFFFFF;
        text-align: center;
}
td#selectedimagezone img          {
        border: medium inset #FFFFFF;
        margin-left: auto;
        margin-right: auto;
        padding: 0px;
}
.copyright          {
        color: #FFFFFF;
        font-size: .75em;
        text-align: right;
}
#thumbnailribbon {
        background-color: #000000;
        height: 480px;
        overflow: auto;
        text-align: center;
        width: 130px;
}
#thumbnailribbon a img {
        border: 1px solid #FFFFFF;
        margin-bottom: 5px;
        margin-top: 5px;
        vertical-align: middle;
}
#thumbnailribbon a:hover img {
        border: 1px solid #FF0000;
}
#thumbnailribbon a:active img {
        border: 1px solid #FFFF00;
}
```

9

Shortcut
Using the id selector: thumbnailribbon

Using the id selector: thumbnailribbon
Wrapped up in a <div> element of the code on the previous page, is the selector 'thumbnailribbon'. This enables produces an independently scrolling list of images. The height of this element is 480 pixels, whereas the width is 130 pixels, preventing the thumbnail images from appearing in anything but a single column. The thumbnailribbon element shares the same height dimension as the table itself. Should the thumbnailribbon element contain more data than is possible to display, the overflow: auto parameter cleverly creates a scrollbar to help the user locate the appropriate image regardless of the actual page size. The images within the list of links are spaced out using top and bottom margins and appropriate CSS styling is defined to show the active link.

Using frames to design pages

Shortcut
Why use frames in your website?

Frames are simply a way of dividing a browser window into sub-windows, each of which displays a different HTML document. They have gained notoriety, unfairly in my opinion, because they can exhibit some interesting side effects. For example, accurately bookmarking a framed site is a challenge; the bookmark only references the top-level window and not the state of any individual sub-windows. Navigation can also be problematic as the navigation history invariably records the entire sequence of sub-window state changes, which you have to unwind through when you wish to back out of a site. Search engines also find framed sites exceedingly difficult to traverse, and if they do find some interesting content the page can often be exposed during a search completely out of context – i.e. on a page by itself.

A good example in the use of frames can be found on www.photowebpublish.com within the contact-centre section. Rather than post my email address all over the site so that every email-spamming robot in the world can pick it up, I prefer to use forms as a method of collecting feedback from visitors. My ISP provides limited form functionality, but does generate simple forms for me through

Why use frames in your website?
None of the problems associated with frames are insurmountable, and if they are good enough for the likes of Adobe (in their website-generation tool) and Google (for image search), they must have some good points. For example, frames offer a fantastic way to unify disparate content. For photographers they also offer a convenient way to aggregate pictures within genres and quickly display only what is relevant to the user's current interest.

the use of a software 'wizard'. My only problem is that I can't put any site branding on the form pages, as the software hasn't been designed to accommodate this.

Creating a frameset page that contains two other pages easily solves the problem. The first sub-page is a thin heading page, situated at the top of the browser window, which displays the prerequisite site branding for overall consistency. The second sub-page is the relevant form page itself, and is situated immediately under the branding header. Although the two pages come from two different sources, the content is unified and the user in none the wiser.

Creating framed pages

To create a framed document, you begin the process by defining a frameset page. This is simply a page that describes the sub-windows or frames within it. Frameset documents differ from your normal HTML document in that they have no <body> section. Instead, they have a <frameset> section that lists only the frames within the page. Frames are arranged in rows and columns, and each frame will have a name and an explicit or implied dimension.

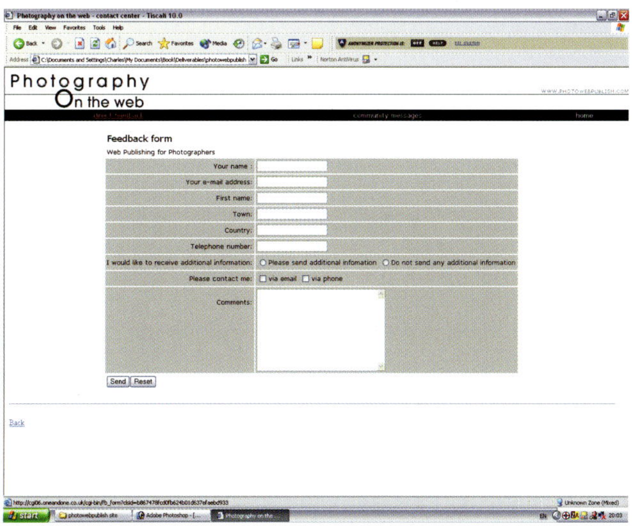

[9.7] Unified content from two different sources appears seamlessly as one in a framed window

To understand frames, you really have to look at worked examples. I've created three layouts that you may wish to use as part of your site designs. These can be seen in Figs 9.8–9.10, and each is accompanied with an analysis of the code used.

Example 1: two-frame layout

The most common of these would be the two-frame layout (Fig 9.8). This is the simplest layout to understand, and is often used to show a column of thumbnail images and correspondingly larger images for each activated thumbnail. The HTML for this example is as follows:

```
<!DOCTYPE HTML PUBLIC "-//W3C//DTD
HTML 4.01 Frameset//EN">
<html>
<head>
<title>A 2 Frame Example</title>
<meta http-equiv="Content-Type"
content="text/html; charset=iso-8859-1">
</head>
<frameset cols="20%,*">
<frame frameborder="1" src="red.html"
name="RedFrame" scrolling="auto">
<frame frameborder="1"
src="yellow.html" name="YellowFrame"
scrolling="auto">
<noframes>Viewing this page requires a
browser capable of displaying
frames.</noframes>
</frameset>
</html>
```

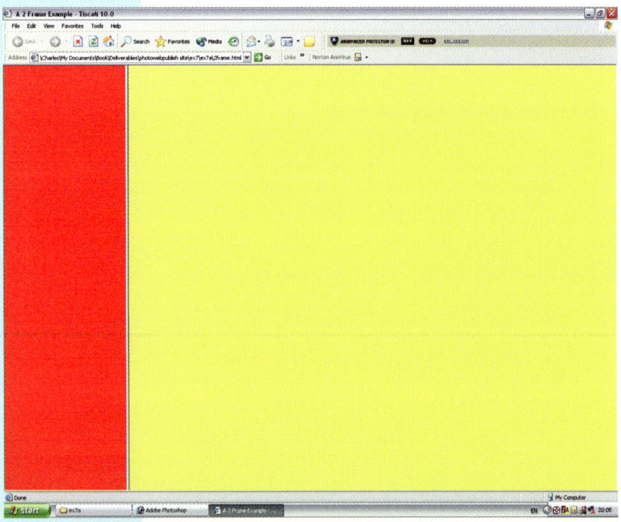

[9.8] The two-frame layout often used to display thumbnail images and larger pictures

The first thing to notice is the DOCTYPE, which has been set to Frameset. The browser should now be aware of how it should interpret what follows. As you can see, there is no body section. Instead, we see the definition for the frameset. In this simple example I have defined two columns for this frameset. The first column is 20% of the overall window width and, as you would expect, this means the dimension is dynamic. The second column has a width of asterisk (*), which is a neat shorthand for 'the remaining space'. In this case that's equivalent to 80% of the browser window. These relative measurements are the most useful, but you could have used absolute pixel values instead, such as <frameset cols="200px, *">, which would have made column one 200 pixels wide.

There then follows a definition of the two frames that occupy each column. Using the <frame></frame> element, frames are defined from left to right for columns and from top to bottom for rows. From this worked example, we can ascertain that the first column will be red in appearance. The frame defines a frameborder, a source HTML document, a name for the frame – which is useful for linking purposes – and whether the frame may scroll or not. The scroll parameter may take the values auto, yes or no. In this two-frame case, we link to an HTML document called "red.html", call the frame "RedFrame" and set scrolling to auto, which means scroll bars will only appear if there is more data within the page than can be displayed. After the first column has been defined, the second column is similarly described by another frame statement. This time the sub-window is yellow in appearance.

Following the frame definition, there exists the standard <noframes></noframes> declaration that allows the definition of text to be displayed should the browser be incapable of displaying frames. It's good practice to keep this statement in the code, but there aren't too many browsers around these days that don't understand the frameset structure.

Example 2: four-frame layout
A second option is to break up the second column into a number of rows, perhaps because you want to include some branding or additional navigation elements. This modification can be achieved very easily. Consider the augmented frameset statement for a four-frame page:

```
<frameset cols="15%,*">
<frame frameborder="1" src="red.html"
name="RedFrame" scrolling="auto">
<frameset rows="50px,*,2*">
<frame frameborder="1"
src="yellow.html" name="YellowFrame"
scrolling="auto">
<frame frameborder="1" src="blue.html"
name="BlueFrame" scrolling="auto">
<frame frameborder="1"
src="green.html" name="GreenFrame"
scrolling="auto">
</frameset>
<noframes>Viewing this page requires a
browser capable of displaying
frames.</noframes>
</frameset>
```

9

Now the second frame is replaced by a nested frameset definition of three rows. The three rows have the dimension of 50 pixels, the remaining portion and a row that is twice the size of the previous portion. You can see just how powerful these relative dimension mechanisms really are in Fig 9.9 (top left). The three rows in the space implied by the second column are then defined as Yellow, Blue and Green frames respectively.

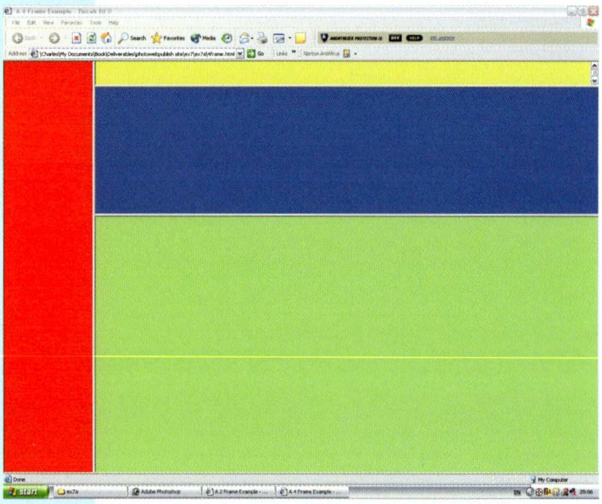

[9.9] A four-frame document

Example 3: five-frame layout

In the last example (Fig 9.10) we see a five-frame layout, which is often used for a branding header, footer and standard three-column arrangement for content and navigation.

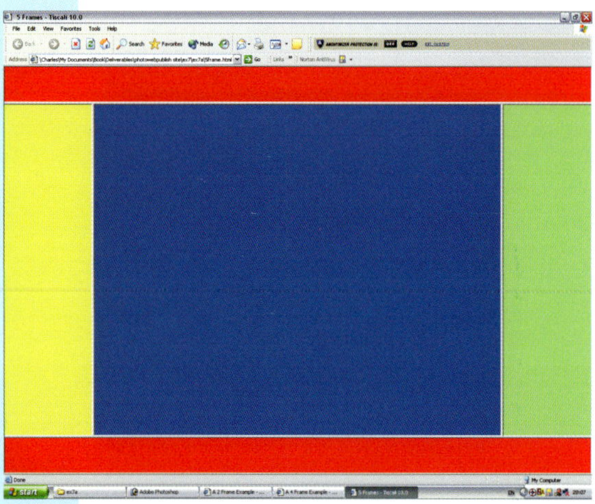

[9.10] A common five-frame layout

```
<frameset rows="75px,*,75px">
<frame src="red.html"
name="headerFrame" scrolling="no">
<frameset cols="15%,*,15%">
<frame src="yellow.html"
name="LeftMainColFrame"
scrolling="auto">
<frame src="blue.html"
name="MiddleMainColFrame"
scrolling="auto">
<frame src="green.html"
name="RightMainColFrame"
scrolling="auto">
</frameset>
<frame src="red.html"
name="FooterFrame" scrolling="no">
<noframes>Viewing this page requires a
browser capable of displaying
frames.</noframes>
</frameset>
```

Simply put, there are three rows, two of which have absolute dimensions of 75 pixels. The centre row is further subdivided using a nested frameset into three columns. I urge you to experiment with your own permutations but I hope you can see from these simple examples how straightforward the definition of frames really is.

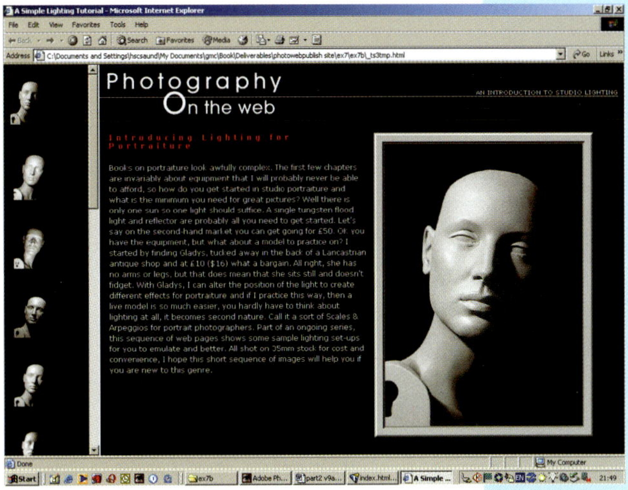

[9.11] A three-frame layout used to display pictures of a model

Disguising frames

Consider the three-frame layout that I have used in Fig 9.11 (right). The code for this example is much as we have seen before:

```
<frameset cols="15%,*">
<frame frameborder="0" src="ThumbnailFrame.html" name="LeftFrame"
scrolling="auto" noresize >
<frameset framespacing=0 border=0 rows="100px,*">
<frame frameborder="0" src="pages/G0.html" name="TopFrame" scrolling="no">
<frame frameborder="0" src="pages/intro.html" name="RightFrame" scrolling="auto">
</frameset>
<noframes>Viewing this page requires a browser capable of displaying
frames.</noframes>
</frameset>
```

The overall page is divided into two columns, and the right-hand column is further subdivided into two rows. The framesets have had their borders removed to create the impression that this is really just one page, even though it is in fact three HTML documents brought together as one. If you really want to ensure that borders are removed, you have to introduce a line of code (which, although redundant, is needed due to browser manufacturer differences). For example, <frameset frameborder=0 framespacing=0 frameborder=no border=0> usually does the trick for all browser permutations. Frameborder should be all you need at the frame level.

In this example, the left-hand column (called LeftFrame) contains a list of thumbnails images. Each thumbnail is an anchor image to another page thus:

```
<a href="pages/G1.html"
target="RightFrame"><img
src="thumbnails/G1.jpg" alt="G1"
height="75" width="54"></a>
```

Notice how the target for the anchor link is defined as RightFrame. This is the name of the second row in the right-hand column. Once the image is clicked on, the RightFrame loads the HTML page 'g1.html' and displays the appropriate larger picture of the relevant thumbnail.

The first row on the right-hand column merely contains some standard branding information for the website and loads 'g0.html' into this TopFrame. Scrolling is switched off for this banner section and the absence of borders makes the transition between the two rows seamless visually.

If you are wondering why it is that you can never seem to load the individual sub-window pages without loading the whole frameset, this is due to a small piece of JavaScript that I have inserted in each sub-page. For example, the branding header g0.html contains the following small script that checks to see whether the topmost frame in the current window is the document itself. If so, then the page must have loaded without its parent frameset and the second line of the script replaces the current document with the whole frameset document (index.html in this case). This is a neat trick and it stops your page frames from being loaded via a search window and appearing out of their frameset context.

```
<script language="JavaScript">
<!-- A piece of clever Javascript to
always keep the page in a frame
if (top.location == self.location) {
    self.location.replace("../index.html")
}
// -->
</script>
```

The last thing of note is that you can stop the user from altering the size of your frames by declaring the noresize attribute in the frame tag.

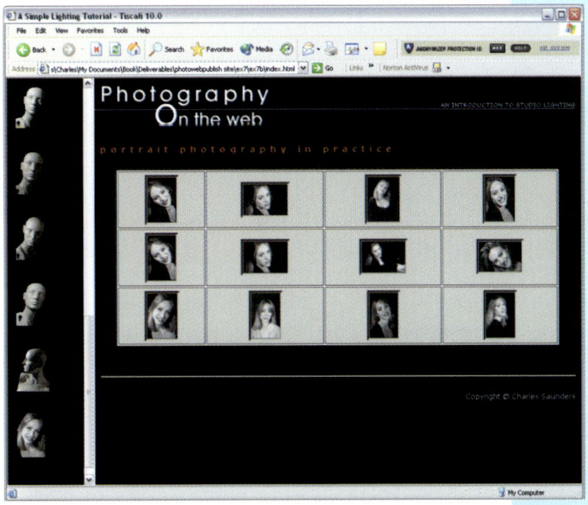

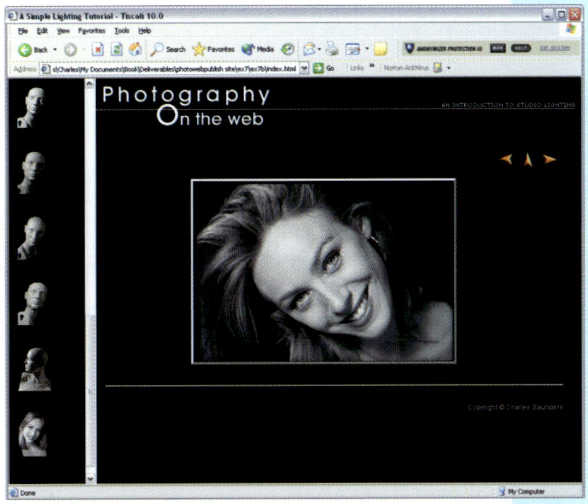

[9.12–13] You can use the frame approach to display tables of other thumbnails and so further arrange your photographic content

10 Enhancing the User Experience

Introduction to JavaScript

Some elements of this book have already provided a short introduction to JavaScript, and this introduction was realistic in that you've seen the language, you know how to incorporate simple scripts in your own pages, yet you probably don't really understand what's going on. Don't worry, this is how we all started.

JavaScript is a very sophisticated language, I cannot possibly hope to teach it from scratch in a single chapter. My aim, therefore, is to give the reader enough knowledge to understand how to reuse the many thousands of JavaScript fragments that are available on the web today and apply it to their own website. For a taste of what is commonly available, simply visit www.javascript.com.

Shortcut

What is JavaScript?

What is JavaScript?

JavaScript is a 'scripting language' used within Internet browsers. It provides simple programming facilities to do things such as open a window, display additional information, validate user input or perform simple calculations. Scripting languages are, in theory, easier to learn than full-blown programming languages because they provide a higher degree of abstraction. In other words, you would have to write more explicit instructions if you were using a programming language.

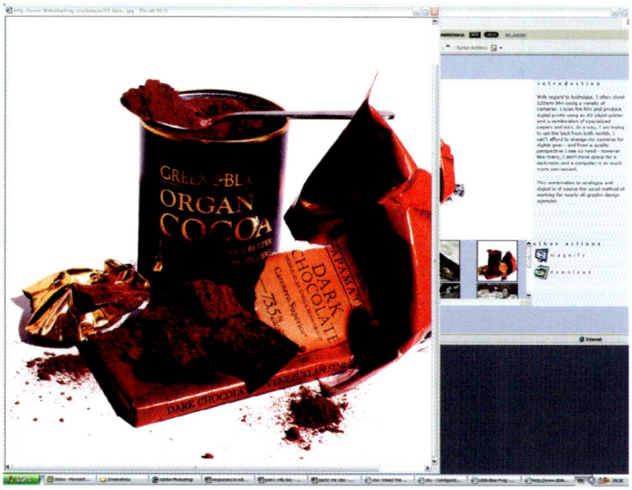

[10.1] The author's own site uses JavaScript extensively to show high resolution images

The history of JavaScript

Although JavaScript and the programming language Java share a similar name, their origins are quite different. The naming convention is a prime example of the computing industry's obsession with the latest fashion. JavaScript was developed by Netscape, and was originally called LiveScript. At around the same time, Sun Microsystems developed a programming language called Java that soon caught the industry's collective imagination as the next hottest technology on the block. The Netscape marketers quickly renamed LiveScript to JavaScript, presumably hoping that some of the Java magic would rub off on LiveScript.

As a marketer, I have to admire this stroke of genius. The trick worked, not least because JavaScript and Java have some syntactic similarities, and that's close enough for most technology journalists. Not wishing to be outshone, Microsoft released their own version of JavaScript, imaginatively titled Jscript, which unsurprisingly has some important differences from Netscape JavaScript. Thankfully, the two parties managed to agree a standard version of JavaScript, currently called ECMA-262.

If you write your examples to the ECMAScript standard, there is a reasonable chance that your scripts will work on several browser platforms. A note of caution, however – some people erroneously believe that JavaScript can leave their computers vulnerable to malicious attack. This is not so, as the language has no capability to write information to a user's computer hard disk. However, they may elect to switch off JavaScript from their browser thereby effectively stopping your page from functioning correctly. It is important to determine a strategy for this eventuality.

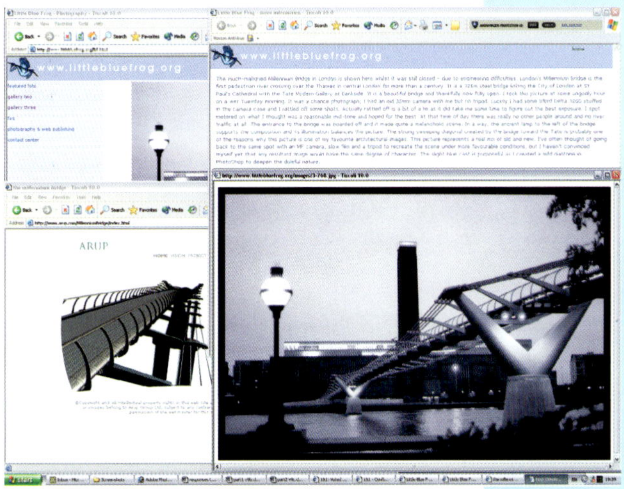

[10.2] Complex content interaction is possible through the use of JavaScript

A simple JavaScript example

As we have already seen, JavaScript is written between one or more <script></script> tag pairs. Scripts are usually inserted in the <head> section of a document, but you can insert scripts into the <body> section should you wish. If the user has a browser incapable of running JavaScript or as is more likely, they have switched off their browser's JavaScript capability, it is possible to communicate this by inserting the appropriate HTML mark-up between a <noscript></noscript> tag pair. You might either urge the user to alter their browser settings, or perhaps direct them using a hyperlink (see page 116) to a variant of your site that does not rely on JavaScript.

Scripts usually call functions that execute a sequence of programming instructions. These functions may be provided with values or 'parameters' to help them in their execution. Script functions are frequently 'set off' by clicking on an HTML link, but that's not the only way they can be invoked. Much more subtle events, such as moving the mouse over an object or loading a page, can also be used as triggers.

In Fig 10.3, the user can either click on the link at the top of the sample page or simply move their mouse pointer over the photographic image object. Either way, a JavaScript function is invoked that tells the user the type of browser they are using and the screen resolution it thinks is available.

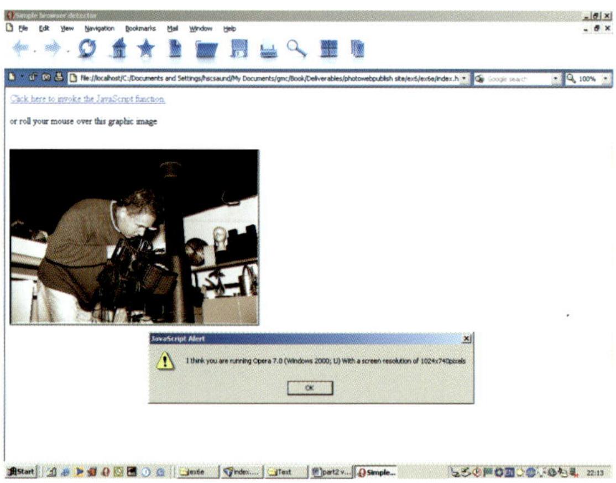

[10.3] Our sample script soon detects the correct browser version and screen resolution

```
<!DOCTYPE HTML PUBLIC "-//W3C//DTD HTML 4.01//EN"
"http://www.w3.org/TR/html4/strict.dtd">
<html lang="en">
<!-- www.photowebpublish.com -->
<head>
<meta http-equiv="content-type" content="text/html;charset=iso-8859-1">
<title>Simple browser detector</title>
<script type="text/javascript">
<!-- Hide script from old browsers
function identifyMe() {
monitorWidth=screen.availWidth;
monitorHeight=screen.availHeight;
browserName=navigator.appName;
browserVersion=navigator.appVersion;
stringa = "I think you are running "+browserName +" " +browserVersion +" With a
screen resolution of "+monitorWidth+"x"+monitorHeight+"pixels ";
alert (stringa);
}
// End hiding script from old browsers -->
</script>
<noscript style="color:red;"><p>This page requires a browser to be JavaScript
compatible.</p></noscript>
</head>
<body>
<a href="javascript:identifyMe()">Click here to invoke the JavaScript function.</a>
<br>
<p>or roll your mouse over this graphic image</p>
<br>
<img src="studio1.jpg" height="282" width="417"
onmouseover="javascript:identifyMe()" alt="" style="border: 3px inset black;">
</body>
</html>
```

The script on the previous page has the function identifyMe(). It takes no parameters and can be invoked via a JavaScript function call embedded within the link's href parameter. Alternatively, simply moving the mouse over the image inserted in the page invokes the event handler 'onmouseover', which then calls the identifyMe() function. Sophisticated editing environments, such as Adobe GoLive or Bradsoft TopStyle, show the events that can affect HTML. It is then quite a simple process to write code for when these events occur.

Shortcut

Understanding the code

The function is simple enough in that it retrieves some parameters from the user's browsing environment, such as browser name and browser version. It stores these parameters in variables that it links together, along with other text, to create the string of characters to be fed back to the user. The system function alert() communicates the string of information to the user within an alert dialog box, and the function then ends. Should the user's browsing environment be incapable of running JavaScript, the <noscript></noscript> tag contains a statement that warns the user that JavaScript is required. You should try turning off JavaScript in the preferences section of your own browser to see how this capability works.

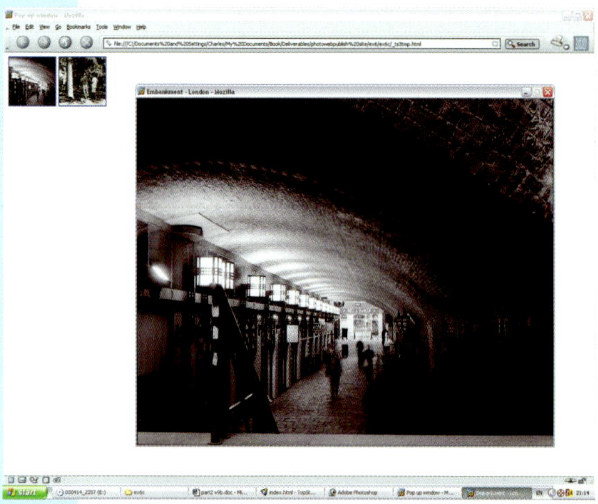

[10.4] Using a pop-up window to display a larger picture from a thumbnail image

Understanding the code

Don't worry if terms like browserName=navigator.appName mean nothing to you. The important thing is that you appreciate how to call JavaScript functions. Indeed, how a function operates should be secondary to your appreciation of knowing how to call it and what parameters it requires. This is what good, component programming is all about.

Creating a pop-up window for large images

One of the most useful things JavaScript can offer the photographer is the ability to provide a pop-up window that can contain a photograph. The advantage here is simply that the image is able to occupy the maximum amount of screen space available, as it doesn't need to be encumbered by large menu and status bars.

```
<!DOCTYPE HTML PUBLIC "-//W3C//DTD
HTML 4.01//EN">
<html lang="en">
<!-- www.photowebpublish.com -->
<head>
<meta http-equiv="content-type"
content="text/html;charset=iso-8859-1">
<title>Pop-up window</title>

<script type="text/javascript">
<!-- Hide script from old browsers
// Just call this function with the name of
the larger photo image and a title
function PhotoViewer(activePhoto,
windowTitle) {
foto = new Image;
foto.src = activePhoto;
stringa =
"width="+foto.width+",height="+foto.heig
ht+",menubar=no,toolbar=no,location=n
o, scrollbars=no, resizable=no"
photoWin =
window.open("","photoWindow",
stringa);
photoWin.document.open();
photoWin.document.write("<html><head
><title>"+windowTitle+"<\/title>");
photoWin.document.write("<\/head><bod
y>");
photoWin.document.write('<div
style="position:absolute;width:'+foto.wid
th+'px;height:'+foto.height+'px;left:0px;to
p:0px">');
photoWin.document.write("<img
src="+activePhoto+"><\/div><\/body><\/ht
ml>");
photoWin.document.close();
//Due to a bug in Netscape you seem to
have to open the window twice on the
first attempt to size correctly, beats me
why.
if (navigator.appName == "Netscape") {
if (photoWin.innerWidth!=foto.width ||
photoWin.innerHeight!=foto.height) {
photoWin.close();
setTimeout("PhotoViewer('"+activePhoto
+"','"+windowTitle+"')", 50);
// if you have problems, try setting the 50
value above to 300 milliseconds
return;}}
monitorWidth=screen.availWidth;
leftOffset=((monitorWidth-foto.width)/2)-
10;
photoWin.moveTo(leftOffset,0);
photoWin.focus();
}
// End hiding script from old browsers -->
</script>
<noscript><p>This page requires
JavaScript.</p></noscript>
</head>
<body>
<!-- to use this function all you need to
do is call PhotoViewer with an image
and a window title. -->
<a
href="javascript:PhotoViewer('p1.jpg','E
mbankment - London')"><img
src="tp1.jpg" height="100" alt=""
width="100"></a> <a
href="javascript:PhotoViewer('p2.jpg','M
adrid Buskers')"><img src="tp2.jpg"
height="100" width="100" alt=""></a>
</body>
</html>
```

The panel on the previous page contains quite a complicated piece of JavaScript, not least because it has to overcome idiosyncratic behaviour in Netscape browsers. The script doesn't resize the pop-up window in Opera, but as only a tiny fraction of users use this browser this is not too much of a problem.

Using the script is really quite straightforward. Simply call the function "javascript:PhotoViewer('p1.jpg','Embankment - London')" with two parameters. The first is the name of the larger image to be contained within the pop-up window. The second parameter is the text to appear in the pop-up window title bar. Notice how both parameters are enclosed in single quotes to avoid confusion with the double quotes that surround the entire JavaScript function call. Assuming you have correctly reproduced the script line for line with no errors, a pop-up window will appear centred on the top of the screen, containing your chosen image.

Of course, you may wish to use this function in several pages on your website. It would be ludicrous to expect you to have this function defined in every page. Instead, you can use the optional parameter of the <script> tag to reference a simple text file that contains just the function itself. In other words, the function is defined once but then referenced many times. For example:

```
<script type="text/javascript" src="pop-up.js"></script>
```

JavaScript source files typically have a '.js' file extension. Simply by referencing the source file 'pop-up.js', you are able to take advantage of the PhotoViewer() function without having to overly complicate your existing pages. Naturally the 'pop-up.js' source file is available for download on the book's accompanying website.

Randomly changing a picture on a web page

Here's a neat trick that you will often see used by websites selling stock photography. To reinforce the belief that content is regularly changing on the site, each time the page reloads a significant image on the page is changed at random from a list of possible photographs. In many browsers you can manually force a reload by pressing the F5 function key on your keyboard, which will allow you to see this change happen. Again, the JavaScript for this facility is not easy, but our analysis can be restricted to the elements you need to modify to reproduce this on your own pages.

We should begin by looking at the code within the <script></script> tags. The very first line of code declares a JavaScript variable called PictureCarousel. Remember: variables are simply places to hold data. PictureCarousel is of a type called 'array', and you can think of it as a logical equivalent to a 35mm slide projector carousel capable of holding a number of photographs. In this example, I have loaded the carousel with pictures taken from elsewhere on the website. Naturally, if you want to use this function you will need to load the carousel with the filenames and locations of the images you wish to use instead.

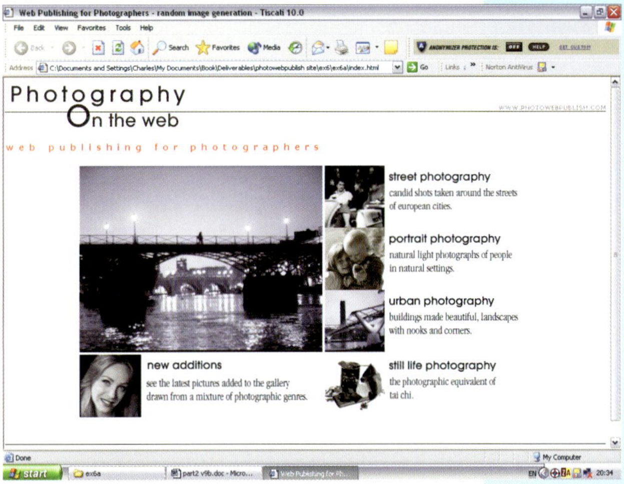

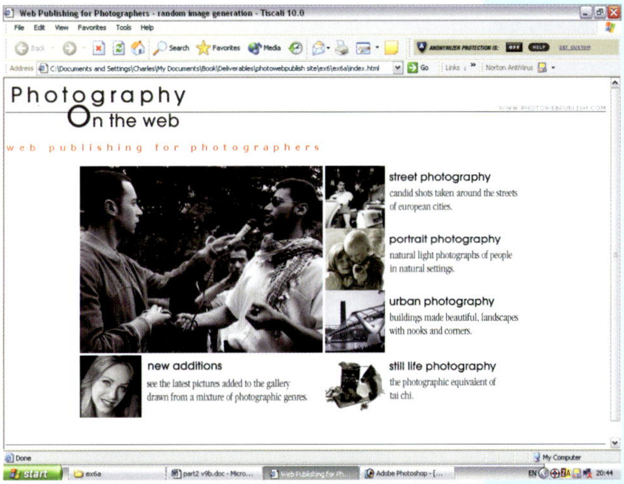

[10.5–6] Switching images on a home page to provide variety requires JavaScript

10

```
<script type="text/javascript">
<!--
PictureCarousel = new Array("../../images/main1.jpg",
"../../images/main2.jpg","../../images/main3.jpg","../../images/main4.jpg","../../images/m
ain5.jpg")
CarouselCount = PictureCarousel.length
function switchPicture() {
    if (document.images){
        randomNumber = Math.floor
            ((Math.random() * CarouselCount))
        document.myPicture.src =
            PictureCarousel[randomNumber]
    }
}
// -->
</script>
<noscript><p>This page requires JavaScript</p></noscript>
</head>
```

When the function switchPicture() is called, a random number is generated and the corresponding image in the carousel variable – whose position equates to the random number – is selected and displayed on the page. How does the function know which picture on the page needs to be switched? Inside the switchPicture() function a line of code changes the src parameter of the <img> reference in the document whose name parameter has been set to 'myPicture'. Therefore, for this function to work in your page one of your images must be called 'myPicture'. The function is called simply by attaching the function call to the 'onload' event for the <body> element of this document. Every time the page loads, the function is called and the picture is potentially switched. I say potentially because the random-number generator can of course generate the same number position as is already set, in which case no visible change is discernible. Incidentally, the initial setting for the myPicture image is a very simple GIF image that simply displays the message 'image loading'. Depending on the speed of your connection, you may or may not see this temporary placeholder. Remember, the switchPicture() function is called only after the page has loaded so you do need a very small and simple image file to occupy this space until the function can be called.

The myPicture image sits among others in a table to give the example an overall visual context.

```
<body
onload="javascript:switchPicture()">
<div class="myheader"><a
href="../../index.html">www.photowebpu
blish.com</a></div>
<div class="bodycopy">
<br />
<h1>web publishing for
photographers</h1>
<table align="center">
<tr>
<td><img src="../../images/main0.gif"
name="myPicture" alt="Welcome"></td>
<td><img src="../../graphics/street.jpg"
alt="street photography"><br>
<img src="../../graphics/portrait.jpg"
alt="portrait photography"><br>
<img src="../../graphics/urban.jpg"
alt="urban"><br></td>
</tr>
<tr>
<td><img
src="../../graphics/newadditions.jpg"
alt="new additions"></td>
<td><img src="../../graphics/stilllife.jpg"
alt="still life"></td>
</tr>
</table>
</div>
</body>
```

10

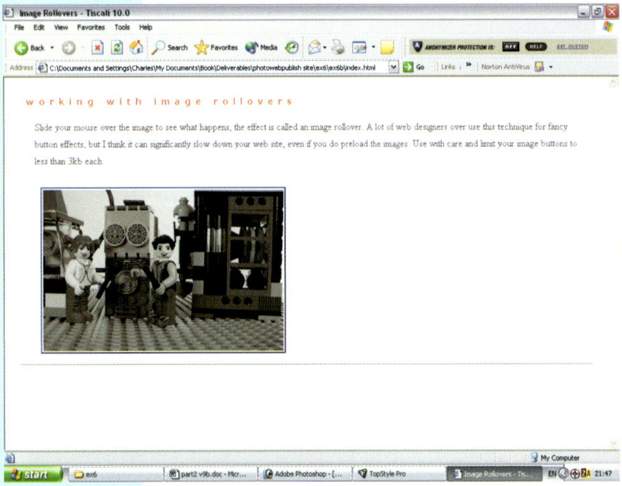

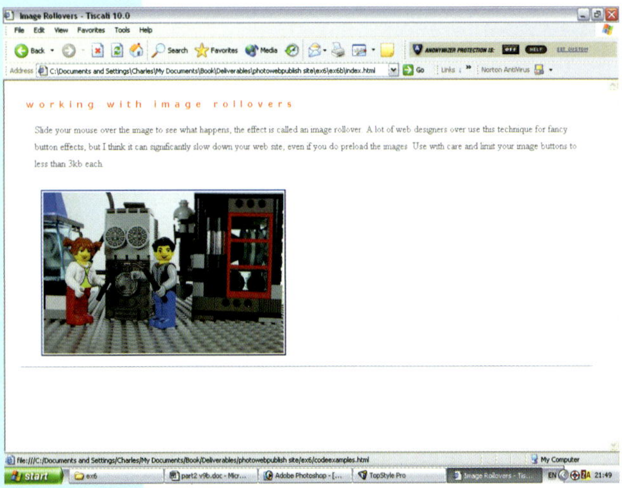

[10.7–8] The main image changes from monochrome to colour as the mouse rollovers the image

Using JavaScript to produce image rollovers

Rollovers probably represent the simplest form of JavaScript and are easily the most abused. They tend to work acceptably with very small image files, but with larger files there is a potential lag in loading and, subsequently, a delay in image switching. The first step is to define the images that are to be switched. This definition has the added benefit of pre-loading the images and making the rollover more convincing.

```
<script type="text/javascript">
bricks0=new Image(400,259);
bricks1=new Image(400,259);
bricks0.src="bricks0.jpg";
bricks1.src="bricks1.jpg";
</script>
```

In this example, I first declare two new image objects called "bricks0" and "bricks1". The numbers (400,259) after the new image declaration are the pixel dimensions for the images themselves.

Using the rollover function

Image rollovers are usually used in the context of anchor links. The idea is that as the mouse rolls over the link, the image changes to give a strong visual clue to the user that a state has changed and that a mouse click here is likely to have an effect. The rollover function can be used to change any graphic object on the page, as long as it is suitably referenced using the name parameter. This approach can be used to great effect when employed with thumbnail images.

After creating image objects, it is necessary to set the src parameter of these objects to the filename of the photograph they will display. The file 'bricks1.jpg' is the monochrome version of the photography, whereas 'bricks2.jpg' is a colour rendition. The aim of this particular rollover is to switch from the monochrome to the colour version of the image as the user moves their mouse over the link (as shown in Figs 10.7–8, far left). This is achieved with the following code:

```
<a href="http://www.lego.com"
onmouseover="myRollover.src='bricks0.j
pg'"
onmouseout="myRollover.src='bricks1.jp
g'"><img name="myRollover"
class="bodyimageleft" src="bricks1.jpg"
alt="My Rollover"></a>
```

To understand this image link, look first at the <img> statement. Here I have declared an image with the name 'myRollover' and whose src parameter is 'bricks1.jpg'. The image therefore starts off displaying a monochrome version of the children's building blocks.

Within the link, two events are trapped. They are 'onmouseover' and 'onmouseout'. The event 'onmouseover' occurs when the mouse travels over the image. When that event occurs, the src parameter of the image file "myRollover" is set to 'bricks0.jpg', thereby displaying a colour image. As soon as the mouse leaves the image zone a second event of 'onmouseout' is trapped and the image is reset to its original monochrome state.

Shortcut

Using the rollover function

Using JavaScript to create a slideshow

In this example we create a slide show capable of displaying a never-ending picture sequence.

Having seen the previous examples, this never-ending slide show is very much a reutilization of the same theory. A table on the page displays an image and two direction arrows. By pressing the arrows, the user can move from one picture to the next in either direction. Once the end of the picture sequence is reached, the selected picture loops around to the beginning or end of the sequence depending upon the direction chosen.

The main image is called onDisplay and the src parameter of this image object is altered by the two JavaScript functions called processNext() and processPrevious(), which can be added to the code as shown opposite.

To reuse this function, all you need to do is load up the Carousel array with the names of your own image files. Assuming you then have an image named 'onDisplay' and a way of invoking the two functions, you should be able to create a sophisticated slide show for your site visitors. Remember, however, to keep the image files small as this last example does carry a significant download overhead.

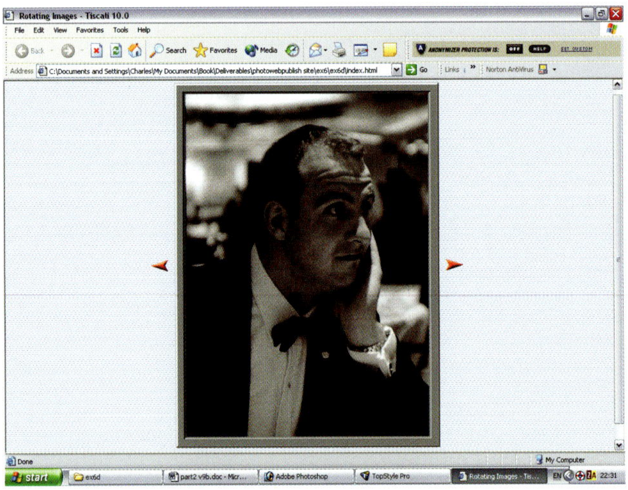

[10.9] A rolling slide show is easily achieved using JavaScript and avoids the need to reload whole pages

```
<script type="text/javascript">
Carousel = new Array ("./images/p1.jpg",
"./images/p2.jpg", "./images/p3.jpg",
"./images/p4.jpg", "./images/p5.jpg")

currentImage = 0
carouselCount = Carousel.length - 1
function processPrevious() {
// This function gets the previous picture
in the carousel and loads it into the
image named onDisplay
   if (document.images && currentImage
> 0) {
      currentImage--

document.onDisplay.src=Carousel[curren
tImage]
   }
   else {
      currentImage = carouselCount

document.onDisplay.src=Carousel[curren
tImage]
   }
}
function processNext() {
// This function gets the next picture in
the carousel and loads it into the image
named onDisplay
   if (document.images && currentImage
< carouselCount) {
      currentImage++

document.onDisplay.src=Carousel[curren
tImage]
   }
   else {
      currentImage = 0

document.onDisplay.src=Carousel[curren
tImage]
   }
}
</script>
</head>
<body>
<table>
<tr>
<td><a
href="javascript:processPrevious()"><img
alt="" src="images/previous.gif"
height="20" width="30" style="border:
0;"></a></td>
<td>
<div id="pictureframe"><img alt=""
src="./images/p1.jpg" name="onDisplay"
id="pictureborder"></div>
</td>
<td><a
href="javascript:processNext()"><img
alt="" src="images/next.gif" height="20"
width="30" style="border: 0;"></a></td>
</tr>
</table>
</body>
```

11 Promoting and Managing your Site

Uploading

You've finally built and tested your site. The next step is to upload the files to your web space. As I have mentioned earlier, the process is remarkably simple.

You can buy specialist software to help you perform this task; the process is called FTP (File Transfer Protocol), and there are many FTP products available to help you get your site online. However, you can just as easily use Internet Explorer to copy your files to the remote location from which the site is hosted. Fig 11.1 (below) shows the point at which I copied the file robots.txt from my hard disk to my website in cyberspace. Internet Explorer will ask me for my username and password to access this space, after all, I don't want just anyone changing my site, but after logging on to the remote location, the copying process is no different from what you do on your own computer. You should consult your own ISP's documentation for specific guidance on uploading files to your chosen web space.

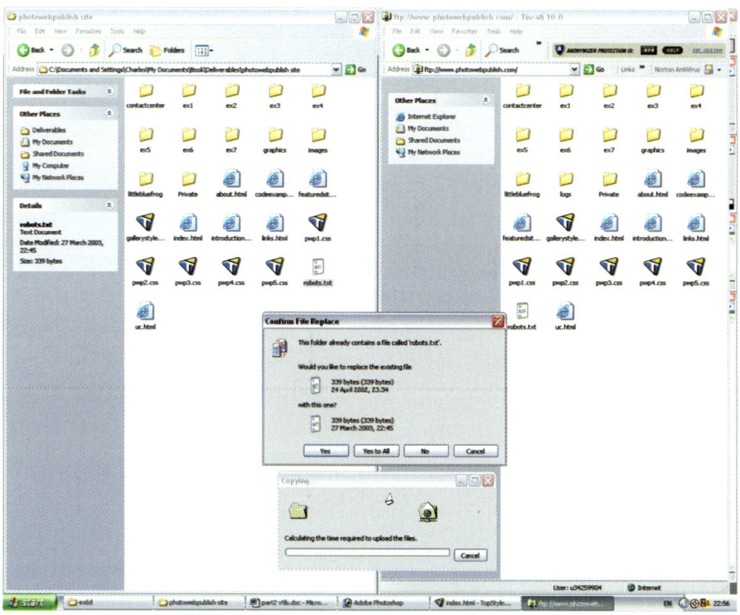

[11.1] Uploading files to your web server couldn't be easier

Promoting sites

Seconds after your site goes live, you'll want people to be looking at it. The question is, how will they find it? Before we get into the intricacies of search engines, don't lose sight of the fact that conventional marketing methods can generate very significant hit rates. If you have a commercial site, this means putting your URL on about anything that moves. Adverts, articles, business cards, email signatures, the backs of photographic prints, even the shop window; the list of potential promotional locations is endless. Even if you are a non-commercial site, don't underestimate the power of word of mouth, though naturally it helps to have a snappy and memorable URL. A great free screensaver or desktop wallpaper featuring the best of your photography can soon spread like wildfire across the Internet. The fashionable phrase for this approach is 'viral marketing'.

Search engines

Failing the conventional marketing approach, most users will find your site thanks to search engines. If you have used them before, you'll have realized how important it is that your site appears in the first couple of results pages delivered by the search engine for any given request. You'll often read that there is no winning formula for achieving a consistently high ranking on search engines for relevant search requests. This isn't true. The answer lies in either having very deep pockets, or

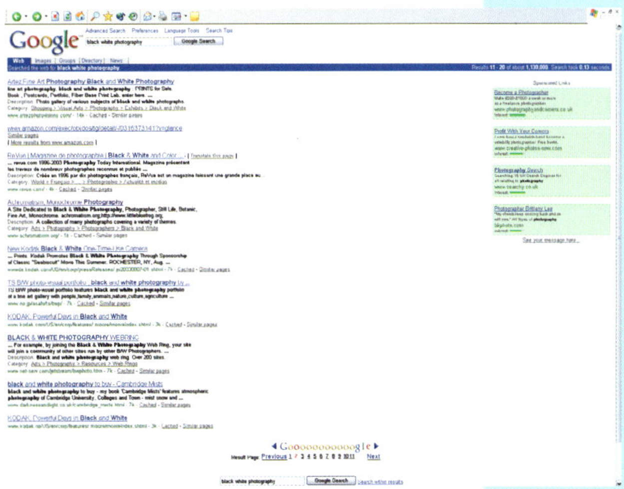

[11.2] Achieving page-two ranking for a search phrase that yields 1,130,000 results hopefully illustrates that the author's search engine submission strategy gets results

Shortcut
Promoting sites

11

Shortcut

Keywords

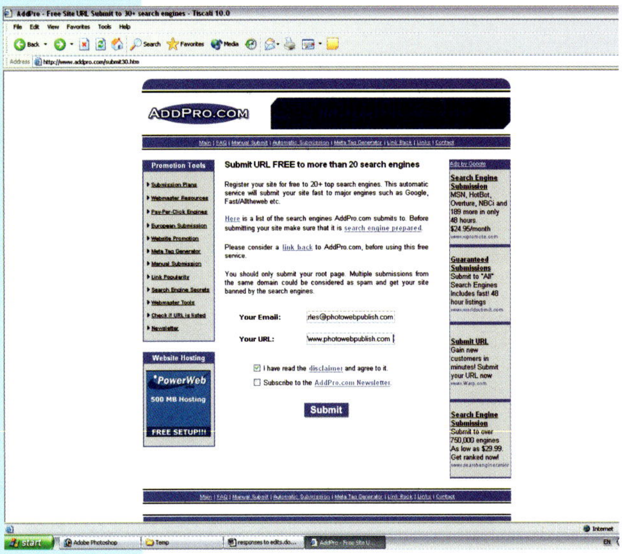

[11.3] Many organizations provide automatic submission to multiple search engines

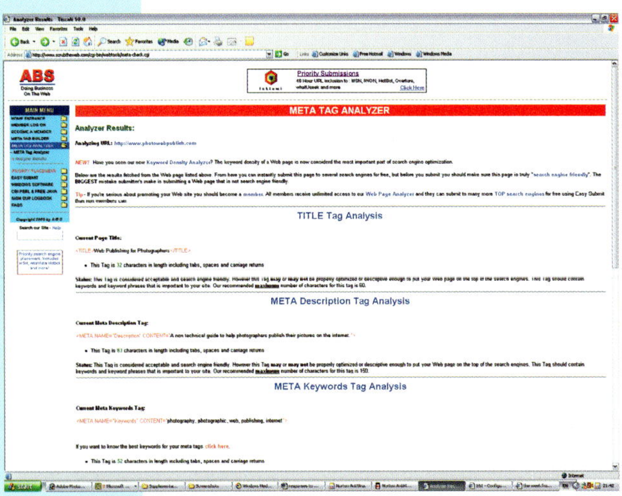

[11.4] Services do exist to help you optimize your likely search engine performance

Keywords

The most important element of this process is to pick the keywords that depict your site very carefully. I was once told that there are 10,000 professional photographers in and around London, UK. A fair number of those will have websites, so what keywords should one choose to help identify, describe and promote a professional photography business in that locale? This can be tricky, and it is vital to think laterally. For example, 'photo' is a fine keyword, but don't forget that in many parts of Europe the correct word is 'foto'.

great website content and lots of it. If you are a commercial venture, the search engines themselves go into great detail about how you can sponsor keywords, phrases and generally part with large sums of cash to assure a good ranking.

Many of the search engines have directories that are compiled by human 'editors'. These individuals have the power to boost your ranking significantly, but are not likely to be fooled by the usual tricks used to gain attention. This is where I think providing your users with something for nothing can score you a dividend.

In addition to this hands-on method of populating search-engine directories, the search-engine providers also use software to find, index and serve relevant content to their users. Some use software programs called 'spiders', which traverse the web looking at sites and reporting back on the content. Massive computers crunch through this data and create complex summaries of the sites from which even more sophisticated algorithms interrogate data to retrieve relevant websites.

Understanding how each of the search engines operates so that you can optimize your ranking in the results is somewhat of a complex art, which is thankfully revealed to a large extent at www.searchenginewatch.com.

Boosting your site's ranking

If like most you have a very small budget for the site's promotion, there are a few tricks you can adopt to help your ranking on search engines. Number one has to be detailed and interesting content. I used to have a non-profit website that 'taught' black-and-white photography using countless articles and worked examples. One day, a human researcher at Yahoo.com found the site and straight away I was on page one of any request for 'black and white photography'. This particular search returns millions of pages, so to rank on page one had me feeling euphoric while I enjoyed my fifteen minutes of fame.

Shortcut

Boosting your site's ranking

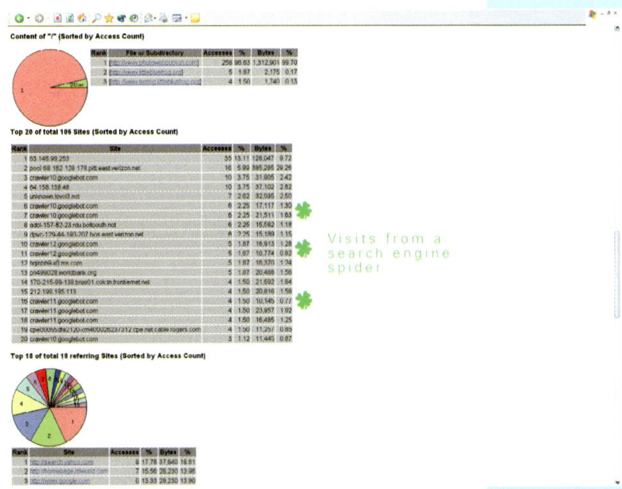

[11.5] Look at your server logs to see whether you have had a visit from a search engine spider program

Imporving your hit rate

The following guidelines should lead to an improvement in your hit rate:

- Give every page on your site a meaningful and descriptive title.
- Select your keywords carefully, and make sure they are included in some way in the upper portion of your web page, perhaps even within heading tags, as well as in the paragraph elements.
- Don't try any of the apocryphal search-engine subterfuge – such as incessantly repeating keywords on a page using the same colour as the background so users won't see it. Search engines are wise to this and many other acts of 'search-engine spamming', and you will be heavily penalized if you are caught trying to be too clever.
- Share reciprocal links between like-minded sites. Many search engines determine a site's standing using the 'Page-Rank' principle, which uses the number of links from one site to others to give an indication of popularity.
- You might consider creating 'landing' pages that automatically redirect the user to your main site. The name of the URL can be long and descriptive, as it is one of the most important criteria for search engine ranking. For example, in addition to www.photowebpublish.com I should also consider buying www.photographyguidewebpublishin g.com. I wouldn't expect anyone to type this in, but it is good search-engine fodder.
- Use meta tags (see opposite) to help further describe any given web page.

Meta tags

Meta tags allow you to include extra information about a page that is not visible to a browsing user. There are lots of different meta tags, but the most important are the Keyword tag and Description tag. The format of their usage is shown below and both appear within the <head> section of your document. The example is drawn from the first page on my site www.photwebpublish.com.

```
<meta name="description" content="A
non technical guide to help
photographers publish their pictures on
the internet.">
<meta name="keywords"
content="photography, photographic,
web, publishing, internet, www, foto">
```

Meta tags are not a panacea for poor search-engine rankings, but their consistent use throughout your site may pay a significant dividend. Above all, try and make sure the first 200 words of text on page contain the keywords you use. Don't be afraid to refine your keywords over time and resubmit them to the search engines every six weeks or so, but not more often.

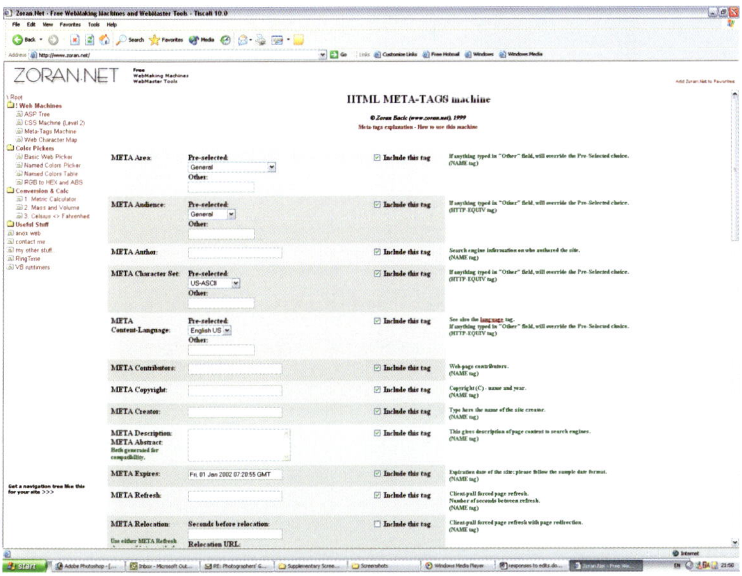

[11.6] A very helpful meta-tag generation machine which should help your provide detailed information for search engine robots

Shortcut

Popular search engines and directories

Keep a track on your server logs. Your ISP might also provide information on what users were looking for when they found your site. Failing that, there are several companies, such as www.webtrends.com, that can provide sophisticated technology to help you understand how your site performs.

Although you can also buy software that submits your site's details to many search engines simultaneously, it is often just as effective to visit each one in turn and better understand their specific submission process. Like most things in life, money talks, and the paid-submission route is the most reliable method of gaining a fast track to getting noticed. Some current popular search engines are listed below, and many have free URL submission sections to help you kick off the process of becoming famous.

Popular search engines and directories

www.google.com
www.yahoo.com
www.altavista.com
www.infoseek.com
www.ask.com
www.lycos.com
www.excite.com
www.dmoz.org
www.webcrawler.com

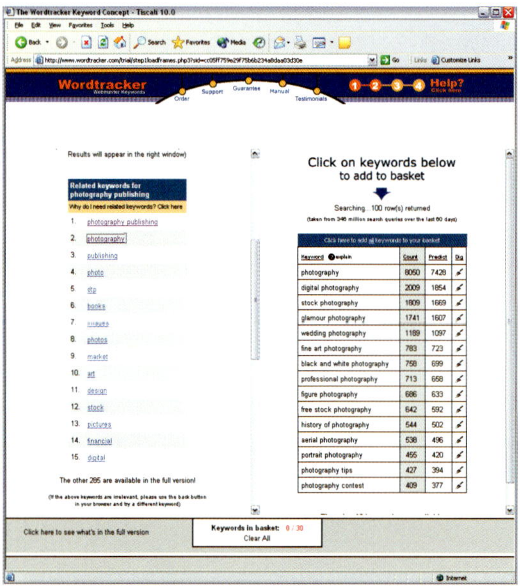

[11.7] Stuck on which keywords to use? Software exists to help you improve your selection

Protecting Yourself and your Website 12

Running a photographic website is a safe-enough proposition. However, it is not without some risk and a responsible publisher of information, whether in the virtual or real world, needs to take some steps to protect themselves from potential liabilities. The two broad areas for consideration are security and the legal/moral aspects of web publishing.

Security considerations

With bizarre terms such as virus, worm, Trojan, spyware and even packet sniffer, you can't help feeling you need protection on the web. Most people are aware of computer viruses and the effect they can have on computer communities as they spread chaos across networks worldwide. The assumption tends to be that you will be safe as long as you have anti-virus software, but this is not the case. There are many forms of attack, and anti-virus software is only one element of your defensive strategy. No computer system can ever be considered impregnable, but the important thing is to cover most of the bases so that the would-be 'hacker' goes for an easier target – of which there are plenty.

Is your website at risk?

The good news is that unless you are hosting your own web server – a task outside the scope of this book – your Internet Service Provider should have highly qualified people on hand to ensure that your website is not damaged by the variety of threats that are out there. However, the question still remains as to whom is responsible for the security of your own computer and the answer is invariably you.

Viruses and worms (which are technically self-propagating viruses) are an extremely widespread nuisance. However, protecting your computer from this form of attack is a relatively simple exercise. Begin by buying anti-

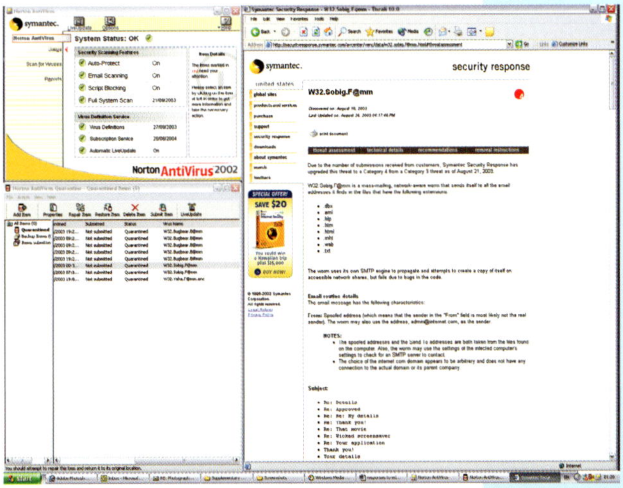

[12.1] Anti-virus software is your first line of defence against attack

Shortcut

Is your website at risk?

virus software from a reputable software vendor, and then ensure that the virus definitions (think of these as inoculations in medical terms) are kept up to date. Virus software that relies on database definitions of known viruses is vulnerable to attack from new viruses for which an antidote has yet to be created and dispersed. The latest software now looks at suspicious patterns of behaviour on a computer system and alerts the user to a potential threat without having to rely solely on a database of known threats.

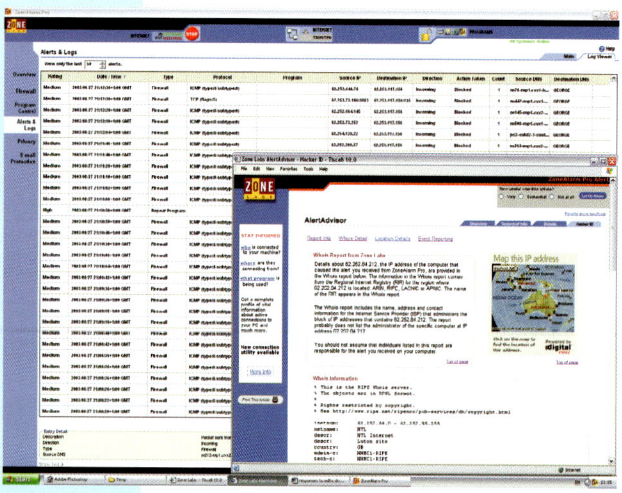

[12.2] A firewall can protect you from all manner of internet contacts and even alert you to where they originate from

Firewalls

To make it harder for hackers to gain access to your computer in the first instance, you should consider installing a personal firewall. Firewalls restrict the entrance and exit of unauthorized information into or out of your computer, and can be thought of as a skin helping to keep out a viral attack. Without one, a hacker has myriad possible entry points into your computer. Firewalls are particularly important if your computer has a broadband 'always-on' connection. Constant connections like these give a hacker enough time to attack your computer at leisure; time they may not have if you only use dial-up access. Firewalls also offer protection from a new and even more malignant form of virus called a Trojan Horse. This is so-called because of the way the Trojan cloaks itself as it goes about its destructive work.

Security loopholes

Even with the best firewall software available, you have to be aware of how to avoid potential security loopholes. The most important is file and print sharing. Most computers come equipped ready to share printers and files across a network. Hackers look for this 'open

12

door' and exploit this feature to gain unauthorized access to your computer. This facility must therefore be switched off if you are to ensure that your network, with or without a firewall, is safer from attack.

Updating software

Another important administration task that you must perform is to check your operating system and browser software regularly for updates and 'patches' (bug fixes). For example, Microsoft constantly release patches for their software. Sadly, users often overlook these fixes, thereby rendering their systems vulnerable to attack. With modern Internet connections to help download and manage software fixes, there really is no excuse for not running the latest and safest version of your software.

Privacy

The last facet of Internet security is concerned with privacy. You would be truly shocked at the amount of facts marketing companies collect about their existing and prospective customers as they surf the web. The vast majority don't do anything particularly intelligent with this data, but it is only a matter of time before better analytical software helps sift this information for 'smarter targeting'. For a start, your Internet browser can give away a great deal of private information if your personal profile information is set up. I haven't yet figured out why your browser needs to hold this information to tell the world as you are surfing. The concern is that many website designers will look to this information for their

Shortcut

Updating software

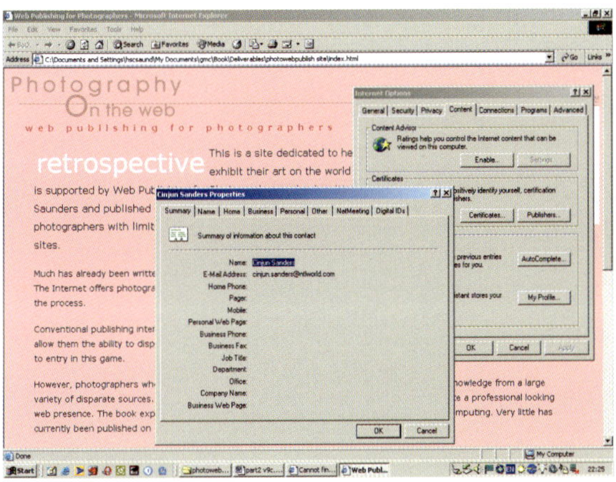

[12.3] Don't share important information by mistake

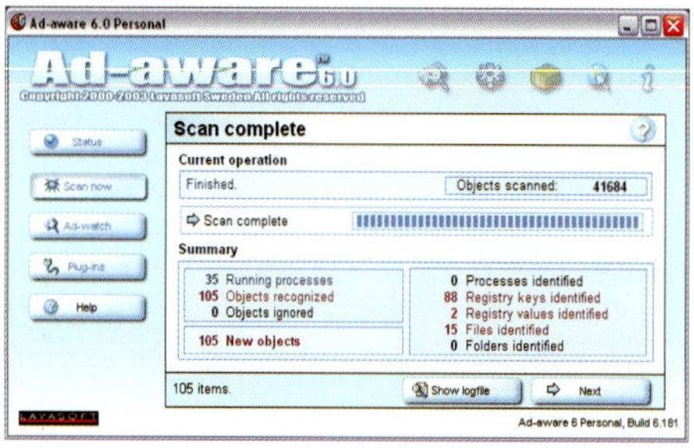

[12.4] Foil the marketers who leave spyware on your computer to monitor your browsing habits and consider adding anti-spyware software to your defence strategy

own purposes, and may also share it with other interested parties. My recommendation would be to delete any personal information in your browser profile that you don't wish to share. The same people can also gain an understanding of your online behaviour by looking at the pages you entered their site from and the pages you went to as you left. Added to this, 'spyware' can be used to take this surveillance process to its ultimate degree. A user might inadvertently download the spyware, which then sits unnoticed on their computer. It can then bore into the unsuspecting user's hard drive and report back to its creator with information the user would surely prefer remained private.

Another growth industry in the security world is anonymous-surfing software. I use it myself to combat the attempts of advertisers to track my surfing and online shopping habits, and to foil those who want to use cookies (small text

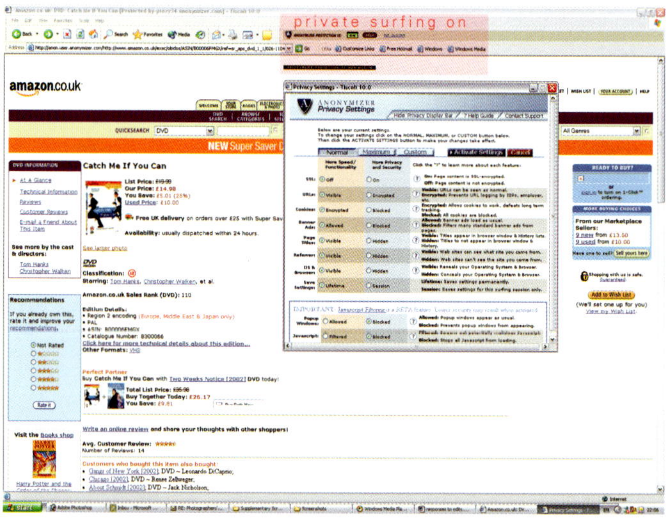

[12.5] Now you see me, now you don't; software such as Annonymizer cloaks your presence from prying eyes on the Internet and protects your privacy

files) to log this behaviour for future reference. Privacy may not seem an important issue, but with ever-increasing data processing power, companies are now merging online data with offline data such as credit-scoring reports to gain a clearer picture of you as an individual. Whether you consider this to be an intrusion worth opposing is a personal decision.

If you do want to surf anonymously, you'll need to sign up to a provider such as www.anonyimzer.com who will act as a proxy server and access the Internet on your behalf. The IP (Internet Protocol) address that uniquely identifies your computer is shielded from view thanks to the anonymizer service, and you can therefore avoid the glare of advertisers who would otherwise use every technical trick in the book to learn your habits.

'Spam'

Another area to consider is that of unsolicited emails, or 'spam', which can choke your inbox. You need to be very careful who gets hold of your email address if you want to avoid a flood of emails selling anything from impotency pills to books on web publishing.

Shortcut

'Spam'

Recently, I had a spate of emails inviting me to help move millions of pounds out of Nigeria via my bank account in

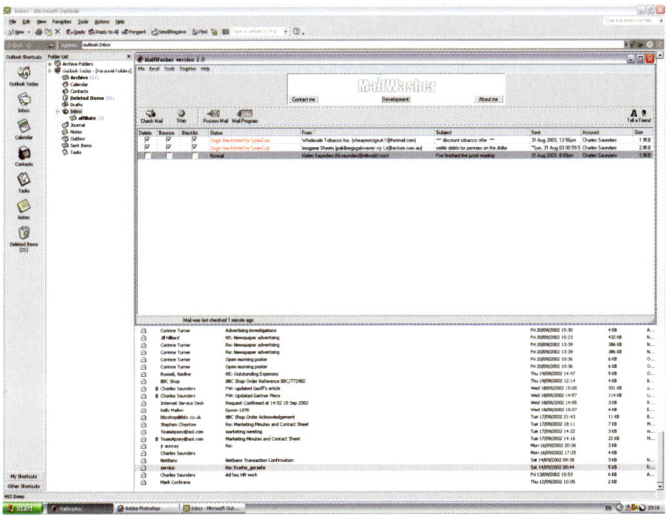

[12.6] Anti-spam software can help you manage and even reduce unsolicited emails sent to your computer

exchange for a large commission. Of course, this is an illegal and well-documented scam that has resulted in many a 'victim' having their bank account emptied by the perpetrators. How did the criminals in Nigeria get my email address? I can only assume that it was on a web page somewhere in the world. The 'mailto:' html link-type is insecure because search engine 'spidering' technology is often used to accumulate email addresses that are then sold on. The cost of emailing is so low that it doesn't really matter if what is collected contains some rubbish. As long as a few email addresses are valid, it becomes just a numbers game.

Shortcut

Protecting yourself from spam

Protecting yourself from spam

To protect yourself from unsolicited emails you should either use your ISP's form facilities to gather feedback or use JavaScript to hide your email address from the average 'spider'. Using the script shown right, rather than the conventional mailto tag, ensures that the spider will be unable to recognize that this is an email link and at a stroke you have achieved anonymity. This example is intended to hide the email address charles@photowebpublish.com. Naturally, you will want to set the initial variables to your own email address to use this small script.

```
<script type="text/javascript">
<!—
// Break up your contact details and enter
the relevant values
var address = 'charles';
var domain = 'photowebpublish';
var ext = 'com';
var tagLabel = 'Click here to contact
Charles';
// Ignore everything from here on
var tag1 = 'ma';
var tag2 = 'il';
var tag3 = 'to:';
document.write('<a href="');
document.write(tag1+tag2+tag3);
document.write(address);
document.write('&#64;');
document.write(domain);
document.write('.');
document.write(ext);
document.write('">');
document.write(tagLabel);
document.write('</a>');
// -->
</script>
```

A simpler approach might be to visit Steve Dawson's automated email-concealment function that can be found within his website: www.stevedawson.com. The appropriate JavaScript code can be generated for you just by entering your email address. My sample code is loosely based on what Steve's page can produce automatically for you.

Summary

So with all these potential sources for attack, what should you do to protect your computer? The following list of guidelines should confer a high degree of protection, but of course there is a cost associated with most of these and you have to balance the cost against your perceived level of risk.

In short, however, if you want to keep a piece of information about yourself private, don't put it on a computer that is hooked up to the Internet.

Online protection guidelines

- Install a personal firewall and virus-protection software. Make sure print and file sharing is switched off.
- Use dummy email accounts for online profiles, newsgroups, e-commerce and so on. Most ISPs give you more than one email address. Save your real address for friends and family, and you can always dump the dummy email address if you find it is being bombarded with junk email or spam.
- Delete the personal information in your Internet browser settings.
- Keep a close watch on cookies and delete these items from your browser cache regularly. You should clear out your cache after each Internet session to ensure privacy.
- Consider using anonymous-surfing technology such as 'Anonyimzer'.
- Delete unopened emails from people you don't recognize, especially if the email has an attachment. Be very careful what you download. For example, promises of screensavers are not always what they seem.
- Make sure that your credit-card information is encrypted before you make an online purchase.
- Be very careful about sharing information such as home addresses, phone numbers or the names and ages of your children. Unless you have a business address I would leave off home details as it just advertises the fact to potential burglars that 'I have a computer and lots of expensive cameras at this address'.

Legal and moral considerations

For those of you who understandably believe that legal and moral issues should be one and the same, I am afraid that vested interests often ensure they diverge. For instance, it is perfectly legal to market to children of whatever age, and as such they are bombarded with clever and sophisticated marketing techniques encouraging them to devour fast food or play with the latest toy. As a parent and marketing professional, I find this practice amoral as children often are unable to separate fact from fiction or perceive the true motives of the 'persuading force'. Likewise, publishing photographs has its own minefields, and what may be legal is not necessarily moral, as we shall see.

I should stress at this point that I have no formal legal qualifications and that the reader would be well advised to consult a member of the legal profession for clarification on the points of interest mentioned in this section of the book.

Despite our familiarity with the Internet, the medium is still very much in its infancy with regard to the law. The lack of much 'case law', from which legal experts would usually take guidance, means that to a great extent web publishers are reliant on their own instincts of what is appropriate behaviour. Added to that, the Internet crosses international boundaries and so you have to ask yourself whose law you are potentially breaking and what potential penalties exist. Let me illustrate this complexity with a couple of cases.

Case 1

If I take a photograph for which I do not own copyright from another site and place the copied file on my server so that I can use the photograph in one of my own pages, this behaviour seems like a very obvious infringement of someone else's copyright. However, the <img> tag allows me to reference an image from anywhere, not just on my own server. In which case, I don't need to copy the photograph onto my server, just link to the file sitting on the other photographer's site. The visual result of both techniques is identical, but have I infringed copyright merely by creating a link? After all, isn't the Internet a mass of inter-linked digital material?

To muddy the waters yet further, don't forget that every time you visit a page on a website, the files are copied to your computer and stored on your browser's cache for fast access. Thankfully there is a concept called 'implied license' that gets us all off the hook on the last point.

Case 2

French privacy laws have become a great deal stronger since January 2003, to the extent that it is now illegal to copy the quintessentially French 'street photography' genre championed by such masters as Cartier-Bresson, Brassai, Riboud and Doisneau. Believe me when I say that the French public are well aware of their new rights and are not afraid to voice their alarm at the sign of a camera. With a very large fine for breaching the new legislation I'm tempted to take my Leica around the streets of London rather than hop across the channel to Paris.

Copyright

As always, a 'common sense' approach to web publishing should protect you from the most serious problems. Case 1 is legal, and morally acceptable if the copyright holder knows what you are doing, has given permission and you make it obvious from your own page that this particular image is credited elsewhere. A good starting point, however, is to publish only what you own. It's important to remember that the Internet is not an unregulated medium where anything goes and all digital content is up for grabs. The ease of copying doesn't make the act any more legal than the act of copying a music cassette or video. Moreover, the absence of a copyright symbol is

The 'fair-use' provision

Within copyright law there is the provision for 'fair use', which is generally limited to allowing people to reference other material in support of an argument or other proposition. If you are a not-for-profit organization, such as a university or charity, the risk of falling foul of the 'fair-use' provision is less than for a commercial organization. Regardless, if you do want to reference copyright material you would be well advised to be explicit about the source, keep your referenced material to an absolute minimum (a subset of the original work), and ideally seek permission from the copyright holder.

Shortcut

The 'fair-use' provision

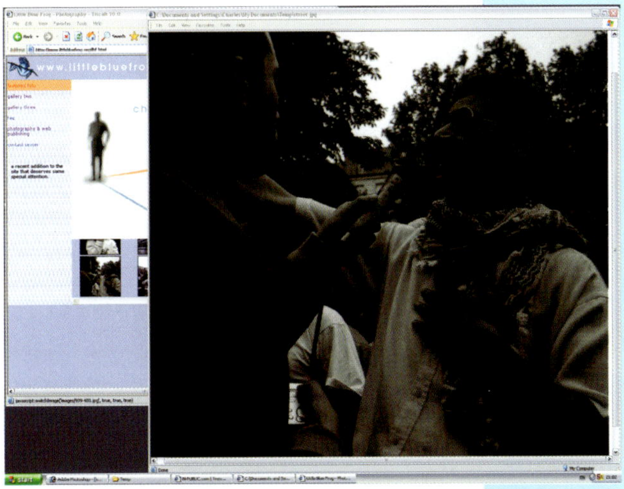

[12.7] Street photography carries its own inherent risks, not least the actual publication

certainly no green light to unrestricted copying, and to do so would infringe copyright law in many countries.

Shortcut

Are graphics copyright?

Are graphics copyright?

Clip art and graphics can be used to bring a graphical element to your site. However, unless you drew the graphics yourself, some other party will own the images. Even royalty-free clip art is usually limited to unrestricted use for non-commercial bodies. Commercial organizations will be expected to pay a fee, albeit lower than rights-managed material. If in doubt, read the copyright notice very carefully.

Although you cannot copyright a URL any more than you can copyright a telephone number, linking to sites also has potential problems. Most webmasters would prefer that you link to their home page only. Deep linking into someone else's site, especially if you do so from a framed window on your own site, can easily create the impression that what's on display is as a result of your own endeavours. As we have seen, with frames it wouldn't take very long to create a website where the branding and navigation pertained to one site, but the gallery of images were obtained elsewhere. This behaviour is perfectly legal in most countries, but quite immoral in my opinion.

Remember: brand your own galleries and provide links to your home page and you can avoid this problem. For the really paranoid, the following piece of JavaScript inserted into the <head> section of your page stops the page from ever being loaded into a framed window:

```
<script type="text/javascript">
<!— Frame break out
if (top != self) top.location.href =
location.href;
// -->
</script>
```

If you really want to link to someone else's content in this way – and you may have a perfectly good reason – it is best to obtain permission beforehand. The linked-to party might also provide a reciprocal link, which as we have seen may help your search engine rankings.

Defamation of character

After copyright, the next potential pitfall is defamation of character. The safest option for publishing pictures of people – especially if related to a product or service – is to obtain a model release form. There are enough examples on the Internet if you search for the term. Of course, model release forms may not be practicable if your favoured genre is 'street photography'. Assuming the pictures were taken in a public place – and outside of France – you should be OK. However, at the very least you should be careful about how you caption your photographs. A dishevelled looking old man may not take too kindly to being referred to as a tramp, and he would be quite within his rights to sue you. Even with no caption against the photograph you have to be careful of context. We all like taking photographs that illustrate interesting juxtapositions, but you still need to be careful. If you were to take and then publish a picture of a man alone in a café bar, sitting beneath a poster that warns 'Date rape: are you sure you're safe?', you could land yourself in trouble placing the subject in an unfavourable light. Perhaps we should all stick to still life?

Nudity

Another tricky topic is that of nudes. In this global publishing environment, one person's nudity is another person's pornography. In some countries, many forms of nudity are strongly legislated against. Interestingly, hosting your site

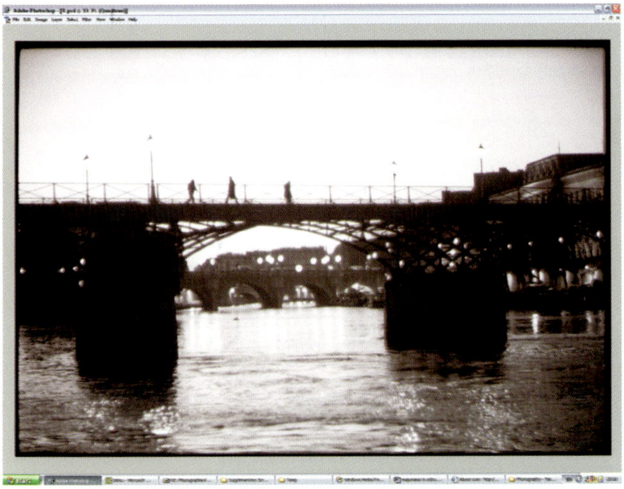

[12.8] After new French privacy laws, is this all that's left of the genre of French street photography?

from a disused oil platform in international waters is no guarantee of immunity from prosecution. Suffice to say that this sort of content does increase the element of risk somewhat. My pragmatic advice would be to use splash screens with warnings of inappropriate content for minors and to use the usual legal wording at the front of the site to warn users from entering the site if it is illegal to do so in their country. I can't say that this is a foolproof plan, but it seems to be the common approach adopted by some 'fine art' sites. Naturally, to qualify as artistic fine art rather than pornography the nudes on display should not be interpreted as participating in any form of sexual act, and genitalia should not feature as the main part of any composition. Needless to say, nude studies of minors are simply irresponsible and thankfully illegal in many countries.

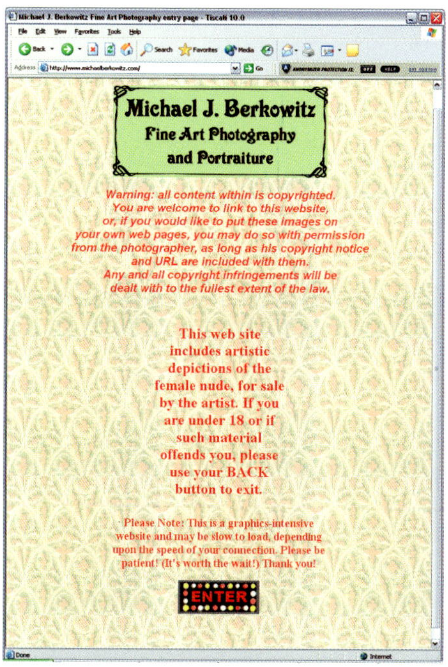

[12.9] A suitable splash screen to warn of nudity is a sensible precaution if you publish these types of images

Protecting your art from theft

One technique you may want to try in order to protect your pictures is to disable the right mouse-button functionality using JavaScript. There are enough examples of this on the web if you want to search for them. I don't like this technique as it also removes useful browser functionality and makes it seem that you explicitly don't trust your user. In any case, a determined thief could simply get the photograph file simply by looking in his/her browser's cache.

Another technique might be to watermark your image files digitally. Software is available that can automate this process, and the watermark can either be visible or invisible. I think the visible option detracts from your original image, and in thc casc of the invisible, how exactly are you going to police the theft? I think a good balance is to make your photographs freely available as long as the image links to your home page and is duly credited. This advertising-based approach is more pragmatic and should at least drive some more traffic to your site.

How at risk are your images?

Put simply, if you don't want it stolen, don't publish it online. In truth, however, you have very little to fear. Even high-resolution web images are of little use to a commercial printer who is more used to dealing with images that are tens of megabytes in size. For printers, 300dpi is an absolute minimum requirement, which means that the resolution of web images is simply too low to be of any practicable use, save for elsewhere online.

Shortcut

How at risk are your images?

13 The Future of Web Publishing

Sixteen years ago, I had barely used a PC and at work I regularly worked with a mainframe system. My colleagues and I interacted with the computer through 3270 'dumb' terminals. The text was green and there was no mouse, but that was all there was on offer. There was one PC in the department. I don't know what it was there for officially, but it was mainly used for playing a popular golf game of the period. On the surface, things seem to have changed a great deal today – or have they?

Shortcut
Maintenance

I still shoot monochrome film on my Rolleiflex, and although quadtone inks can produce some wonderful inkjet prints, I still feel that you can't beat seeing prints appear before your eyes in the darkroom. Similarly, IT may return to its mainframe origins, albeit in a much modified form. Mainframe computers have tremendous processing power, but back in 1988 they needed constant attention from highly trained technical staff. Moreover, access to this processing power was strictly limited and controlled. Every time I wanted to perform an analysis, I had to plan my request carefully, design a report and then submit my 'job' to the data-centre experts. At some later date I might get the answer I was looking for, but more often than not the results threw up a list of more unanswered questions.

Then came personal computing. PCs brought spreadsheets and adhoc analysis. We took data from the mainframe, and were able to manipulate it without recourse to other parties. Data-centre staff hated the PC revolution, and for good reason. They lost the power of centralized data, processes become more complex, and worst of all they had to fix the PCs that we had broken. Their protestations fell on deaf ears because the spreadsheet empowered middle management to make some quite incisive decisions. Adhoc analysis was here to stay and the client/server revolution was born.

Maintenance

If you have owned a PC for any length of time you'll have realized that from time to time it needs maintenance. All computers, no matter what their size, need some form of ongoing tuning and maintenance. Unless you have your very own IT department, this means that you have to learn to be an administrator. You'll need to know about device drivers for computer peripherals, to clean out temporary files, optimize your disk, fix your registry when software doesn't upload properly, even perform major surgery if you need a memory or chip upgrade. You either learn this stuff yourself or buy in the expertise. Either way, there is a cost involved in running a computer system.

The network is the computer

What if a computer was like a telephone? You plug it in, switch it on, and it works – end of story. Of course, computers are a great deal more complex than telephones, but this plug-and-play set-up is to a large extent reality for some corporations today. The mainframe era revisited sees a high-resolution full-colour graphical device on every desktop. This device is connected via a high-speed network to a powerful server computer that performs all of the data processing, storage and security aspects of the system. The user has no need for a separate computer on their desktop. There is no need for constant memory or software upgrades and very little software resides on the device itself. Users have to perform no system maintenance at all and, more importantly, new economies of scale kick in as revolutionary methods of software licensing are introduced. Finally, unique smart cards allow users to access any device within the organization without worrying about where their data is stored and which programs they have installed.

This might sound a long way off, but to see some proof of this PC-less world simply visit the Sun Microsystems website at www.sun.com.

Consumer-market developments

Of course, the model outlined above is unlikely to predominate in the consumer market. However, I do feel that the convergence of high-speed network providers and software companies will enable this proposition to become commercially viable for the average person in the street. There is no technical reason why this method of computing won't enable photographers to work on their digital images in this way, and some well-known multimedia companies with private high-speed networks are doing precisely this. Who knows – you may end up renting Adobe PhotoShop one day rather than buying it.

Improved image quality

Another trend of increasing relevance to photographers is one of increasing image fidelity. High-speed networks coupled with increasing processing power on display devices means that increases in resolution will continue apace. So far we have moved from 600x480 to 800x600 and now 1024x768 as the standard monitor resolution. In time, as resolution quality continues to increase the web will become a significantly more important environment for exhibiting our art. This situation will be fuelled yet further by the increased market penetration of high-resolution digital cameras.

Shortcut

Buying images online

Increased market penetration

Two other developments are important to contemplate. The first is the growth of ubiquitous computing where network-aware appliances appear throughout the home. The second is the increasing adoption of wireless networks. How long before we see picture frames that hang on our wall and display images taken directly from the Internet? When you realize that companies such as GE are considering putting an Internet address within every light bulb, the notion doesn't seem that fanciful.

The number of photographic websites will balloon, with sadly a corresponding lack of overall quality. Just look at cable television for a comparison. However, the advent of more digital material will fuel a market aimed at selling these images to a much wider audience than has hitherto been possible.

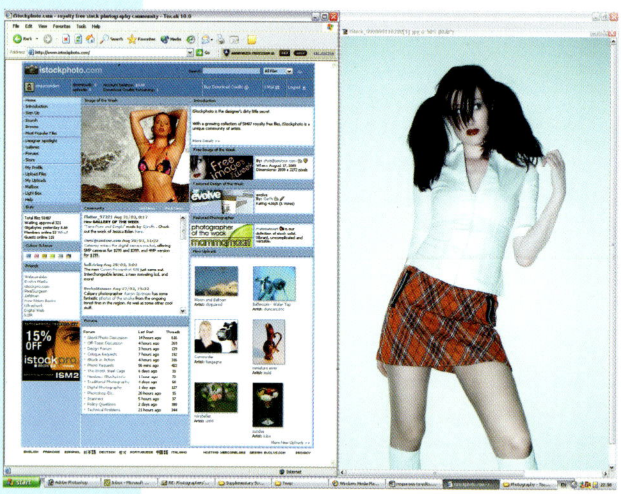

[13.1] With www.istockphoto.com now everyone can become a stock photographer and earn good money from their craft. © istockphoto.com Inc

Buying images online

If you have ever worked in marketing, you'll be only too aware of the cost of licensing images. One recent campaign of mine potentially required a huge budget to license three images around the world. Needless to say we re-shot the concept for a fraction of this price. Stock image libraries seem to be going through a period of unusual market consolidation with the result that prices are equalizing 'upwards' in this less competitive environment. Perhaps in response to this, companies like www.istockphoto.com provide a vehicle for photographers everywhere to upload their material and sell it to whoever wants to license their image, at remarkably competitive rates. Print on demand will undoubtedly be the next phase, where amateur and professional photographers alike can sell their prints and earn commission without the need to establish sophisticated e-commerce and marketing/distribution infrastructures. The theory has already been proven with other digital media such as music. Just check out www.mp3.com to see how it could work.

Short-term considerations

Few can pretend that photography is a cheap hobby. There's always another piece of equipment to buy or film to experiment with. Naturally you want your site to be a profitable experience, so the next natural step is to begin selling your images. Do a quick search on 'shopping cart software' and you will discover a wide range of pre-built services that you can readily incorporate into your site with only limited technical knowledge. Simultaneously, you may decide to look at creating a site that is database-driven. This book helps photographers understand how to build static sites – i.e. sites that don't change greatly in appearance.

However, if you are a prolific photographer with plenty of content on offer, a database-driven site is your next step. This will allow you to present the images that your user has requested, perhaps based on some search criteria.

Database-driven websites

Database-driven sites require a quantum leap in technology investment, both in terms of money and knowledge. However, if you are a wedding photographer with aspirations of selling photographs of a particular wedding to the guests after the event via an online portfolio, this is precisely the next step that could provide a profitable new source of revenue.

Shortcut

Database-driven websites

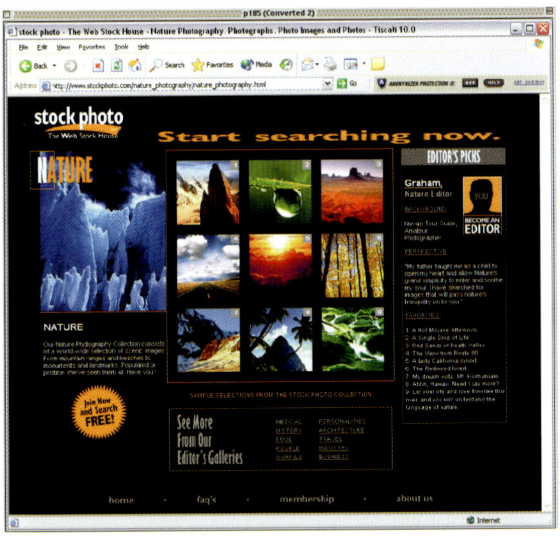

[13.2] Database-driven websites such as www.stockphoto.com require a quantum leap in technology to create from scratch.

© Stock Photo, NY, USA

About the Author

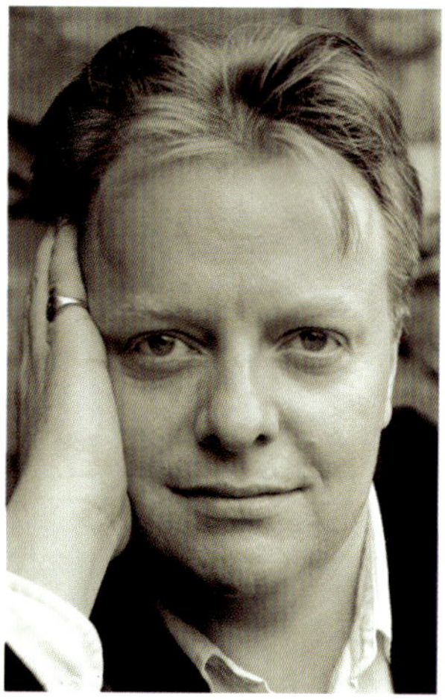

Charles Saunders is a highly qualified guide to the world of web publishing. In 1990, he graduated with a first-class honours degree in computer science, and subsequently studied e-commerce at the University of Berkeley, in California. Having worked for several leading IT companies over the past twelve years, he has developed a number of successful websites.

Charles is also a skilled photographer, having keenly pursued his interest in photography since the age of thirteen. His preferred medium is monochrome reportage, although he has extensive experience in many different genres from portraiture to sports photography.

Index

photographers' pip institute press

TITLES AVAILABLE FROM

THE PHOTOGRAPHERS' INSTITUTE PRESS

The Photographers' Institute Press, PIP, is an exciting name in photography publishing. When you see this name on the spine of a book, you will be sure that the author is an experienced photographer and the content is of the highest standard, both technically and visually. Formed as a mark of quality, the Photographers' Institute Press covers the full range of photographic interests, from expanded camera guides to exposure techniques and landscape.

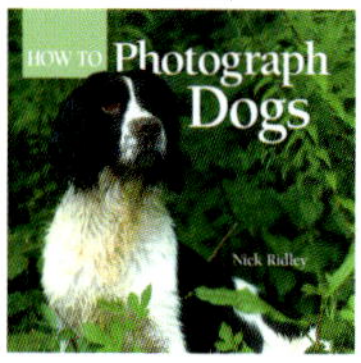

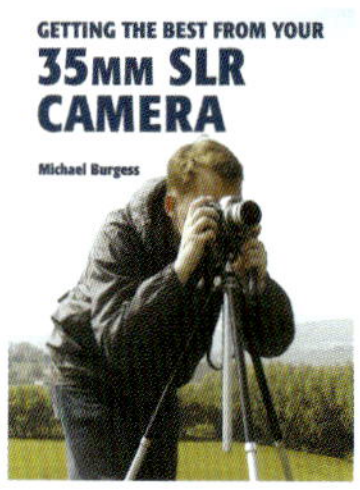

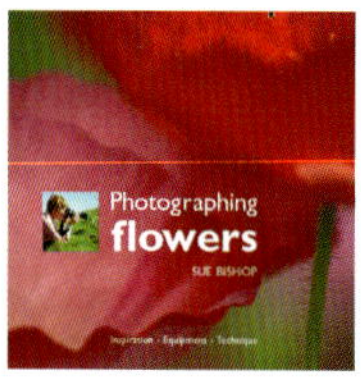

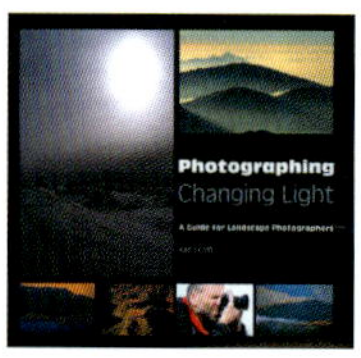

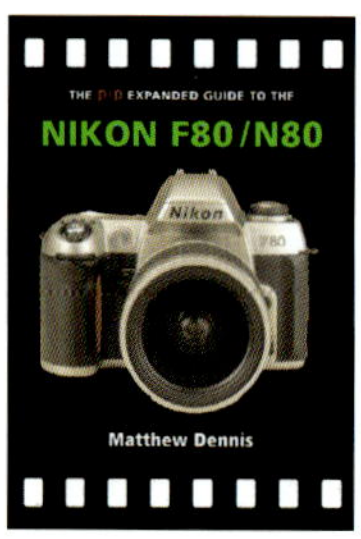

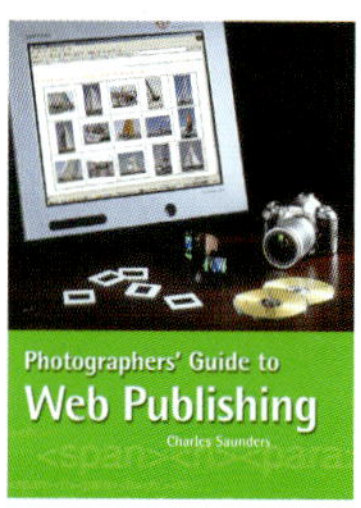

Animal Photographs: A Practical Guide
Robert Maier
ISBN 1 86108 303 3

Approaching Photography Paul Hill
ISBN 1 86108 323 8

Bird Photography: A Global Site Guide
David Tipling
ISBN 1 86108 302 5

Digital SLR Masterclass Andy Rouse
ISBN 1 86108 358 0

Garden Photography: A Professional Guide
Tony Cooper
ISBN 1 86108 392 0

Getting the Best from Your 35mm SLR Camera Michael Burgess
ISBN 1 86108 347 5

How to Photograph Dogs Nick Ridley
ISBN 1 86108 332 7

Photographers' Guide to Web Publishing
Charles Saunders
ISBN 1 86108 352 1

Photographing Changing Light: A Guide for Landscape Photographers
Ken Scott
ISBN 1 86108 380 7

Photographing Flowers Sue Bishop
ISBN 1 86108 366 1

Photographing People Roderick Macmillan
ISBN 1 86108 313 0

Photographing Water in the Landscape
David Tarn
ISBN 1 86108 396 3

The Photographic Guide to Exposure
Chris Weston
ISBN 1 86108 387 4

The PIP Expanded Guide to the: Nikon F5
Chris Weston
ISBN 1 86108 382 3

The PIP Expanded Guide to the: Nikon F80/N80 Matthew Dennis
ISBN 1 86108 348 3

The PIP Expanded Guide to the: Canon EOS 300/Rebel 2000 Matthew Dennis
ISBN 1 86108 338 6

Travel Photography: An Essential Guide
Rob Flemming
ISBN 1 86108 362 9

The list represents a selection of titles currently published or scheduled to be published.

All are available direct from the Publishers or through bookshops and specialist retailers.

To place an order, or to obtain a complete catalogue, contact:

Photographers' Institute Press,
Castle Place,
166 High Street, Lewes,
East Sussex BN7 1XU
United Kingdom

Tel: 01273 488005
Fax: 01273 402866
E-mail: pubs@thegmcgroup.com

Orders by credit card are accepted

Comp
Cameras

How to get the best from your point and shoot camera

John Garrett

EBURY PRESS
LONDON

First published in 1994
1 3 5 7 9 10 8 6 4 2

First published in the United Kingdom in 1994 by
Ebury Press
Random House, 20 Vauxhall Bridge Road,
London SWlV 2SA

Random House Australia (Pty) Limited
20 Alfred Street, Milsons Point, Sydney,
New South Wales 2061, Australia

Random House New Zealand Limited
18 Poland Road, Glenfield, Auckland 10,
New Zealand

Random House South Africa (Pty) Limited
PO Box 337, Bergvlei, South Africa

Random House UK Limited Reg. No. 954009

A CIP catalogue record for this book is available from the British Library.

ISBN O 09 178359 3

Edited by Cindy Richards
Designed by Jerry Goldie
Printed, typeset and reproduced by
Butler and Tanner, Frome

Contents

Washday in Venice

Venice is a walking place, around every corner there is something even more beautiful to experience and photograph, and so you walk on and on all day. To be able to walk all day without the weight of a heavy camera bag on my shoulders but still be able to take good quality pictures with my compact gave me a great sense of freedom and in fact encouraged me to take more pictures than I would have with all my usual camera equipment.

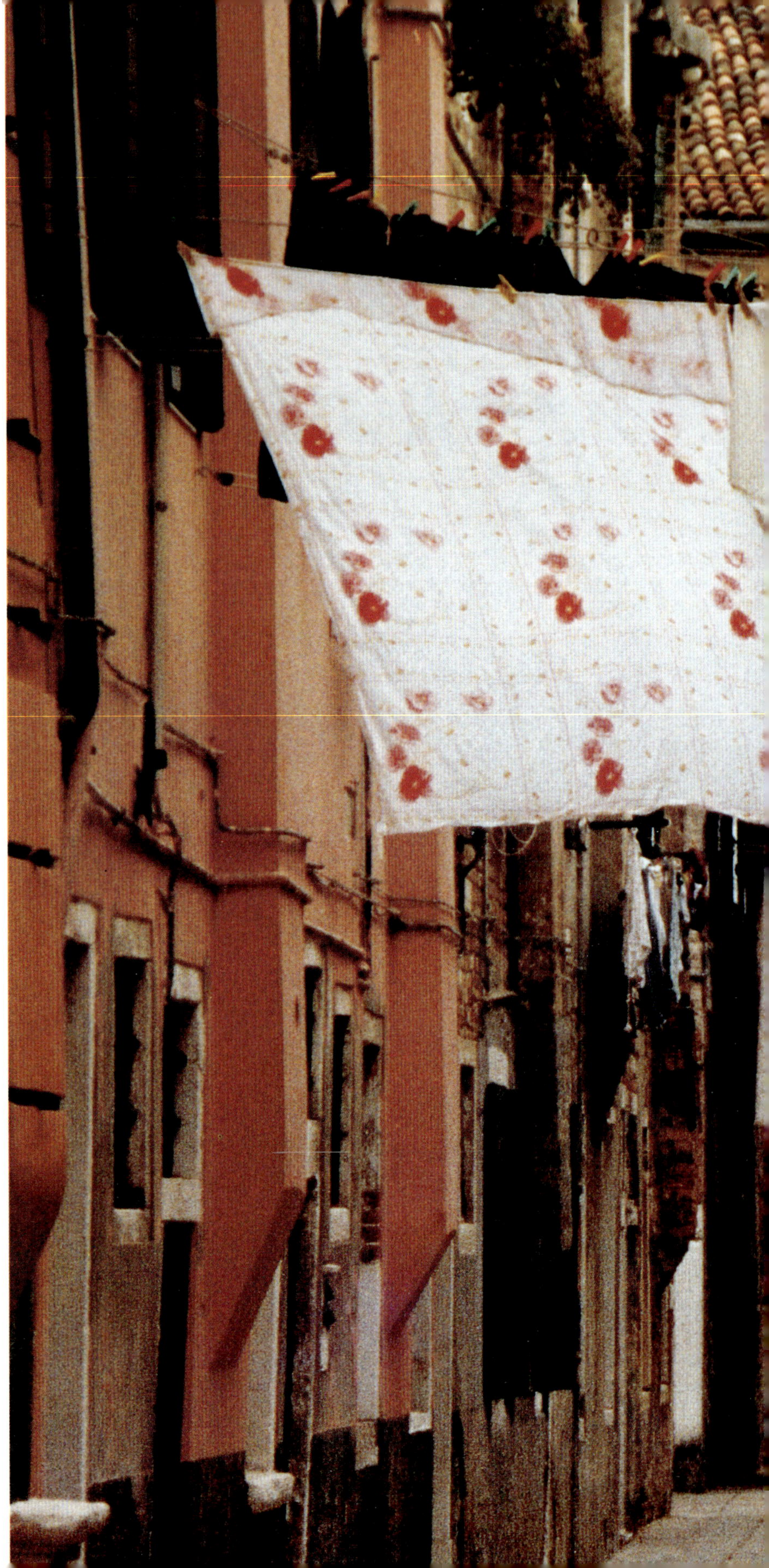

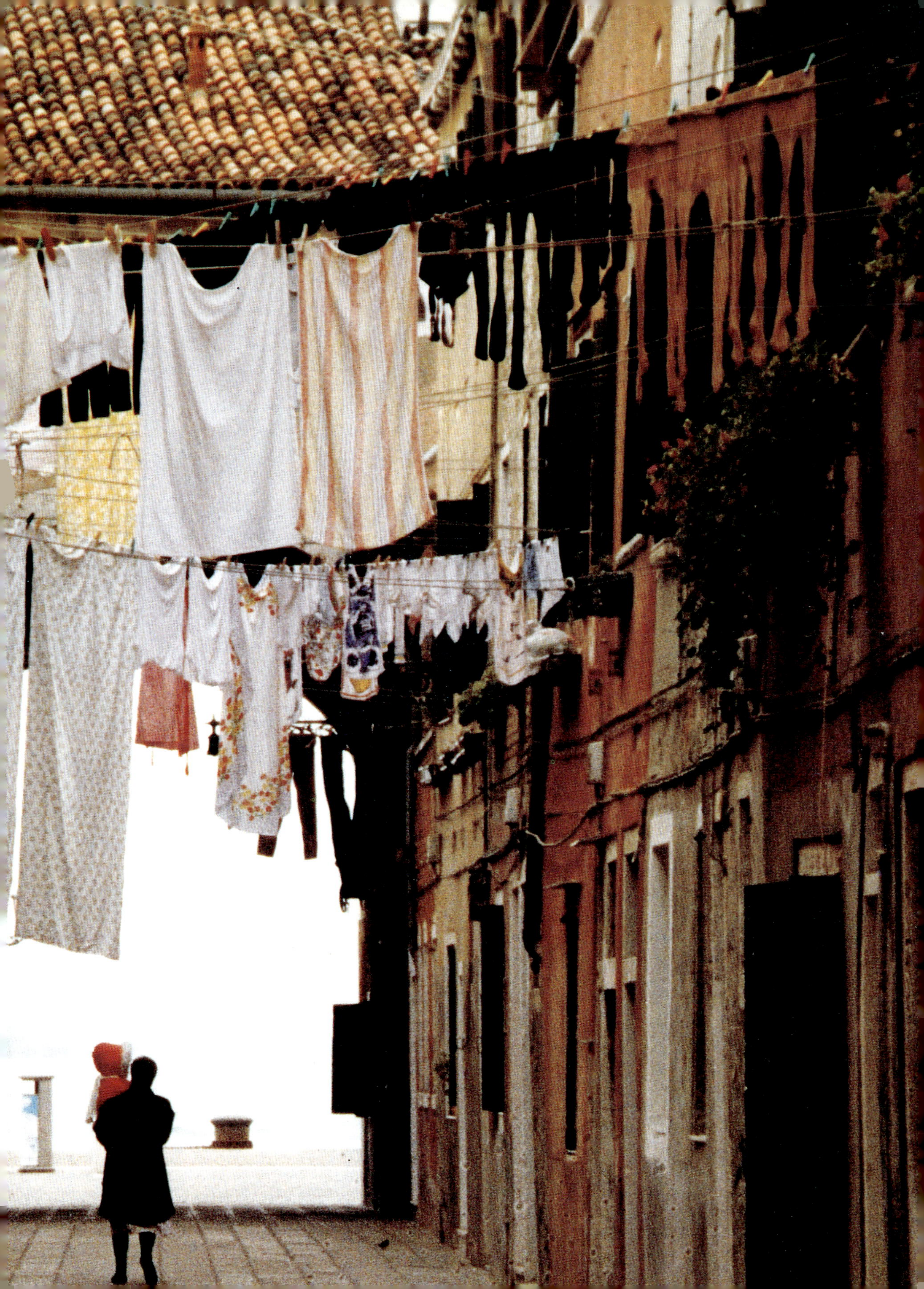

Introduction

'I only have a compact camera, but I want to take good pictures'.

I was in New York recently doing a series of photographic clinics and many people who asked my advice prefaced their questions with that apology. The time has come to stop apologizing for your compact camera. Many of the great photographic images of the past were taken on far less sophisticated cameras than a compact. Compacts are serious cameras capable of taking excellent pictures. I realized by the end of my New York trip that the time had come to write a book on how to use a compact camera.

The technology built into compacts has galloped ahead in recent years: the lenses are sharper, the viewfinders brighter and more accurate, exposure is better and the zooms zoom even further. But, as with our stereo equipment and video recorders, they are also becoming laden with USPs (unique selling points) which complicate their primary function. I have written this book in order to clarify the technology by explaining how a compact functions, what all the various modes are for and whether they are worth having. With a little extra knowledge, we can make this wonderful technology work for us rather than against us. We can then concentrate on what a camera is really all about – taking satisfying pictures.

I have not discussed the pros and cons of all the various makes and models of camera because they are changing daily. But all the leading manufacturers make similar models and the principles are the same. This book concentrates as much on the techniques of reading the quality of light, choosing the appropriate film and how to increase your visual awareness as it does on camera techniques.

For this book, I took myself out of my usual professional photographer mode and put the Hasselblads and Nikons in

Boy with a bucket and spade
We see this situation on holiday beaches throughout the world. The setting on my zoom compact enabled me to get close enough to fill the frame without the little chap sensing my presence and I was able to take the picture without disturbing his concentration.

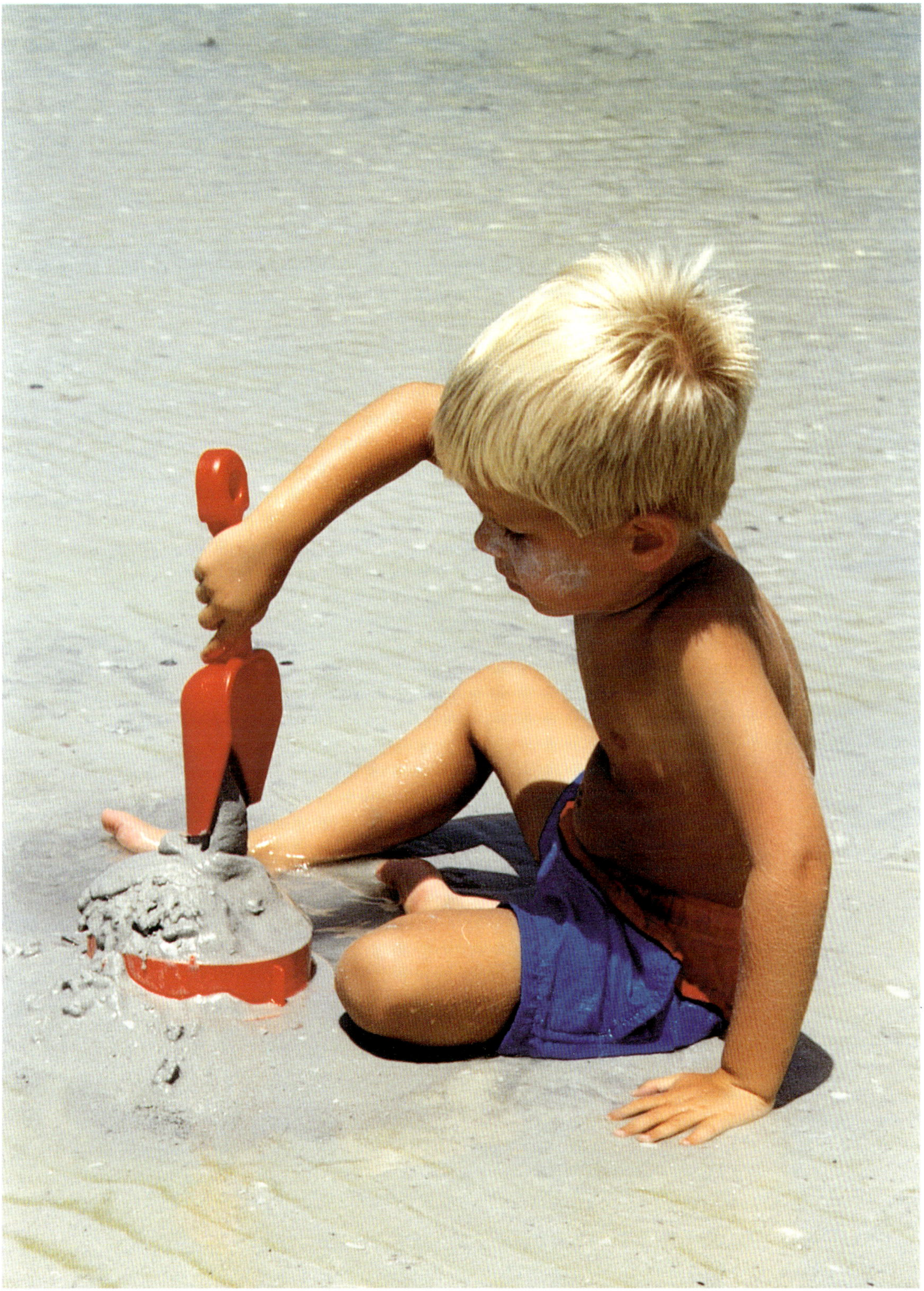

the cupboard and went out armed with my compact. I found to my surprise that shooting on compacts was quite difficult at first. The camera and I were locked in a battle for control over the pictures – I was not programmed to just 'point and shoot'. Once I became more familiar with the auto-focusing system, the various flash modes, and all the other functions, I began to relax and enjoy the contribution the camera was making to my pictures. I was in control again, which I believe is the fundamental requirement for taking good pictures with a compact, once you understand what it is doing and why you can be in charge instead of the camera.

I chose four locations for the majority of the photographs: a beach holiday on Sanibel Island, Florida; a week in the Welsh mountains; a long weekend in Venice and my home town of London. These four places enabled me to cover the situations that you are most likely to come across when taking pictures. All the people who were brave enough to feature in the pictures are friends or family.

Taking the pictures for and writing this book has been an interesting learning experience. Photography at its richest and most worthwhile is about people recording their own lives and those around them and I hope that the tips and advice passed on in the book will help you to improve your photography and so add to your enjoyment.

I finish with the philosophy on which this book is founded – it's people who take pictures, not cameras.

History of the Compact Camera

Compact cameras are nothing new really. In 1925, the German Leica Company revolutionized the hand-held camera market by introducing a camera – the Leica 1 – that used the 35mm film already commonplace with cinema cameramen. The result was a camera a fraction of the size and weight of the old-fashioned 'press' cameras that had used large glass plates and sheet film. The new 35mm cameras were precision-built with high-definition lenses and manual focusing (by reckoning, as there were no range finders). The aperture and shutter speed were also manual and exposure times had to be judged from experience as light meters were not yet on the market. These early 35mm cameras were called miniatures rather than compacts but they were the parents – or great grandparents – of our modern compacts.

The Leica, however, was very expensive, so Kodak, the champion of photography for the people, mass produced a much cheaper 35mm camera in the early 1930s that made the 35mm format universally popular, as it remains today.

At the same time (from the late 1930s onwards), there grew a great fad for subminiature cameras or, as they were popularly termed, 'spy cameras' which produced very small negatives on 16mm and 8mm films. Many were the size of, and even disguised as, cigarette lighters. The fad went out of fashion, however, because it was difficult to produce satisfactory prints from such small negatives although some precision high-quality versions were used for espionnage work.

The single lens reflex (SLR) was launched in 1960 and for many years has been the most versatile and popular 35mm camera with its range of lenses and accessories plus built-in electronic programming. But while this was happening, the photographic industry was aware that there were millions of happy snappers out there who wanted to take pictures but did not want to learn the relatively involved techniques required to use the SLR successfully.

Kodak, of course, pursued the simple alternative. They came out with a 126 cartridge camera in 1963, in 1972, the 110 cartridge, and in 1982, they brought out a disc camera. All these types of camera came under the popular title of 'Instamatics'. The electronics were developing and they were producing better exposed pictures in daylight and with the introduction of an auto-flash unit, at night too. But the ultimate quality was limited to the smaller negative sizes.

In 1976, Konica marketed the first 35mm compact, as we know it, with an automatic focusing and exposure facility, and a built-in flash. The next development was in 1980 when Minolta brought out a compact with a zoom lens that had two focal length positions, 38mm and 60mm (now called a twin lens compact). Up until then all compacts had a fixed focal length, 35mm lens (see Lenses and Depth of Focus, page 17). From then on, the development of zoom lenses has exploded and compacts are now available with a variety of continuous zooms: 28–80mm; 32–85mm; 35–70mm; 35–105mm and 38–115mm. Alongside this development came auto-exposure and auto-focus programming, fill-in auto-flash, remote shutter buttons, DX coding and so on. The compact had come of age and it is now possible, as never before, to take excellent pictures of almost anything without having to take a night school diploma and without – rejoice, rejoice – having to carry around a huge bag of gear. Compacts, in all their many and varied forms, are really here to stay!

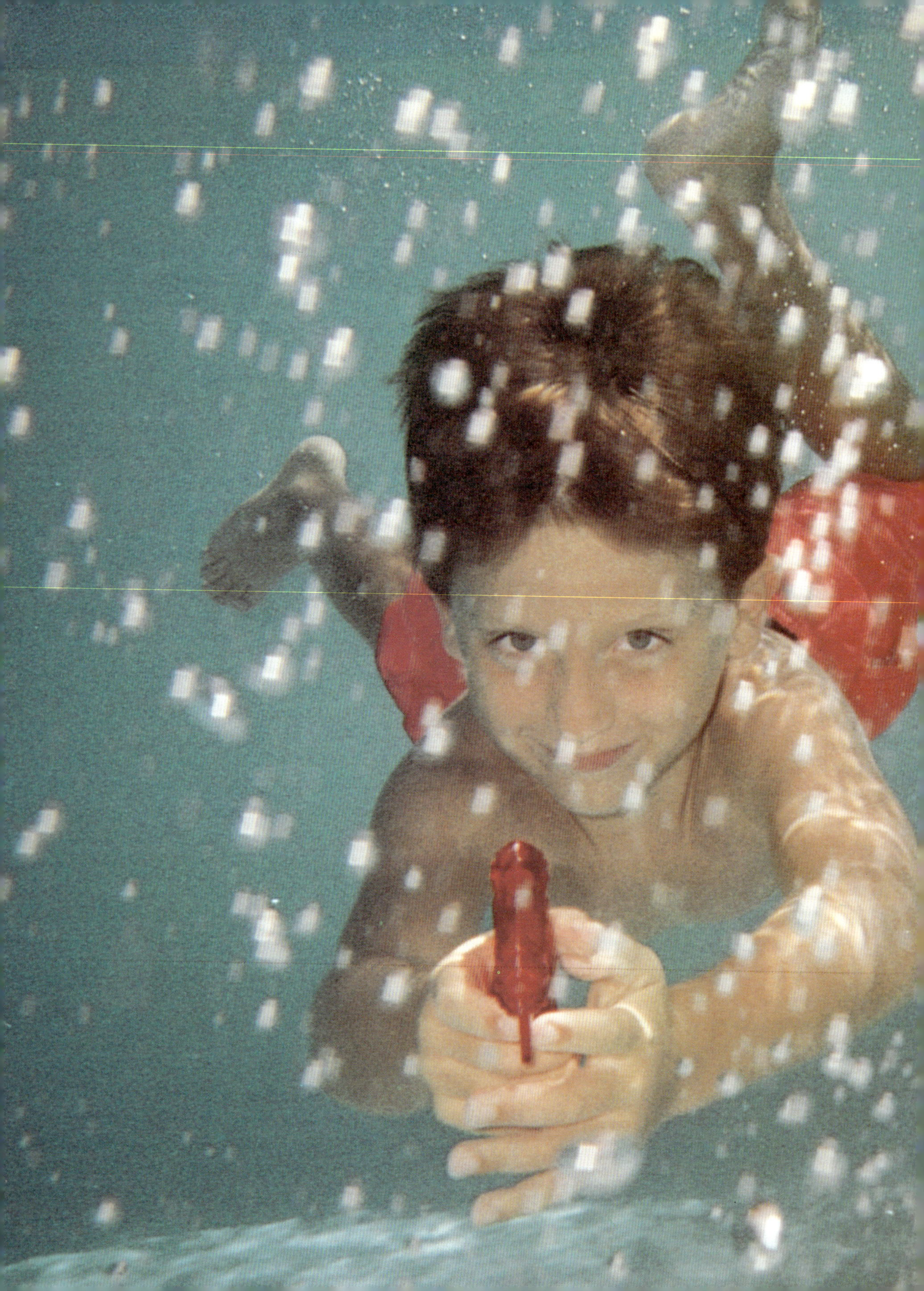

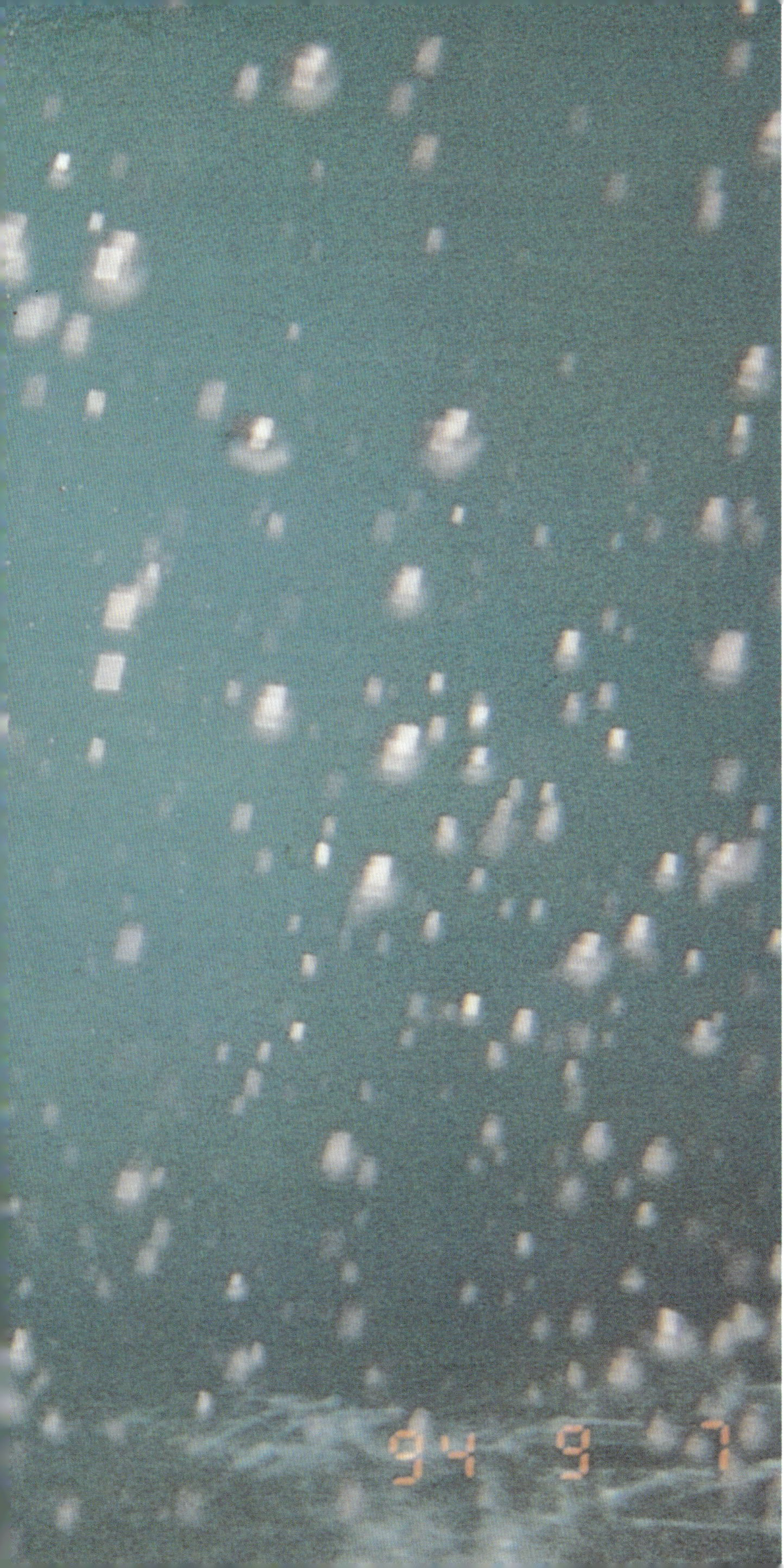

SECTION

1

Technicalities

CHAPTER ONE

How it Works

A camera is basically a light-tight box with a hole on one side placed opposite a light sensitive surface (the film). When light enters the hole and strikes the film an invisible, upside down photographic image is left on its surface. Think of it in terms of a pinhole camera which I'm sure most of us made while at junior school. The only fundamental difference is that a lens has been substituted for the hole in order to focus the image sharply (see Lenses and Depth of Focus, page 17) and to correct the upside down image.

Despite all the buttons and gadgetry, a compact camera is still just a light-tight box which fortunately for us, includes a number of automatic functions. However, to get the most from your camera it is worth having an understanding of what you can do to control it and what factors are beyond your control.

Exposure

The amount of light that strikes the film, the 'exposure', is controlled by two mechanical devices, the aperture and the shutter, which are mutually dependent on each other, so that if your camera changes one the other changes too.

The aperture controls the amount of light that passes through the lens and onto the film. The wider the aperture, the greater the amount of light entering the camera and vice versa. To photograph a dimly lit subject, therefore, you need a wide aperture setting (or slow shutter speed) to admit as much light as possible: for a brightly lit subject you need a small aperture setting (or fast shutter speed).

The aperture size is measured by f numbers or 'stops' which are fractions of the focal length of the lens. So f2 means that the aperture is one-half of the lens' focal length and f4 one-quarter, and so on. A high f stop gives a small aperture and a low f stop a large one. The maximum aperture of a lens is written around the rim and for most compacts this is somewhere in the region of f3.5 or f4, although some of the most expensive compacts have maximum apertures of f2 or f2.8. When choosing a camera it is important to know that an f2.8 lens will allow you to take pictures in lower light conditions than an f4 lens without the need for flash.

When the aperture goes from f4 to f5.6 or from f5.6 to f8, the amount of light entering the camera is halved each time right down to the smallest aperture setting of f16. This process is called stopping down. When the reverse happens and the lens moves from f11 to f8, the amount of light entering the camera is doubled and this is known as 'opening up'.

The aperture also controls the depth of focus or field which means the area behind and in front of your focal point (the subject of your photograph) that will also be in focus. The smaller the aperture, the greater the depth of focus that the lens produces. The aperture is an important creative device as it allows you to select the areas you wish to be in focus, as can be seen from the photographs on page 16. (See also Lenses and Depth of Focus, page 17).

The shutter controls the amount of time the film is exposed to light; the slower the shutter speed the greater the amount of light reaching the film. Shutter speeds are measured in fractions of one second: 1/250 sec, 1/125 sec, 1/60 sec, 1/30 sec, 1/15 sec and one second. Some compacts in the medium to top end of the price range, however, give a shutter speed as slow as 15 seconds for night shots.

The shutter speed is critical to the 'sharpness' of an image, for example a moving object taken with a slow shutter speed will appear blurred, whereas a fast shutter speed ensures a sharply focused image (see page 14). Compact cameras do not have very fast shutter speeds: most have a maximum speed of between 1/250 sec and 1/360 sec, so if you wish to freeze fast moving subjects you need to 'pan' or move the camera as your subject moves (see page 15).

The shutter speed is also important when looking at the most common reason for out-of-focus pictures – camera shake. This is caused when the camera has selected a slow shutter speed and the photographer cannot hold the camera steady enough during the exposure time. It can also be caused by pressing down too hard on the shutter release button (see Problem Solving, page 79).

Fortunately with the compact camera, the aperture and shutter speed are controlled automatically, so you don't have to worry about them. However an understanding of the above enables you to assess what your camera is doing in different lighting conditions and enables you to manipulate and control the automatic functions, if you wish. One of the most effective ways of controlling the exposure is to use the right film for the result you want (see Film, page 36). For example, on a sunny day with a 200 ISO speed film, the camera will choose the smallest aperture with the maximum shutter speed. In bright light you will therefore achieve maximum depth of focus. This means if you focus on a point about 10 metres (33 feet) away from the camera, the picture will be in focus from about 2 metres (6½ feet) to infinity. You will also be able to capture some movement because the bright light will mean that a fast shutter speed has been chosen to achieve the correct exposure. On a bright overcast day you would require a 400 ISO speed film to achieve the same effect and on a dull, overcast day, you would require a 1000 ISO speed film.

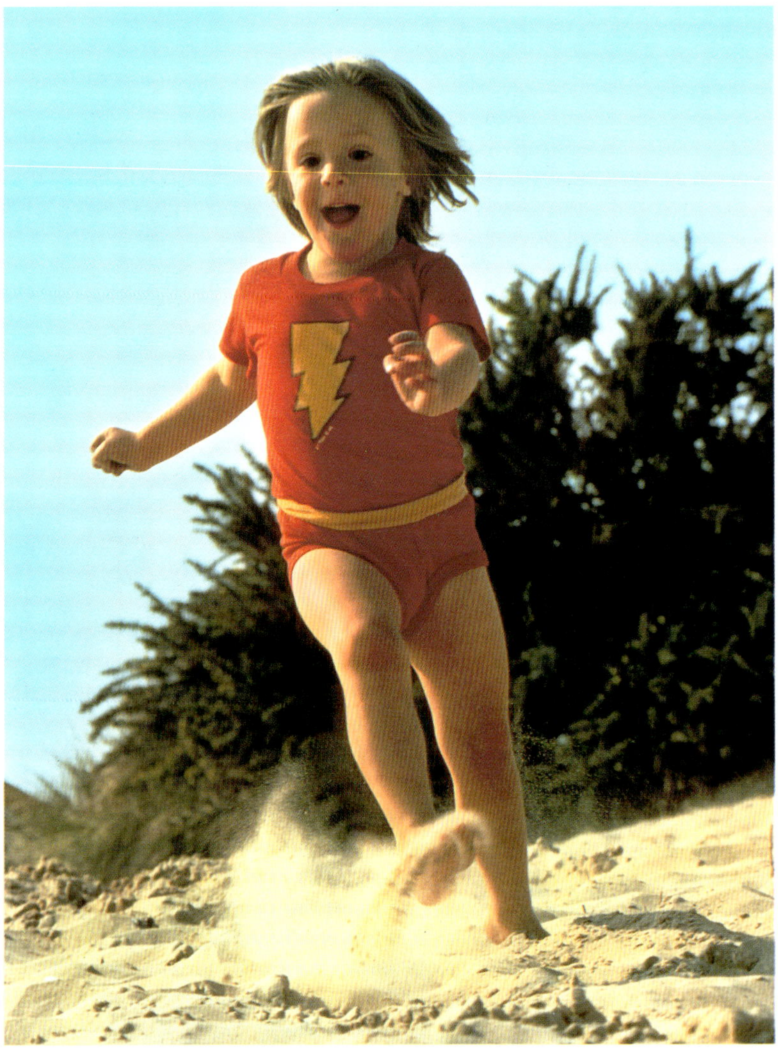

Freezing movement: Matt in Captain Marvel gear

It is easier to freeze movement coming towards the camera than it is movement going across the camera. This shot of my son (taken several years ago) was shot on a bright sunny day on 200 ISO film. The camera has chosen a shutter speed of about 1/250 sec and the lens was stopped down to an aperture of about f8. I pre-focused on a spot in the sand that I knew he would come racing over by pushing the shutter button down to its first stage and held it there. When he came running in and hit the spot, I pushed the button the rest of the way down to fire the shutter.

• Shot on 200 ISO film with zoom at 35mm.

Capturing movement: the runner

The first picture of the runner (right) was shot with the camera still. Because the lighting conditions were quite poor and I was using a slow film, the camera selected a fairly slow shutter speed (about 1/30 sec) and the moving image appeared as a blur across the film.

With a compact, you cannot manually change the shutter speed, so to capture movement under those conditions, I had to use a technique known as panning. This means moving the camera from left to right, or vice versa, so that the moving subject is kept within the frame as you press the shutter. Using this approach, I was able to hold the runner quite sharp (below) even with a slow shutter speed. The panning had blurred the background adding to the feeling of speed.

This time I ran with the camera (centre right), panning in the opposite direction just to produce a feeling of speed. The background and subject both appear blurred but it gives a very atmospheric shot.

I deliberately shot all these pictures on 100 ISO film on an overcast day so that the camera would choose a slow shutter speed as it is the best way to illustrate the panning technique. By using a fast film (1000 ISO) or shooting the action on a sunny day, the camera would choose a shutter speed of about 1/250 sec which would enable me to hold the action sharper and also to take pictures of faster moving subjects, for example, a horse galloping, someone cycling or playing tennis.

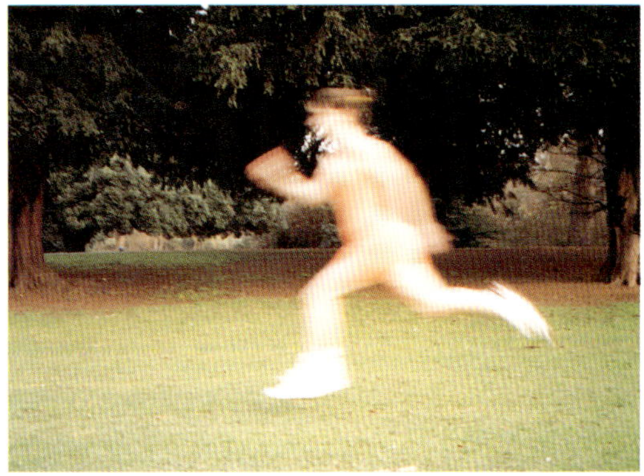

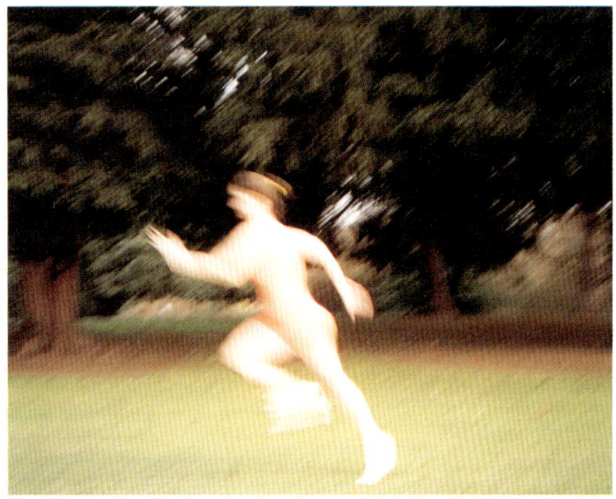

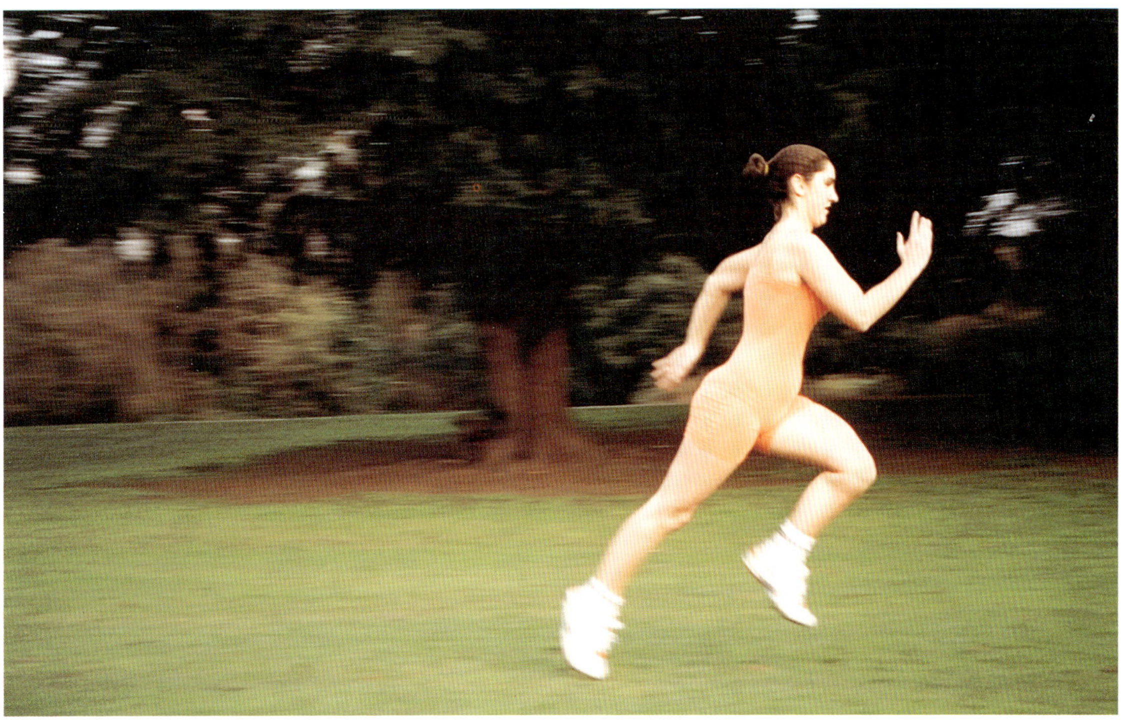

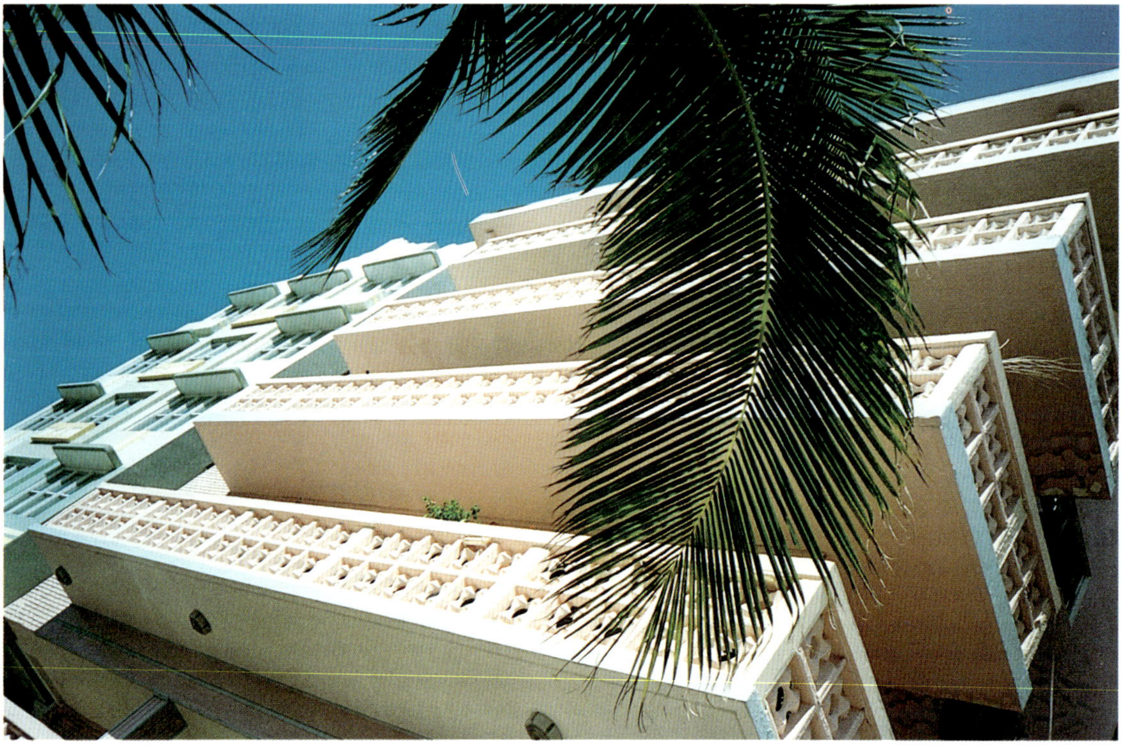

Depth of focus

This picture (above) was taken in the bright Florida sunshine. The lens was stopped down to its smallest aperture (f16 in this case) to give the ultimate depth of focus. The palm frond in the foreground which was $1\frac{1}{2}$ metres ($4\frac{1}{2}$ feet) away from the camera is sharp as is the top edge of the far building which was about 20 metres (60 feet) away. (See opposite for the effect of focal length on depth of field).

Bird on beach

This is an example of a lens shooting on a wide aperture, between about f3.5 and f5.6, and giving a shallow depth of field. The bird is sharp but the background is out of focus.

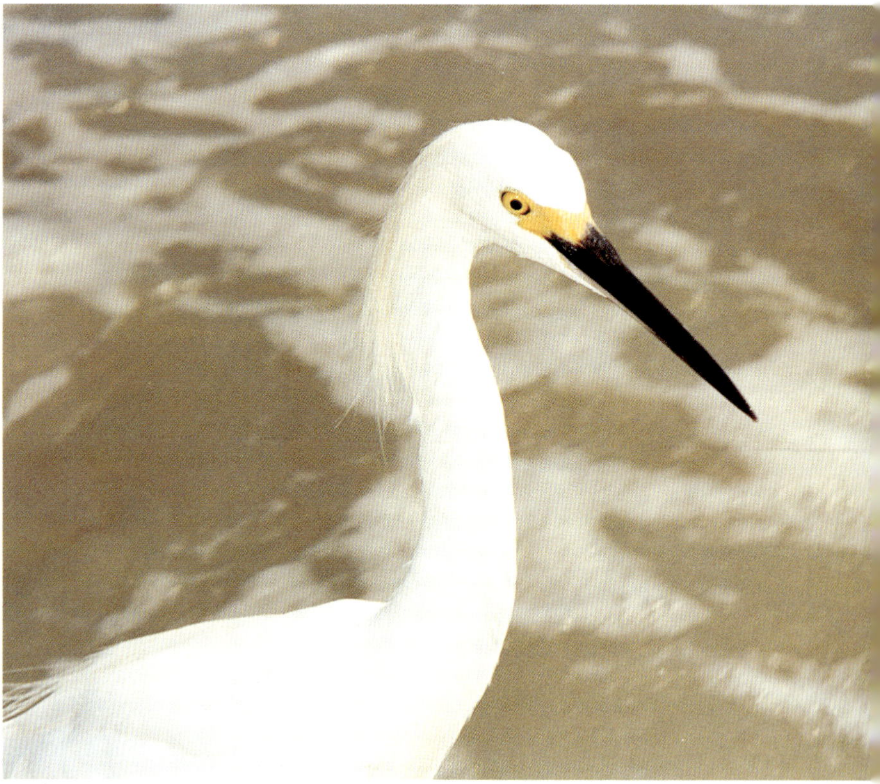

Lenses and Depth of Focus

You can buy a compact camera with either a fixed-focal-length lens or a zoom lens which has a number of different focal lengths. Fixed-focal-length compacts usually have a slightly wide-angle lens with a 28mm or 32mm, 35mm or 38mm focal length, while zoom lenses come in a great variety of combinations: 28-80 mm, 35-70mm, 35-105mm and 38-115mm.

There is a temptation with a compact camera to use the shortest focal length (say 35mm) just to get more of a scene in or zoom in to get closer to your subject. I'm not saying this is wrong but you should also be aware of the creative effect such decisions will have on your picture. First consider the effect this is going to have on your depth of focus: a wide-angle lens has a much greater depth of focus than a zoom lens set at a focal length of say 80 or 105mm. In addition, if you are focused tightly in on a subject then you have small depth of focus, whereas the further you are away from your subject, the greater the depth of focus. If you want the maximum possible depth of focus, use the wide-angle setting in bright light with the foreground about 6 metres (20 feet) away and, for the minimum depth of focus, shoot close up with the zoom on its maximum 'telephoto' setting on a dull day.

You need to remember, too, that the wider the angle of your lens,

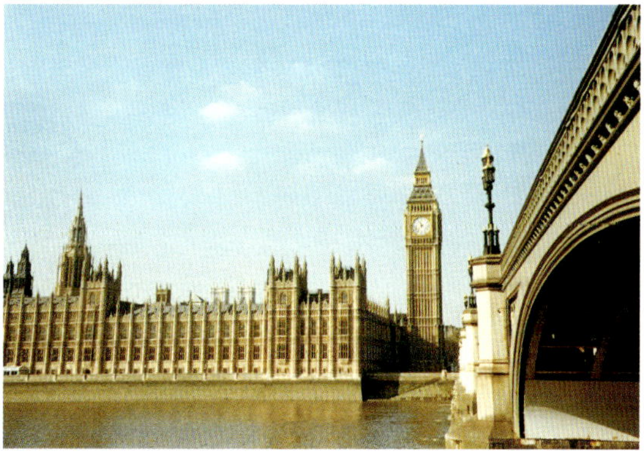

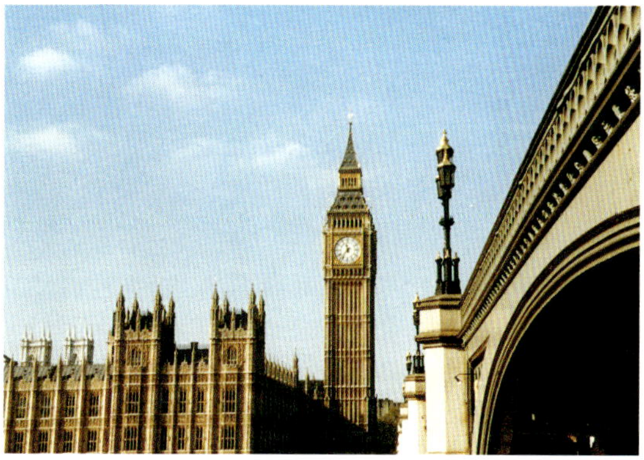

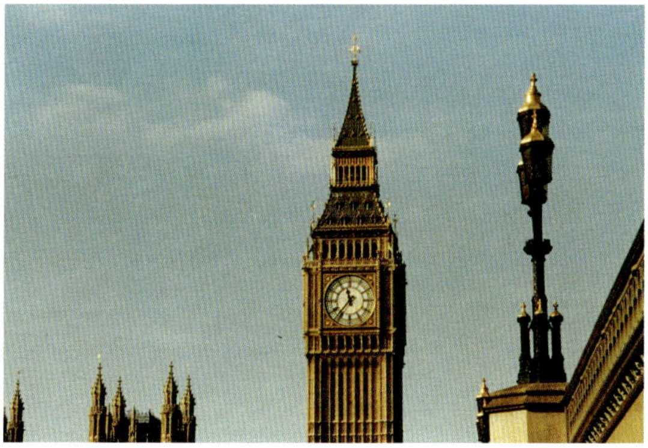

Angle of view of a zoom lens

The Houses of Parliament (above left) taken with the zoom on the wide-angle setting of 35mm.

The scene (above) taken from exactly the same spot with the zoom lens set at 50mm.

Exactly the same picture again (left) with the zoom on 105mm.

the greater its ability to exaggerate perspective, and the longer the focal length of a lens the greater its ability to foreshorten perspective. This has an enormous effect on the composition of your picture as you can take the same subject at each end of the zoom lens and achieve two very different photographs, as can be seen from the pictures on page 17. You should also be aware that fixed-focal-length and wide-angle lenses are not good for head and shoulder portraits because they tend to distort facial features. The longer focal lengths of a zoom lens (70mm or longer) ensures more flattering and natural looking portraits. It's also important to realize that the zoom lens on a compact will have a larger maximum aperture on the wide-angle setting than on the zoom settings. In fact, the wide-angle setting will allow four times the amount of light onto the film as the longest zoom setting. So while the 35mm setting will have an aperture of f3.5, the 105mm zoom setting will only have an aperture of f8. This means you can take photographs in much poorer light conditions with the wide-angle setting than you can with the zoom.

Depth of focus

The smaller the aperture, the greater the depth of focus that the lens produces. In bright sunny conditions, therefore, you will achieve maximum depth of focus.

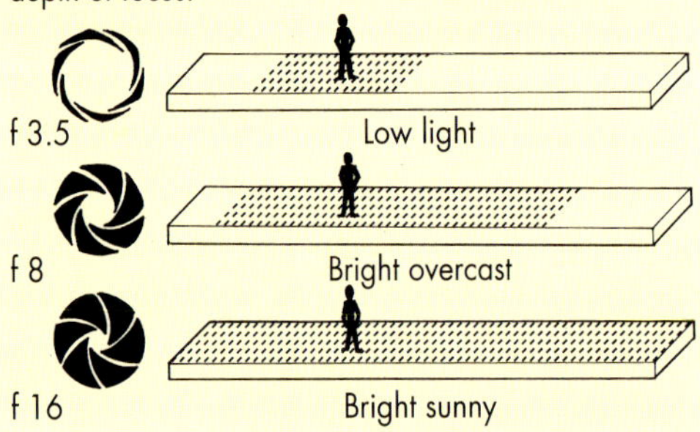

Auto focus

Nearly all compact cameras focus automatically, all you have to do is to make sure you know how to use this system correctly. When you look through the viewfinder on your compact you will notice a pair of brackets in the centre: these are the focusing brackets. In order to get a correctly focused picture you must ensure your subject falls within the area marked out by the brackets. I found the compact auto-focus system difficult at first because I was used to looking through an SLR viewfinder in which the image goes in and out of focus as you move the lens, whereas everything in the viewfinder of a compact looks sharp.

Be aware also that the central positioning of the focusing brackets can lead you into the trap of taking pictures in which the main subject is always in the centre of the frame. If you want to take a shot with your main subject off centre, first compose your picture with the subject inside the brackets. If you are taking a close-up shot, make sure your subject falls within the close-up auto focus brackets (see page 35). Press the shutter release button lightly and keep it down. This locks the focus on and allows you to recompose the picture with the subject off centre

When to use the focus lock

In order to get a correctly focused picture you must ensure your subject falls within the area marked out by the focusing brackets. In some situations this is not possible and you should use the focus lock.

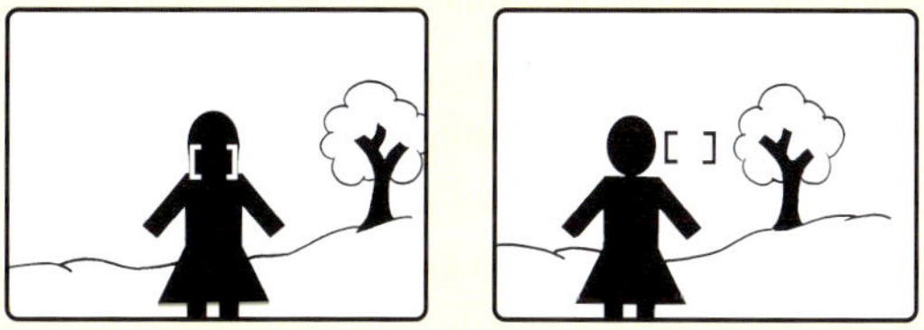

If you wish to compose a photograph with the subject off centre then first compose your picture with the subject inside the focusing brackets like this (above left). Press the shutter release button lightly to lock the focus and recompose(above).

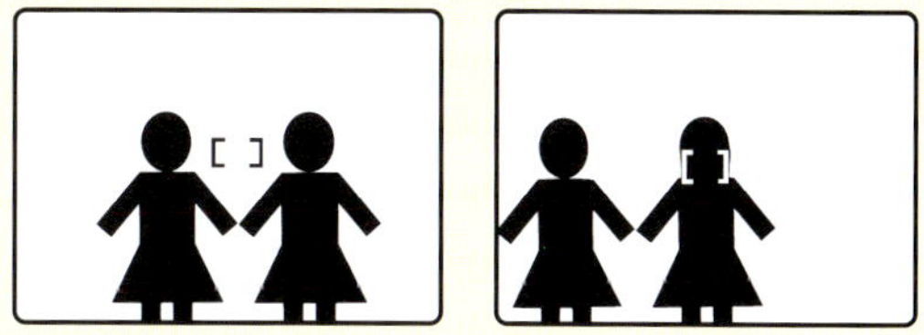

When photographing two people the focusing bracket may fall between them (above left). If a shot is taken with the brackets in this position, the background will be in focus but the two people blurred. Use the focus lock on one of the subjects only (above right), then recompose.

before finally firing the shutter. Do use the focus lock, it is useful and enables you to make interesting compositions.

Another useful function to have is an infinity setting. This not only allows you take sharp pictures of faraway objects such as distant mountains but also allows you to take photographs through glass without interfering with the auto-focus mechanism. When photographing through glass, for example, a train or car window, position yourself as close to the glass as you can and drape a coat or rug over your head and the camera to prevent unwanted reflections. If you are trying to photograph a stationary object from a moving vehicle then focus on a point ahead or behind the object to reduce the movement and therefore the chance of blur on the picture.

Some compact cameras boast of a 'tracking focus mode', which is supposed to hold focus on a moving subject. To be honest, however, I didn't find it of much use as it couldn't even hold the sharpness of a child running towards the camera let alone anything really quick. My advice is to prefocus (see Freezing Movement page 14).

Most of the auto-focus systems on compacts work using an infra-red light signal which bounces off the subject and returns to the camera. The distance is measured by the auto-focus sensor and the lens elements adjust in order to focus accurately on the subject.

Overcoming Exposure Problems

A compact camera automatically sets the aperture and shutter speed to give the correct exposure (the total amount of light that is allowed to reach the film) for the light conditions and type of film you are using. This, combined with the versatility of colour print films means, that you will nearly always be able to get a print from your negative. Occasionally, however, there are certain situations where the automatic

Overcoming exposure problems

A compact camera automatically sets the aperture and shutter speed to give the correct exposure, but occasionally there are situations where the automatic exposure may give the wrong reading. In these situations you will need to use the exposure compensation mode or backlight button if you are:

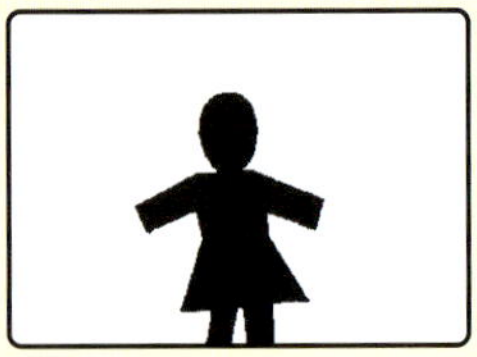

Photographing a small figure against a light background.

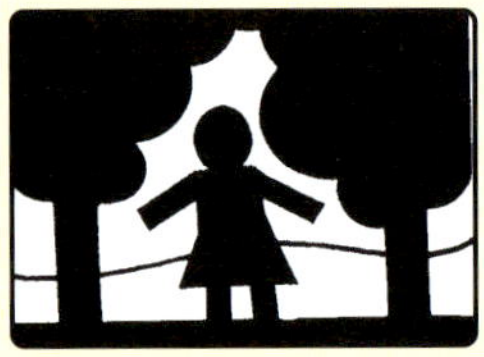

Taking a portrait under a tree.

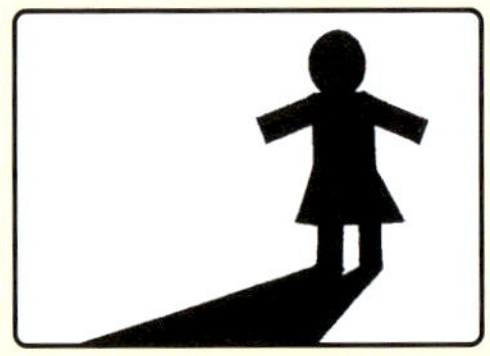

Taking a shot where there is strong backlighting, for example, into the sun.

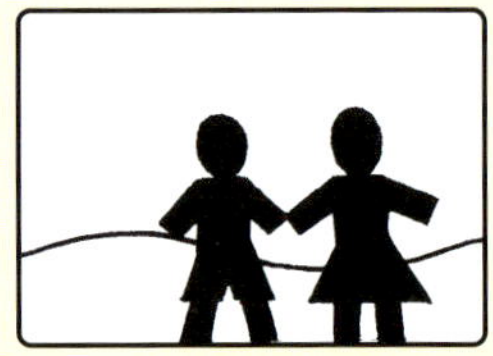

Taking a picture where the sky is the dominant feature.

exposure may be fooled into giving the wrong reading.

If you wish to photograph a relatively small dark figure against a large area of white, for example, the automatic exposure will correctly expose for the background but in so doing underexpose for the figure. The reverse is also true: if you are trying to photograph a small light figure against a large dark background the figure will be over exposed and the background correctly exposed.

There are several ways of overcoming this problem. If your compact has one, you can use the exposure compensation mode. This overrides the automatic exposure and either increases or decreases the exposure time by altering the size of the aperture by + or - an f stop. It will normally go down a maximum of two f stops and up a maximum of two f stops: -2, $-1\frac{1}{2}$, -1, $-\frac{1}{2}$ or $+\frac{1}{2}$, + $1\frac{1}{2}$, + 2, + $2\frac{1}{2}$. For the situation above you would need to set the exposure compensation at + $1\frac{1}{2}$ for the white background and - $1\frac{1}{2}$ for the dark background. With experience you will learn the values you need to use.

If your compact doesn't have exposure compensation then it may have a backlight button which is the equivalent of opening the aperture another $1\frac{1}{2}$ f stops. Alternatively, some compacts have a spot focus mode whereby the camera reads the exposure off a small area, marked by a spot in the viewfinder. Place the spot over the subject, push lightly on the shutter release button to lock the exposure, then, holding the button down, recompose and shoot.

You may also have problems with exposure if the subject is unevenly lit. This can happen if you are trying to take a portrait in the shade with a brightly lit area in the background. If your compact is set on fully automatic then the flash will probably go off to throw more light on the subject being photographed. However, if you do not want flash then turn if off and use the exposure compensation, backlight button or spot focus modes of your camera to solve the problem.

Other Modes

The list of modes on some compact cameras is almost never ending. Apart from the essentials such as automatic exposure, focus and flash there are many other gimmicky devices available; some are useful some are not worth having (see Choosing A Camera, page 32). Listed below are the more usual facilities:

- Mid-roll rewind with memory, which is useful if you want to take a few shots on an ultra-fast film, for example, and then go back to your normal film. By pressing a button the film rewinds and takes note of how many exposures were used on the film and when replaced rewinds to the number of exposures that were previously taken.
- Self-timers that allow you time to get into the picture before the shutter fires (about 10 seconds).
- A remote control device that fires the shutter from about 5 metres (16 feet) away.
- A multiple exposure mode that shoots two or more exposures on the same negative for special effects photography.
- Continuous shooting mode that keeps taking pictures for as long as you keep the button pressed down (up to two per second).
- Interval exposure that sets the camera to fire automatically at intervals without anyone present.
- A TV mode that allows you to take pictures off the screen.
- A clock and date code that automatically records and prints on the picture when it was taken (too far in for my liking).
- A print-a-message mode that will print 'Happy Birthday' or some such message across the picture (available in four languages).

Remember don't buy facilities you don't want, they cost money and make the camera far too complicated.

Exposure: Summary

- The aperture and shutter are linked together to control the correct exposure: the aperture controls the depth of focus (how much of the picture will be in focus) and volume of light falling on the film while the shutter controls the length of time that light is allowed to expose the film and controls movement of the subject. For example, a fast shutter speed freezes a moving subject and a slow shutter speed blurs.
- You can influence the camera's choice of shutter speed and aperture by your choice of film. A fast film will make the camera choose a faster shutter speed and smaller aperture. Therefore on a bright sunny day, when the camera has set an aperture of approximately 16 at 1/550 sec (on 200 ISO film), you will have maximum depth of focus and be able to freeze movement.
- If the light conditions deteriorate sufficiently, the flash will automatically switch on. If you wish to turn off the flash you must be aware that the camera will choose a slow shutter speed and will need support to avoid camera shake resulting in out of focus pictures.
- You can override the auto exposure on many compacts by using the exposure compensation mode or the backlight button.
- The wide-angle zoom setting admits 4 times the volume of light onto the film than the telephoto setting.

CHAPTER TWO

Taking a Picture

Loading an automatic compact is simplicity itself. All you have to do is open the back of the camera, pop the cassette in the left-hand compartment and lay the film leader across the back to the take-up spool. You do not even have to attach it to the spool as with manual cameras. Shut the back of the camera (make sure it snaps shut) and the film will automatically wind on to the first picture although do check that the counter has moved to 1 and is not still on S or E, which would mean the camera had not loaded correctly.

Some compacts won't take a picture unless loaded correctly, which saves any disappointment. Another wonderful advantage of the compact camera is that it adjusts the automatic exposure system to suit the speed of the film that has been loaded. It can do this because of the special coding on all films, called DX coding, which the camera's electronic contacts can recognize.

Holding the Camera

There are two vital points to remember when holding your camera: the first and most important is to hold your camera absolutely still when taking a shot. Most out-of-focus prints are caused by camera shake. This can be avoided if you gently squeeze the shutter release button rather than pressing down hard and jerking the camera out of position.

Holding the camera

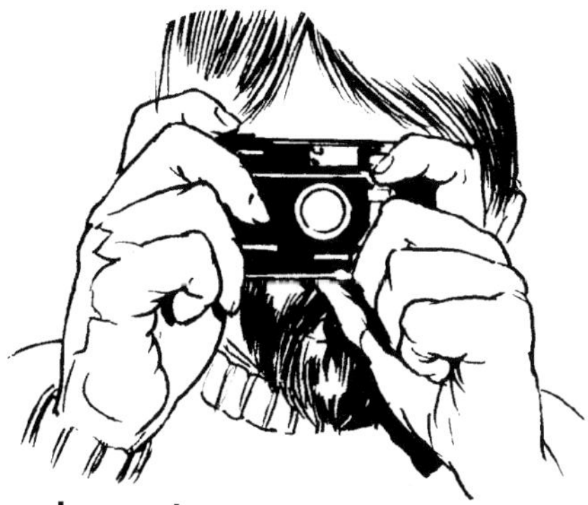

Incorrect

The fingers of the left hand are obstructing the flash and auto focus windows, and are too close to the lens.

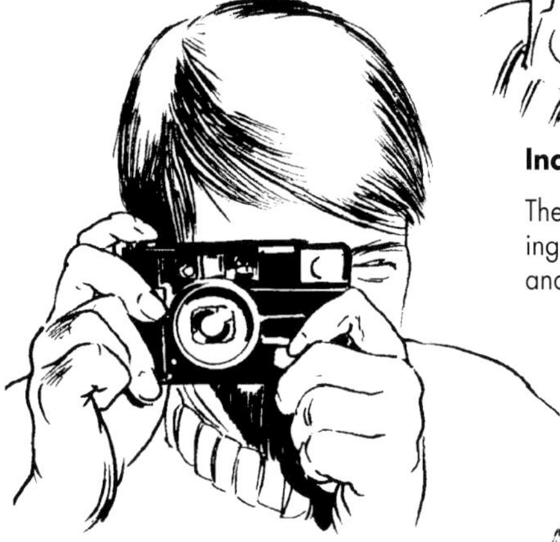

Correct

The camera is well supported and the fingers are clear of the flash and the auto focus windows.

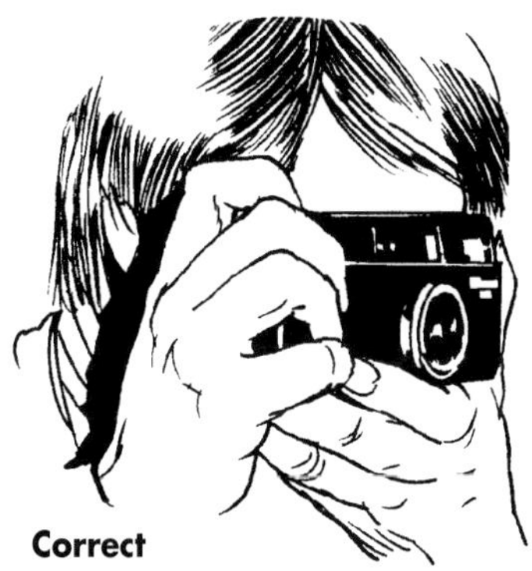

Correct

When the camera is on the tele setting you can provide greater camera support using the forefingers under the lens.

Camera Care

Heat and dust are a camera's two worst enemies.

• Never leave your camera in the glove compartment or boot of a car in full sun.

• In dusty or sandy conditions, keep your camera in a self-sealing plastic bag and remember to replace it in the bag after use.

• Keep film in the fridge as heat and humidity cause it to deteriorate, especially if it has been exposed.

• In cold weather, the camera's battery will have to work much harder, so it won't last as long. Help preserve battery power by keeping your camera warm in the pocket of your coat.

• Always take a spare battery (or two, in the case of some compacts) with you and keep an eye on the battery charge indicator on the LCD.

• Most cameras take approximately 22 roles of 24-exposure film, with 50 per cent flash use, per set of batteries.

(Camera shake can also be caused by a slow shutter speed, see Problem Solving, page 79).

If you wish to take still life photographs or other shots that would require slow shutter speeds then you should consider buying a tripod.

The second point to remember is to keep your fingers away from the lens, the flash, the viewfinder and also the small auto-focus, self-timer and auto-exposure windows. If you cover any of these you will prevent them from functioning properly and, in the case of the lens, you will end up with a picture of your finger (see Problem Solving, page 76).

CHAPTER THREE

Flash

Every compact camera on the market has a built-in flash. The power of the flash, or the effective distance at which it can correctly expose the film, varies greatly between camera models and you should check this out before purchasing any camera.

Basically, the more you spend on a camera, the more powerful the flash. The chart opposite is divided into three groups: low-cost, medium-cost and high-cost cameras. It shows how the effective working distance of a flash varies according to the speed of the film. You can see that the faster the film the greater the 'throw' (the distance at which the flash is effective) of the flash. Make a similar chart for your camera and keep it with you at all times. If you don't have the information, then ask at your camera shop.

It's worth noting that when working at a normal flash distance of between 5 and 12 metres (16 and 40 feet), the flash recharges more quickly the faster the film you use. This is because the flash needs to produce less light to expose fast film than it does to expose slower film. It is also more effective over greater distances if the camera lens is on a wide-angle setting rather than a zoom one because the lens aperture is larger when used on the wide-angle setting that it is on zoom and therefore more flash light reaches the film (see page 18).

I'm constantly amazed at the time and money wasted by people flashing away with their compact cameras at night from too far away from their subject for the little flash to have any chance of making an exposure. If you want to take night shots at, say, a football game then use fast film (ISO 1000, 1600 or 3200) and turn off the flash. You will need to support the camera by leaning against a post or seat as the shutter speed will be relatively slow but it is worth trying as you can produce some very atmospheric shots. It's also a good way of taking pictures at concerts or plays where flash photography is forbidden.

If you can't switch the flash off on your camera, hold your finger over the flash instead. This is just as effective.

Modern compact cameras have several different flash modes to select from, each identified by a different visual symbol that appears on the LCD (liquid crystal display) panel (see page 35). Unfortunately, different manufacturers have different symbols for each function, so you will have to check with your manual what the symbols are for your functions.

Auto flash

When set on automatic, the flash fires automatically if the camera assesses there is insufficient light to expose the film correctly. It is important to note that your camera's assessment of insufficient light assumes that it is being hand-held and that the slow shutter speed required would make it difficult to hold the camera steady enough to keep the picture in focus. Don't assume, therefore, that the flash is only going to go off at night or when you are shooting indoors. You may find, for example, that the flash fires if you are trying to take a picture which is in dark shadow.

Flash off

Some compacts have a flash off or flash cancel mode. This is very useful as it means you can switch the flash off in a situation where the camera would normally fire the flash automatically. Remember, if this is the case, the shutter speed may be slow so make sure you can hold the camera steady using a support, if necessary. I often turn the flash off as can been seen from many of the examples in this book. Remember, if your camera doesn't have a flash off mode, cover the flash with your fingers.

Flash Shooting range

For a fixed-focal-length camera look at the wide-angle column. Tele-zoom refers to the longest zoom setting.

Low-cost cameras

ISO film speed	Wide-angle zoom in metres (feet)	Tele-zoom in metres (feet)
100	3.5 (11)	2 (6)
200	5 (16)	2.5 (8)
400	7.5 (25)	3.5 (11)
1000	10 (33)	5 (16)
1600	15 (49)	7 (23)
3200	20 (66)	10 (33)

Medium-cost cameras

ISO Film speed	Wide-angle zoom in metres (feet)	Tele-zoom in metres (feet)
100	5 (16)	2.5 (8)
200	7 (23)	3.5 (11)
400	10 (33)	5 (16)
1000	16 (52)	8 (26)
1600	20 (66)	10 (33)
3200	29 (95)	14 (46)

High-cost cameras

ISO Film speed	Wide-angle zoom in metres (feet)	Tele-zoom in metres (feet)
100	7 (23)	3 (10)
200	10 (33)	4.5 (15)
400	14 (46)	6 (20)
1000	22 (72)	10 (33)
1600	28 (92)	12.5 (41)
3200	40 (131)	17.5 (57)

Red-eye reduction

Everybody has examples of pictures taken with flash where everybody appears with bright red eyes. It is caused when light conditions are poor and the pupils of the eyes enlarge to allow more light to enter the eye so that we can see better. As a result, when the flash on a camera goes off, the light is reflected off the red blood vessels behind the pupil back into the camera. The result — red eye!

The red-eye reduction mode aims to reduce this effect by firing off several small flashes to make the pupils of the eyes contract before the full power flash takes the picture. You can also help to reduce the effects of red eye by photographing in a brightly lit room.

The only way to eliminate red eye completely, however, is to prevent your subjects looking directly at the camera, which isn't always possible. Alternatively, use a fast film (1000, 1600 or 3200 ISO) and turn off the flash. You will be surprised at how good the results can be. Remember to set the zoom on a wide-angle setting to ensure the camera uses its largest aperture.

Anytime flash

This function allows you to use flash whenever you wish, so it is for you to decide if you feel a subject needs the extra light from the flash to 'fill-in' an area that might otherwise be in shadow. The camera automatically balances the daylight and flash to ensure the correct exposure, which is actually a technically difficult decision to make and took a lot of experience and knowledge to achieve using manual flash guns — now all you have to do is press a button.

It is different from auto flash as you have to make a creative decision to use it. Auto flash may well fill in areas of shadow but it may not necessarily be when you want it.

Auto flash with slow sync.

If you are taking a portrait of a group of people at night against a background of city lights, for example, the flash will normally give the correct exposure for the figures but the background will be underexposed. The slow sync. (synchronization) mode gives a longer exposure for the background while also exposing correctly for the flash to produce a correctly balanced exposure. This is another technique that used to be extremely difficult with hand-held flash guns.

When on slow sync. mode the camera will select a relatively slow shutter speed (about $\frac{1}{4}$ of a second) so you will have to lean against a sturdy object to prevent camera shake.

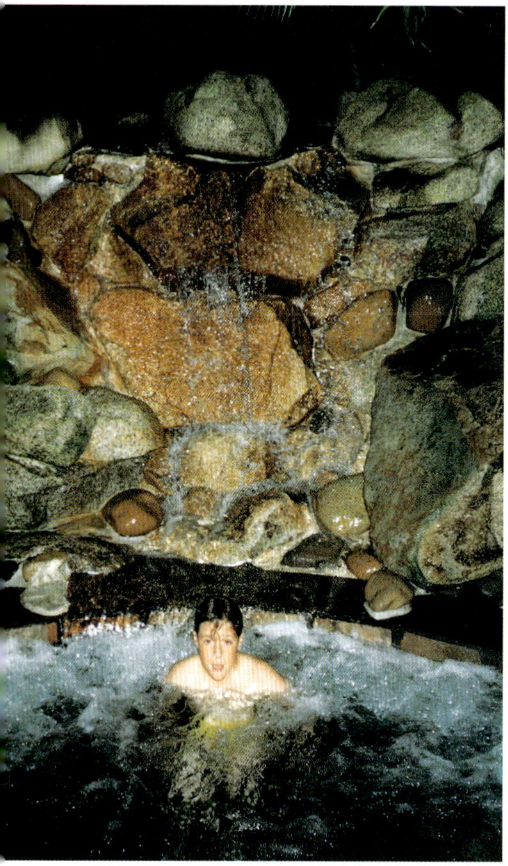

Swimming pool

This picture is of my son Matt in Queensland. I shot this photograph in the middle of the night and as there was no light available, only flash would do. The resulting red eye was unavoidable, but I still like this picture because of the memories it has preserved. Not even a really fast film (3200 ISO) could have produced an image in the light conditions available.

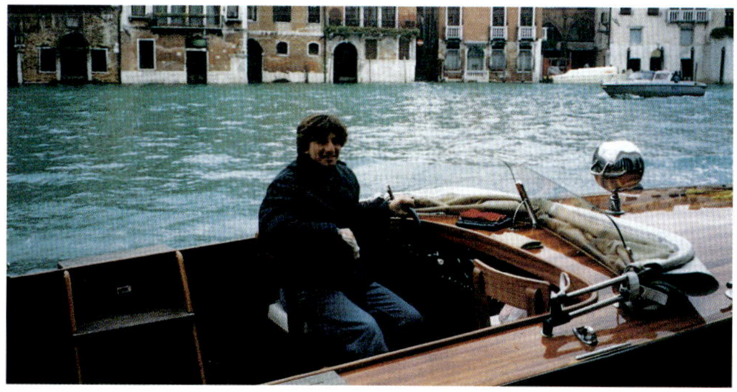

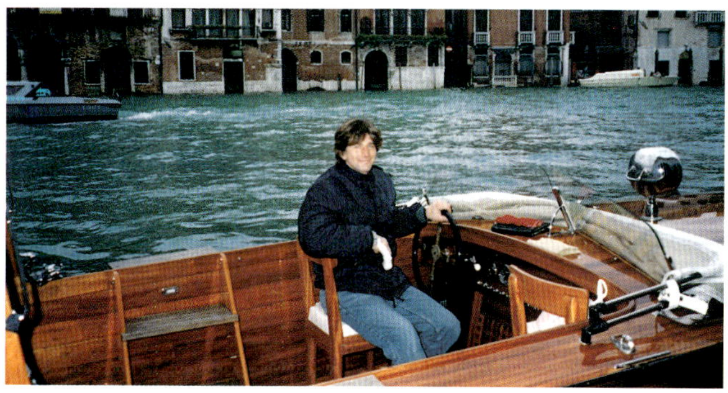

A Venetian chauffeur

This chauffeur was waiting for his wealthy employers to return. I took the first shot (top) on automatic expecting the camera to fire a fill-in flash because of the contrast between the foreground shadow area and the background. However, the contrast was not great enough for the camera to detect and the flash did not go off and so the foreground appears very dark. For the second shot (above) I used the anytime flash mode to throw extra light onto the man's face and the boat.

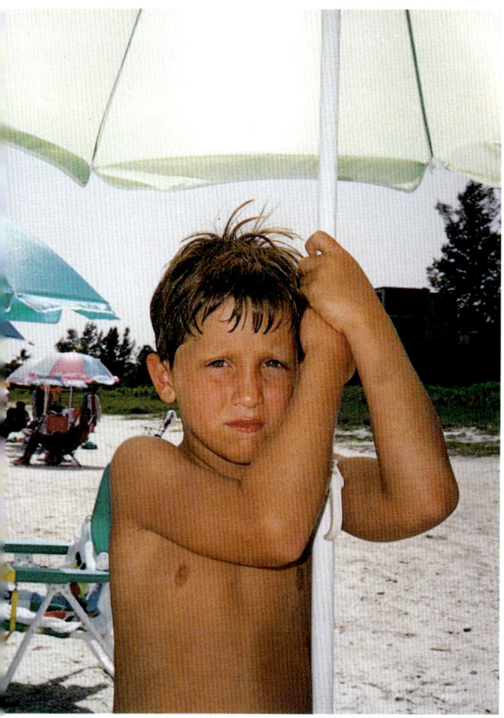

Young boy and brolly

This portrait shows how the camera can very successfully provide fill-in flash on the fully automatic setting. The little boy was actually in shadow and, because the contrast between him and the brightly lit beach behind was so great, the camera fired a fill-in flash. Without the flash the little boy's face would have been underexposed. The camera has also automatically provided the correct balance of light between foreground and background.

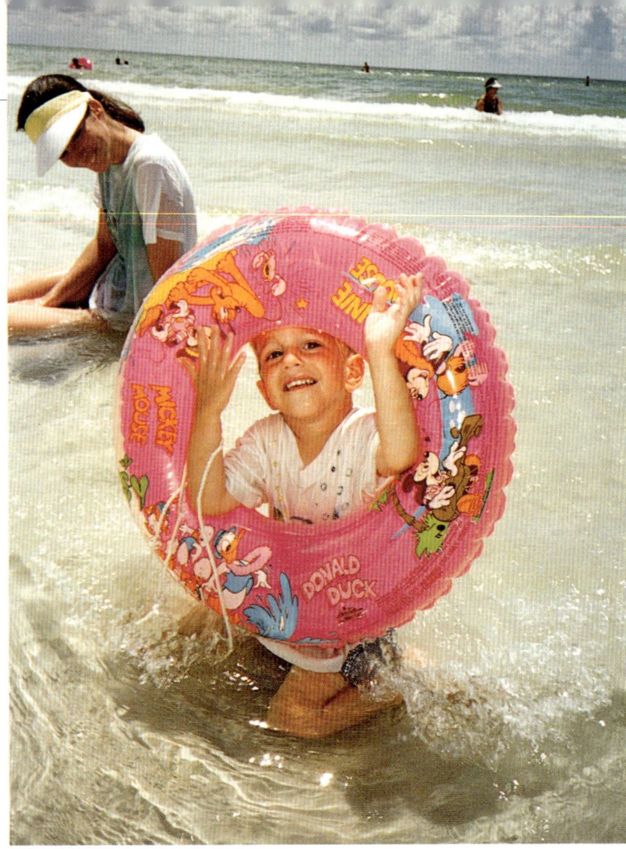

Boy in a ring

You wouldn't expect to have to use flash in the midday sun on a beach in Florida. But, in fact, photographing in such hard overhead light is very difficult because the faces are in dark shadow. I therefore decided to use the anytime flash mode to create some highlights in the boy's face. Look how his mother's face, which the flash could not reach, is still in shadow. Do experiment with flash on sunny days, you will achieve some interesting effects.

White Swan

This shot was taken with the camera on automatic and it has used a fill-in flash to reduce the contrast between the brightly lit background of the setting sun and the poorly lit foreground area with the swan to produce a perfectly balanced photograph. It also shows how the flash can pick out detail so precisely, for example, look at the droplets of water and the bird's feathers.

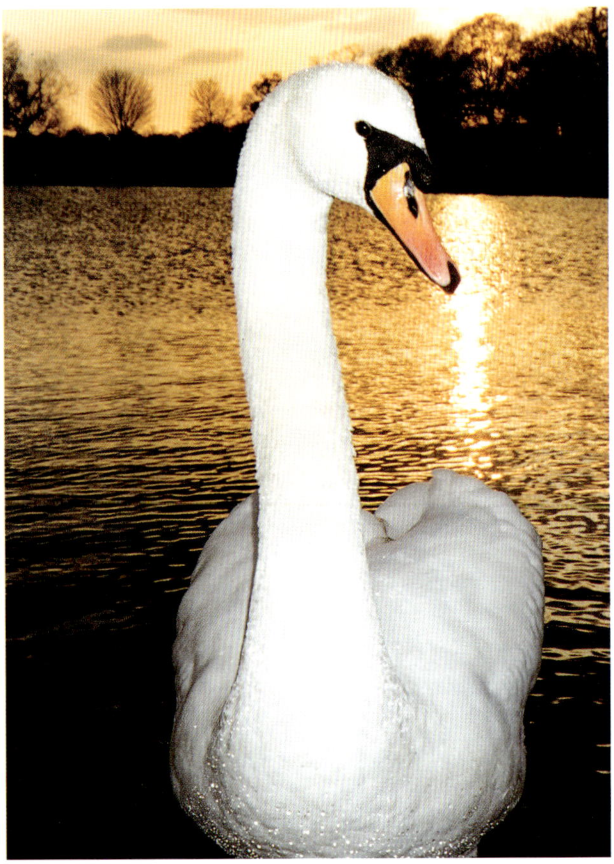

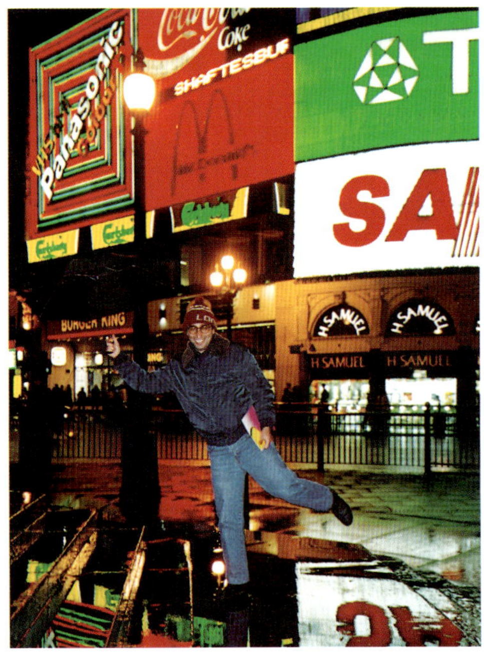

Nighttime in Piccadilly Circus

I shot this picture using the slow sync. flash mode. The slow shutter speed (1/15 sec) ensured the correct exposure for the background lights while the flash has correctly exposed for the man in the foreground.

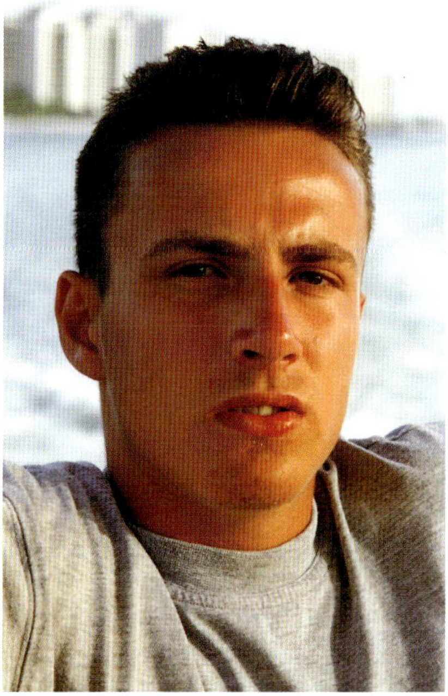

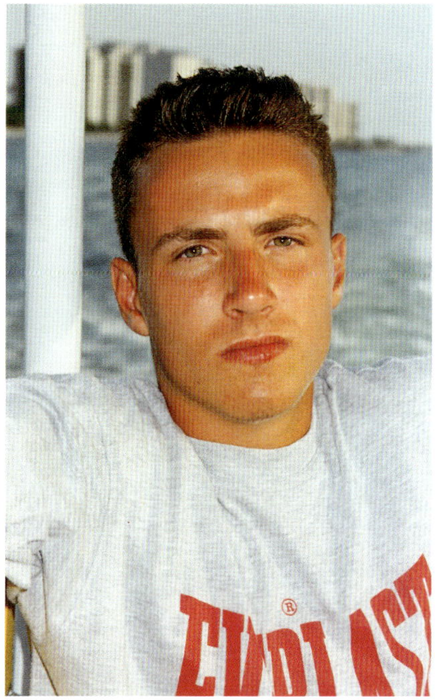

Young Man in T-shirt

These two portraits show how using flash can change the atmosphere of a shot. The first portrait (far left) was taken in the strong crosslight of the afternoon sun. For the second shot (left), I used the anytime flash mode to give a more even light, which gave a much flatter result. I'm not saying one is better than the other — it all comes down to personal taste.

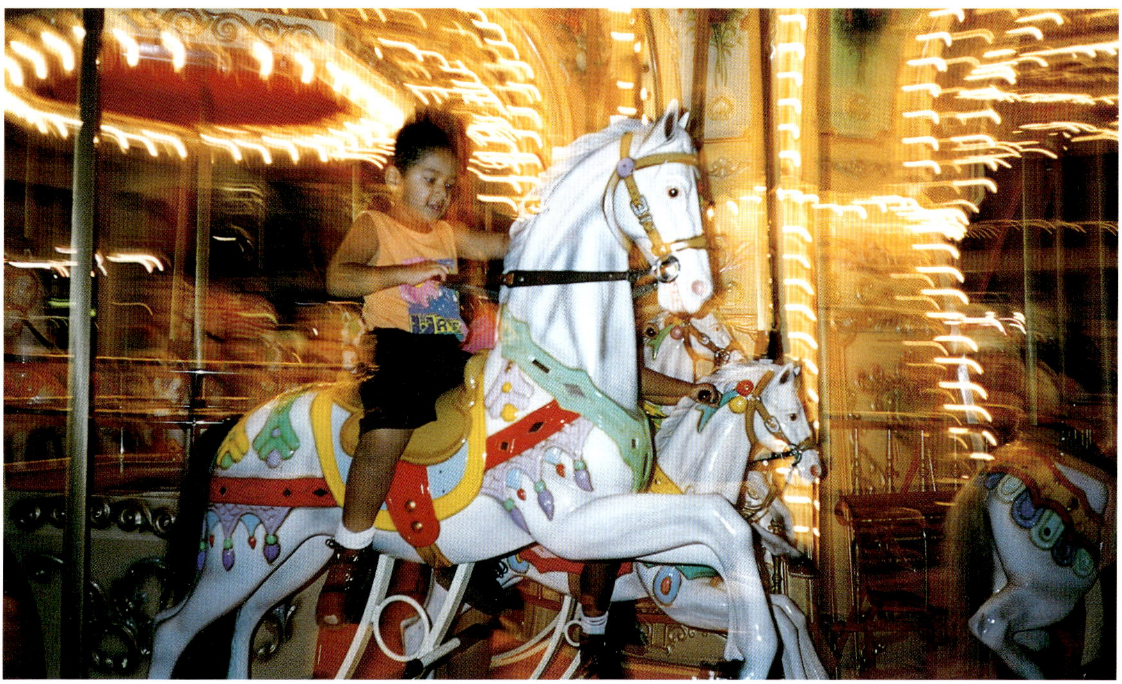

Carousel

This is another example of slow sync. where the flash has correctly exposed for the figure and because of its speed has captured and frozen the movement of the child and horse. The slow shutter speed (about 1/8 sec) has correctly exposed for the background carousel lights which have streaked because of the slow shutter speed.

Mother and daughters

In the first portrait (right), the flash has unevenly lit the faces because they were all at different distances from the camera, so in the second shot (below) I made sure the trio were all the same distance away. The result was an evenly lit shot.

When taking shots like this indoors try to ensure that people's heads are as close together as possible so you have more chance of achieving an even lighting.

I used the red-eye reduction mode on these shots, which worked very well here.

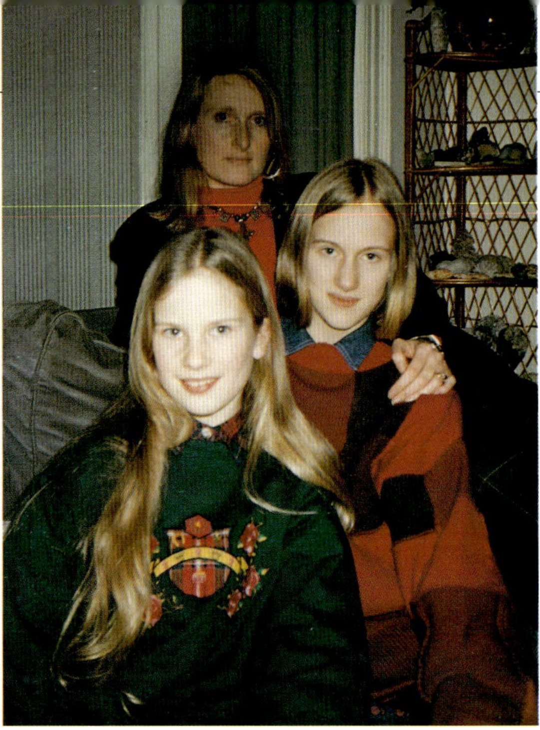

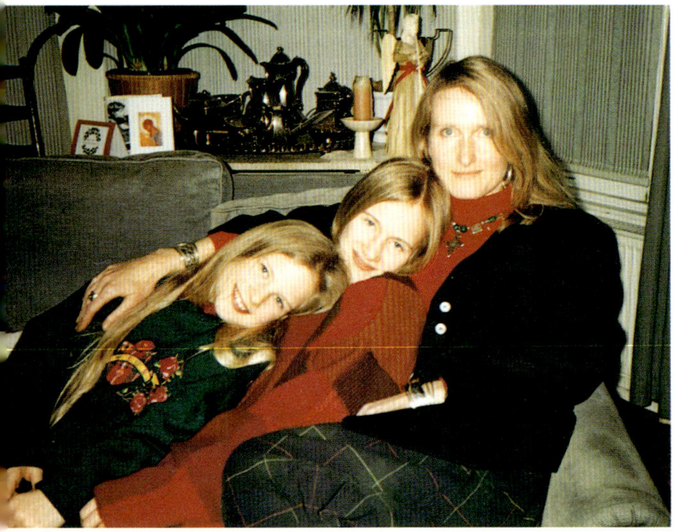

Tips

- If you are planning to take lots of flash pictures, take a spare battery (or batteries) with you as flash uses them up quickly.
- Before you take a shot, make sure the flash ready light has been on for a few seconds to ensure the flash is fully charged.
- When taking pictures of people inside, remember that the flash works most efficiently between 1.8 and 3.6 metres (6 and 12 feet). Any closer and you risk burn out (over-exposure of the faces) and beyond 3.6 metres (12 feet) you risk under-exposure.
- Use fast film (400 or 1000 ISO) as your normal indoor flash film. As you can see from the chart on page 25, you gain a greater throw and use up batteries more slowly because the flash recharges more quickly with fast film. However, don't shoot too close to faces on 1000 ISO as you will over expose (nothing closer than 1.8 metres (6 feet), preferably 3 metres (10 feet).
- The flash duration on a compact is very short – anything from 1/2000th sec to 1/6000th sec and produces a very sharp image on the film. This means that when there is no background light you can freeze a rapidly moving subject.

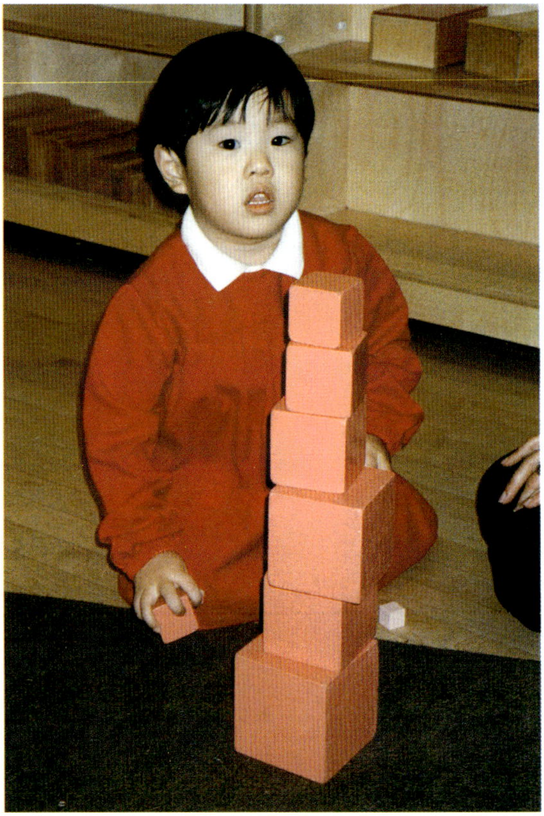

Chinese boy

I managed to prevent the dreaded red-eye here by taking this shot in a brightly lit room, which reduced the size of the little boy's pupils.

Girl in a red sweater

Take care when taking flash shots against any reflective surface such as a mirror or a window. Try not to shoot straight on to the reflective surface as it will bounce the light of the flash straight back into the camera, causing flare on the print (see right). Take the shot from an angle instead.

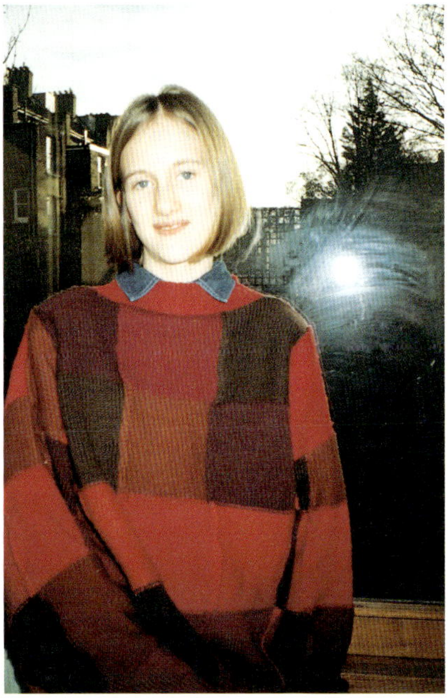

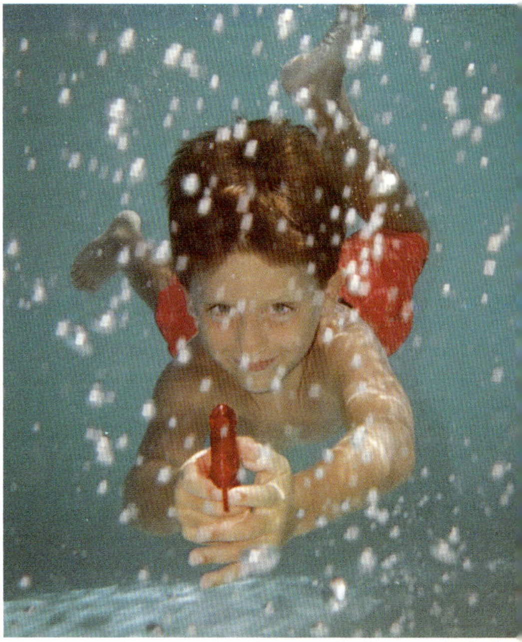

Three lads

This is a typical case of burn-out (overexposure) caused by shooting too close to the subject against a poorly-lit background. To avoid this burn-out I should have taken this shot from no closer than about 8 metres (26 feet) against a properly lit, light background. I could, of course, have avoided using flash by using a fast film (1600 or 3200 ISO).

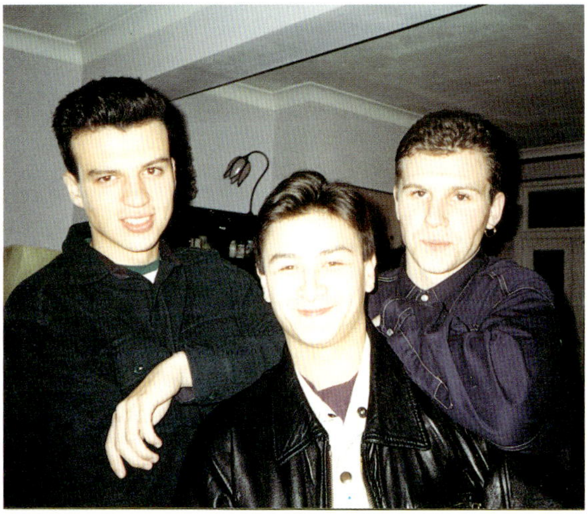

Boy under water

There was actually enough light under the water to take this picture without using the flash, but I wanted to experiment, so I used the anytime flash setting. I was very pleased with the result and like the way the flash has thrown highlights on the air bubbles, creating an almost surreal effect.

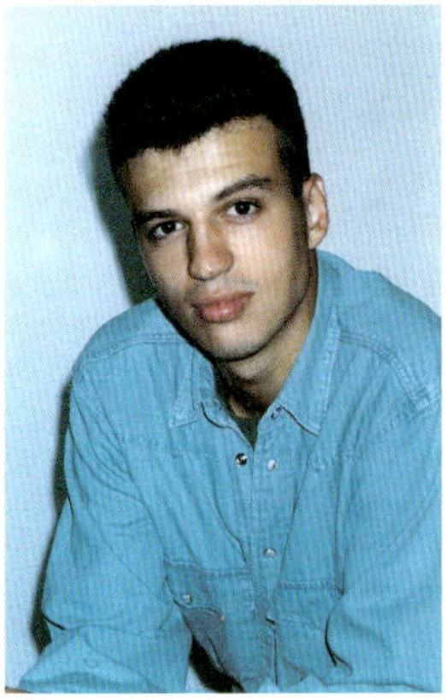

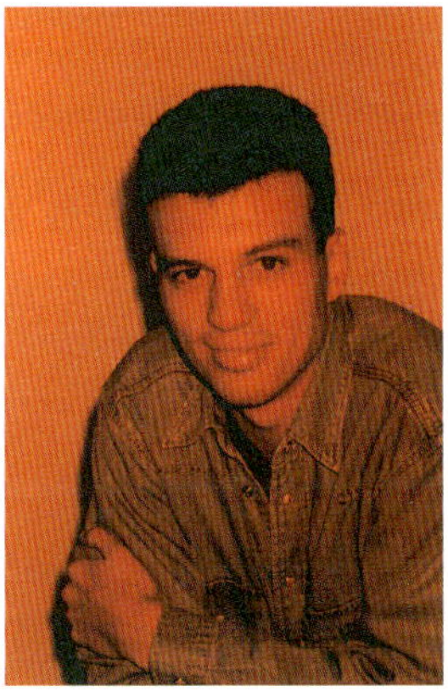

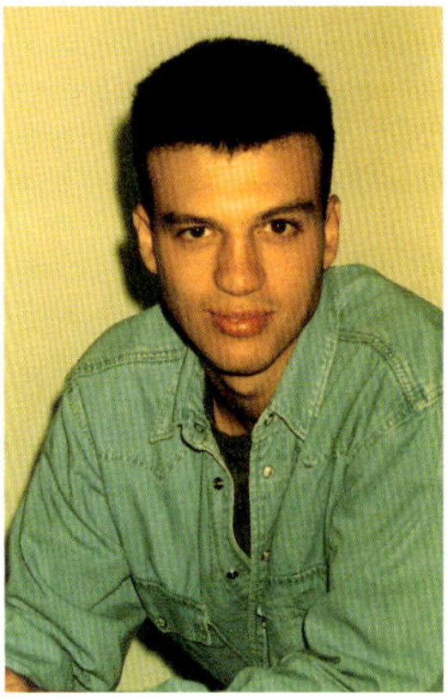

Filters

By placing coloured filters over the flash you can change the colour dramatically as can be seen from these three photographs. The one on the far left is a normal flash photograph, the one in the centre was taken with a red filter and the one on the left with a yellow filter.

CHAPTER FOUR

Choosing a Compact Camera

There is a huge range of compact cameras now on the market and trying to make a choice can be a confusing business, so, before you walk into a camera shop it's worth asking yourself a few questions. How much do you want to spend: compacts range in price from a few pounds to over a thousand? What do you want the camera for: holiday snaps, family portraits, sports photography, landscapes or a bit of everything? Do you want to be able to carry it around with you at all times?

Once you've answered these questions you will at least have narrowed the choice down slightly. I have divided the compact cameras available into five groups according to their cost and listed the pros and cons for each. There is also a fifth group of special cameras which includes underwater and disposable cameras. I hope this will help you to make the right choice. You may also find it helpful to look in photographic and consumer magazines as they are constantly testing and reporting on the latest models available.

Low-cost Compacts

In this price range you will get a fixed-focal-length lens around about 35mm; a fixed focus and aperture (between f5.6 and f8); and one shutter speed (about 1/125 sec) plus an automatic flash. Although the facilities are limited they produce surprisingly good results but you have to be aware of the camera's limitations.

+ Very compact because of the fixed-focal-length lens so are easy to carry round in a pocket.

- To get the best out of this type of camera you need to be able to judge distances quite well because there is no auto focus.

Low- to medium-cost Compacts

In this price range you will now get an automatic focusing facility; a variable shutter speed (between 1/250 sec and 1/15 sec); better lens with a variable aperture; more powerful flash and a more accurate viewfinder. The more basic twin lens cameras (a zoom with two settings, wide angle and telephoto) and those with a zoom lens begin to sneak into this group.

+ The cameras in this group are really good value for money and are simple to use.

- They don't all allow you to override the auto flash, which is a useful facility to have (see Flash, page 25).

Medium-cost Compacts

The range of cameras available in this group is mind-bogglingly vast and again you can find some very good value cameras. You will have all the facilities listed before plus a greater range of zoom lenses. Such facilities as multiple exposure, infinity auto-focus, macro, anytime flash and exposure compensation become available (see Other Modes, page 21).

+ I would recommend buying a camera from this group as there are some useful modes available such as anytime flash and exposure compensation but they haven't become over complicated. In addition the lens quality improves dramatically as does the power of the flash.

High-cost Compacts

This group just has more of everything than the previous group. The lens quality has improved but this is only evident on large prints over the 30 x 20cm (12 x 8in).

+ If you are into flash photography, you do get a more powerful flash.

- There is a danger in this group of paying a lot of money for USPs (unique selling points). As with video cameras and stereos, the camera manufacturers are adding lots of gimmicks that, in my opinion, hinder good photography rather than help it.

Very Expensive Compacts

This group covers the range of super compacts that are targeted towards the professional photographer and rich amateur. The cameras tend to have fixed-focal-length lenses with large apertures (f2.8 and f2). The automatic functions can be manually overridden, so the photographer can control the shutter speed and aperture: the settings for these two are displayed in the LCD at all times.

+ Lovely to use particularly good for low-light photography.
- Very expensive!

Special Cameras

Underwater There are several weather-proof compacts on the market with underwater capabilities. They are water-proof, sound-proof and dust-proof and can take underwater pictures down to a depth of about 5 metres (16 feet). They relieve you of the worry of sand and water destroying your camera – you can just drop them on the beach and wash them off later. They perform very well above water too.

+ An ideal camera for holidays: extremely versatile and great fun to use.

Sport or off-road cameras These are resistant to water, sand and dust. They are useful for outdoors enthusiasts but are not suitable for underwater photography.

Disposable cameras Most of the film manufacturers are now marketing disposable cameras, which come loaded with film (usually 400 ISO). They are not re-usable and have a fixed focal length and one shutter speed (usually 1/100th sec).

In good, bright light they produce surprisingly good results. The built-in flash works efficiently up to 4 metres (13 feet). This is the fastest growing market in photography and there are now underwater versions available.

+ Useful if you forget your camera or to take to the beach to avoid ruining your compact. I think the underwater models are great fun to take on holidays as an extra, especially if you anticipate doing some scuba diving or snorkelling. They are very reasonably priced, and a welcome addition to the photography scene.

The Liquid Crystal Display (LCD) Panel

The modern compact identifies its numerous modes and programmes by visual symbols that appear in the liquid crystal display panel (LCD) on the back of the camera. On one camera, forty different symbols appeared in the LCD panel.

I could never remember what functions they all performed or which button or combination of buttons I needed to push to recall a particular programme, so I wrote down all the symbols on the back of one of my business cards and kept it in my pocket for reference. You could stick it to the back of the camera.

Remember to READ YOUR INSTRUCTION MANUAL CAREFULLY, AND DON'T LOSE IT. Every camera is slightly different and this book will not replace your instruction book.

LCD Panel

The symbols illustrated below are representative of those that will appear in your camera's LCD display panel. Make sure, however, that you know what the symbols on your particular camera represent.

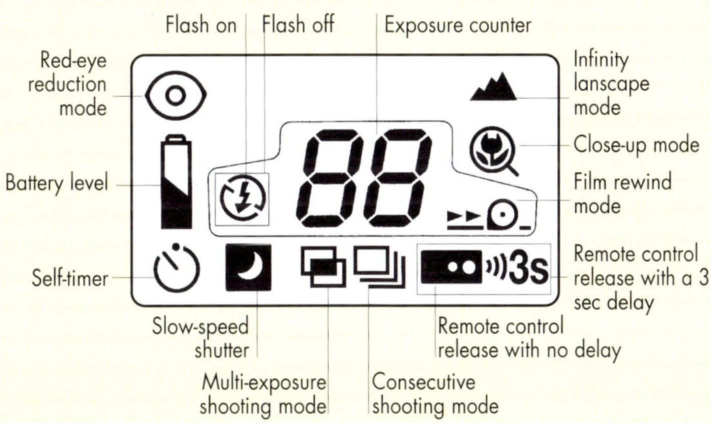

Viewfinder

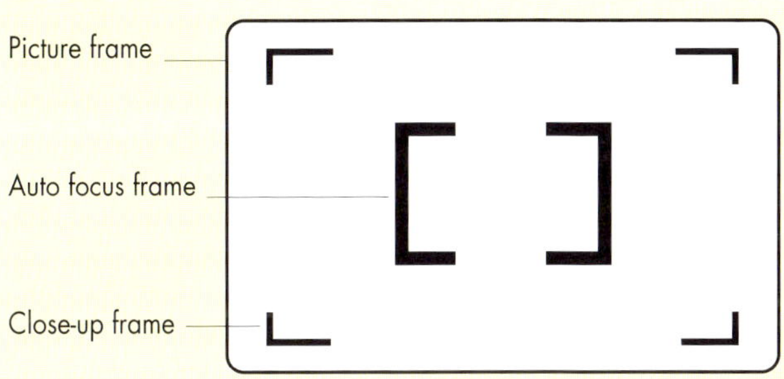

CHAPTER FIVE

Film

There are three types of film available to the photographer: colour negative or print film; colour transparency or slide film; and black and white negative film. Compact cameras were primarily designed to use with print film. Apart from the fact that most people prefer to look at prints rather than set up a projector and screen for the slides, there is also an important technical reason; print film has far more exposure latitude than slide film, which means that the automatic exposure on your camera can be 2 stops overexposed or 2 stops underexposed but the resulting negative can still produce an acceptable print.

This flexibility is one of the main reasons why cheap compact cameras can produce good-quality photographs.

Colour print film has also improved greatly in the last few years. It is faster, sharper, finer-grained and the colour balance is better. The quality of colour print paper has also improved. Both these factors have made compact cameras even more popular.

Professional photographers mostly use transparency (slide) film because they can control the final result in the camera and don't have to rely on their film processor's printing machine.

However, with the improvement in print film and the move of daily newspapers to colour, more professionals are now using print film.

Black and white photography was almost dead ten years ago, but has made a great come-back with professionals and enthusiastic amateurs. The joy of developing and printing your own black and white pictures is still to many (including myself) the ultimate photographic experience (see Black and White section page 122). The compact camera is ideal for shooting black and white film because it also has considerable exposure latitude.

All films are measured according to their sensitivity to light. A film that is very sensitive to light and can produce a good result in low light conditions is called a fast film and a film that needs bright lighting conditions is called a slow film. As a general rule of thumb, slow films produce sharper, finer grained prints that have greater colour saturation than those produced on medium or fast films. The faster the film the grainier the effect that is produced, the softer the colour gradation and the less sharp the image.

A film's sensitivity is measured in ISO numbers, which appear on every film box, for example, a slow film will read 50 ISO and a fast film 1000 ISO.

There are roughly four groups of film speeds (see below). You can choose your film not only to match the lighting conditions but also to achieve a specific visual effect. Remember your choice of film is a creative decision, not just a technical one.

Slow (25–64 ISO)

This group gives extremely sharp detailed images with very little grain and the high contrast saturated colours are outstanding. It is the ideal choice of film for architectural or still-life shots. Unless the lighting conditions are extremely bright, however, you will need a tripod. The excellent quality of the negatives means you can make enlargements without any appearance of grain, up to 51 x 61 cm (20 x 24in).

Medium (100–200 ISO)

This is the most popular group of films. The resulting prints are sharp and fine grained, and the colour saturation is excellent with good reproduction of skin tones. It is the ideal film for summer holidays in the sun when you can anticipate good light conditions. Colour balance is very much a matter of personal taste, you need to experiment to find which manufacturer's film pleases you best.

Fast (400 ISO)

This is the group that I find I use most with my compact, especially in the UK where we often have overcast skies and the light conditions are therefore quite subdued.

Although the print quality is not as fine grained or as sharp as the medium and slow films, the quality of 400 ISO films has improved dramatically over recent years and there are huge benefits to be gained from using a fast film. The extra speed enables the camera to use a faster shutter speed, thus keeping a moving subject sharper, and also enables the lens to stop down further, gaining greater depth of focus (see How It Works, page 17). It also enables you to take pictures in poor

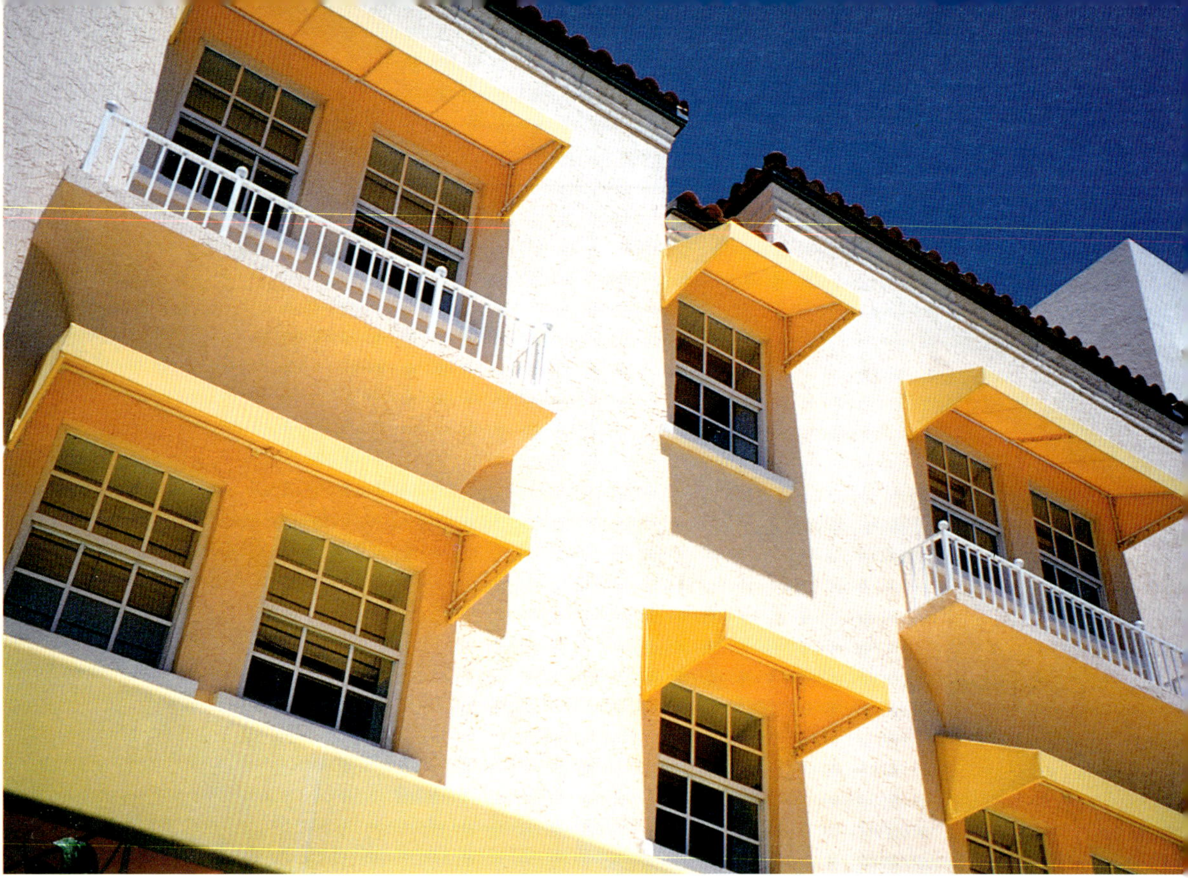

light conditions without flash. Photographs taken in natural light are generally softer and more attractive (see Light, page 54). When the flash is in use, however, the faster film has the effect of increasing the range of the flash so you can use the flash on subjects further away. When working close to a subject, the faster film uses less flash light for exposures which means the flash will recharge more quickly for the next exposure (see Flash, page 24).

As you can see from the examples on the following pages, unless you are making big enlargements, the difference in quality is not very noticeable between prints made from medium and those made from fast films.

Ultra Fast Films 1000–3000 ISO

This group of films has been designed for low light or available light photography without flash. The results are grainier than the fast film group but the quality has improved over the last few years.

I use this group not only because of the photographic possibilities of low-light photography, but also because of the creative possibilities. The soft colours and the grainy texture have a rather painterly look which you can use for many subjects. However, don't use these films in bright light conditions as the negatives will be overexposed.

Yellow windows

This house (left) was shot using a very slow film (25 ISO), which is ideal for architectural shots when you want an ultra-sharp, hard-edged result. It worked particularly well here because the saturated colour has emphasized the yellow canopies. Remember, though, slow film needs lots of light. If there isn't much light, use a tripod as the camera will use a slow shutter speed.

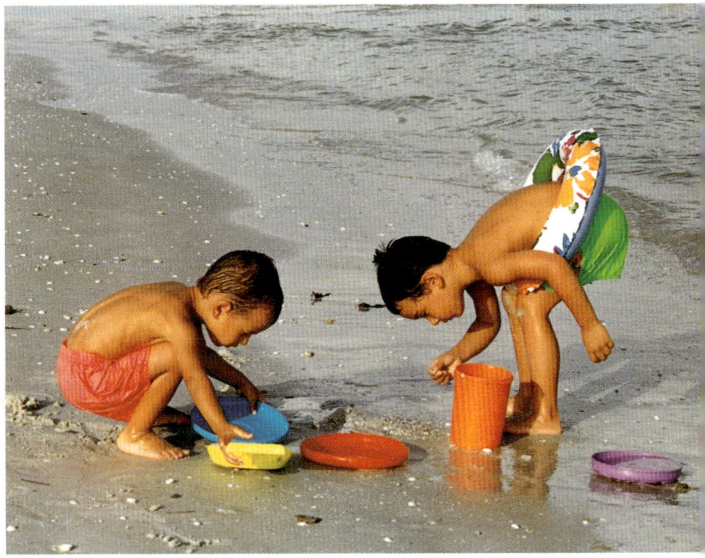

Boys on beach

This is ideal subject matter for medium-speed (200 ISO) film. The resolution (sharpness) is good and the colours at each end of the spectrum are saturated and the skin tones are very natural.

In most instruction books and articles, the 100 and 200 ISO films are discussed as the 'normal' films for compacts. I believe this is only the case if you live in a sunny climate and shoot mostly outdoors in bright conditions. For the average British and North European photographer, the 400 ISO films are much more appropriate for our often overcast and subdued conditions. This range of films is also excellent for producing large prints.

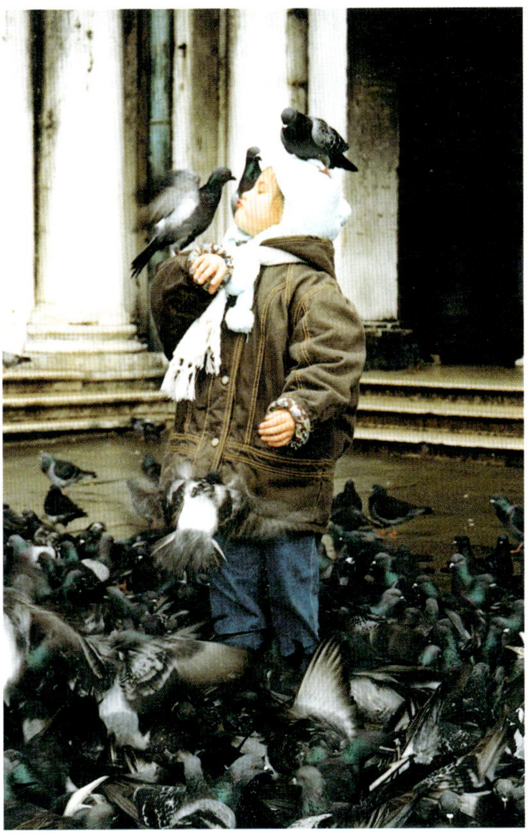

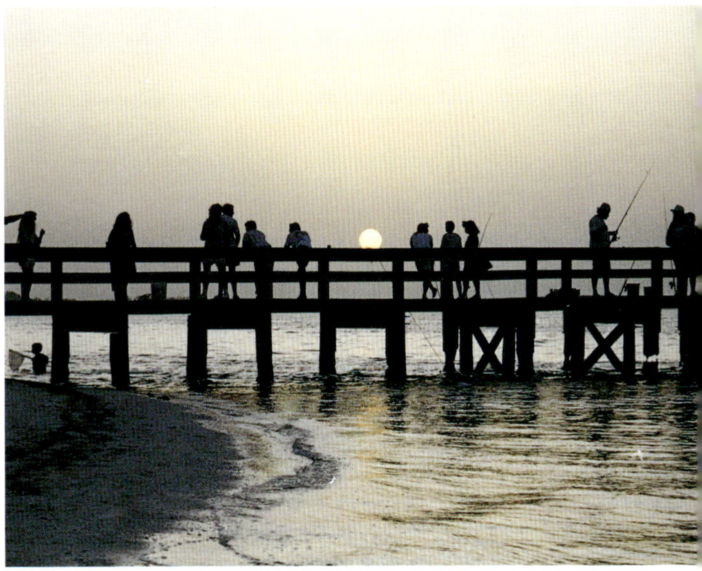

Girl with pigeons and silhouettes

I have chosen these two pictures (left and above) to illustrate the all round versatility of 400 ISO film. The little girl with the pigeons is a typical reportage picture. It was shot on an overcast day but the film has produced a print of good quality and soft colour balance. The fast film enabled me to shoot action with the zoom at 70mm. Using a slower film I would have needed to use a wide-angle setting. If the sun had come out, the film would have coped well with that too. The evening silhouette was also shot on 400 ISO film, and has produced an excellent quality image at the end of the day in poor light conditions without flash.

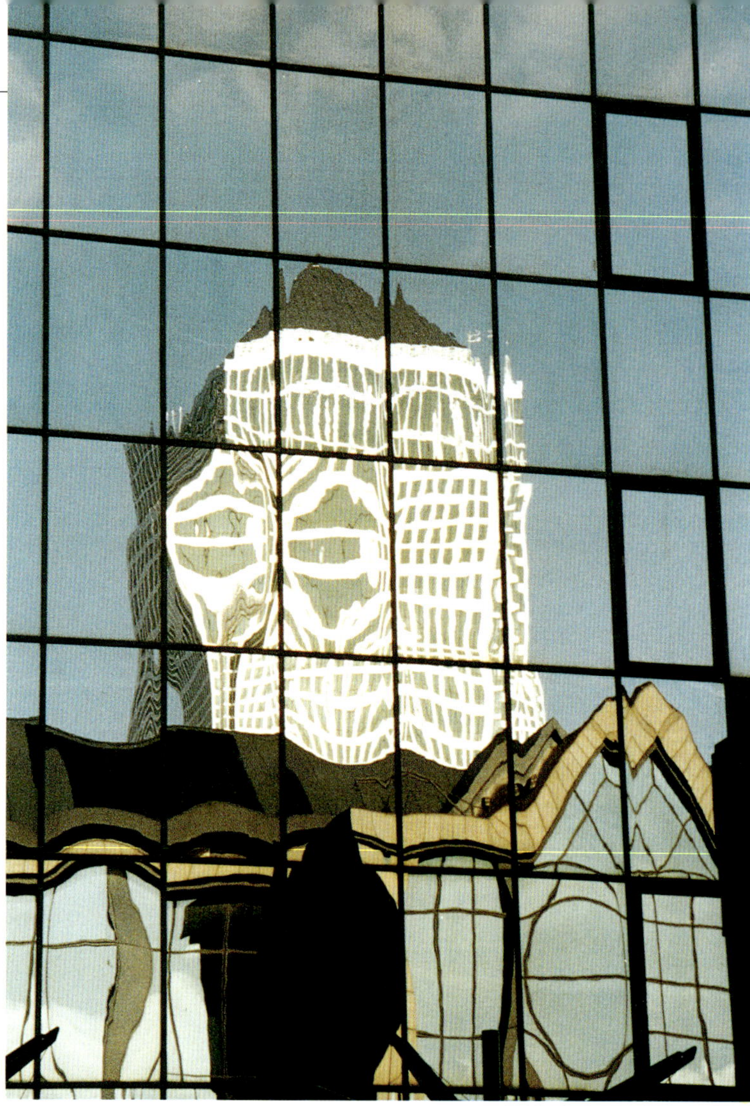

Dockland Reflections
The 1000 ISO films are very versatile indeed. In recent years the grain structure has become finer and the sharpness and colour balance have improved. They can be used for outdoor photography in normal light conditions and then on the same film you can shoot indoors using the available light. I had to check the negatives to be sure that this picture was indeed shot on 1000 ISO film because the quality is comparable to 400 ISO film of a few years back.

Little girl in chair
The contrast in this portrait shot on 1000 ISO film is softer than it would have been on 400 ISO film and the texture is a little grainer, but I took this picture without flash or a tripod and that is very important to me.

Waiter
Don't just think of 1000 ISO film as an emergency film, to use when there is almost no light; use it as your normal indoor film as I have here. It is also effective with flash because you get a longer throw with the flash and a faster recycling time.

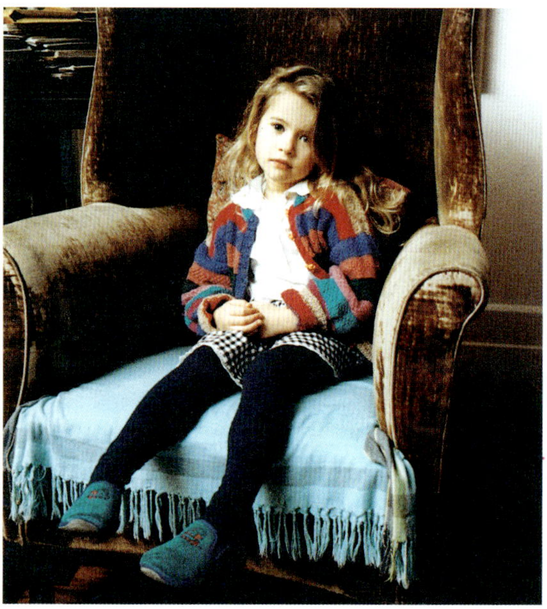

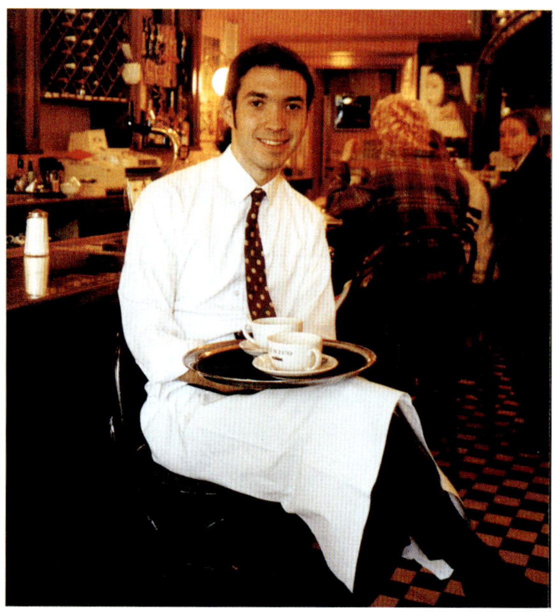

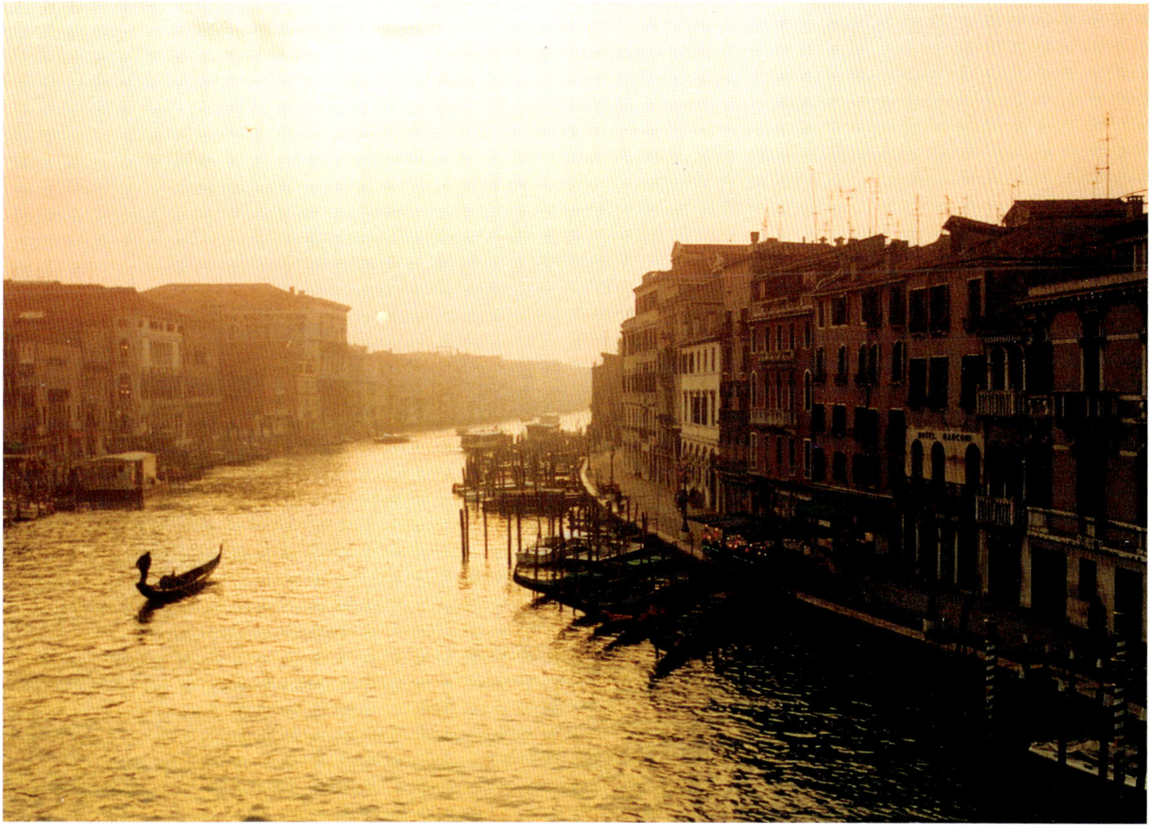

Grand Canal

I chose the ultra-fast 1600 not only because the light was low and, therefore, the shutter speed was slow, but for the effect. I like the soft colours produced by the 1600 ISO film in this picture and also the grainy texture adds an Old Master feeling to the picture.

Mother and Children

This ultra-fast (3200 ISO) film can produce images in very low light conditions but it is, as you can see, very grainy. This grainy effect is worth experimenting with for its creative possibilities. I prefer to use the 1600 ISO film in low light because it is less grainy and if you keep your zoom on a wide-angle setting (see How It Works, page 12), you can produce a good image in most indoor situations.

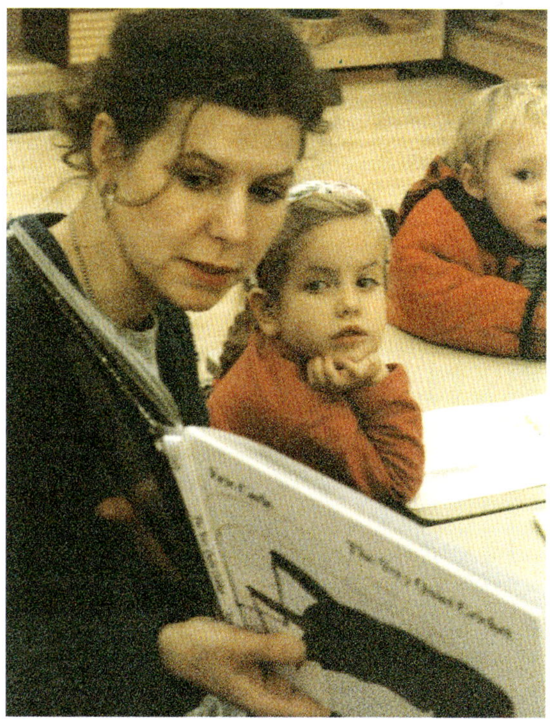

CHAPTER SIX

Framing and Composition

The most important aim to have when you compose a photograph is to keep it simple. What you leave out of the picture is just as important as what you leave in. This means you have to be constantly aware of what is in shot and make sure that you haven't included anything ugly or distracting in the background. Photography is as much about eliminating the unsightly as it is searching for beauty.

Remember too when composing a shot that we have a frame 36 x 24mm which we can use either horizontally or vertically. Look at your subject both ways before shooting. It is so easy to go with the horizontal format, whereas the vertical format may be more appropriate.

Lenses too can have an enormous effect on the composition of a shot. If your camera has a zoom lens, look at the picture at different zoom settings so you can see how the different focal lengths alter the composition of a picture as you can see from the pictures of Westminster. You also have a choice of camera angle: the same shot can look entirely different from a low angle to a high, overhead angle. Don't just put the camera to your eye and shoot. Take time framing your subject (if that is possible) and teach yourself to really look at everything by moving the camera round, to the left, right, up and down. Photography is all about seeing things with a fresh, clear vision.

The next step is to look at the shapes and colours of your subject and to organize them within that 36 x 24mm format. Where you place them is dependent on the visual story you wish to tell. I hope the examples in this chapter will inspire you to try out new techniques – there are no rules, only tips and suggestions of different ways of looking at things. Every photographer composes differently; your approach will be different to mine and is equally valid.

Filling the frame

The most common fault of inexperienced photographers is that they do not fill the viewfinder with the subject. The resulting pictures are therefore a disappointment because the subject fails to dominate the print.

The eye sees the little girl (below) as much bigger in the frame than she really is, hence the result. In the second shot (right), I made sure my subject filled the frame. So the first rule is to look carefully in the viewfinder to make sure your subject is large enough. I think it is a good idea to make the subject bigger in the viewfinder than actually feels comfortable.

A zoom is very useful for close cropping, but if you don't have one, remember that your legs will work just as well. Both pictures were shot on 200 ISO film with the zoom set at approximately 80mm.

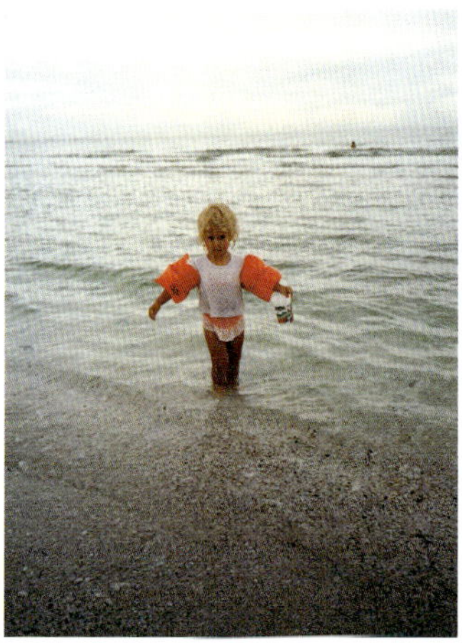

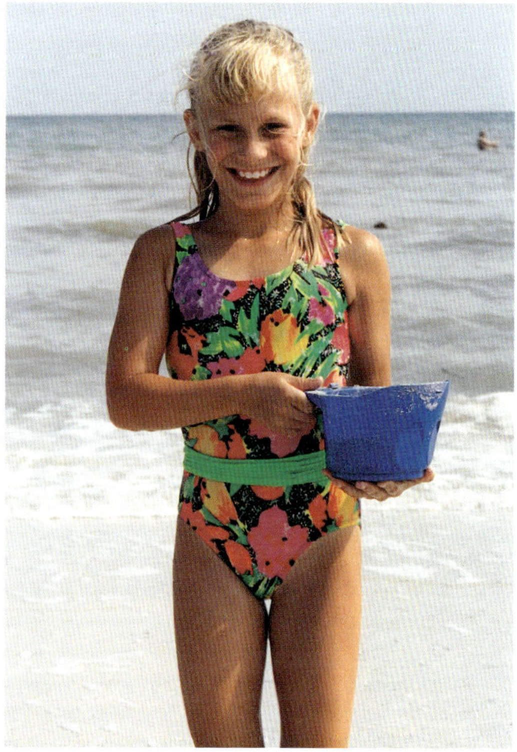

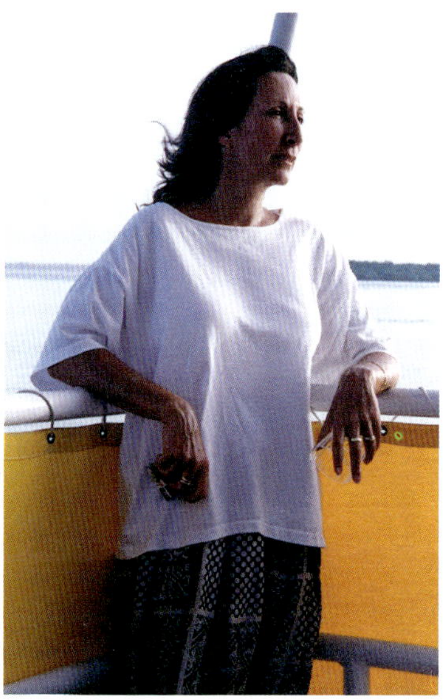

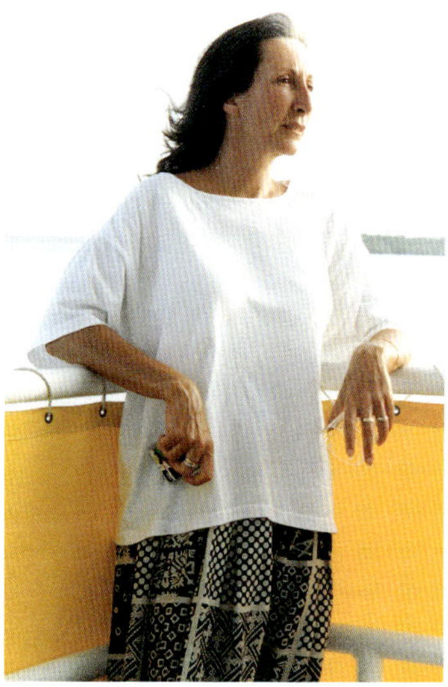

Removing rubbish

A photographer should always be aware of exactly what is going to appear in the final picture and make sure that any ugly or distracting objects are removed. However, sometimes we forget, as in this portrait of my wife Michelle, where it looks as if a pole is growing out of the top of her head. I had the pole removed (retouching, not surgical) just to show how much better it looks. I wish I had asked Michelle to move along slightly before I took the picture.

Format: horizontal or vertical

The rectangular proportions of 35mm film means we have a choice of whether to hold the camera vertically or horizontally. This can have an enormous effect on the final composition and yet it is surprising how often we automatically choose to take a horizontal or a vertical picture without even turning the camera around to look at the alternative.

I initially shot this picture of the gondolas and the church with the camera in the horizontal position (below). It was not a decision I made by choice, but an automatic response. I then took another shot using the vertical composition (right) and discovered that this framing gave a much simpler and effective image. Remember, the choice of format gives two dramatically different possibilities, so you have to make a creative decision for each picture.

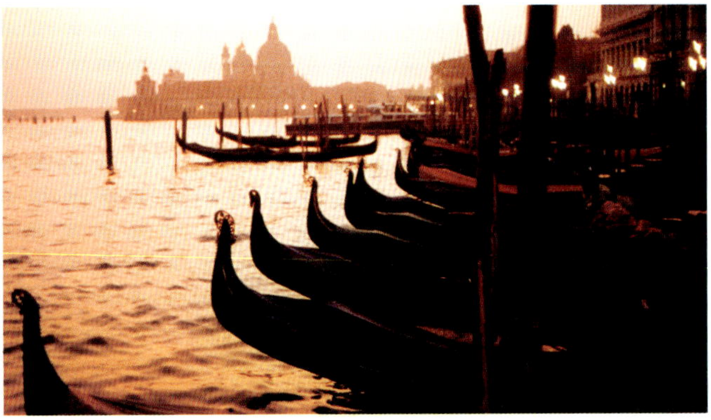

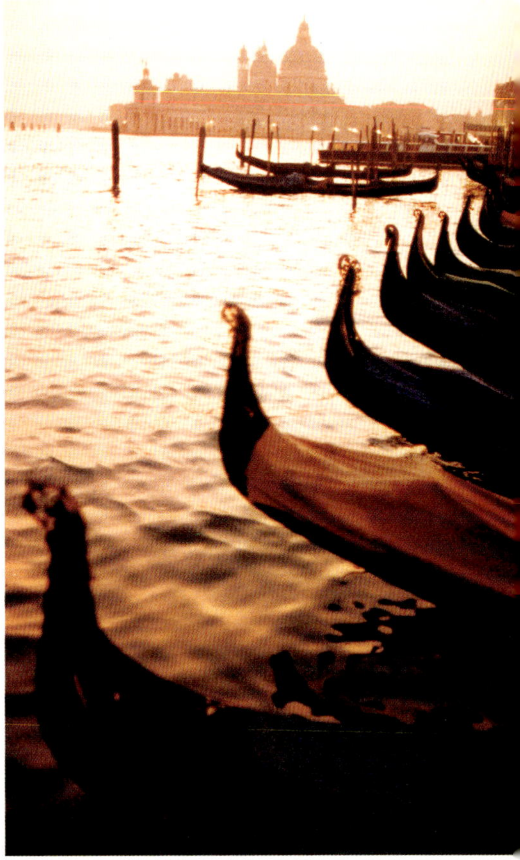

Lenses

The focal length of the lens affects the perspective of the picture (see How It Works page 17) and therefore the length of the lens used on the zoom has a significant influence on the composition of a photograph.

I set the lens on 32mm for this picture of a group of schoolboys (right), then I changed to 85mm for the shot below. (I had to move back several metres to keep the group roughly the same size as the first shot. You can see that Westminster is much larger in proportion to the boys in the second picture than it is in the first. The boys also appear to be closer together in the second shot, whereas in the first picture the emphasis is on the boys, with Westminster away in the background. Make sure you are aware of the compositional effect that each end of the zoom has on your picture before you push the button, it can change the story that the picture is telling.

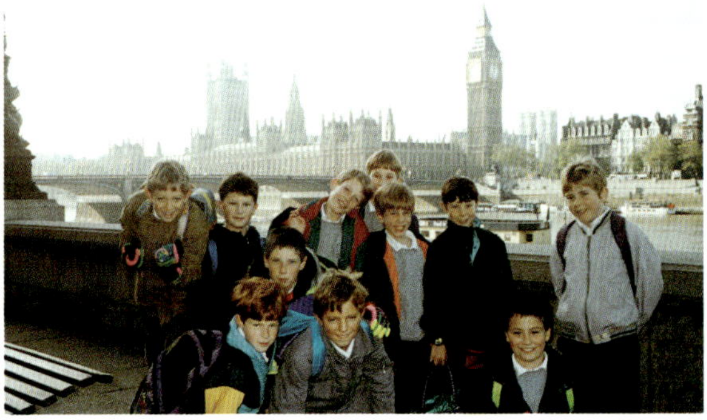

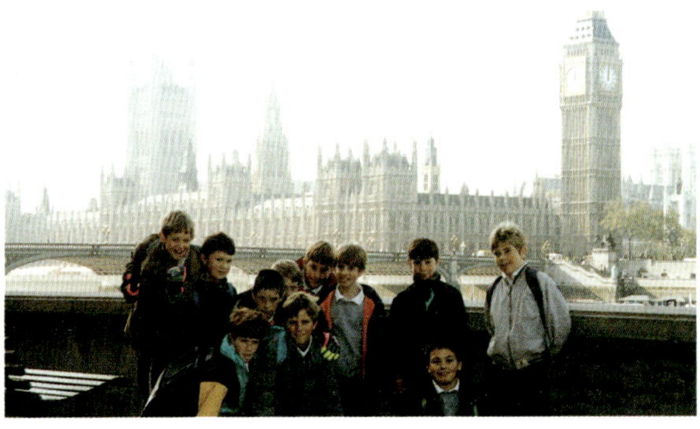

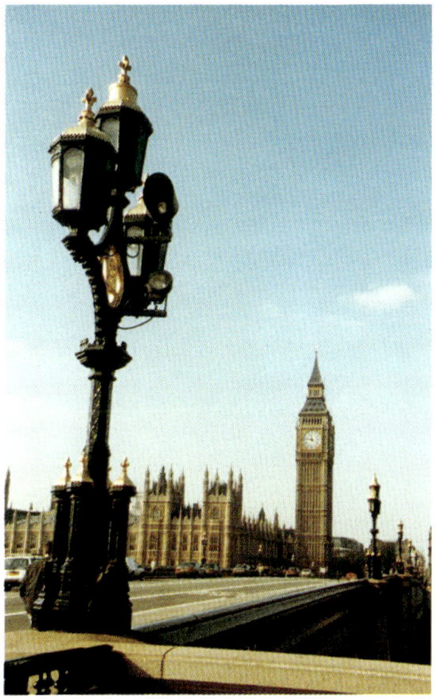

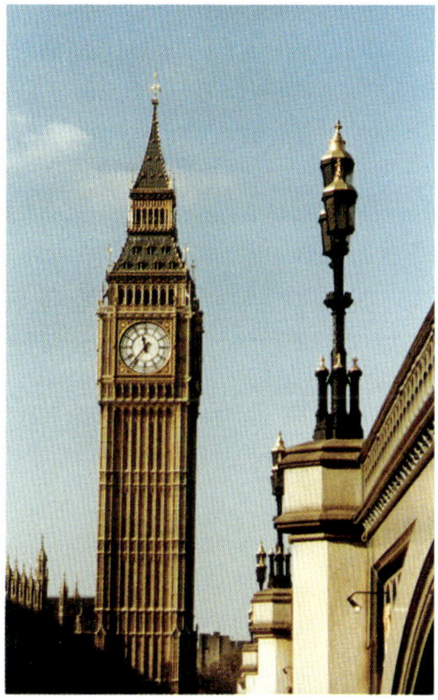

Lenses

This photograph (far left) was shot on a 28mm fixed-focal-length compact whereas the photograph (left) was shot on the 115mm end of a 38–115mm zoom. They were taken from different sides of the bridge, but equal distances away from the Houses of Parliament.

The different focal lengths have produced dramatically different compositions because of the change in perspective they each give to the picture.

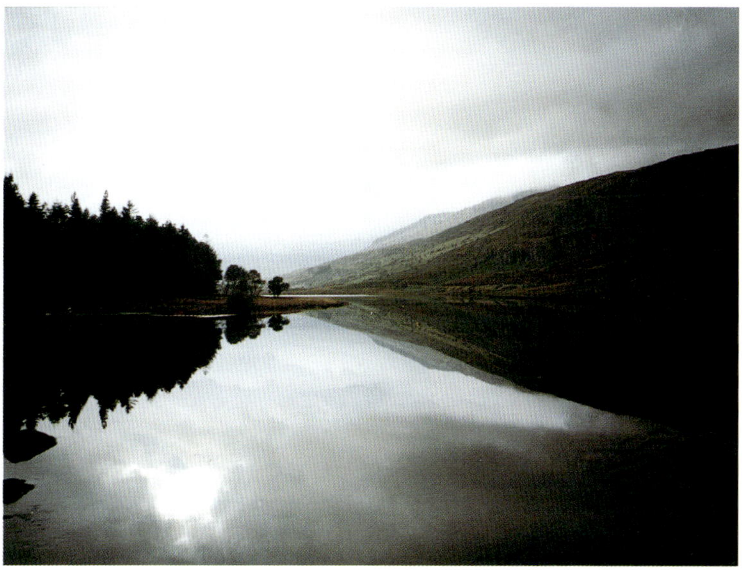

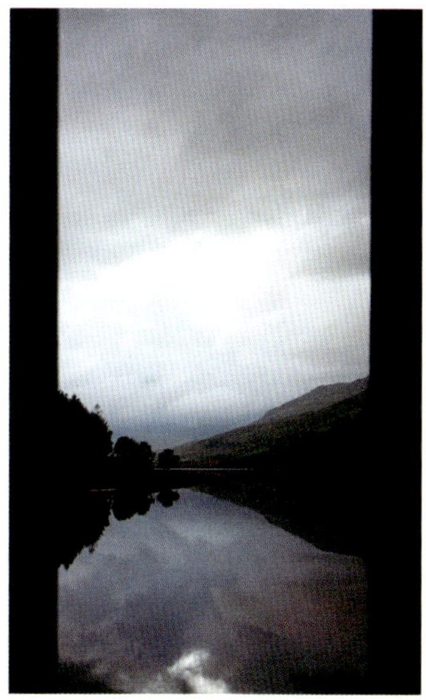

Panoramas

Many compacts now incorporate what they call a panorama format. This isn't a true panorama format but a masking system that cuts the top and bottom off the picture. It offers an interesting additional shape in which to compose pictures. This landscape picture was shot with normal framing (above left) while the pictures above right and right were shot using the panorama setting. Remember to switch this off once you have taken the picture – I forgot and messed up a whole set of pictures.

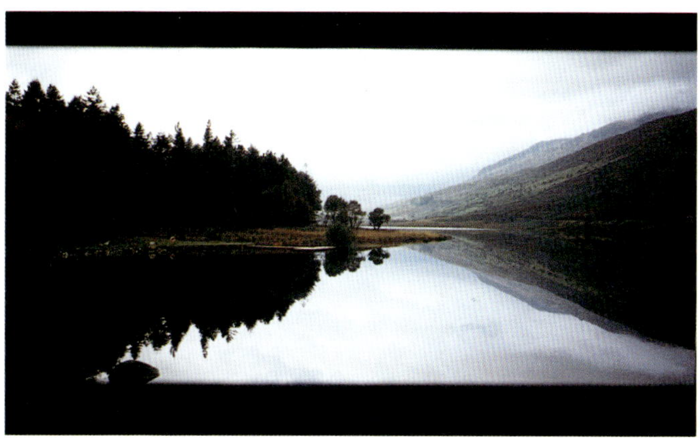

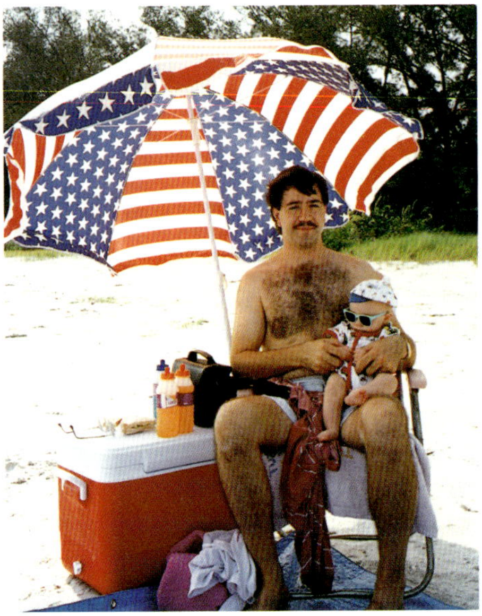

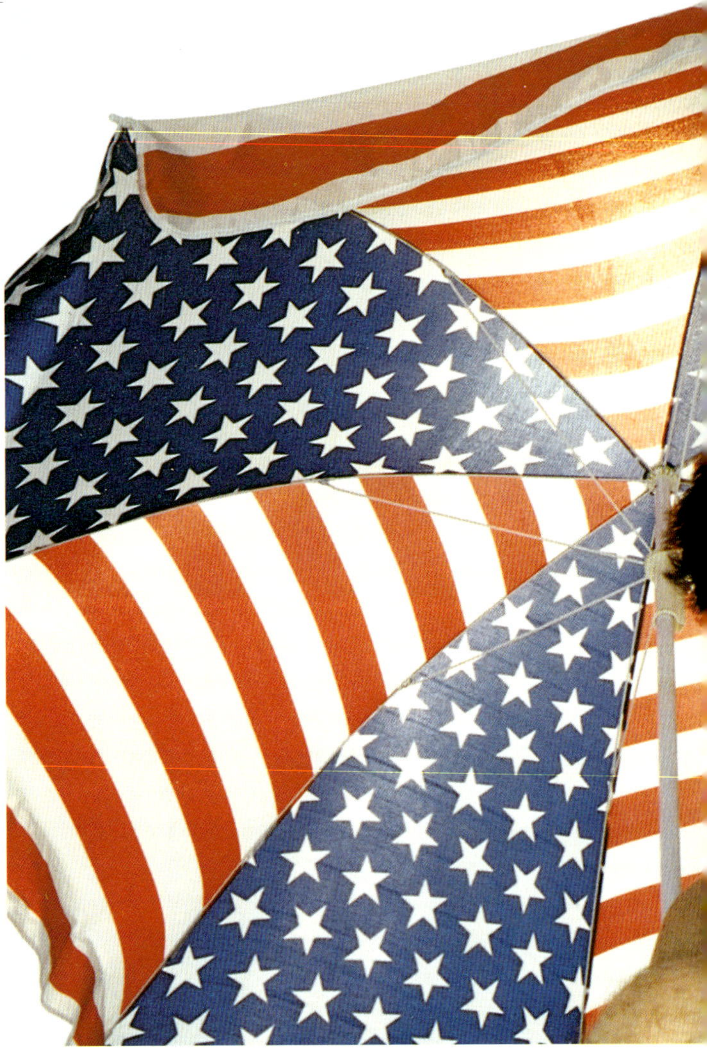

Camera angle

Interesting compositions usually result from the desire to be as descriptive as possible rather than from a burst of creative inspiration. My first interpretation of this father and son portrait was pleasant enough (above) but I wanted to frame the father and son inside the shape of the patriotic stars and stripes umbrella. To achieve my final composition (right), I had to lie down and shoot up towards my subjects. The low angle made a more dramatic picture as well as a more descriptive one. Note that I have used a flash fill-in (see Flash, page 26) to get light into the faces.

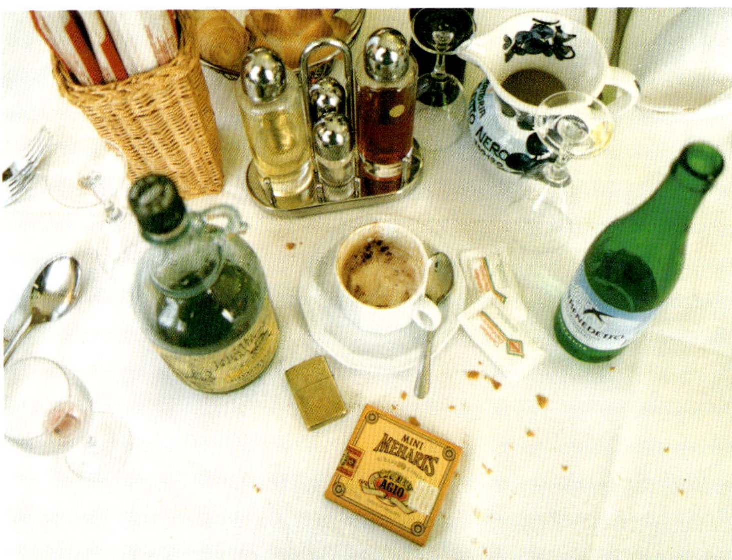

Different viewpoint

Whenever you feel that your composition is looking boring, try a complete change of camera angle. I had just finished a memorable meal in Burano and wanted to record the final scene. The composition from a sitting position looked uninspiring. The waiter loaned me a small box and I found that the high angle was graphically more interesting as all the shapes were clearly defined to give an image that summed up the end of the meal. High camera angles are useful if you wish to take in the whole of a scene, for example at a football match.

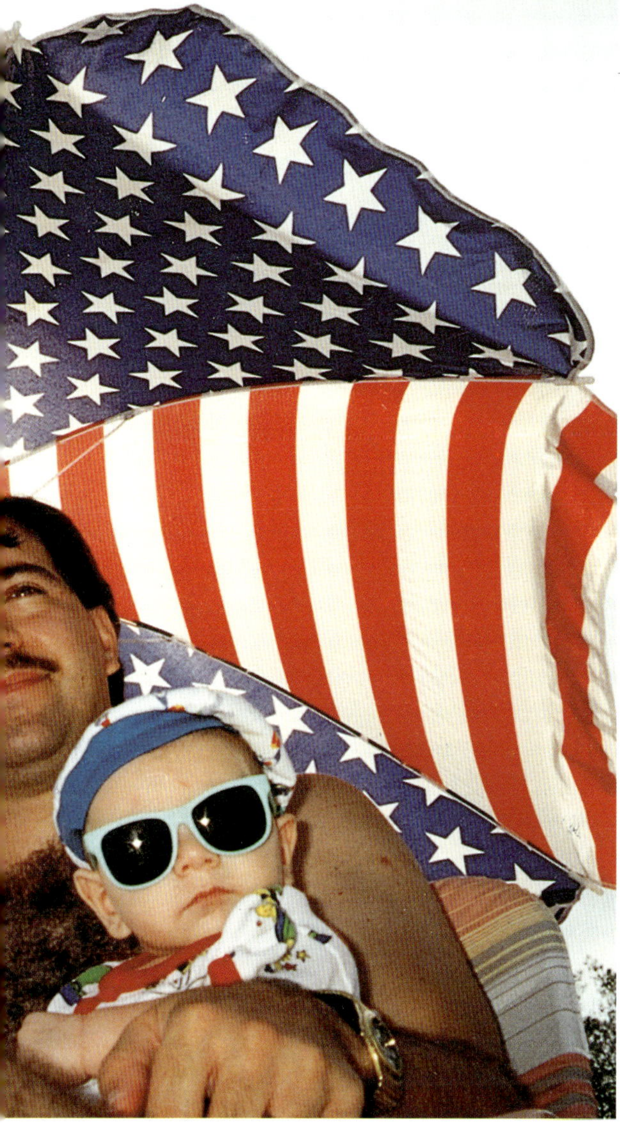

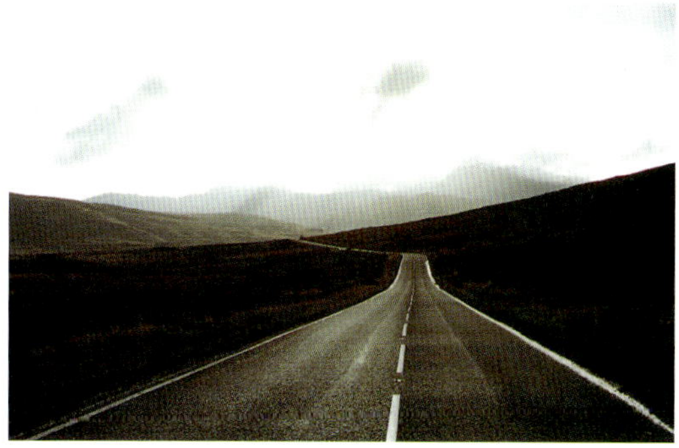

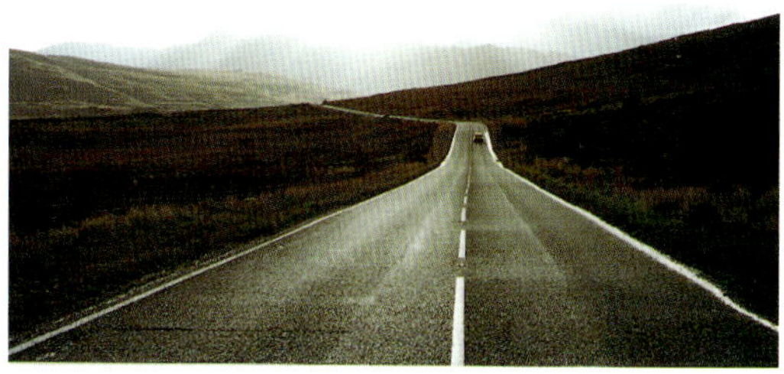

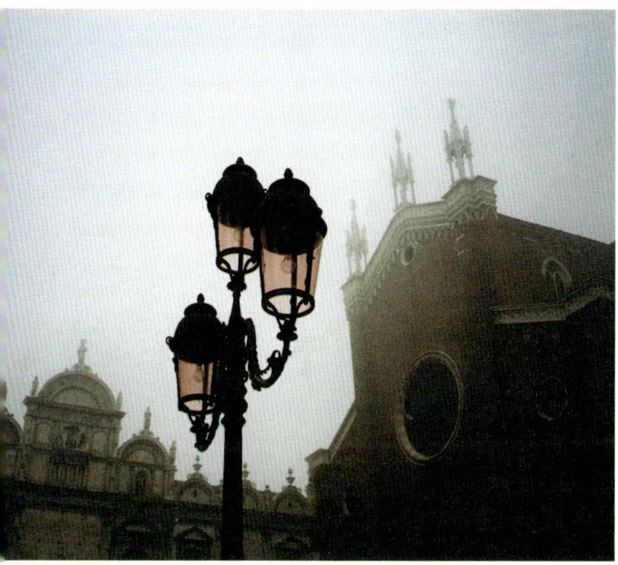

Focal Point

Pictures require a focal point to capture the viewer's attention and hold it in the frame. The problem with the composition in the first shot (top) is that there is no focal point and the eye moves along the road but sails off the end without stopping. In contrast, the eye is immediately drawn to the car in the shot (above) and as a result the viewer spends time observing the wet road and the desolate moorland.

I had to wait for quite some time before the car came into view but it was worth waiting for. This method of treating a composition and then waiting for a focal point to move into the space you have left for it is a tried and tested way of achieving excellent results. You need patience, however.

Frame within a frame

By moving around and organizing the shapes within the viewfinder, I have been able to frame the pink street lamps within the U shape of the church in the background. The shape of the lamp and the line of the roof are almost repeated and, therefore in harmony one within the other. The result is that the outline of the church holds the lamps in the picture. This creation of a frame within the frame of the viewfinder is often used by photographers and painters. Another common example is the house framed by the branches of a tree, which provides a protective safe feeling as a result of the composition.

Space

I left about the top one-third of this picture (right) empty. This gives the impression that the mother is lifting her baby up into the space and that I have caught her in the middle of an action. In the second shot (below), I have closed right in and the result is a static shot of a mother holding her baby. Space is used here to tell a story.

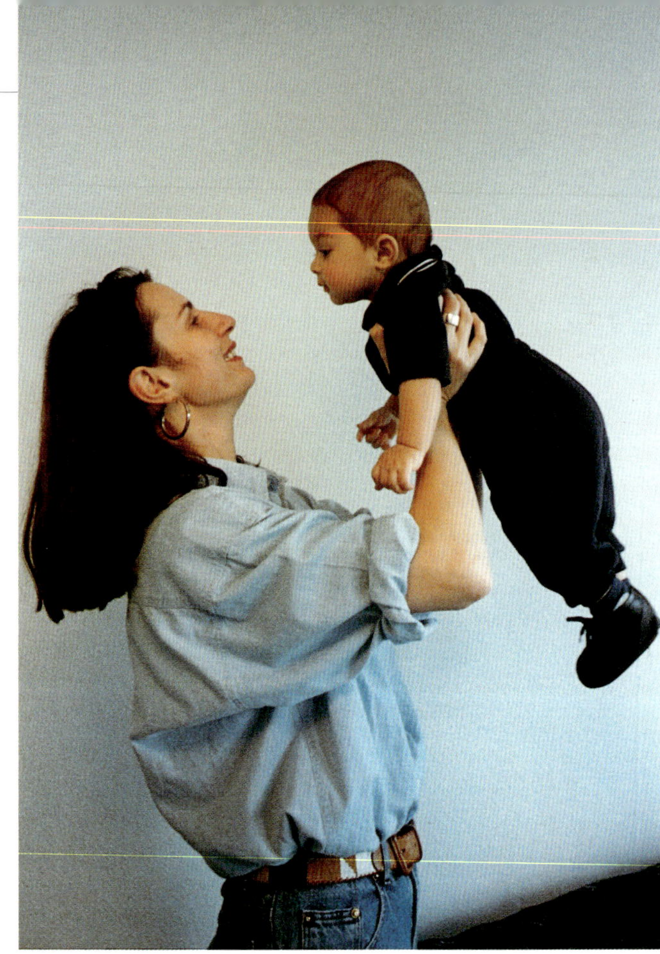

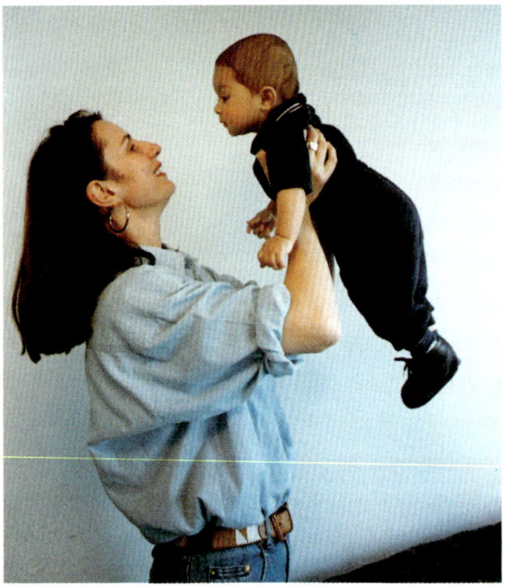

Originally I photographed this little chap (right) in the centre of the frame. I later discovered that when I masked off the space in front of the ball, it looked as though he was just about to catch it (below), and when I masked off the area behind him it looked as if the ball was running away from him (below right).

You make fascinating discoveries about the graphic tension within a photograph by masking off areas as I have done here. You can get a print made of the new composition by a lab that does printing by hand.

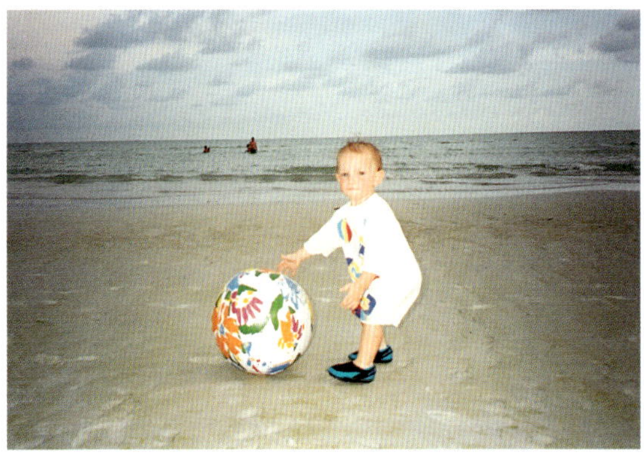

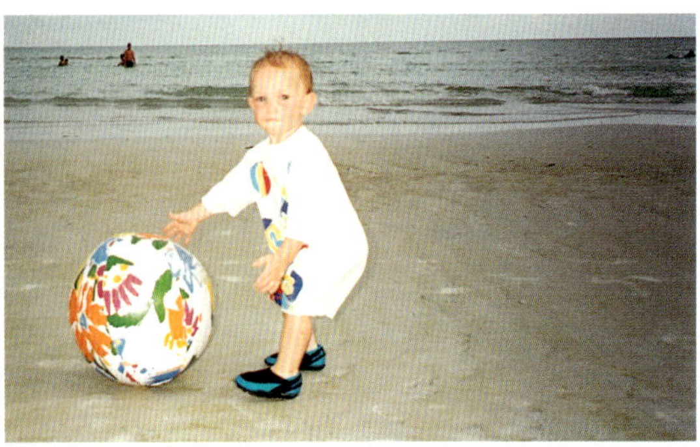

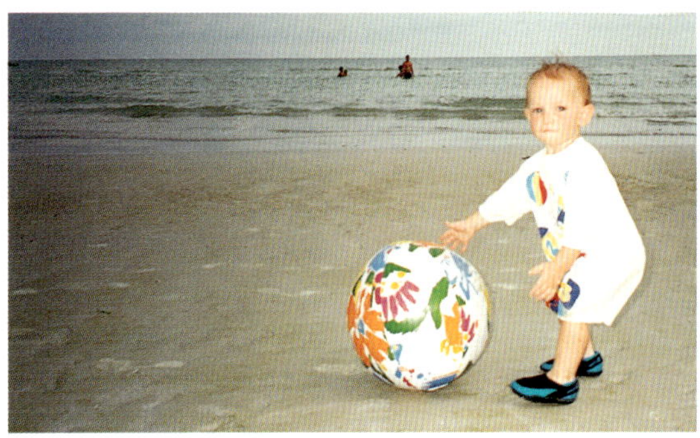

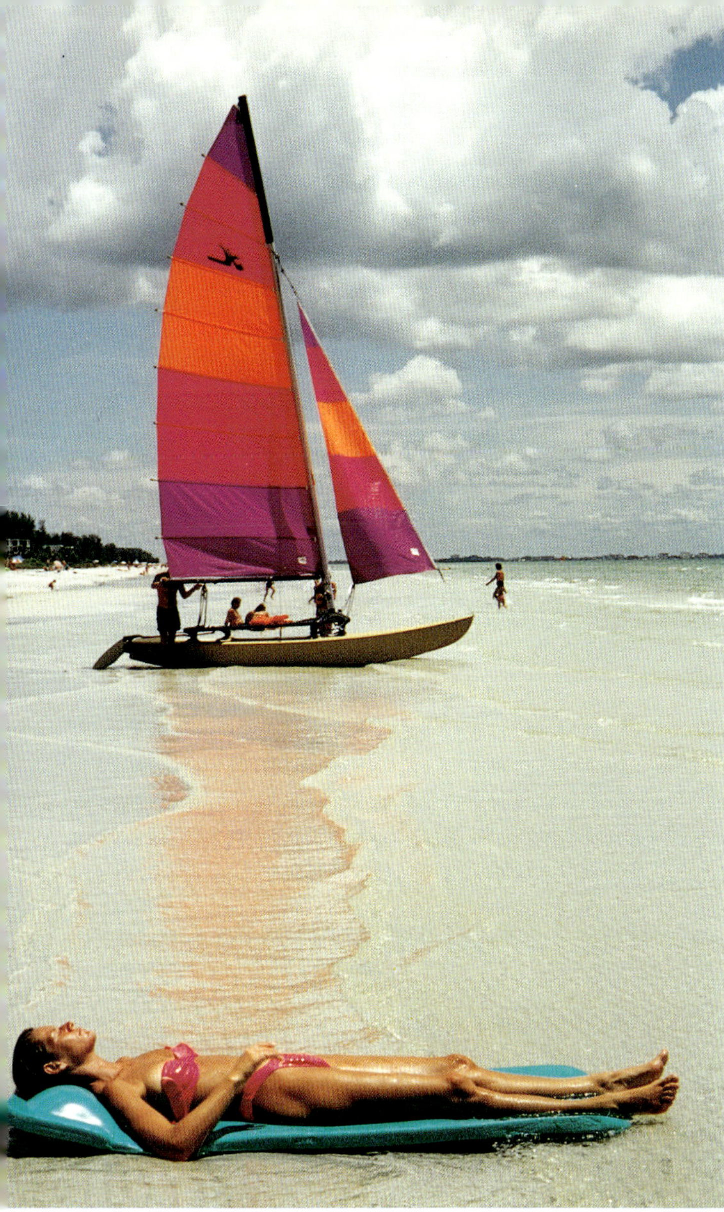

Life buoy

The red life buoy really zings out of the monochromatic, dark background to suggest a mood of danger. Although it is a good example of selecting colour to induce a mood, the reason it works so well is because of the absence of any other colours. Often what we leave out when composing a photograph is more important than what we select – especially in terms of colour.

• Shot on 1000 ISO film with the zoom at 50mm

Sunbather and yacht

This picture of the sunbather and the yacht should really be two separate pictures. However, they work together because the colour of the woman's bikini echoes those of the sails and the reflection of the sails link the two together. Try to view your subjects as coloured shapes that you are trying to arrange in the best way possible inside the viewfinder (usually by you moving the camera, not the subjects).

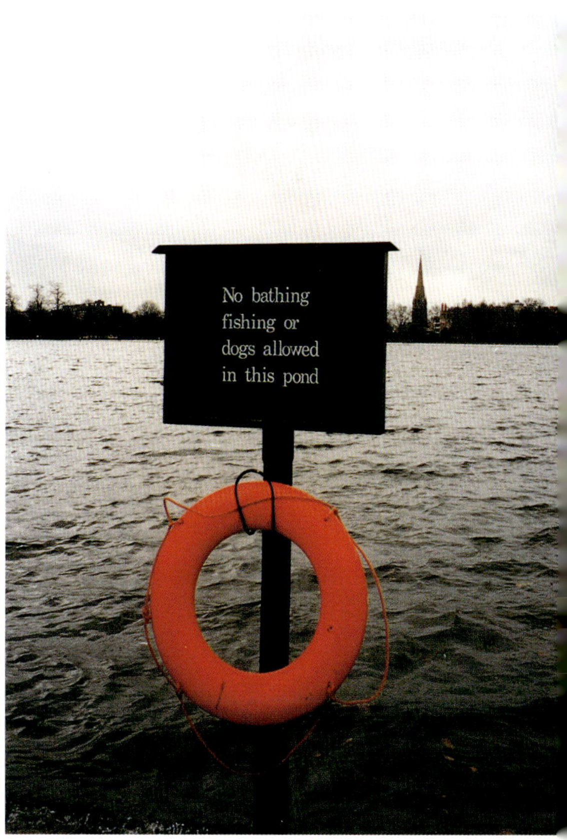

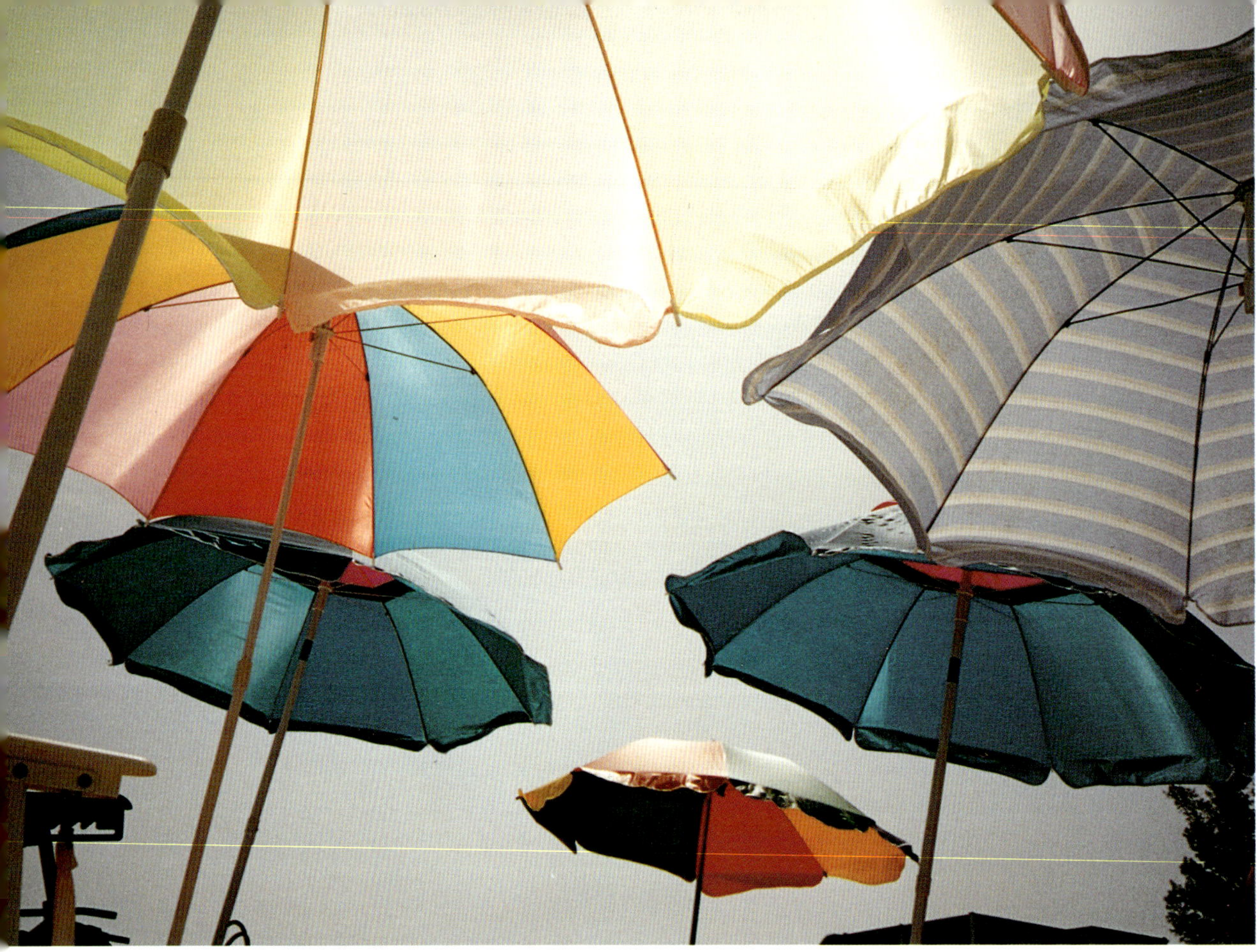

Composition, Colour and Pattern

The colours we select and how we organize them in the viewfinder profoundly affects the composition of the finished picture.

Colours are often used to convey emotions and moods and in everyday language we use phrases such as 'feeling blue', 'browned off', 'green with envy', 'a yellow streak', 'red-light district', 'black mood', and so on. Combinations of colour can create a variety of moods, for example, red and green vibrate when placed against each other to give an agitated, excited feel, while green and yellow combine to create a harmonious, more peaceful feeling. It is important to be aware when you are composing your picture that colours are not just pretty but can create strong feelings in the person looking at the picture.

We are surrounded by an infinite number and variety of patterns. Unlike a painter, the photographer does not have to create patterns but he does need to train the eye to select and discover the patterns already there. Training the eye in this way is crucial to successful photography, so take care to *look* carefully at whatever you are photographing. The photographs on this and the following pages illustrate the interesting and beautiful images that can be achieved when you concentrate on and emphasize colour and pattern.

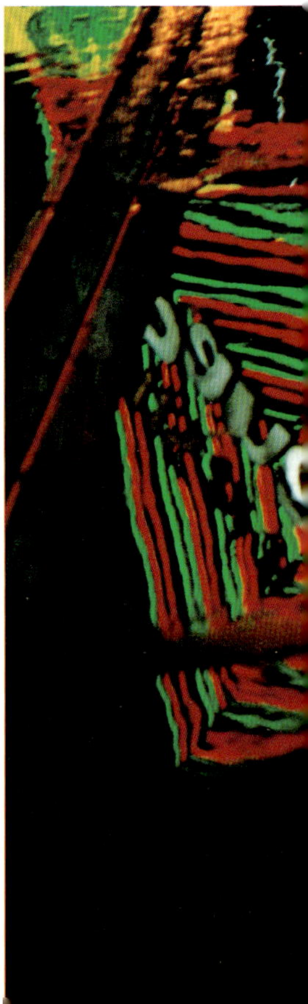

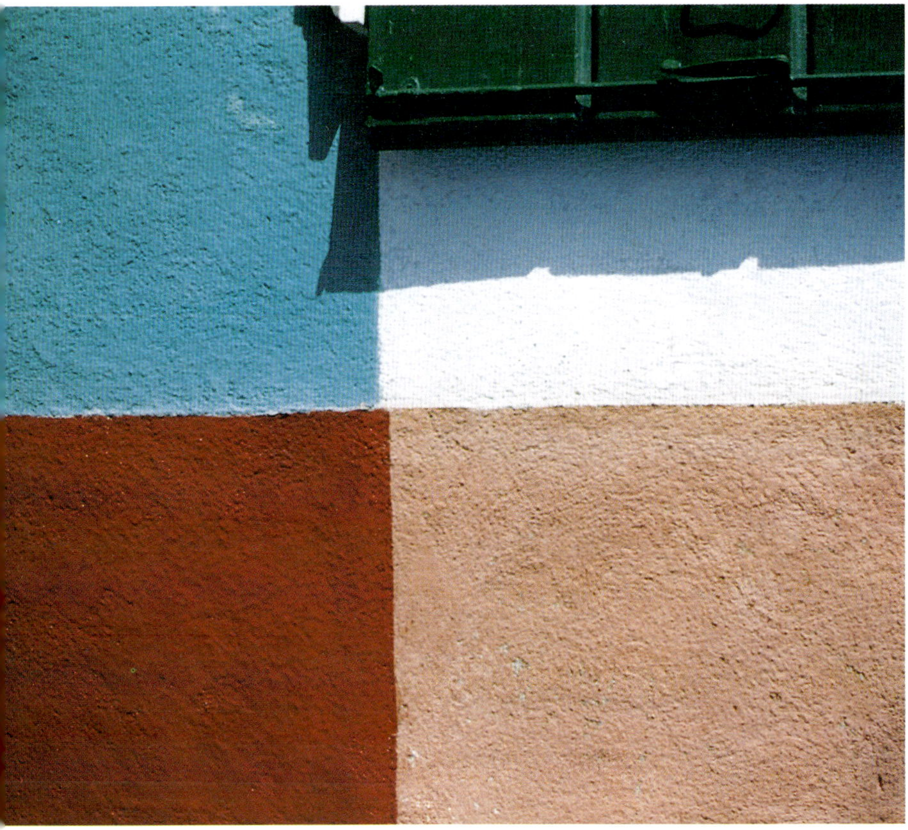

Beach umbrellas of Sanibel Island (opposite)

Burano wall (left)

Wet pavement, Piccadilly Circus (below)

Reflections of Burano (overleaf)

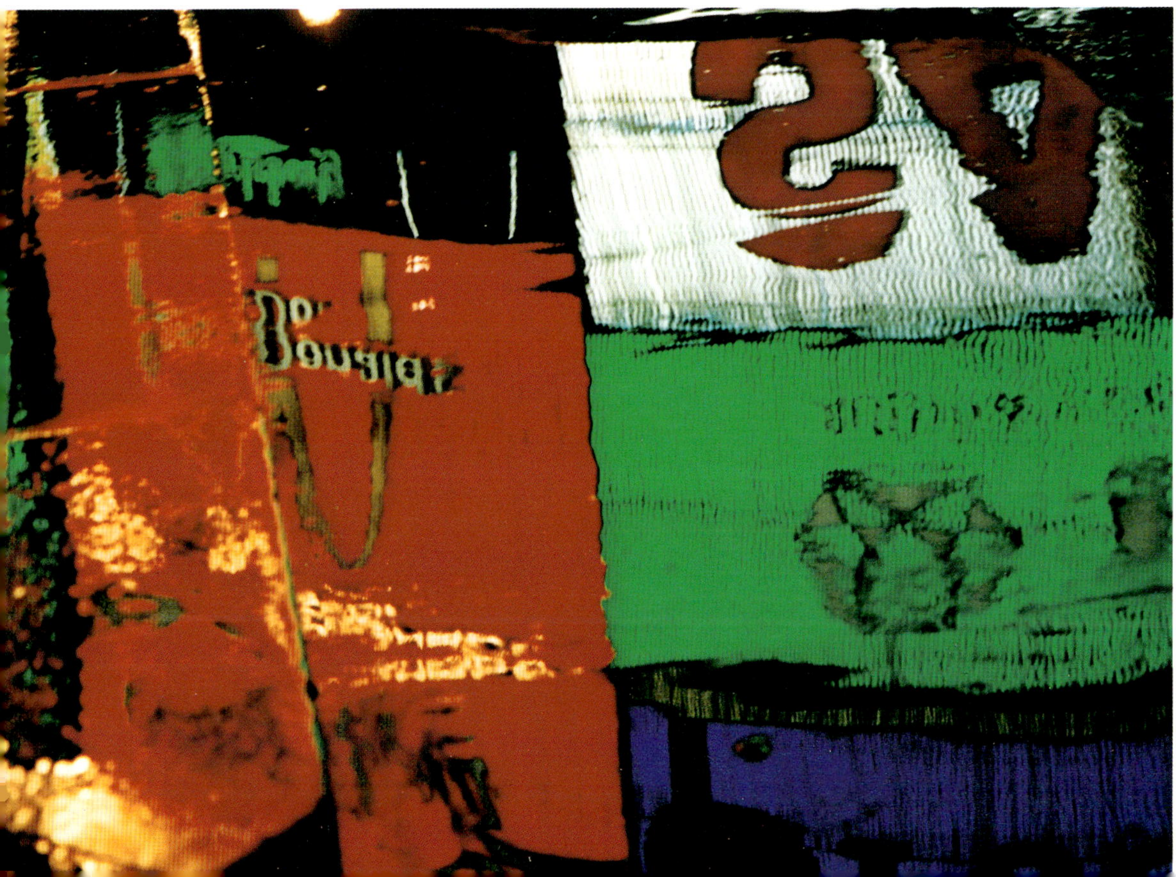

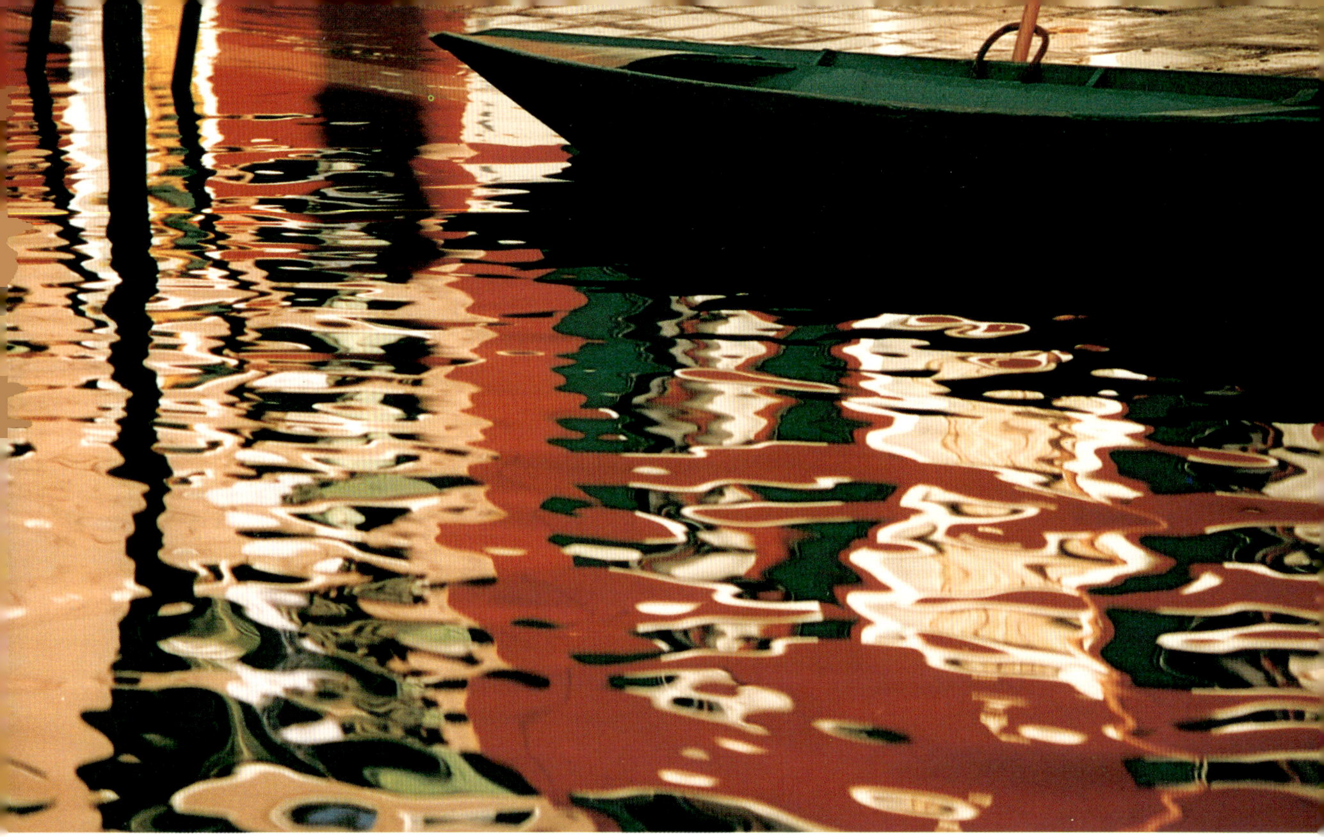

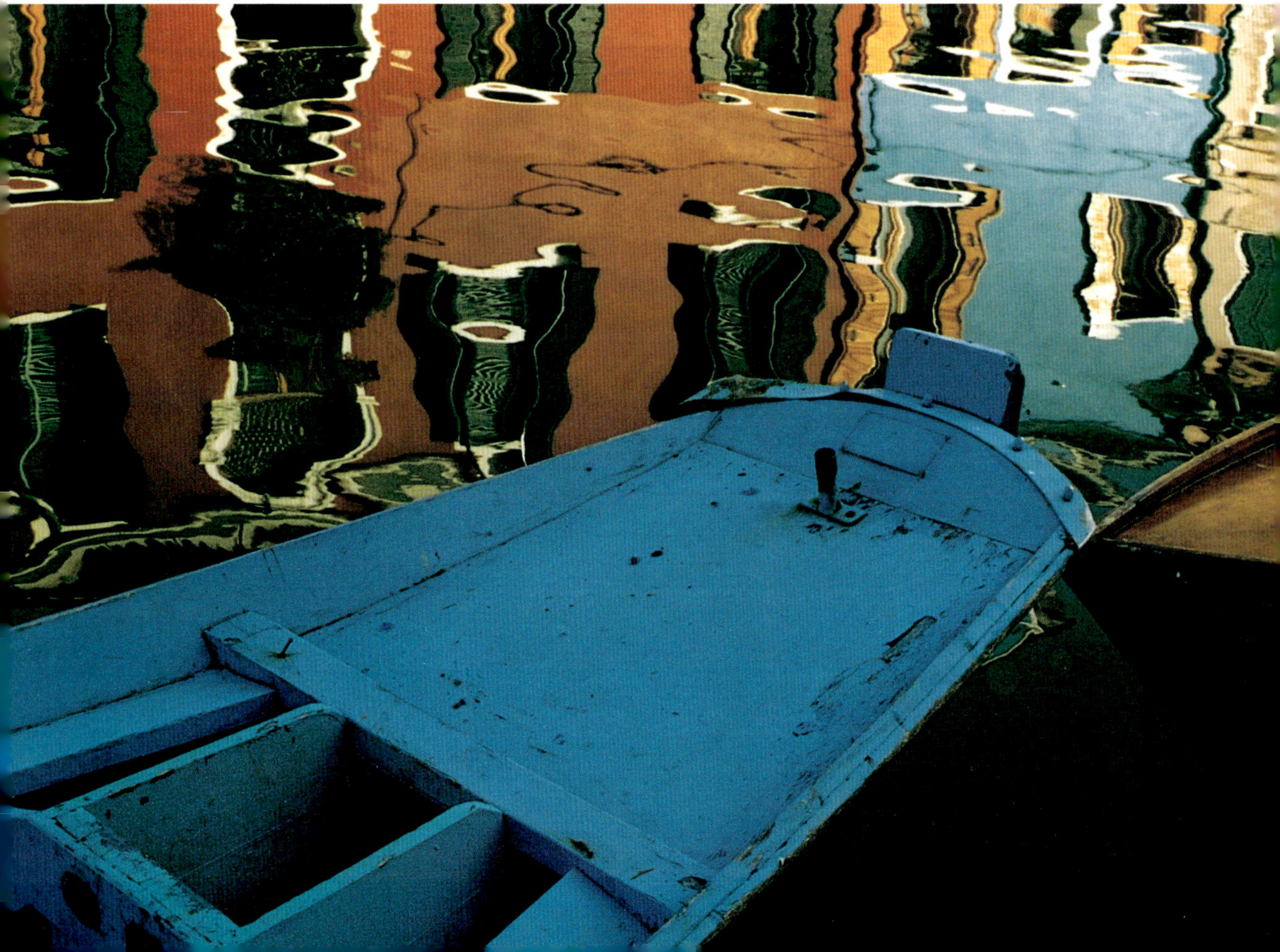

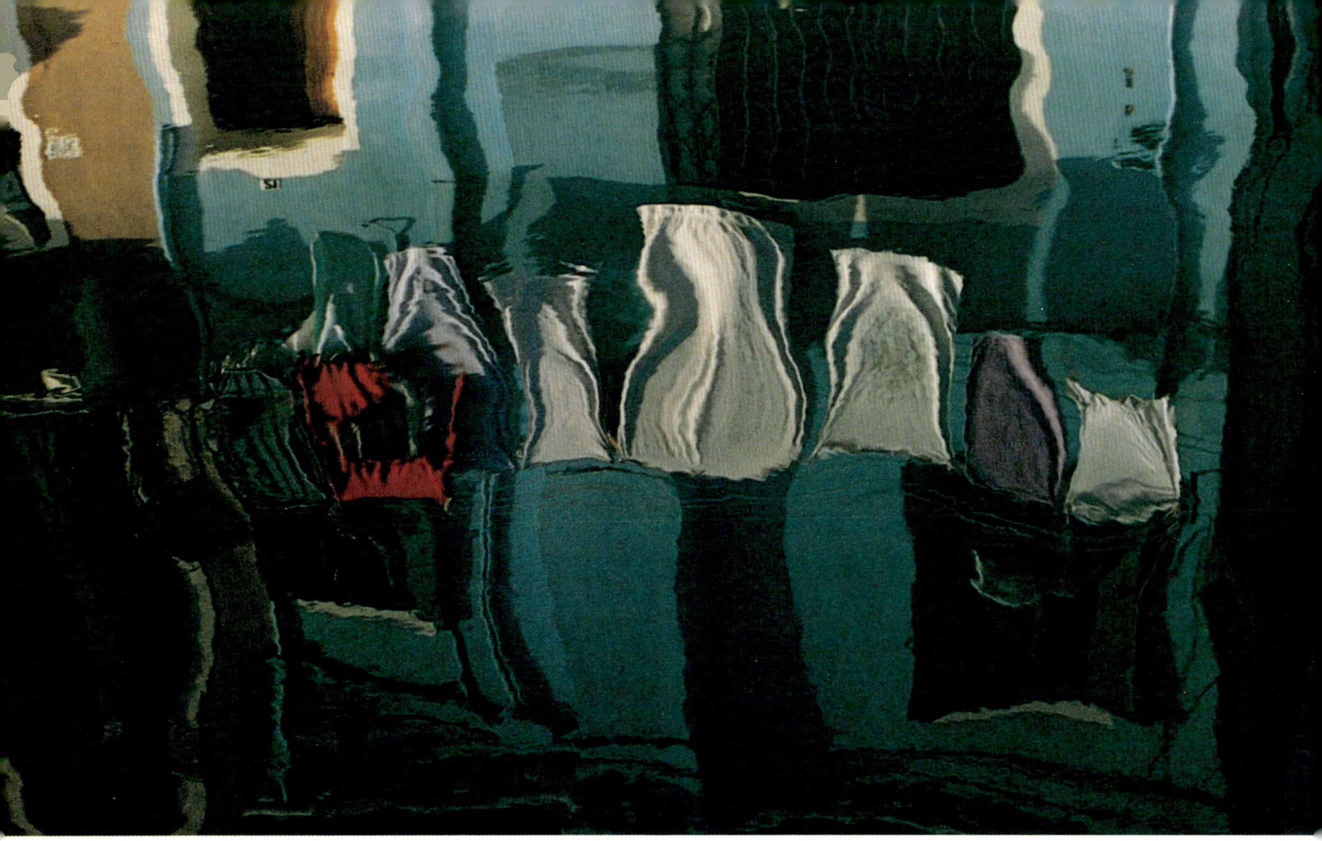

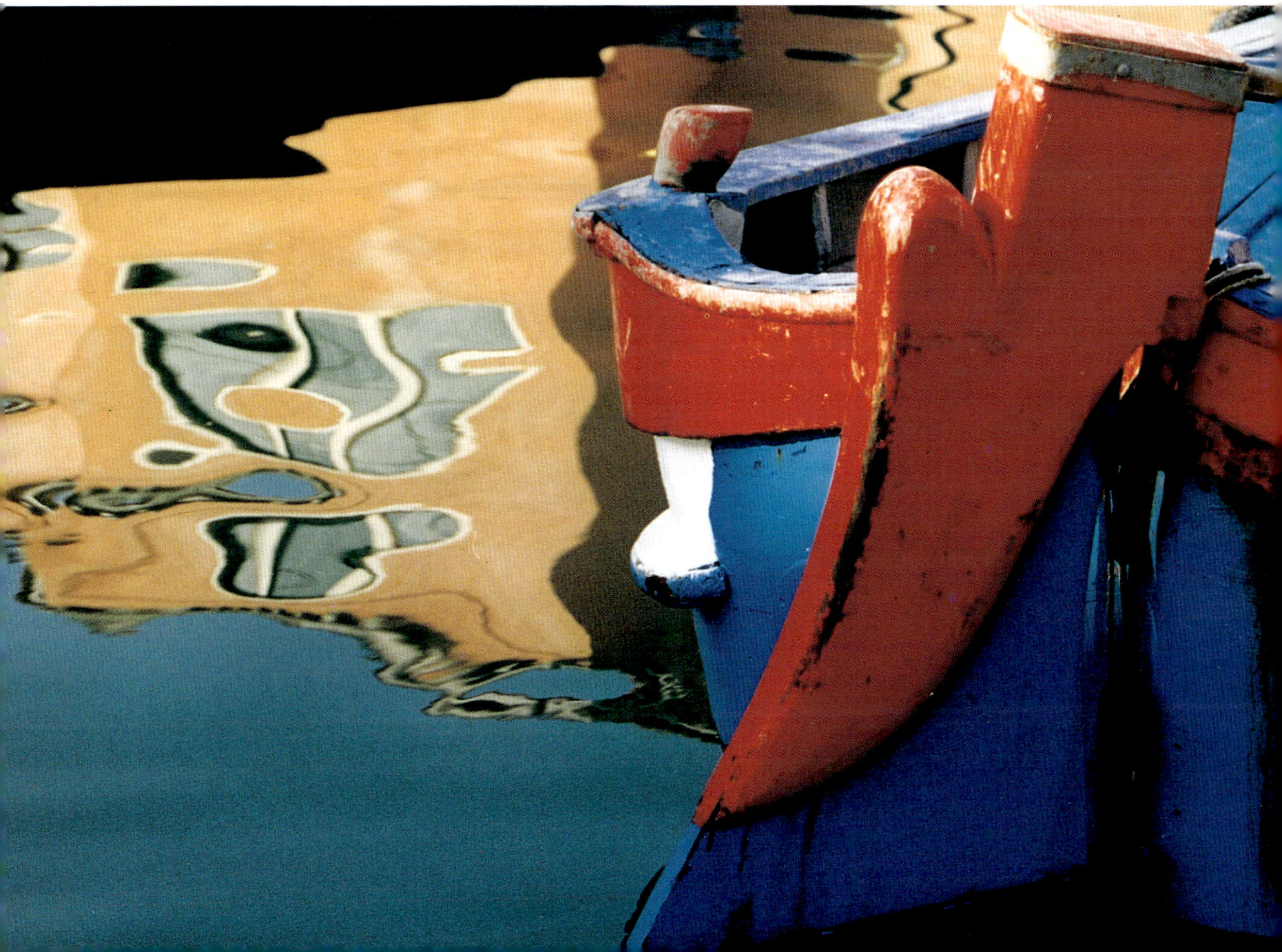

CHAPTER SEVEN

Light

If I were to describe photography in cooking terms, I would undoubtedly name light as the magic ingredient that transforms the mediocre into something magical. We all must have shared the experience of going out on an overcast day when everything looked drab and uninspiring, only to return a few hours later to find the scene transformed because the sun had come out: where before everything had looked flat and lifeless, light now streaked across the face of buildings and bounced off the road as if a team of painters had splashed the place with gold leaf.

One of the most important things for a photographer to learn is how this magic ingredient affects all aspects of what we see from perspective and mood to texture and colour. We have to learn to 'read' light and understand the effect it is going to have on the type of film we are using, the subject we are photographing and how, at different times of the day, the same picture can look completely different. Early morning light, for example, is sharp and clear although sometimes an early-morning mist can give a soft mysterious quality to a shot. The light is low in the sky and the way it picks out objects can be dramatic: a good light for landscape photography. By midday the light is much harsher, the sun has risen over-head, the shadows are short and dense. It is a difficult light for portraiture (see Flash, page 28) but it is good if you are looking for hard-edged shapes and dense colours. In the late-afternoon and evening, the light becomes softer again and the low angle gives more form and texture. The light levels can drop dramatically, however, to give large areas of deep shadow with no detail.

The direction of light is also important, as has been said, the harsh overhead light of the midday sun causes the face to be in shadow and a fill-in flash needs to be fired to give detail (see Flash, page 26). Side-lighting or 'crosslight' can give interesting shadow areas and drama while backlighting gives a flattering halo-effect.

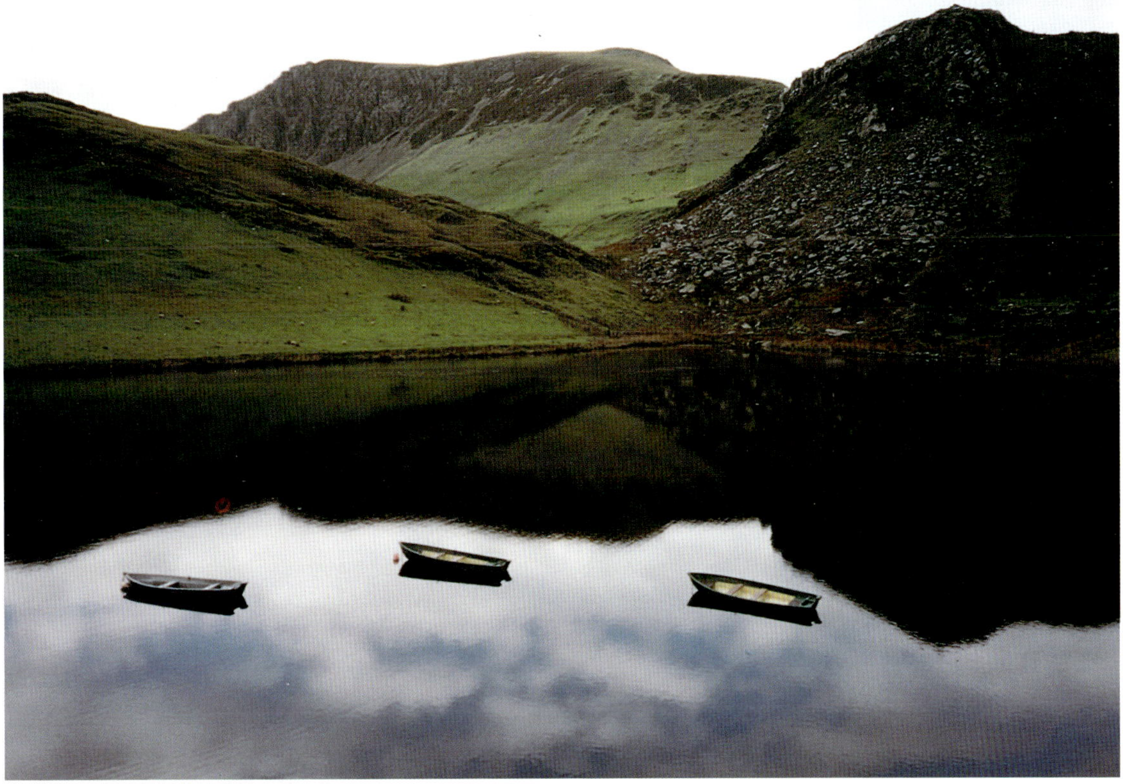

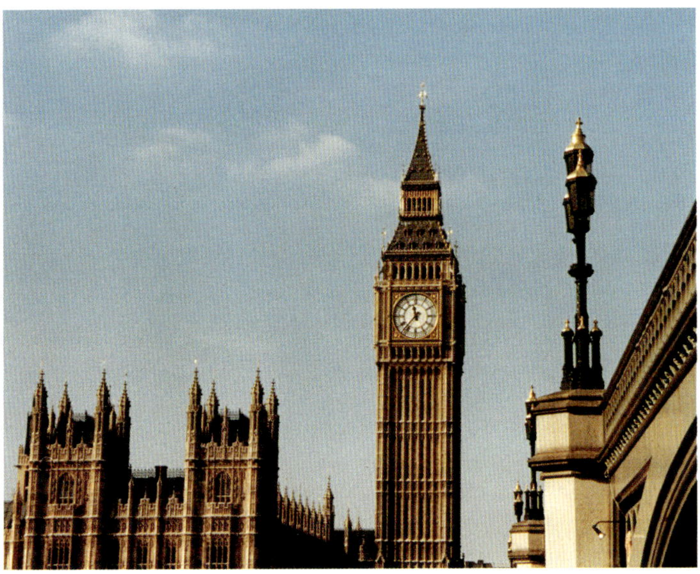

Early morning light: boats on the lake

Dawn, the sun had risen in the lowlands, but had not yet appeared over the mountains. The air was clean and sharp, and very still. Because the sun was still behind the hills there was no direct light and therefore no shadows which made it an ideal light for picking out texture and detail, as can be seen from the distant hill. To photograph in such low light conditions you either need very fast film or some sort of support for the camera to avoid camera shake. I rested mine on the top of a convenient rock.

• Shot on 200 ISO film with the zoom at 50mm.

Westminster

This shot was taken early one morning (about 7.30am) in late Summer. The light was clean as the city dust had not yet been stirred up by the traffic. The strong crosslight enabled me to bring out the texture and details on the building. Early morning conditions like this are ideal for photographing buildings and city skylines.

• Shot on 200 ISO film with the zoom at 60mm.

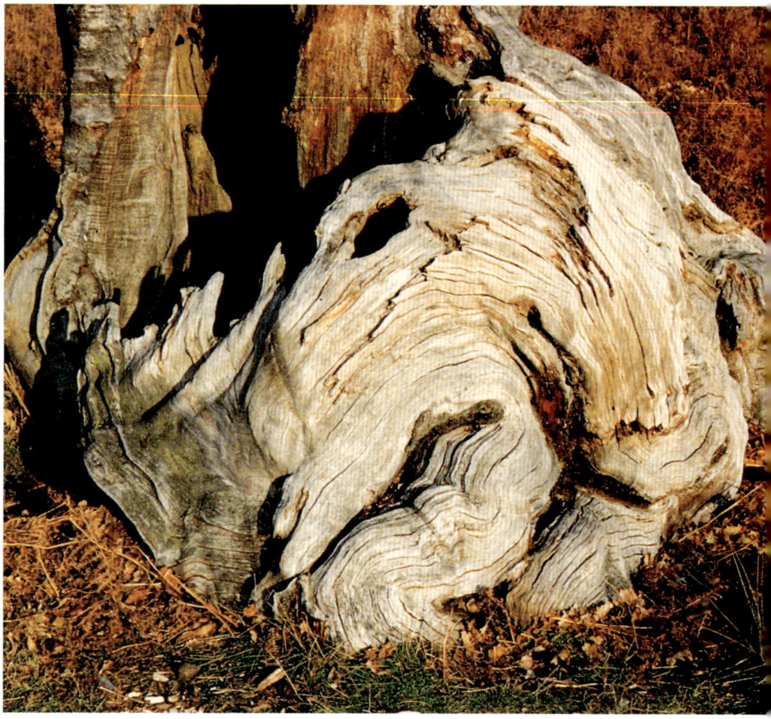

Late afternoon light: tree stump

This close-up was shot in the crosslight of the late afternoon sun, which has given it a warm, golden glow. It has also emphasized every grain of the old tree stump.

• Shot on 400 ISO film with the zoom at 50mm.

Midday: father and child

Midday on a Florida beach with the sun directly overhead. This is a difficult light for portraits (see Flash, page 28) and for any pictures which require detail. However, it can be most effective if you are looking for hard-edged shape and primary colours with high contrast between the highlight and shadow areas.

• Shot on 200 ISO film with the zoom at 80mm.

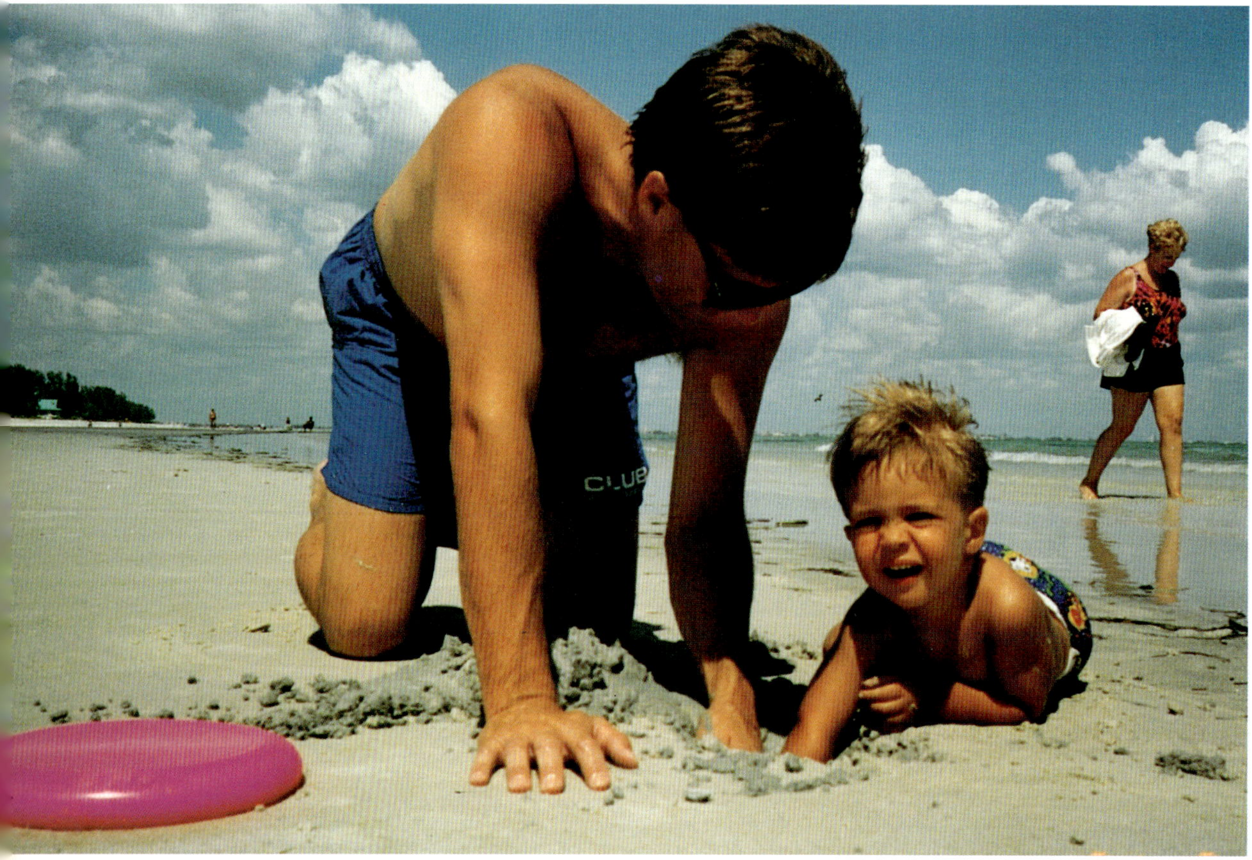

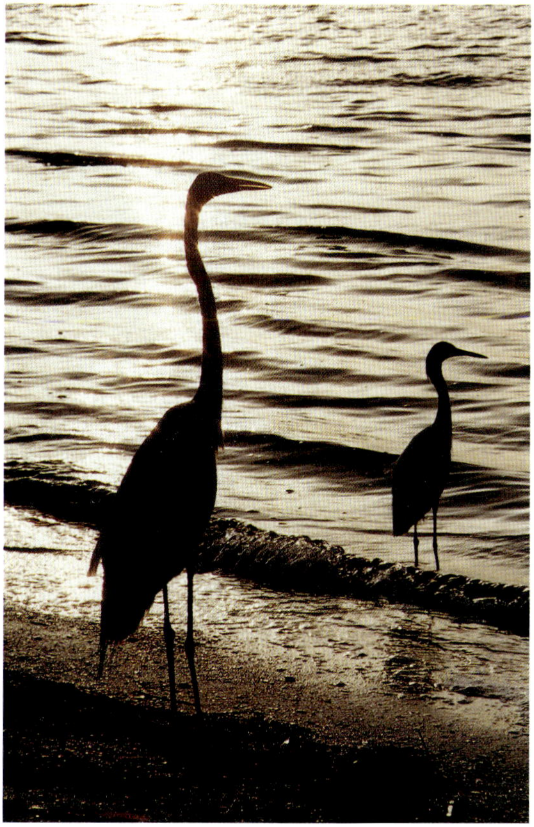

Birds on the seashore

You can also use the late afternoon sunlight as a backlight to create a near silhouette effect as I have done here. Make sure you turn off the flash otherwise it may fire a fill-in flash and destroy the silhouettes you were trying to create.

• Shot on 400 ISO film with the zoom at 50mm.

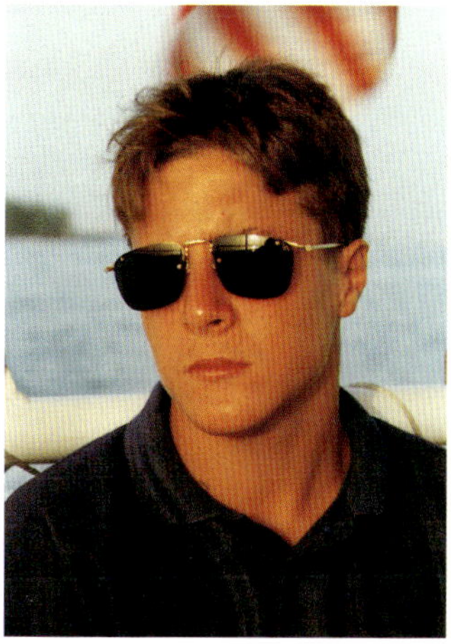

Young man in sunglasses

Late afternoon sunlight is great for portraits. The sun bouncing off the water has thrown a golden glow across my son Matt's face. The warm colours from this time of day flatter most subjects.

• Shot on 200 ISO film with the zoom at 105mm.

Backlight: Michelle in smoke

My wife Michelle was sweeping up the autumn leaves. The late afternoon sun created a dramatic backlight as it poured through the fencing and was diffused by smoke from the incinerator. It was the quality of the backlight that drew my attention to the scene; the same scene at midday would have had none of these qualities. I used a fill-in flash (see Flash page 26) to throw some light into the foreground shadow areas.

• Shot on 400 ISO film with the zoom at 35mm.

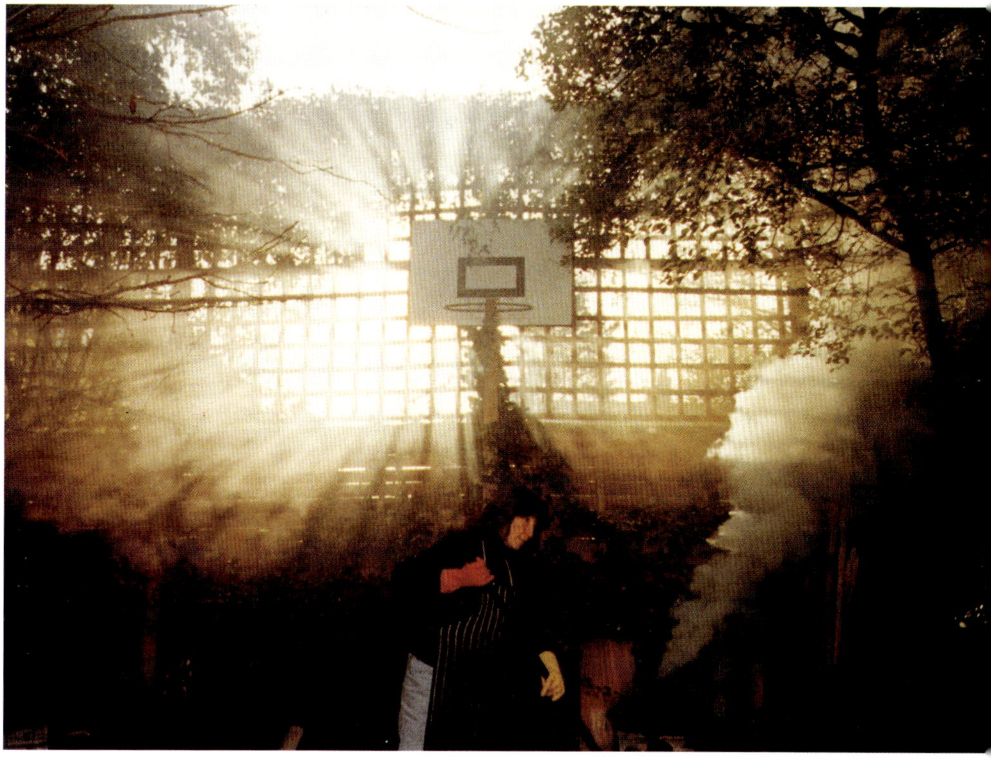

Light through a fence

The strong backlight shining through the fence created an interesting pattern down the side of Leryn's head, but it left most of her face in deep shadow. I didn't want to use fill-in flash as it would have killed the lighting pattern, so I bounced light back onto her face using a white reflector which I asked her to hold. With a reflector you can see exactly what effect it is creating, so I managed to achieve the perfect balance between light and pattern. You can make your own reflectors with white card or sheet (see Artificial Light and Reflectors, page 69).

• Shot on 200 ISO film with the zoom at 105mm.

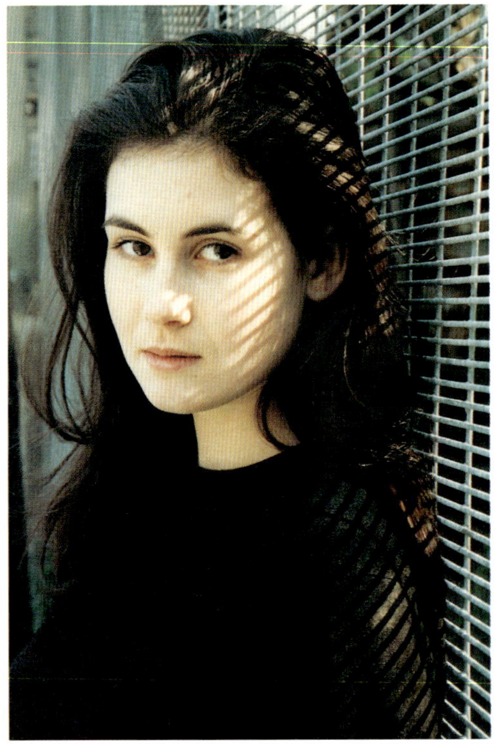

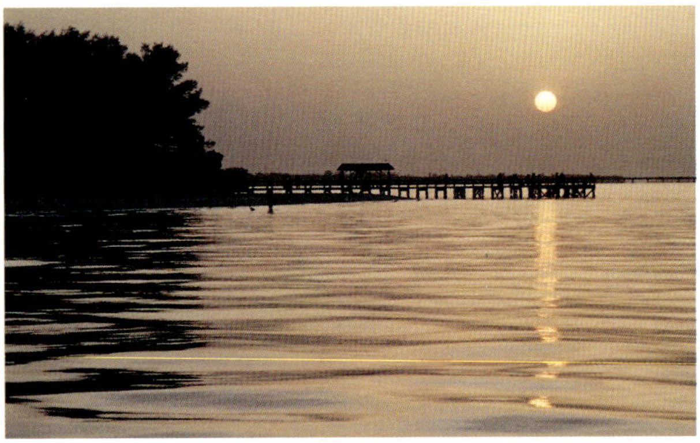

Florida sunset

Sunset is one of the most romantic of lights and I guess more pictures have been taken at this time than at any other. My only tip when photographing a sunset is to make sure there is a strong feature in the composition and, if by the water, try to capture the sun's reflection trail. Beware of pointing the camera directly at the sun, because you could pick up flare (see Problem Solving, page 77). Try to compose your shot with the sun left or right of the centre of the frame (see above).

• Shot on 400 ISO film with the zoom at 28 mm.

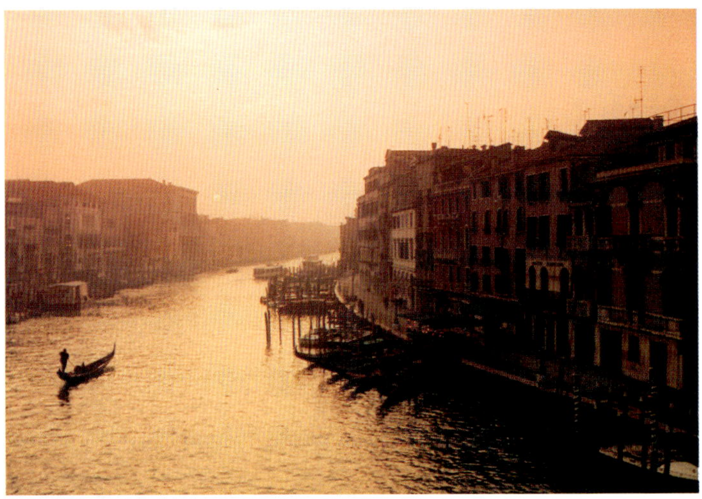

Dusk: Grand Canal

Dusk is one of my favourite times for taking pictures. After the sun has set there is an afterglow for about fifteen minutes. It is a magical time because there is still enough light, using a fast film, to take a picture without a flash; the colour from the sunset is lingering in the sky but the street lights have been turned on. I captured this shot during that time, so remember not to put your camera away too soon, but grasp the moment while you can, it doesn't last long.

• Shot on 1600 ISO film with the zoom at 32 mm.

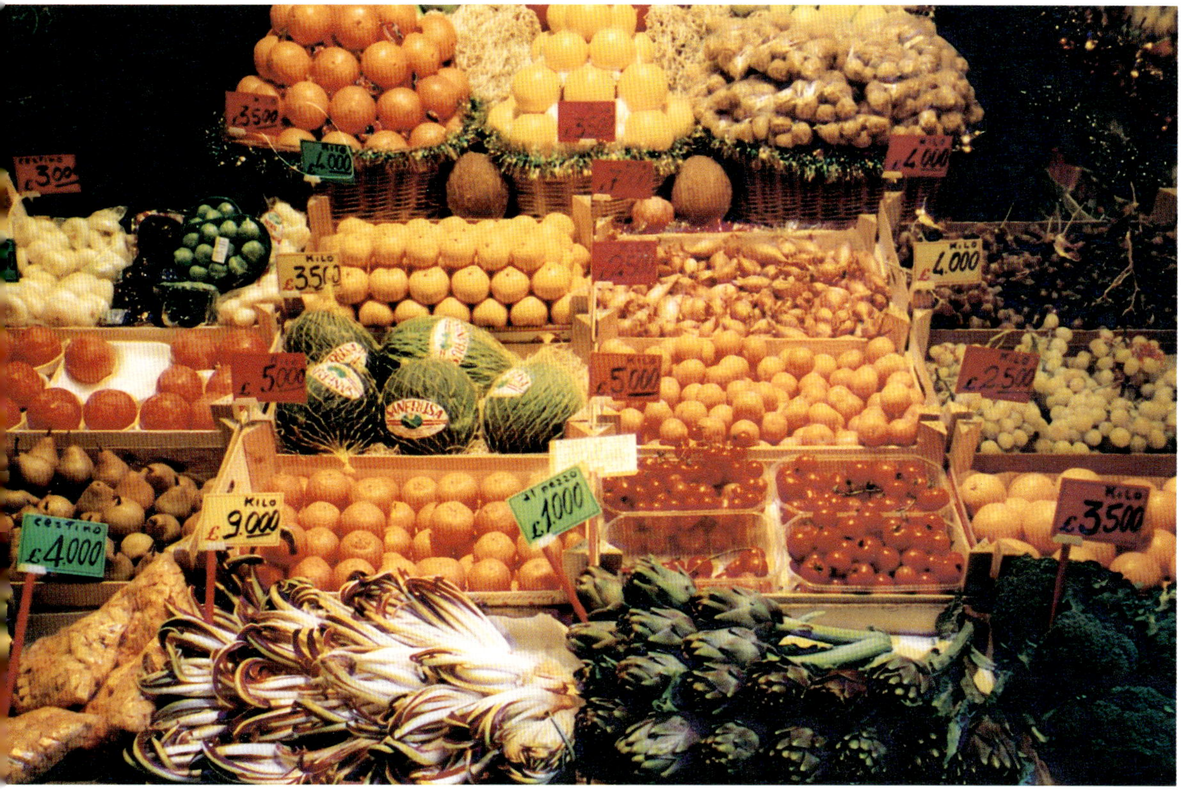

Fruit market

I took this first picture (right) as I entered the fruit and vegetable market in Venice; there was plenty of daylight and the colour balance is just right. However, as I went further into the market, the natural daylight was replaced by the market's artificial tungsten lighting and there is an orange cast over the whole picture (above). If you are shooting under artificial light then this unnatural colour can be avoided by placing a blue filter over the lens (see Using Filters, page 62).

• Both pictures were shot on 400 ISO film with the zoom at 32mm.

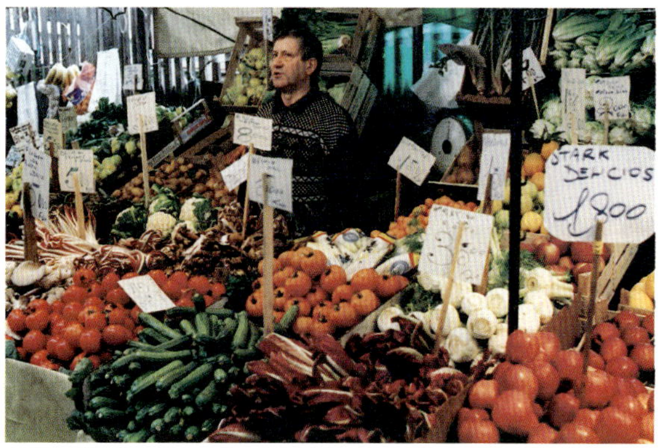

Window light: girl against wall

The light coming through a window is one of the most beautiful lights for portraiture as you can control it like an artificial light by using it as a side- or back-light and yet it is daylight. You can either use it direct as the sole light source or with a reflector to fill in the shadow areas. Make sure you turn off the flash (or cover it with your fingers, see Flash, page 25) and support the camera because, if the light is low, the camera will choose a slow shutter speed. This portrait was taken without a reflector.

• Shot on 400 ISO film with the zoom at 50mm

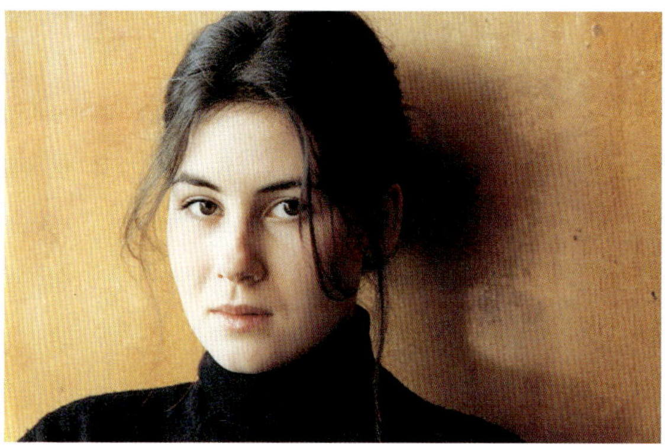

Umbrella in Hyde Park

This dark winter's day provided this stark photograph. Don't be put off by extremes of weather: I was dog walking in Hyde Park in the pouring rain when I took this picture. A plastic carrier bag with a hole in the bottom to push the lens through works fine to protect your camera from the rain. You can view through the open end.

- Shot on 1000 ISO film with the zoom at 32mm.

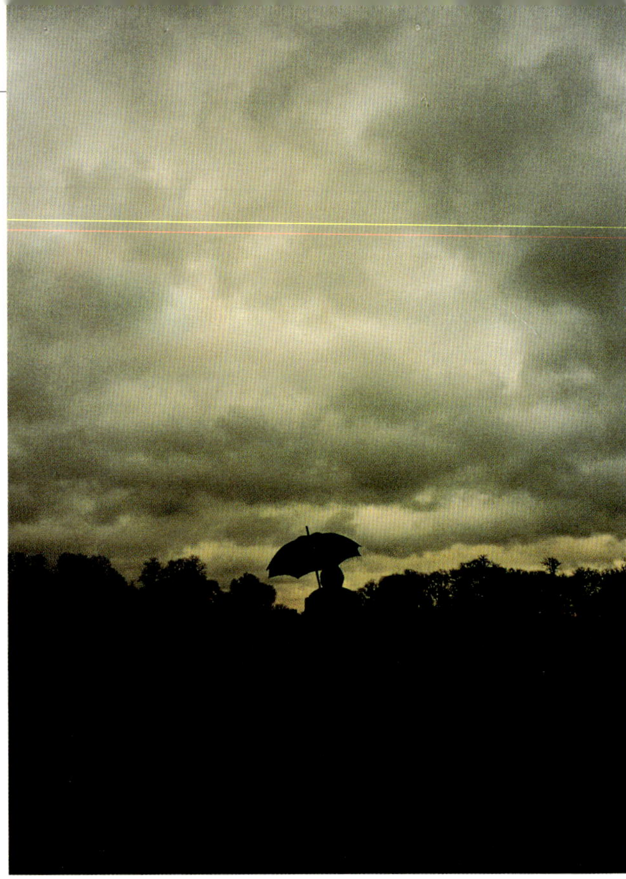

Stoplights in Welsh valley

I was driving through this Welsh valley in the early morning. The rain was coming down and I was attracted by the stoplights of the car ahead of me as it slowed down for the temporary traffic lights. I stopped the car and leapt out to capture this moment. Don't automatically put your camera away when the weather looks forbidding as extreme conditions can provide exciting results.

- Shot on 1000 ISO film, with the zoom at 38mm.

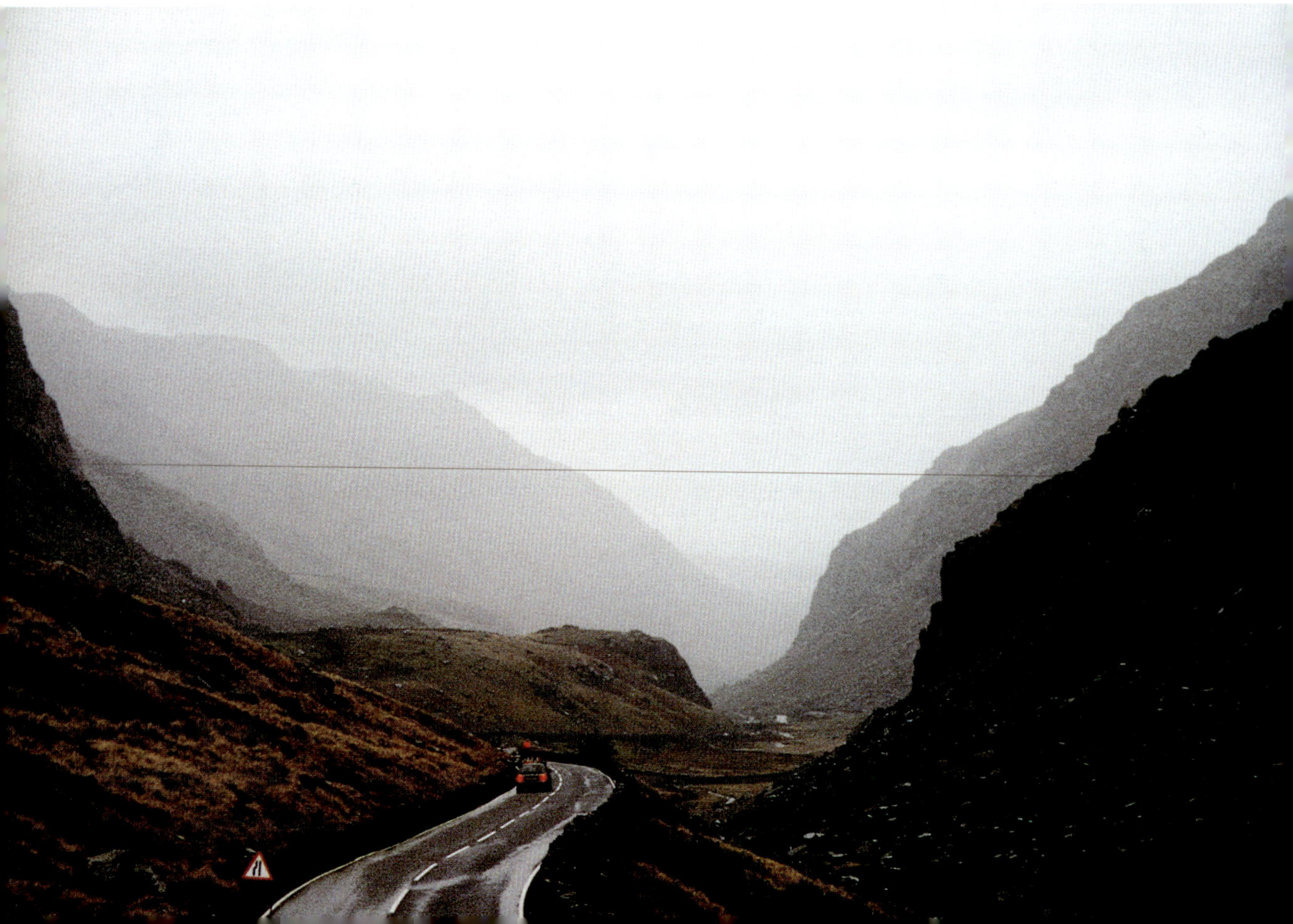

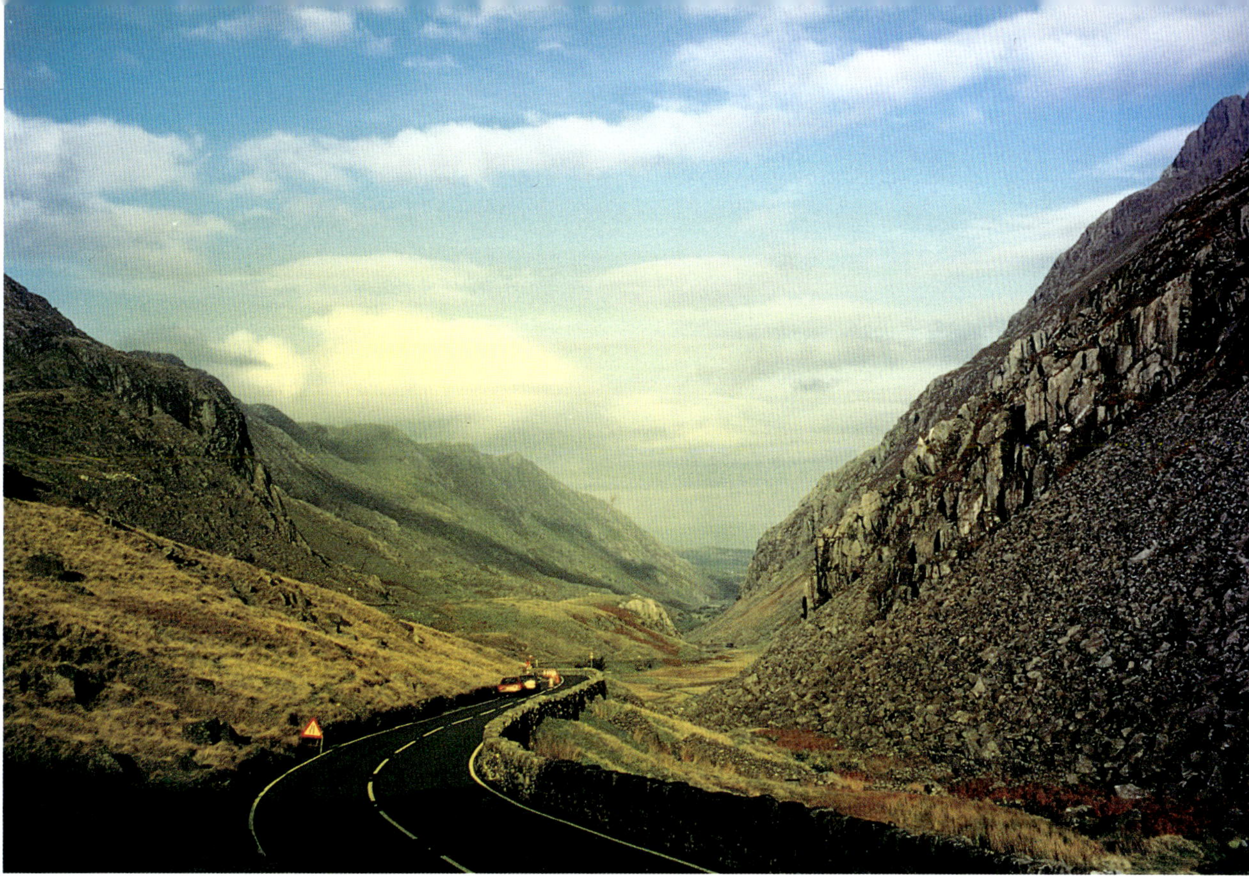

Sunlight in Welsh valley

The same spot photographed in the afternoon when the sun had come out in what we are programmed to think is ideal light. I much preferred the morning version, however, with its juxtaposition of monochromatic colours and the red of the stop lights. I have used these two extremes to show what effect different lighting conditions can have on a photograph.

• Shot on 400 ISO film with the zoom at 28mm.

Rainbow

Autumn is generally the best season to photograph rainbows, especially against a dark sky like this, which is when they look most effective. On a stormy day, the sun is likely to break through the clouds and combine with the rain to produce the most spectacular rainbows. But you must have the camera ready because these special moments are fleeting ones.

• Shot on 1000 ISO film with the zoom at 80mm.

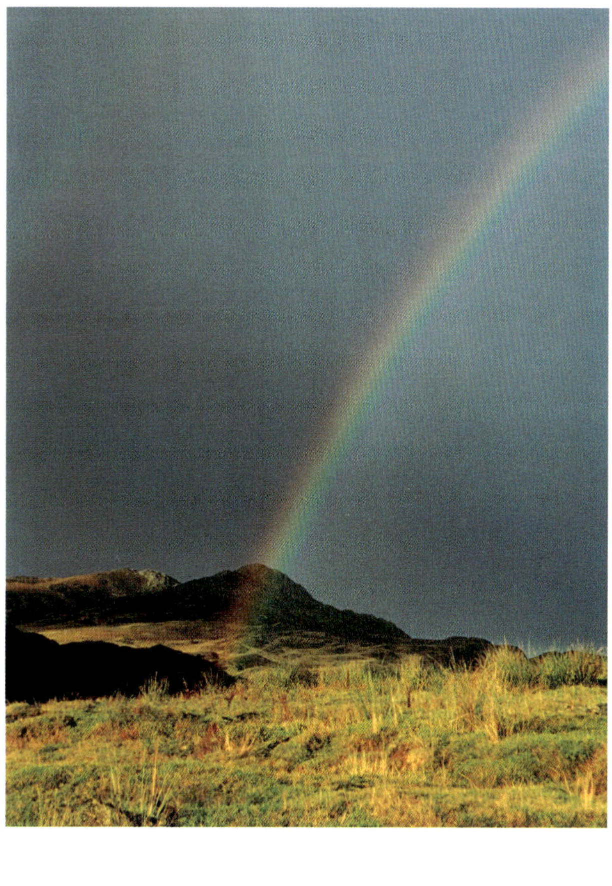

CHAPTER EIGHT

Using filters

Filters are not normally associated with compact cameras. The very thought of using filters seems to be a 'turn off' to many people and they see it as rather 'pro'. Filters, however, are really very easy to use and work on very simple principles. There is a filter system available for compact cameras, produced by Cokin, which includes a holder into which you can slide the various filters. This system only works when the zoom is in the wide-angle position, but as this is the position in which you are most likely to use filters it is not really a problem. However, I use gelatin filters that you can buy cheaply from professional camera shops. I cut them to the size of the lens and just stick them on with pieces of Blu-Tak.

The most useful group of filters are the 'warming' filters that literally warm up the colours in a picture. The Kodak Wratten 81 series is particularly useful and starts with the 81 filter which gives a little added warmth to a picture through the 81A, 81B, 81C, 81D and the 81EF filters. If you use an intense warming filter such as the 81D or EF filter, you can produce the equivalent in lighting terms of a late-afternoon sun on a cold grey morning and a sun tan to a mid-winter pale face. There are other systems, including the KR series, which goes from KR1.5 to 15 and the 1A and 2A series. Warming filters have a sepia and pinkish hue that intensify most colours in a photograph – except blue. They work very well on dull days, giving life to colour and enhancing skin tones. You can also use filters to produce a sunset or fog and there are numerous special effect filters that will create star effects, halo effects, even mask the picture to produce a keyhole shape. The blue 80B filter is useful for correcting the colour of daylight film shot under household tungsten lighting. Although not essential to good photography, filters can add a new dimension.

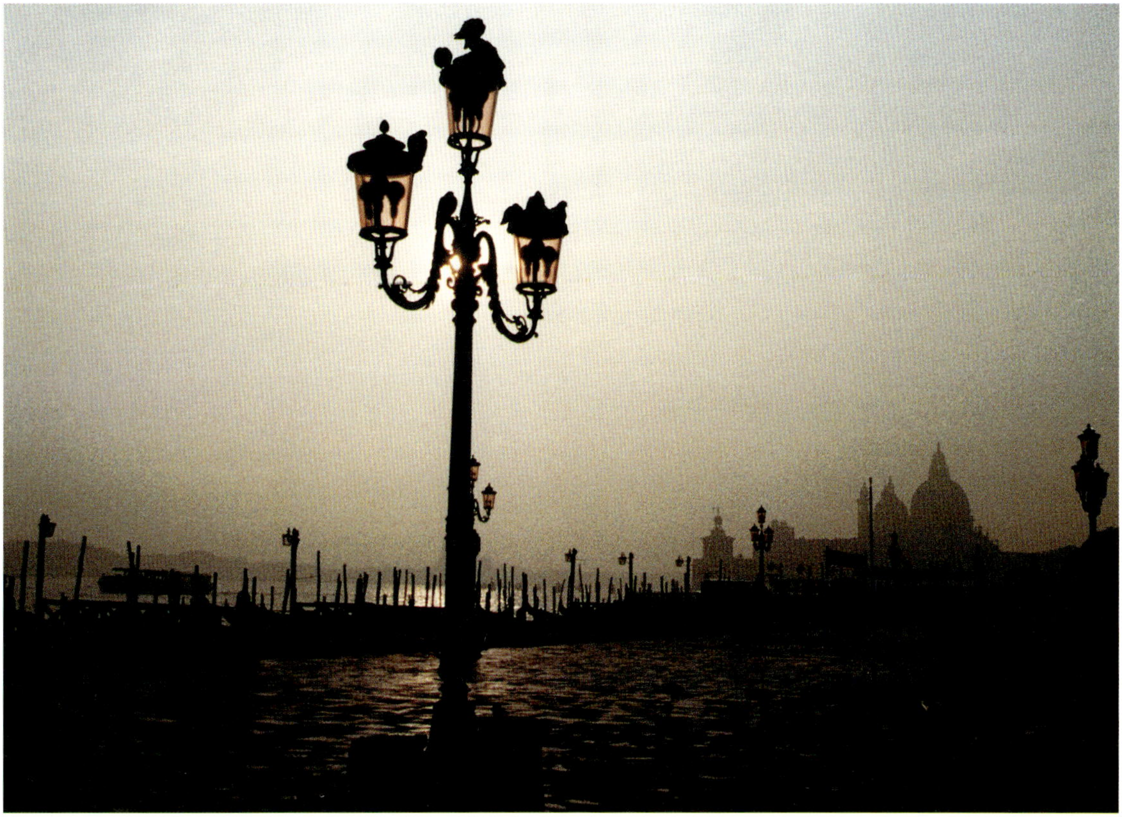

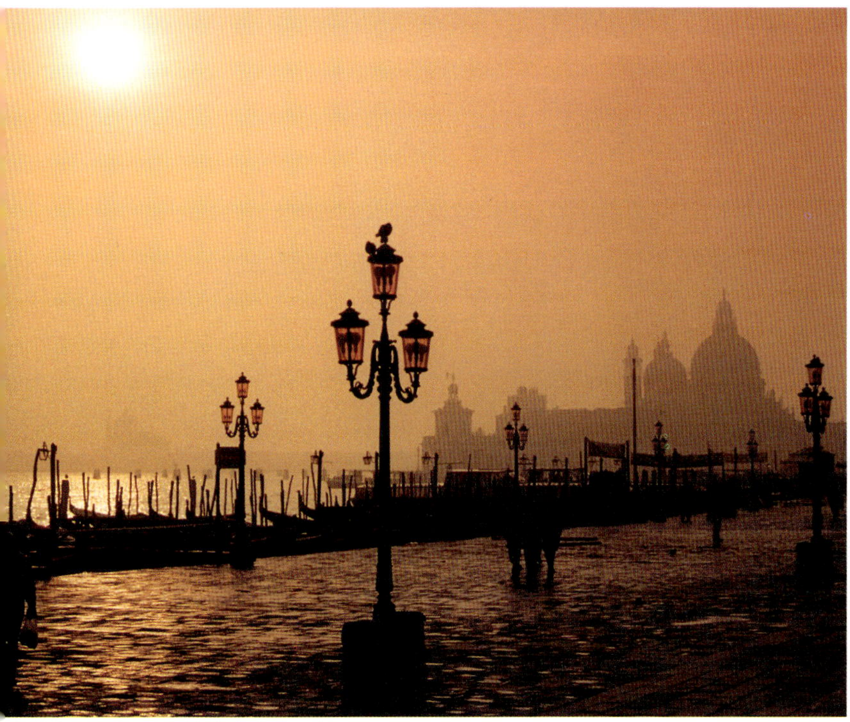

Venice street lamps

This first shot (above) was taken late in the afternoon on a grey day before the sunset had coloured the sky.

• Shot on 1600 ISO film with the zoom at 35mm.

For the second shot (left), I used a sunset filter, which created the romantic changes of hue.

• Shot on 1000 ISO film with the zoom at 70mm.

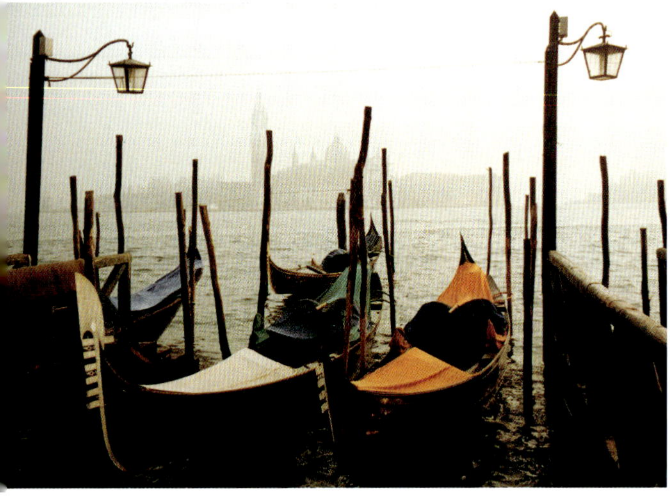

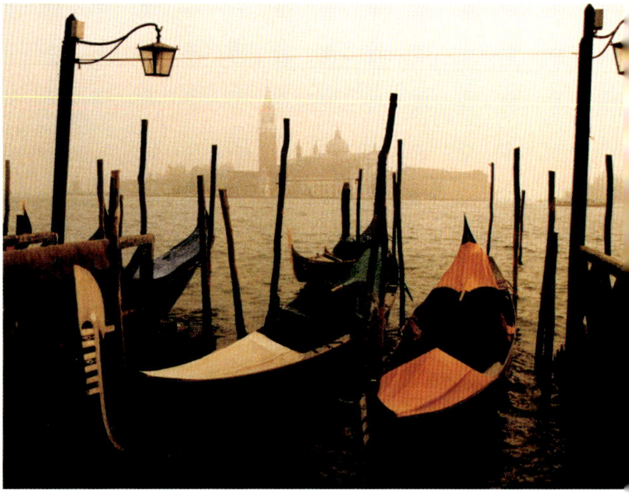

Gondolas

It was a wet, grey morning in Venice. I shot the first photograph in this series during a pause in the rain (above). This is actually the way I saw the picture with no filtration. For the next shot (above right), I stuck an 81C gelatin filter over the lens with Blu-Tack and produced a more saturated, warmer colour. Then I added a graduated filter (centre right) which has colour in the top half (in this case pink) but which gradually clears in the bottom half. Graduated filters come in many colours and can be used to make blue skies, green grass or any other colour you wish to half of the picture. Because you don't view through the lens on a compact like you do on a single lens reflex camera, graduated filters are tricky to use. I shot this picture several times to achieve this one, which I think is about right. In some, the graduated pink came too low into the picture and in some it was too high.

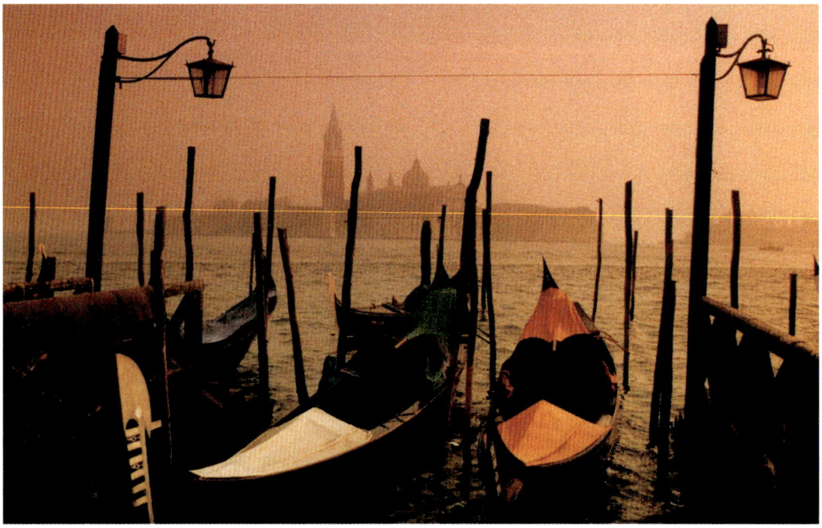

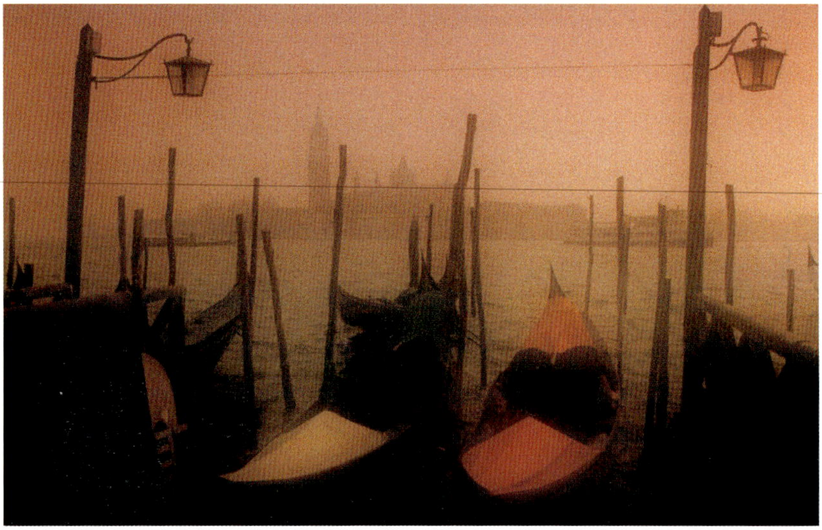

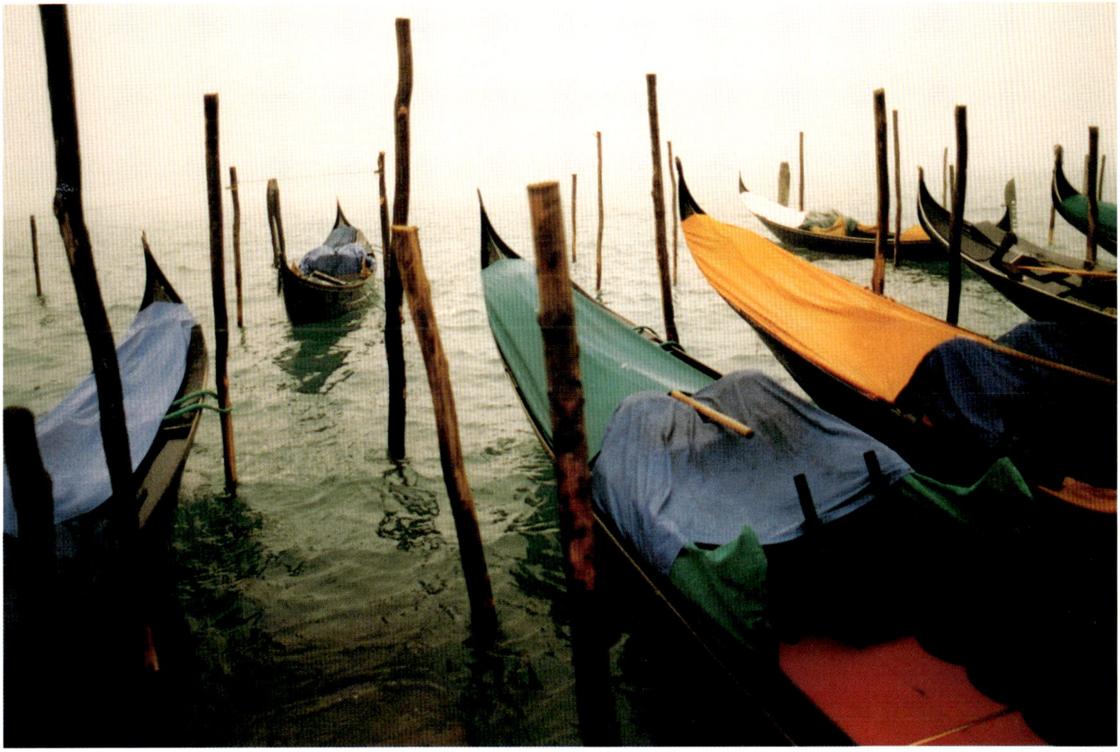

Finally, I added yet another filter, this time a diffused filter, which has given this a misty effect (opposite below). So we have here, through the use of a variety of filters, built a picture quite different in feeling to the real life scene. And who says the camera doesn't lie?

• Shot on 1000 ISO film with the zoom at 50mm.

This first shot (above) was as I saw the view, for the second shot (below) I used the cheapest and one of the most effective filters available to the photographer, a quick breath over the lens. The condensation created as a result gives a misty effect.

• Shot on 400 ISO film with the zoom at 32mm.

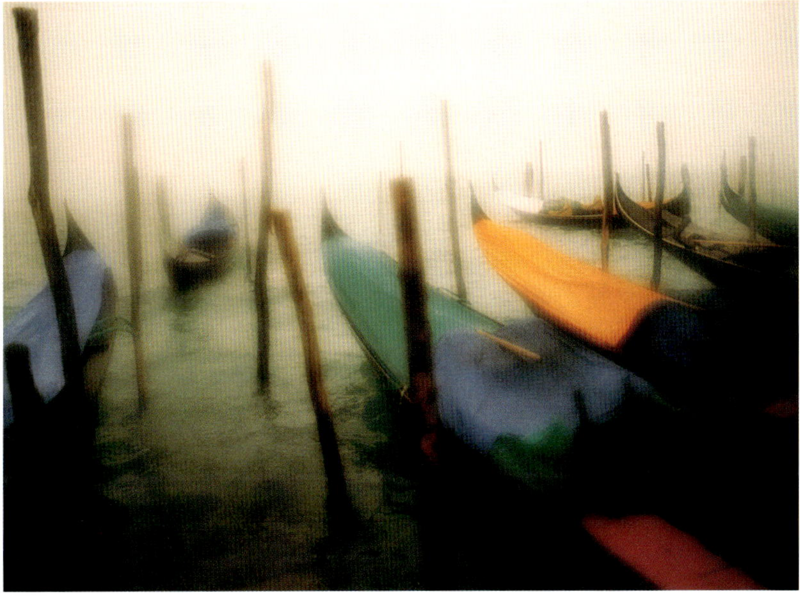

TIPS:

- Hold a filter up in front of your proposed subject matter to get a good idea of how the photograph will actually look.
- Treat the Kodak gelatin filters with care and you can use them again. Remember to keep them stored in the sleeves.
- When taking pictures using room lights, the colour will go an orangey, warm hue. You can correct this and create normal daylight by covering the lens with a blue filter.

CHAPTER NINE

Artificial Light and Reflectors

God's light is best, but even He has his off days and there may be times when you are forced or want to take a still life or portrait indoors. In this section, therefore, I have described several simple lighting set-ups which will enable you to experiment with studio-style lighting. The arrangements I have shown, aim to re-create natural daylight as closely as possible, because I like lighting to look natural. But, as you can see from the single light exercise (opposite), light can change the apparent shape of an object and create different atmospheres, so with a couple of artificial light sources you can create many interesting effects. Owing to the fact that most print film is daylight-balanced, when photographing under artificial lights you will either need to filter your lens with an 80B (blue) filter or use daylight balanced light bulbs which are blue – these are available from specialist art shops. You can also buy mirror back floods that are daylight balanced. Alternatively, you can buy tungsten light print film from professional photography shops.

Single Light Source

The pictures below show how you can apparently change the shape of a face by using a single light source in different positions. I used a 250-watt photoflood.

1. **Front lighting:** this produces a flat straight likeness much the same as the auto flash on a camera but without the red-eye.
2. **Lamp 1.53 metres (5 feet) over the camera:** the face looks narrower and the cheek-bones and jawline are more defined. This was the style of lighting favoured by Hollywood cameramen and is flattering to most folk.
3. **Three-quarter top lighting:** this is the lighting set-up used for most male portraits because the face appears narrower than in the front-lit portrait.
4. **Side-lighting:** this makes the face appear long and thin and is good if someone has a very round face.
5. **Side-light used with a reflector opposite:** this gives detail to the area in shadow and broadens the face, although it is still a flattering light for round faces.
6. **Light from 61 centimetres (2 feet) below the camera:** the face appears very wide. This was the standard lighting effect for the old horror movies.

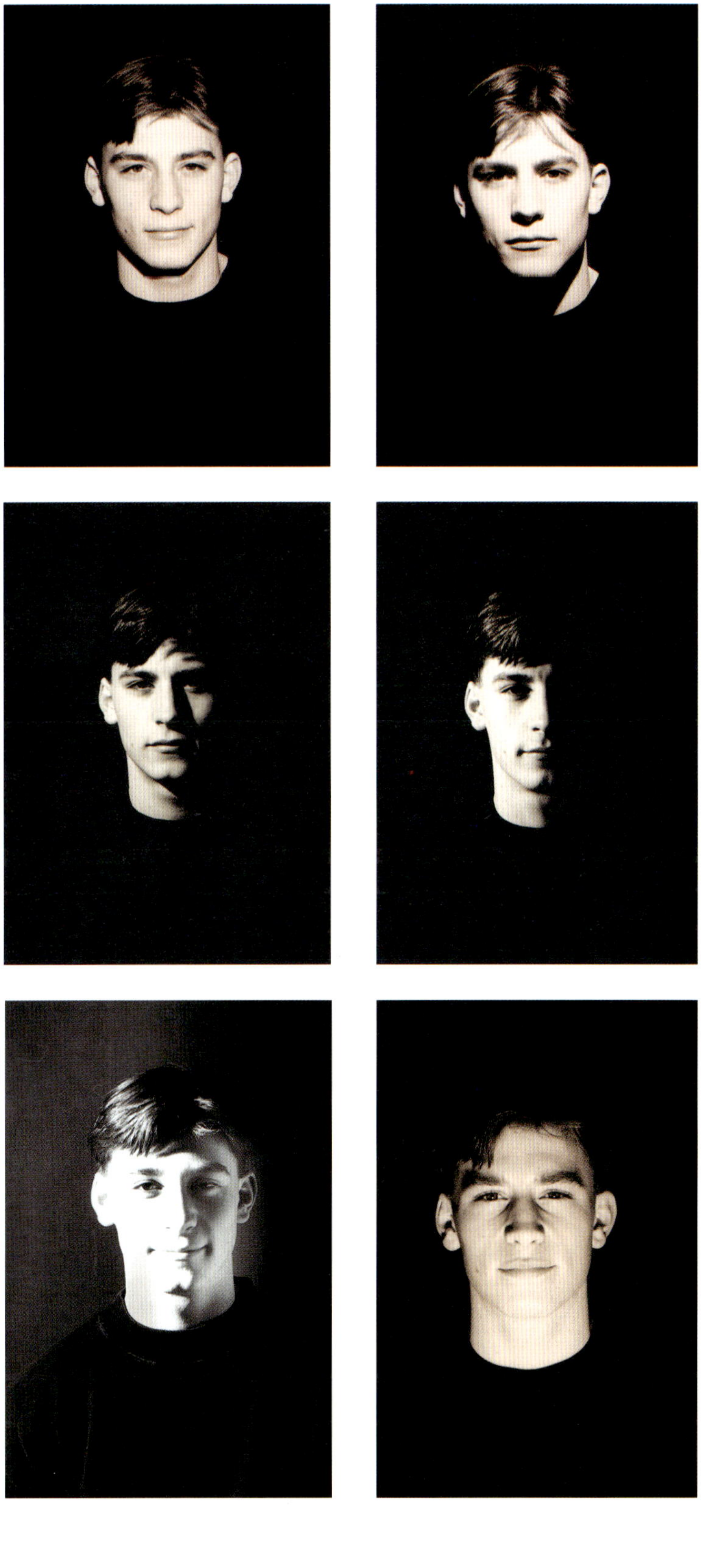

Portrait of man with a beard

I used a continuous grey background for this shot. I have a collection of different-coloured backgrounds in my studio which you can buy from professional photography shops: this one was 1.5 metres ($4\frac{1}{2}$ feet) wide. I used a 250-watt photoflood which I diffused to create a soft light by hanging a sheet of tracing paper 1.22 x 1.22 m (4 x 4 ft), 61 centimetres (2 feet) in front of the light. I then placed a white card 92 x 61cm (3 x 2ft) on the shadow side in order to bounce light into the shadow area. I used side lighting to avoid highlights reflecting off my subject's beard.

• Shot on 1600 ISO film with the zoom at 80mm.

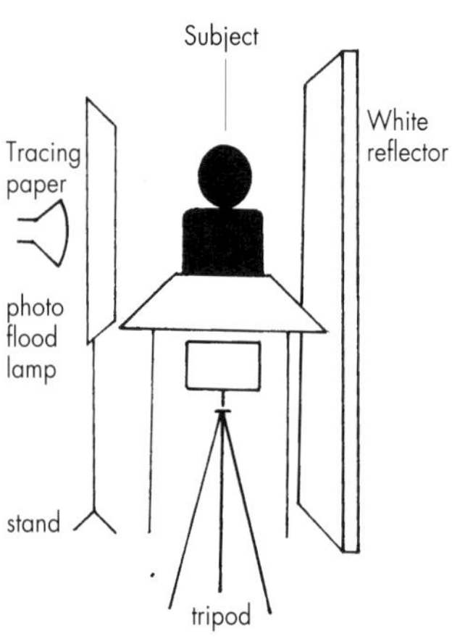

Note: the 250-watt photoflood made by Kaiser Fototechnik was daylight balanced and is available from professional shops. It is a very powerful lamp and most effective for use with compacts. The lamp holders (if you can buy them with reflectors) are also available from pro shops and are not expensive.

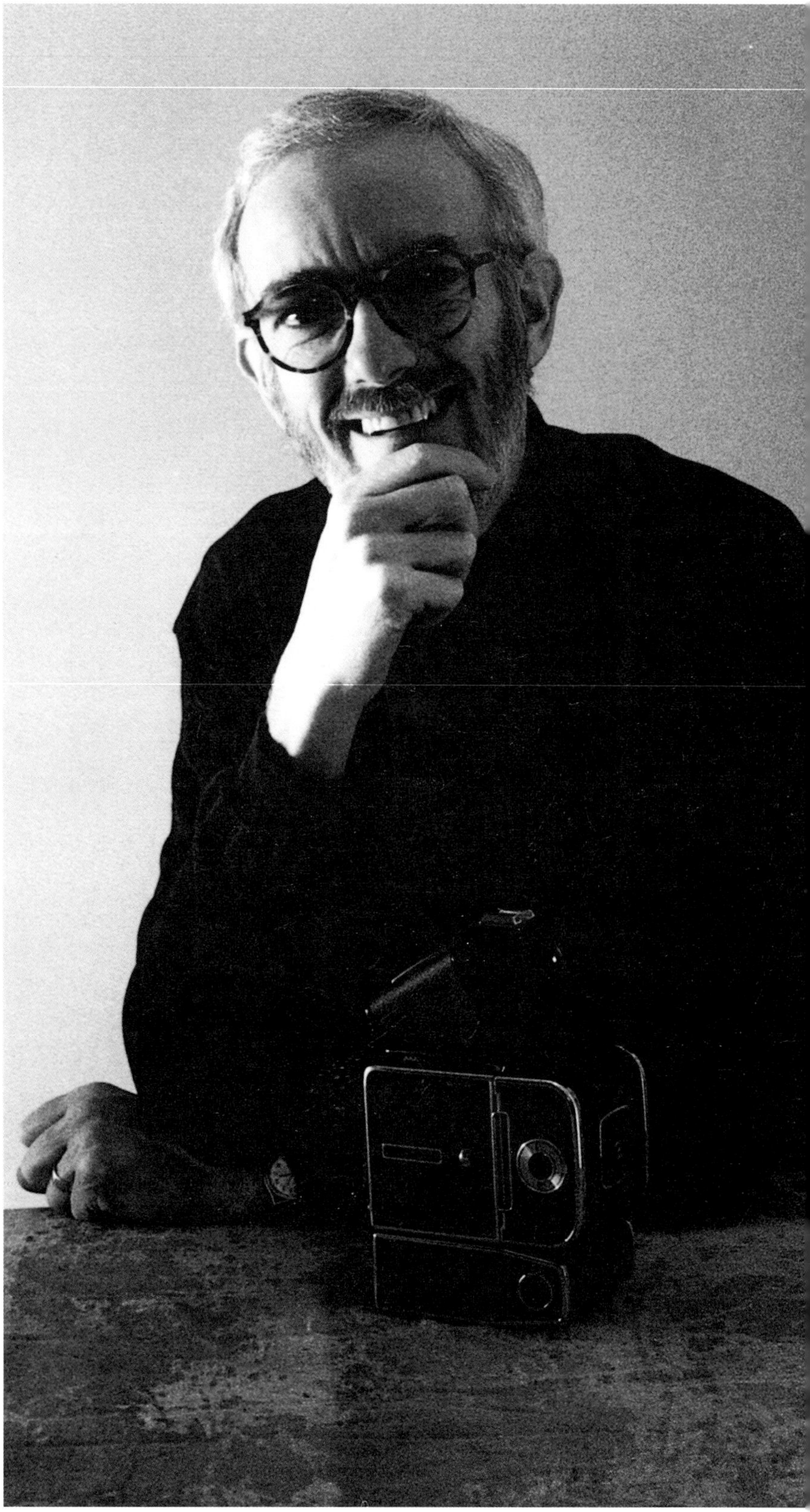

Still life

I decided to use an Italian cum-Mediterranean pasta theme for this still life which I shot in our glass-topped conservatory and framed right of centre. As you can see from the photograph (below), I asked a friend to hold a bright-gold reflector on the opposite side to the light source. This provided a golden 'Mediterranean' glow to the shot and I used a brolly to simulate daylight. For an alternative still-life, lighting set-up, use backlight as the main light source and then fill in with a white (or gold) reflector between the camera and the subject matter (see illustration below).There is no reason why you can't shoot still lifes such as this one in the garden if you have a good table top and a backboard you can clamp behind it. You can then experiment with all kinds of light – bright sunshine from the side or behind, backlight, overcast light, and so on. To light a still life effectively you need to use reflectors in order to bounce light into the shadow areas. This softens the light and so emphasizes the form and shapes of the objects. Make your own using baking foil, white cards or the aluminium lids from take-away containers.

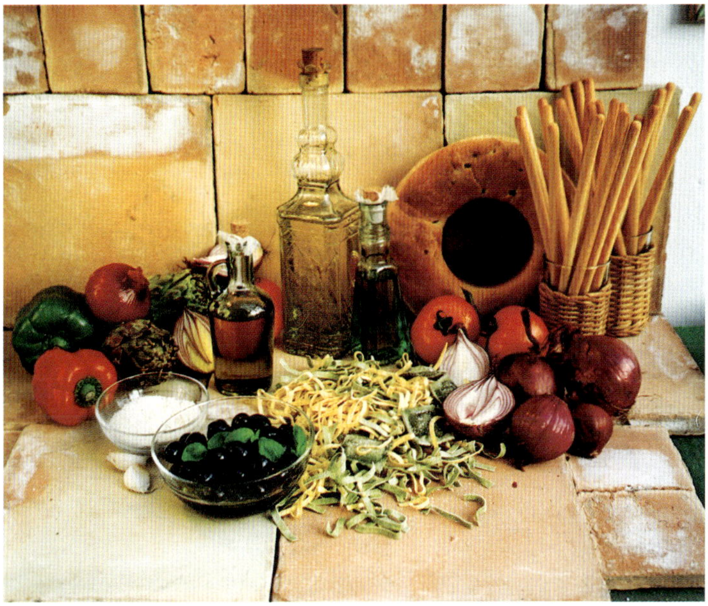

- Shot on 400 ISO film with the zoom at 35mm.

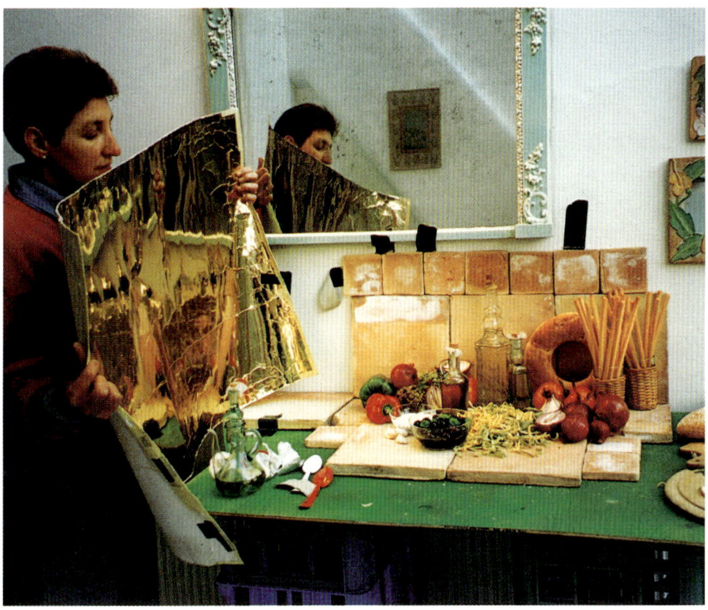

Backlight

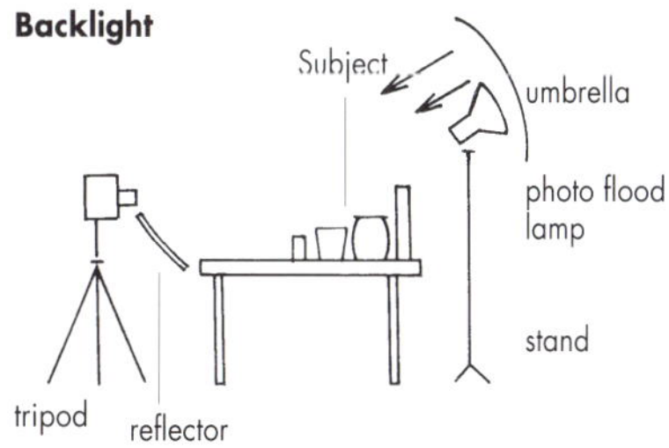

Sidelight

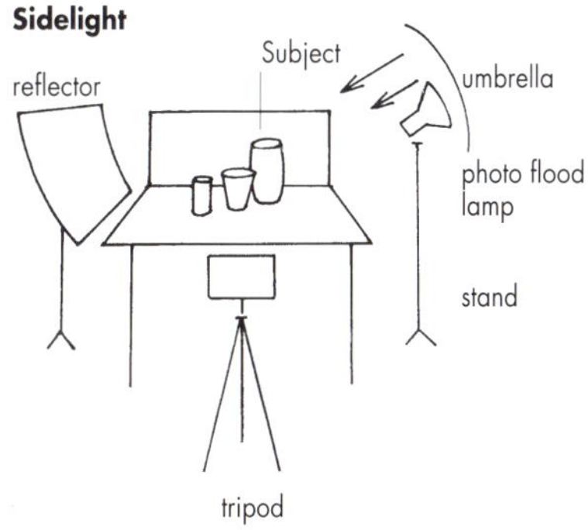

CHAPTER TEN

Developing and Printing

There are now many High Street developers and printers, which is good news for the customers as the competition has made them sharpen up their service. There seems to be a much better attitude towards the general public with most processing labs genuinely trying to get the prints right and willing to reprint if a customer is unhappy. In fact, most said they would prefer that their customers brought in disappointing prints rather than go away feeling dissatisfied. Unfortunately, most people don't know if a poor print is the result of their photography or the lab's developing, so hopefully this section will provide you with the answers and the questions to ask.

I would encourage you to go to a developer that also does hand prints for those really special shots. The quality of a hand print, although more expensive, is far superior to that of an automatic machine. Look in the phone directory for a list of firms in your area that offer a hand-printing service. Most are fairly small businesses and so you can build up a good personal relationship with them. Most of the High Street labs also process and print black and white films now, although the service takes a few days instead of hours.

Here are some examples of negatives and prints that I trust will work as a guide for your developing and printing. The final result is actually in the hands of the film processors, so it is important to get it right or to know the questions to ask if it isn't.

Correctly exposed negative

This is an example of a well-exposed colour negative. I chose it because it has a large range of clean pure colours. Note that the negative colours become their complementary opposites in the positive print, so, for example, green prints as red, blue as yellow, etc.

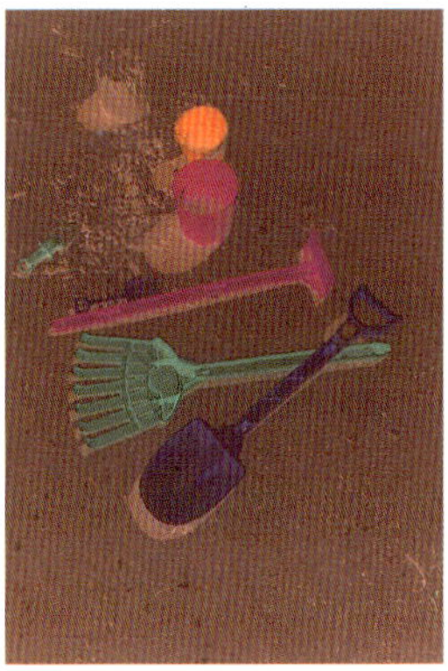

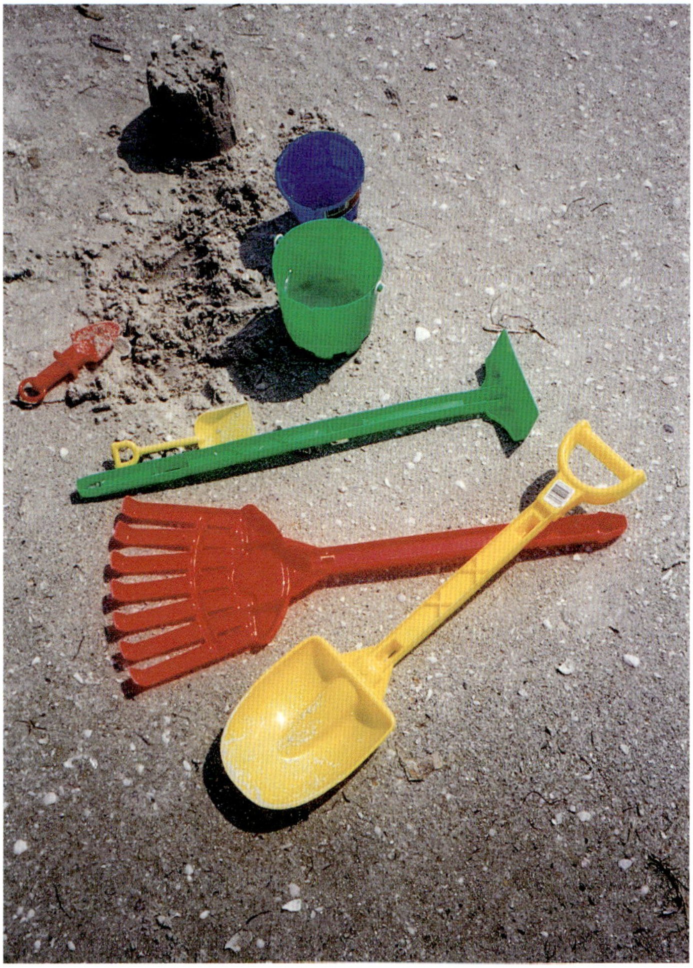

Underexposed negative and print

This negative is underexposed because the flash was too far away. It is important to be able to recognize underexposure in a negative so that you will know when a dark print is your fault or the film processors. An underexposed negative will look very light, so if you think the negative may be underexposed ask the processing lab to 'push' the development of the negative by one stop. Hopefully, the extra development time will give extra detail and save the picture. It is not generally recommended as it increases the grain and unbalances the colour, but is worth the risk for a special image.

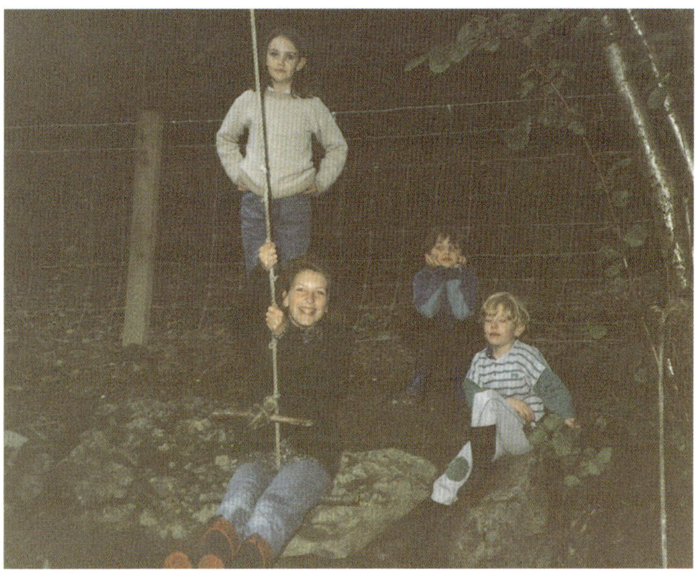

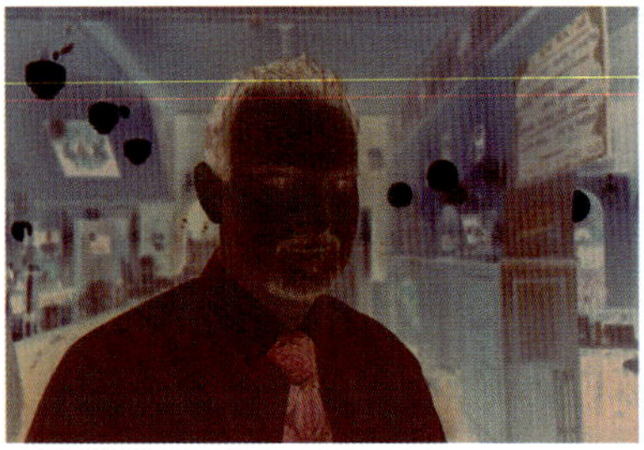

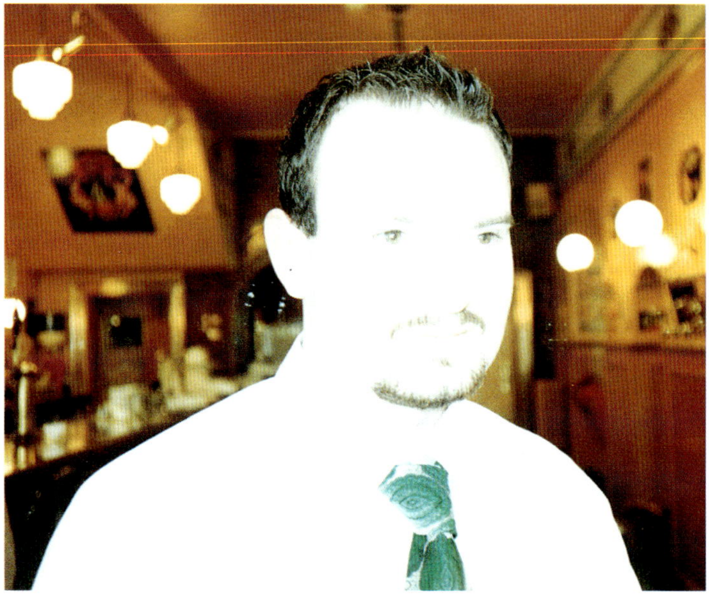

Overexposed negative and print

This overexposed print was caused by flash burn-out (see Problem Solving, page 78). You can tell the negative is overexposed because the faces appear very dark. As with the underexposed negative, all is not lost, ask the lab to reprint darker and to put some tone into the faces.

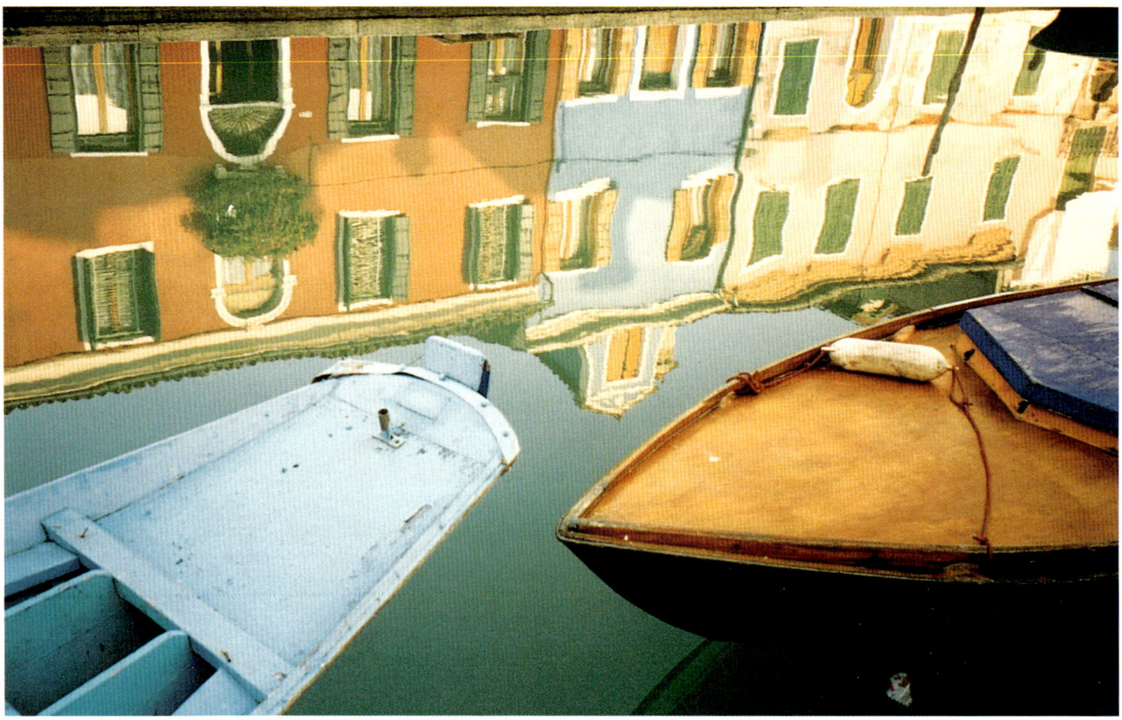

Good negative: bad print

The negative was actually correctly exposed but the print is washed out and grey because the lab have not replenished the chemicals adequately. Take it back and ask for another print, explaining what you think the problem is. Talking to them from a position of knowledge helps considerably.

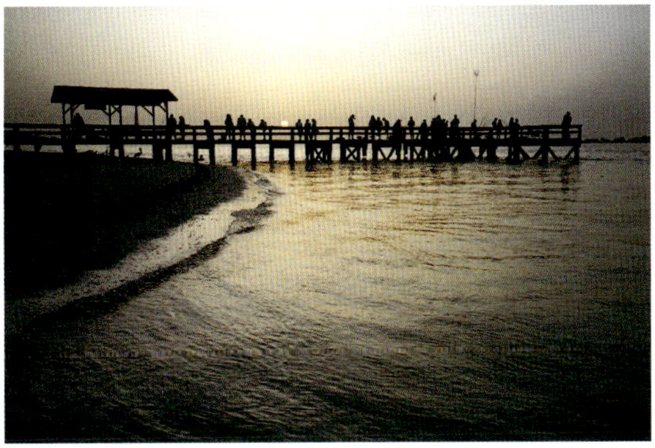

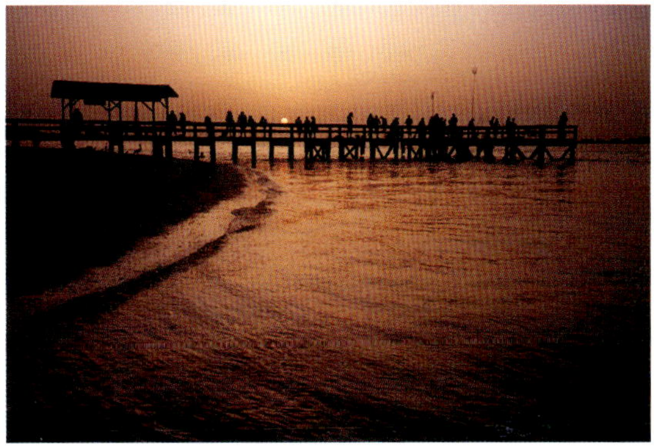

Pier

The machine print was accurately developed (above left) but I wanted to add more sunset colour to the print, so I asked the printer to add more colour (above right). You can change the colour tone of a picture when hand printing so don't just hand over the negative to the printers but discuss what can be done. They prefer to print for people who really care and want to create interesting prints.

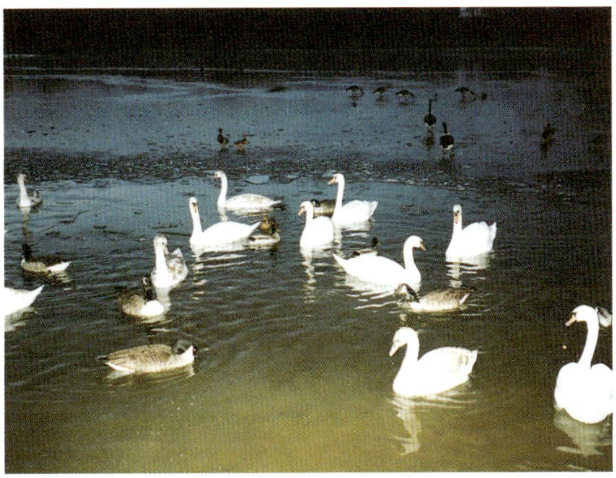

Swans

I knew the negative for this print would provide problems for an automatic printing machine because there is a huge exposure and tonal contrast between the background and the foreground (left), and therefore had it hand printed (below). This enabled the printer to shade light off the background while exposing the foreground more to produce an even print. A machine could have printed darker for the birds but the background would have appeared black. I also had the picture reframed on the enlarger which is another great advantage of hand printing as it means you can recompose the picture and have it framed any way you want.

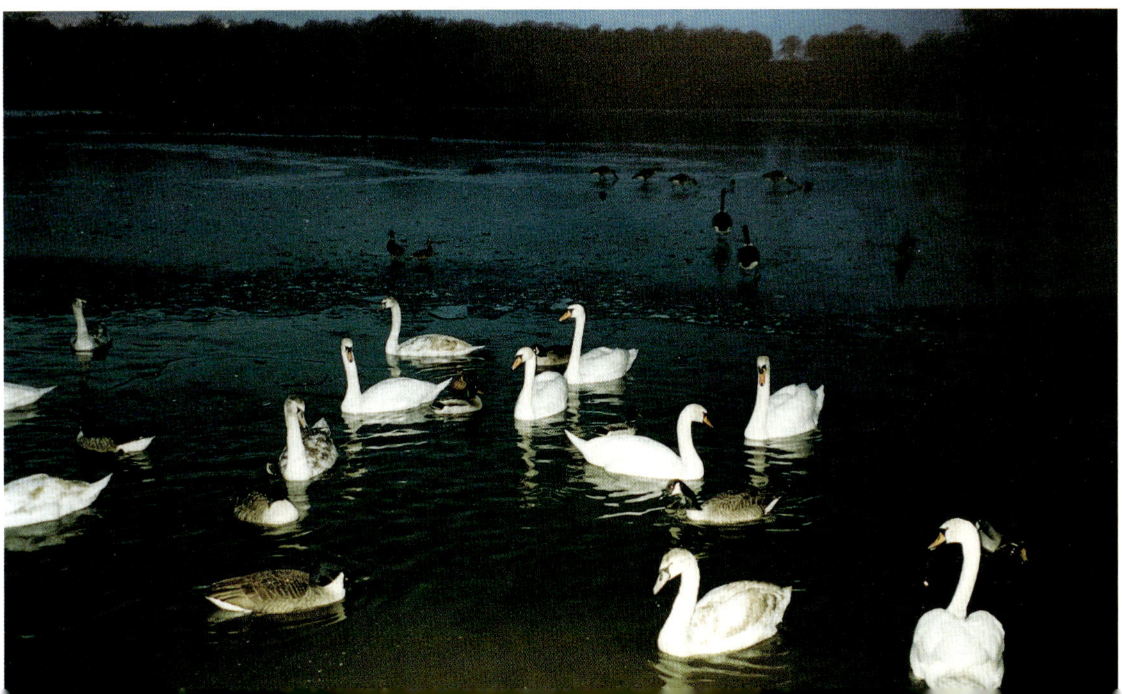

Black and white tones

These four prints were all produced on an automatic printing machine using different filtration values. The negative was black and white. If you want similar results, explain to your processing lab that you want to emphasize tones rather than solid colours.

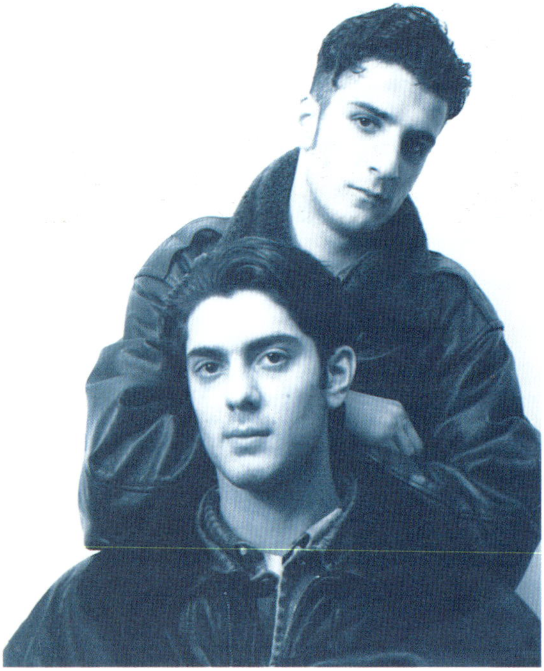

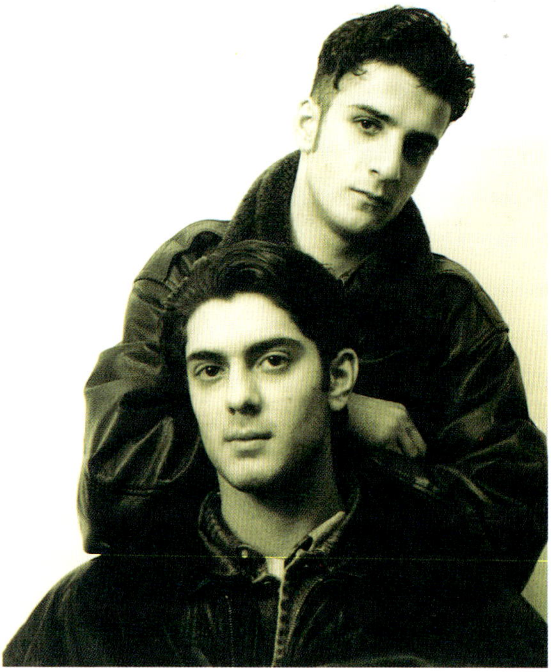

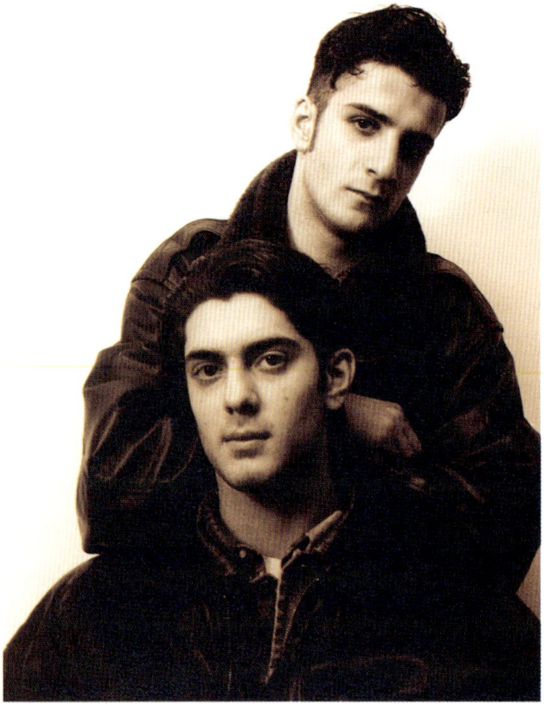

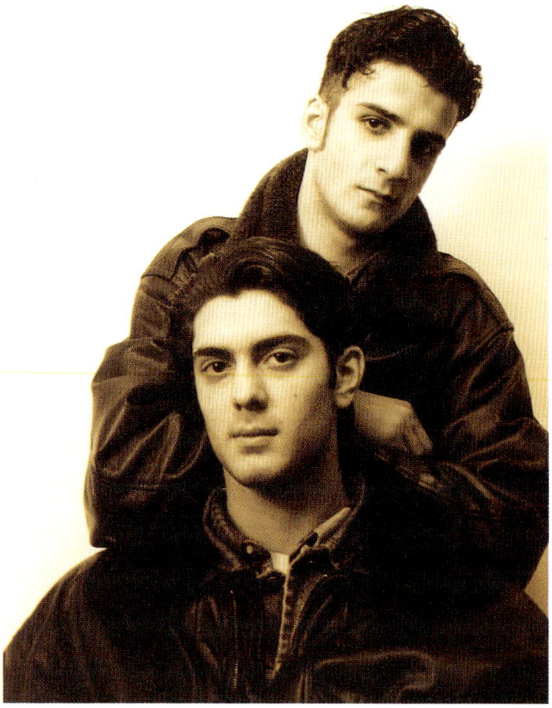

CHAPTER ELEVEN

Problem Solving

We have all experienced the disappointment of getting back an eagerly awaited set of prints from the film processing lab only to find that the majority of them are no good for some reason or other. This chapter, I hope, will prevent such disappointments in the future by outlining the most common faults experienced by amateur and professional photographers alike and how to avoid them. At least in the future if things do go wrong you'll know why and whose responsibility it is. It is not always the fault of the photographer, so don't be afraid of going back to the film processing lab if you think it's their mistake (see also Developing and Printing, page 70).

Sloping horizons

If the horizon is sloping down from the left to the right of the picture it usually means that you've pressed down too hard on the shutter release button (which is on the right of the camera) and moved the camera off line.

An alternative cause of sloping horizons in either direction is that you have become too absorbed in your subject matter and just haven't noticed the sloping horizon line.

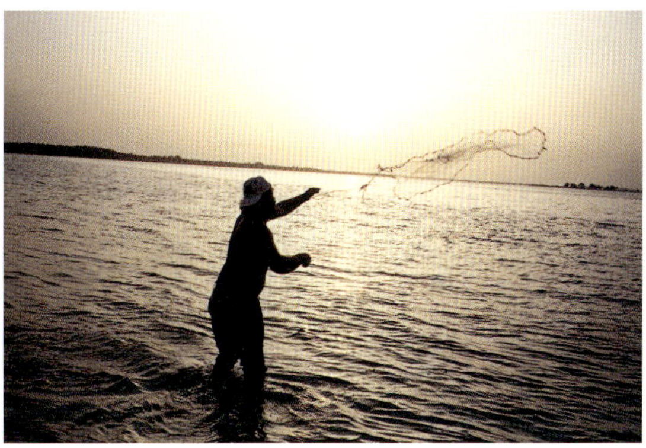

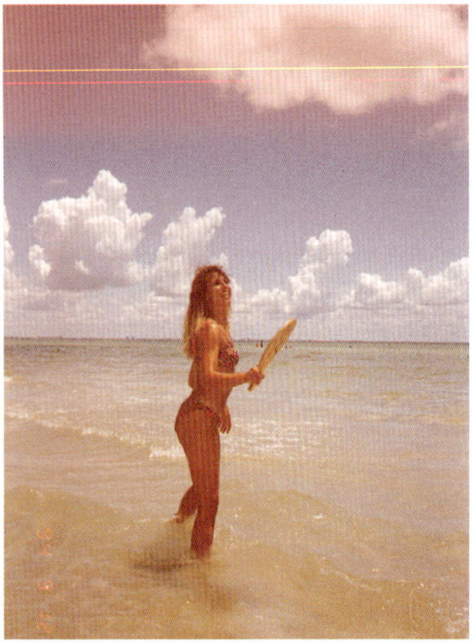

Foggy cast

The foggy magenta cast (left) over this picture has been caused by light leaking into the camera. Check the back of the camera is locked securely. If the problem still occurs then have your camera checked out by a camera shop.

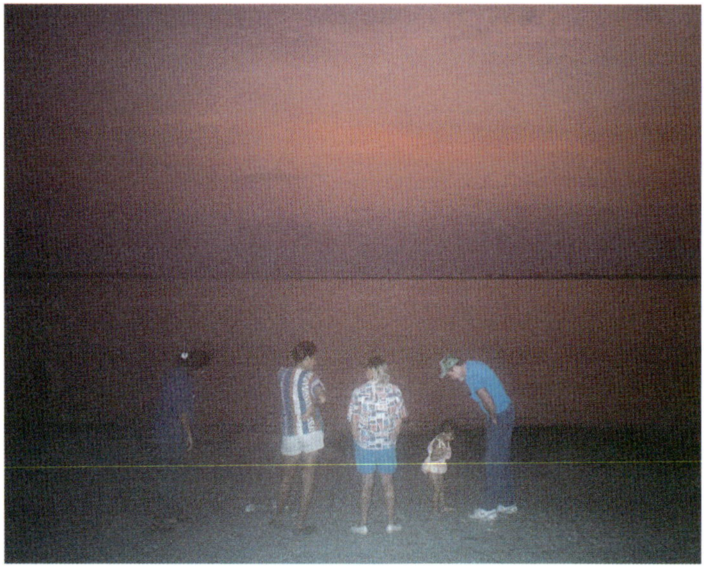

Underexposed flash

The group of people (right) were too far away from the camera for the flash to light them sufficiently for a correctly exposed print. Either the camera needs to be moved closer or a faster film used (see Flash, page 24).

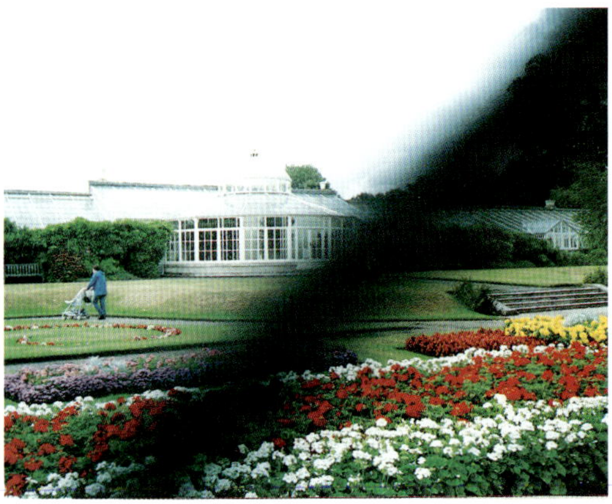

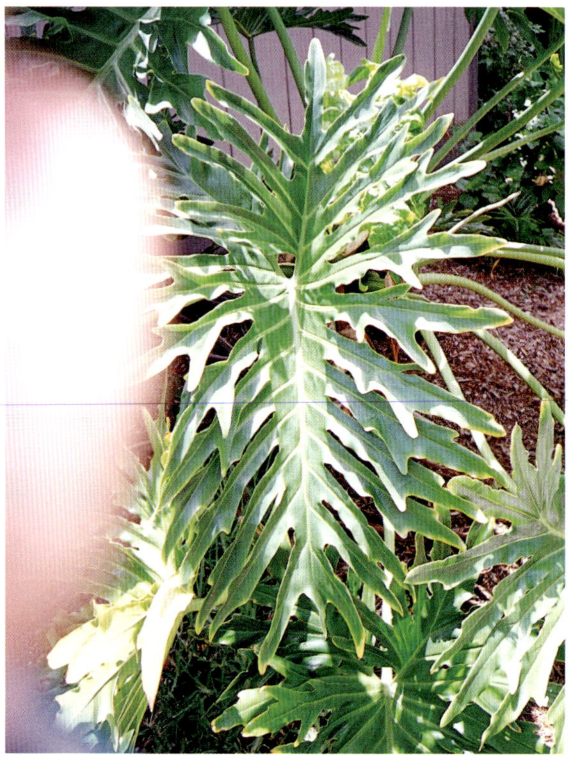

Obstructions in the frame

In the shot above, the hand-strap appears across the print and in the one on the right a finger. Both problems are extremely common, as on a compact camera the viewfinder does not show you what the lens is seeing. Always check before you take a shot, therefore, that nothing is obscuring the lens.

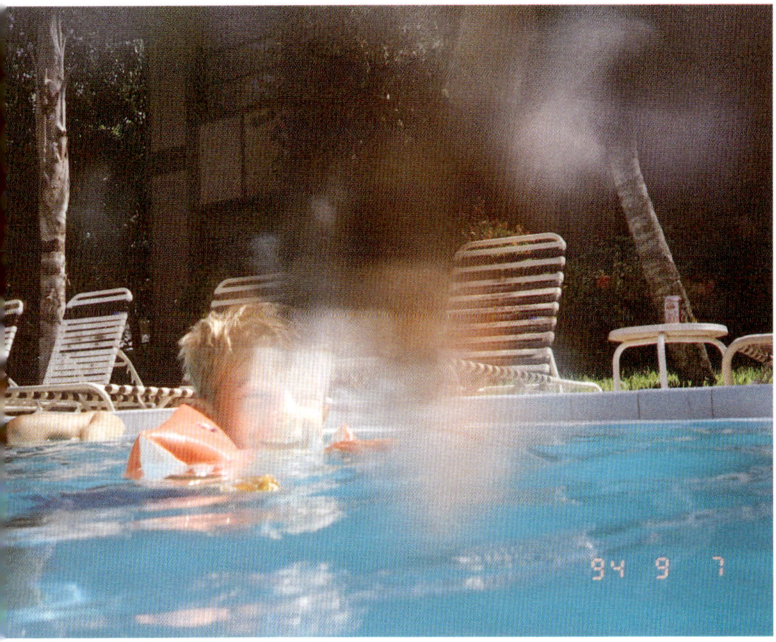

Blurred spots

This foggy result (left) has occurred as a result of a drop of water on the lens that has caught the light. This is a particularly common problem when using underwater compacts above the water, so take care and make sure the lens is water free.

Flare

The overexposed areas of this picture (below) have been caused by shooting into the sun: the rays have bounced directly onto the lens and caused this flaring effect. The best way to avoid this is to change position so the sun is not shining directly onto the lens. If you can't move, then use your hand to shade the lens, being careful not to get your hand in the picture.

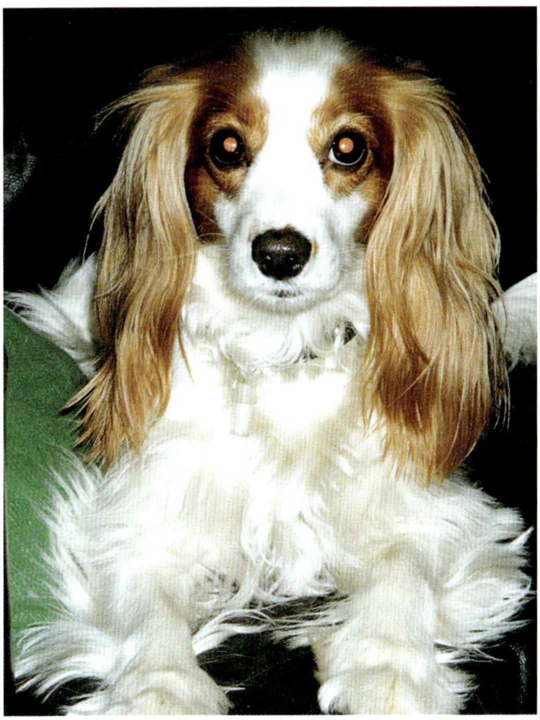

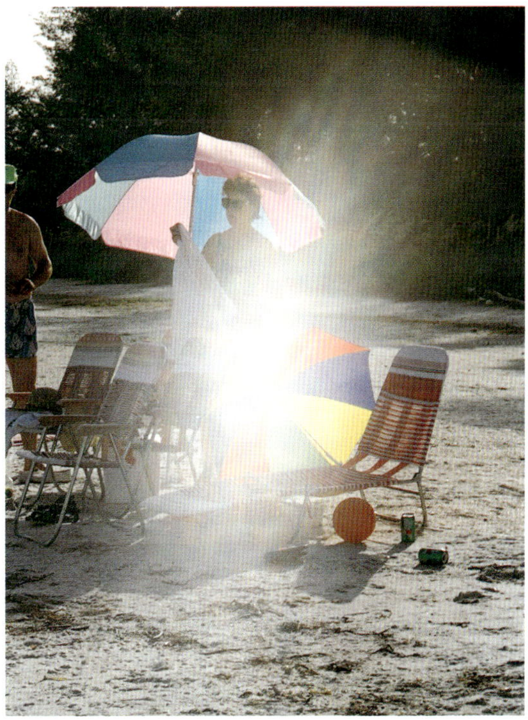

Red-eye

In low light, the pupils of the eyes enlarge to allow us to see more. Under these circumstances if you take a picture with flash the flash is reflected off the red blood vessels behind the eye and the pupils come out bright red (above left). Some cameras have a built-in red eye reduction facility (see page 26) which does help to reduce but not eliminate red-eye. You can also help prevent red-eye by photographing in a brightly lit room, which will make the pupils of the eye contract thus reducing the risk of red-eye.

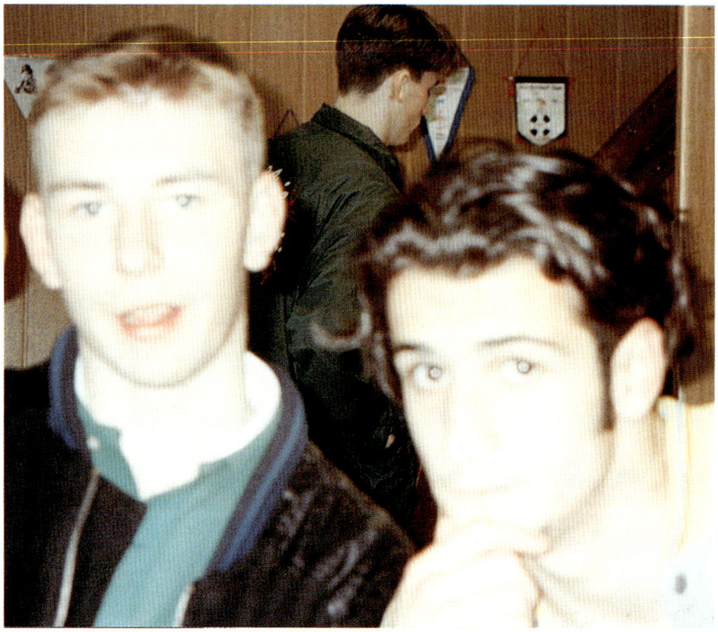

Flash burn out

This picture was taken too close to the subjects, who are overexposed while the background figure is perfectly exposed. This picture also illustrates a classic focusing mistake which is easily made using a compact. In order for the subject to appear in focus it has to appear within the focusing brackets on the viewfinder (see How It Works, page 19). In this example, the focusing bracket has missed both figures and focused right down the middle of them onto the background figure, who is in perfect focus. To avoid this you must make sure the focusing bracket is over the subject you want photographed. This means you may have to use the focus lock (see How It Works, page 19).

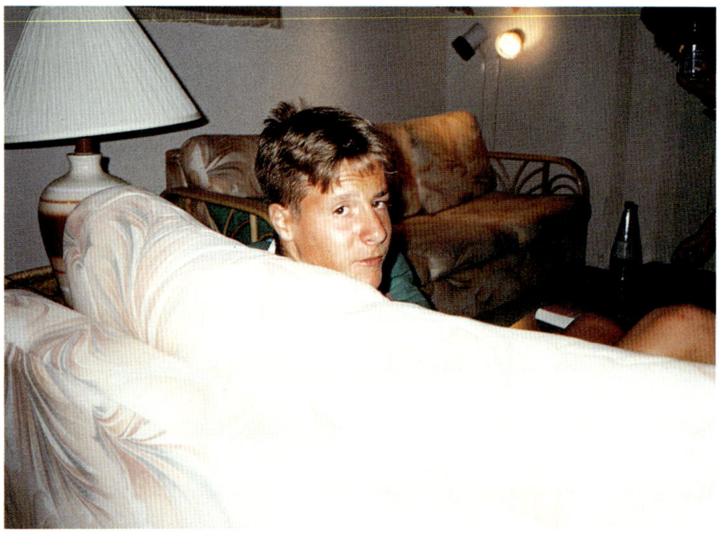

Drying mark

The mark to the left of the rainbow has been caused by drying the negative incorrectly and is the fault of the film processing lab. Ask them to reprint it and retouch the drying mark.

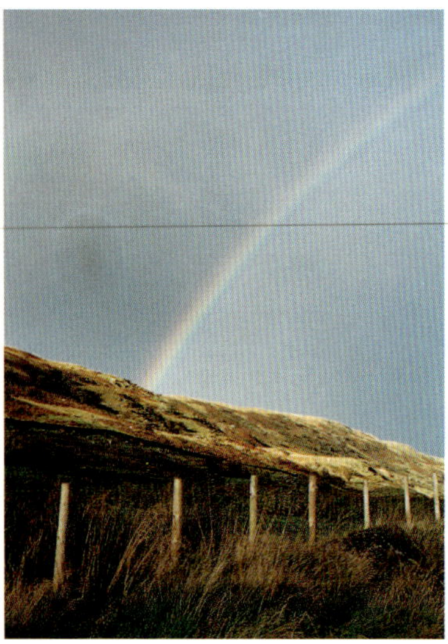

Uneven flash lighting

The right-hand side of the settee is too close to the flash and is therefore burning out (see Flash, page 31). In order to photograph this correctly you need to move further back or recompose the shot so that everything is the same distance away from the camera.

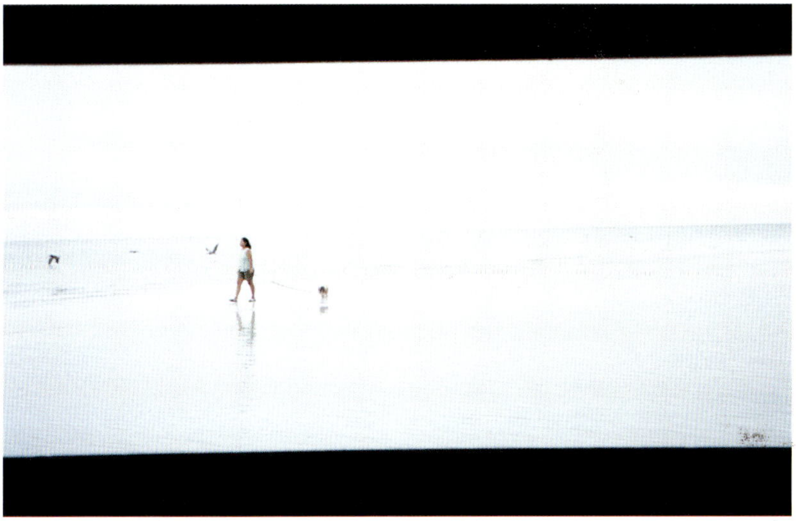

Washed-out panorama

If the lab prints panorama masked negatives without the correct masking facilities, underexposure occurs. You should return it to the film processing lab and ask for a reprint.

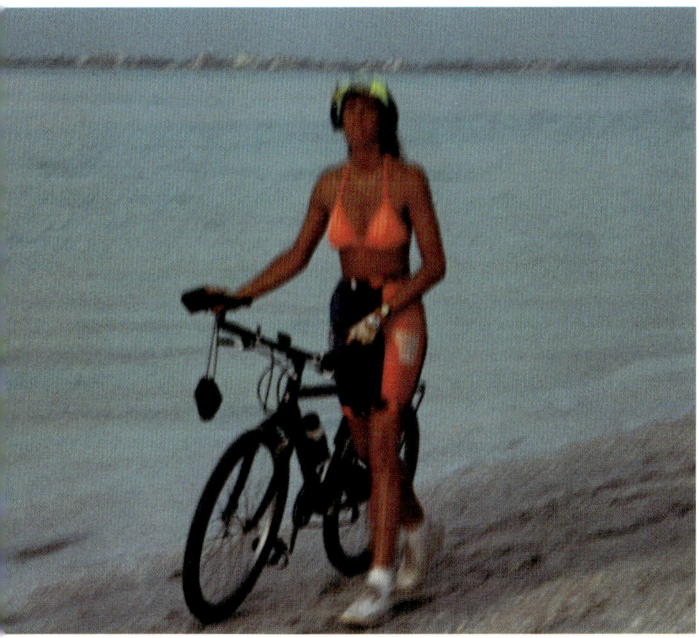

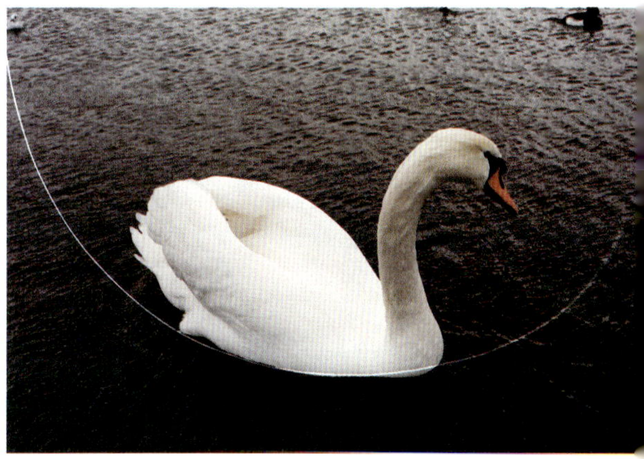

Hair mark

The white hair mark has been caused by a mark on the negative which the processing lab should have wiped clean before printing. Again ask them to reprint.

Camera shake

I tried to take this picture in low light conditions with a slow film (100 ISO). The camera selected a slow shutter speed (about 1/15 sec) but I couldn't keep the camera still enough and the image was blurred. If I had been using a faster film (400 ISO) the result would have been fine.

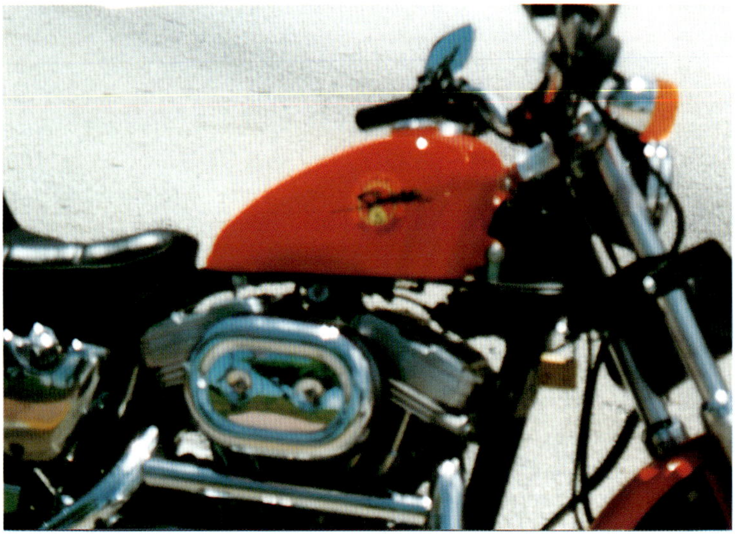

Out of focus

I had just taken a picture of a landscape with the focus set on the infinity mode and had forgotten to reset it for this shot of the bike. The camera has therefore focused behind it. Always check that you have the correct focus programme for your shot.

Out of focus and out of frame

The camera was too close to the flower (below left) to focus correctly and because I didn't use the close-up framing lines the flower was also cut in half.

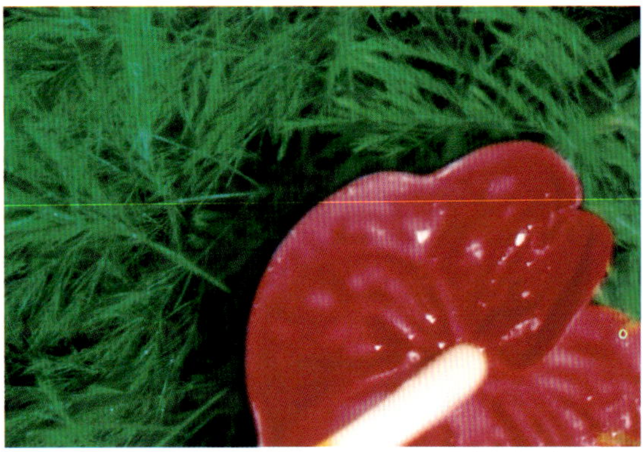

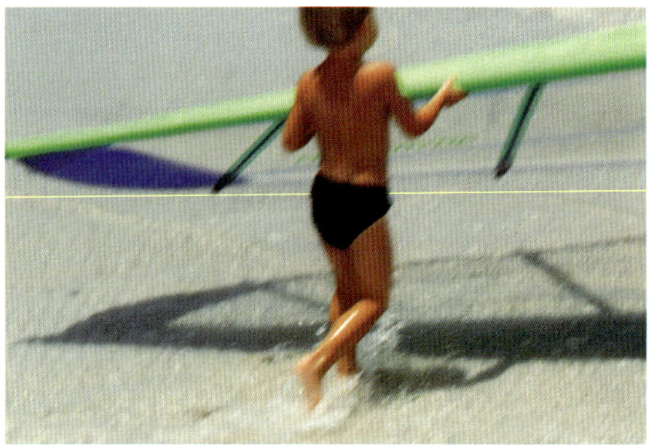

Out of focus

The boy was moving from left to right (above right) and I was moving the camera from right to left. If I had moved the camera with him I would have been able to freeze the movement (see How It Works, page 15) instead of getting this out of focus image.

In this shot (right), the bird is off centre and therefore did not appear within the focusing brackets and so the camera has focused on the background water. Make sure you always frame your subject within the focusing brackets and if you want if off centre then use the focus lock (see How It Works, page 19).

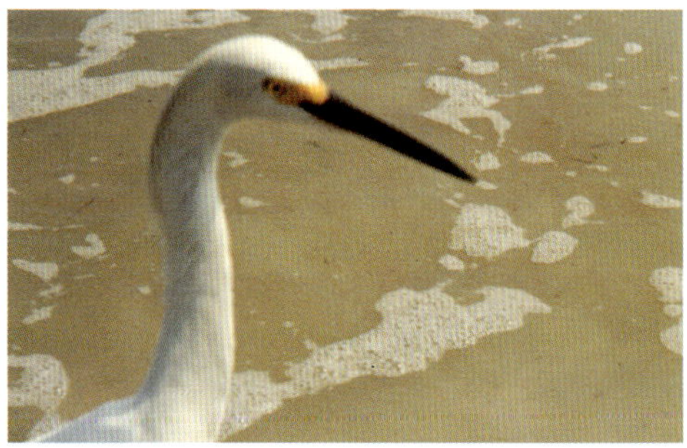

Head cut off

The printing machine cuts off about 15 per cent of the frame so always allow extra space above the head of your subjects to compensate for this loss (see Developing and Printing, page 70). Unfortunately, I had not taken this into account and therefore the bird's head is cut off (right).

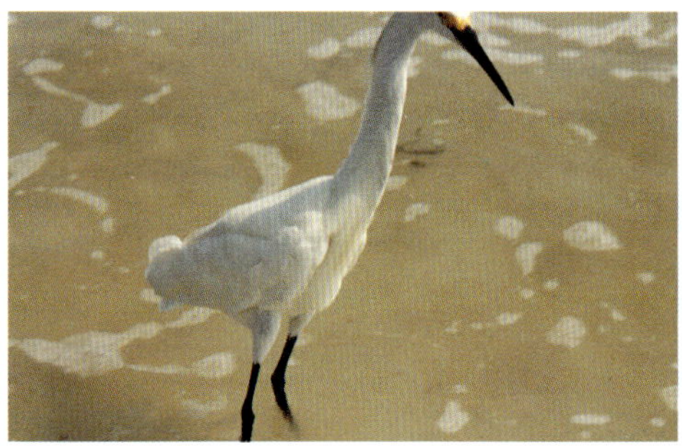

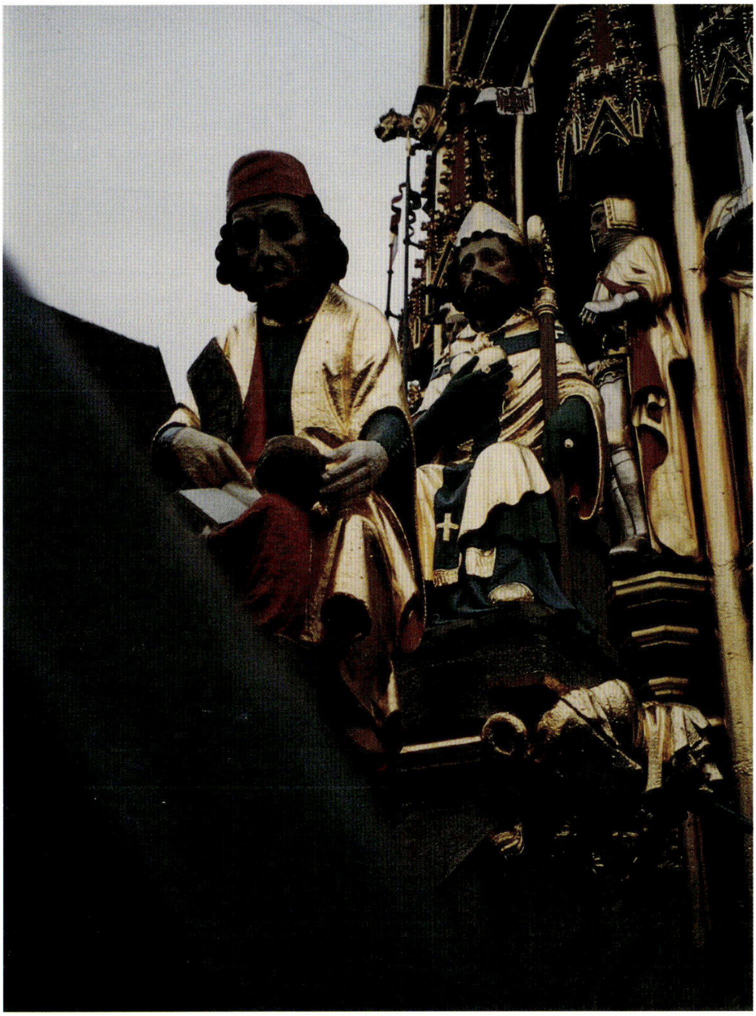

Image cut off

When shooting between railings or bars, remember to put the lens through the gap not the viewfinder otherwise you will get a cut-off shot like this.

Dark face, light background

The white screens in the background of this picture have thrown out the camera's automatic exposure system and the young man's face is underexposed. Using the anytime flash mode would have thrown some light into his face and solved the problem. If the picture you had taken was important you could always try asking the film processing lab to try to make a lighter print.

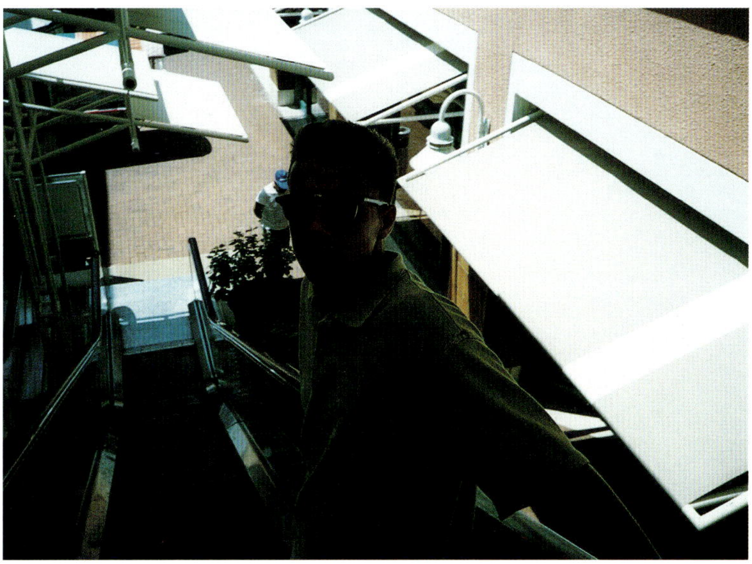

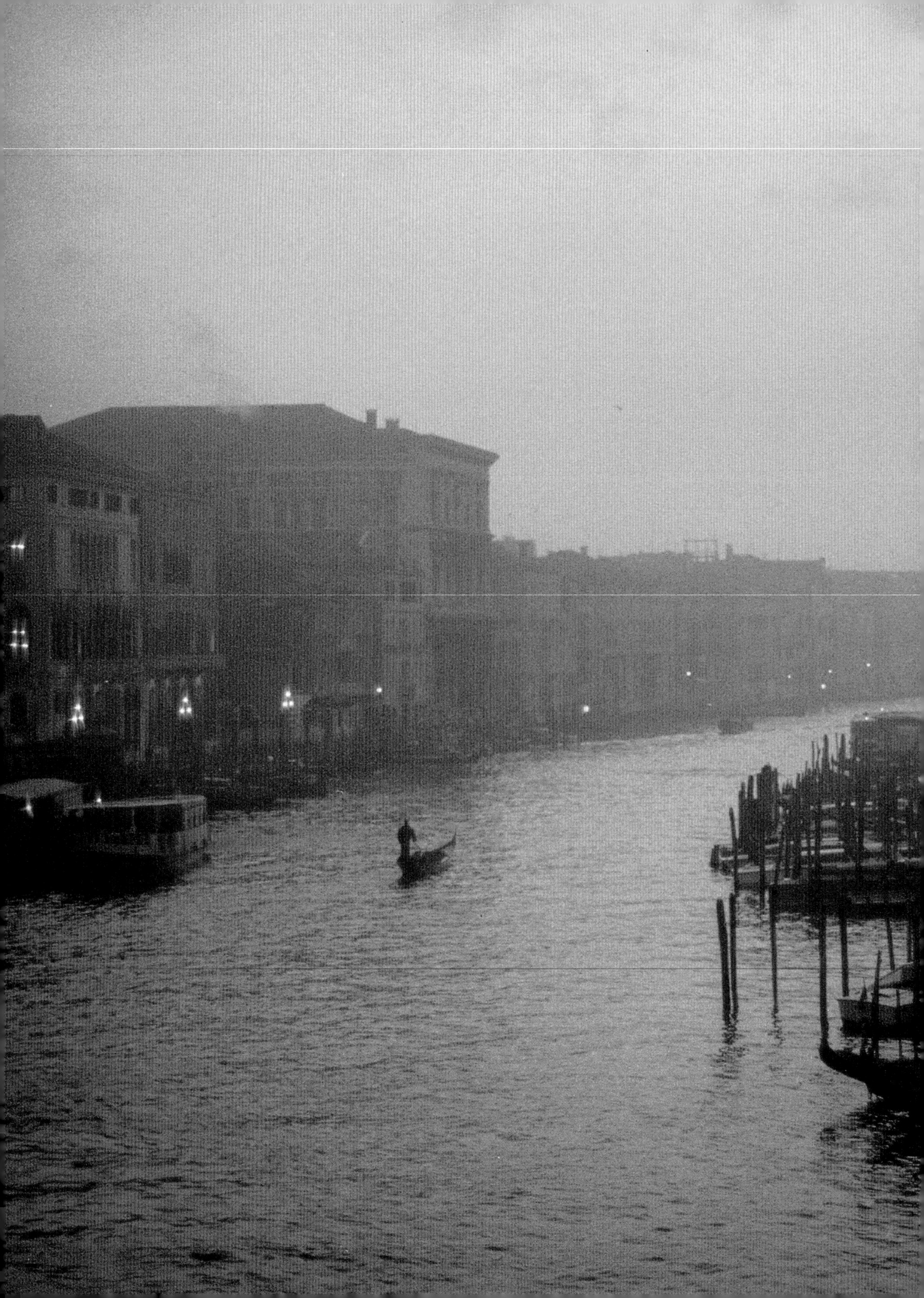

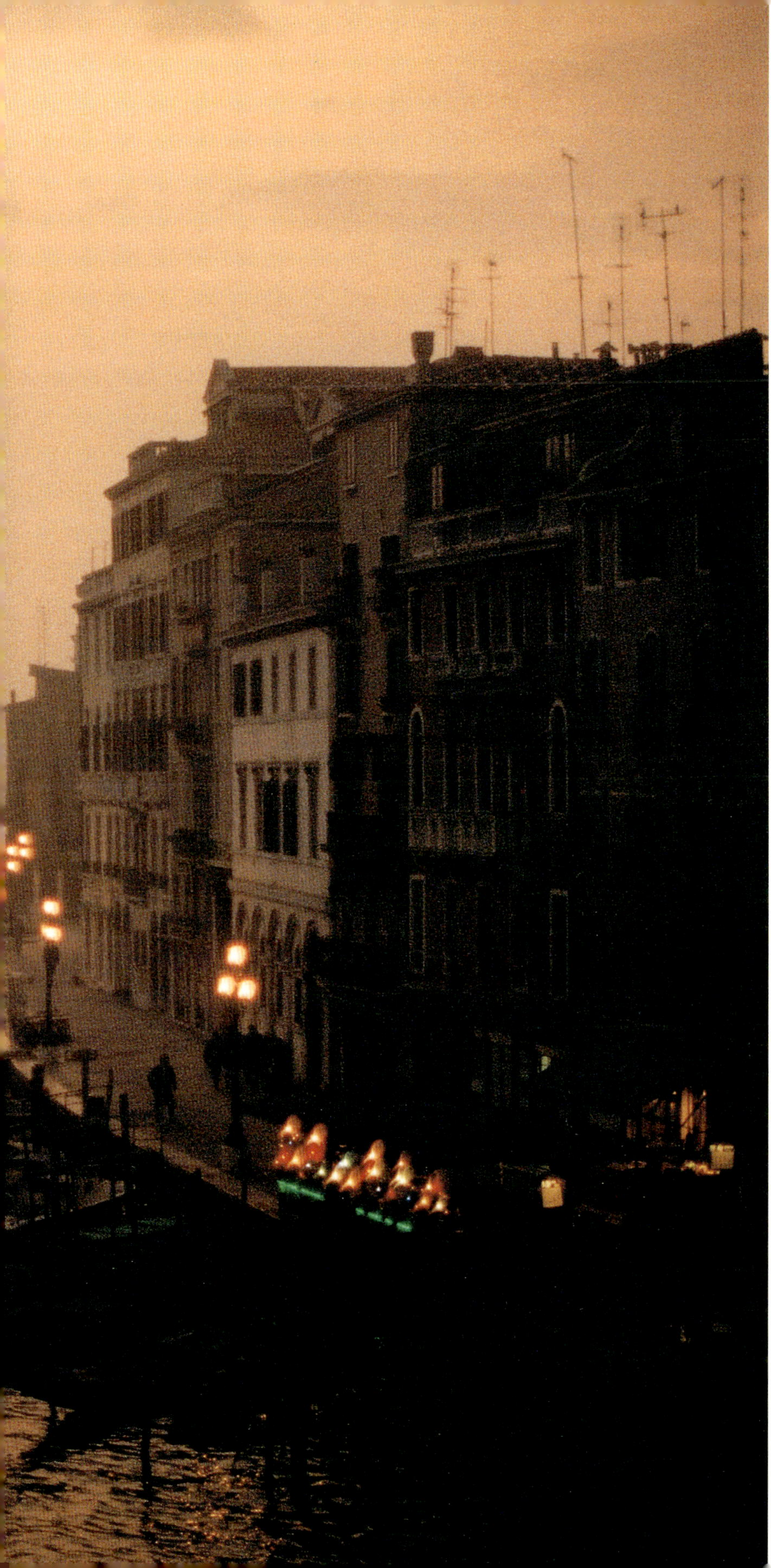

SECTION

2 The Themes

CHAPTER TWELVE

Portraits

Most of the portraits we take are of people we know – friends and family. We therefore want to produce a flattering image of them and yet we expect to be able to do this by taking a quick snapshot. No wonder we are disappointed with the results. I believe a fundamental change of attitude is required by the photographer who wants to move from snapshots to successful portraiture and that is to recognize the need to spend more time taking the picture.

Past generations of amateur photographers took great care over family portraits because camera technique was so difficult. But the results were worth it as we can see from the boxes of wonderful dignified family portraits they left behind. We are lucky because we have the freedom to take snapshots effortlessly but let's not leave behind boxes full of grimacing red-eyed monsters.

Having made the momentous decision to spend twenty minutes instead of twenty seconds on a portrait, you need to take the following into account:

- Do you want a background?
- If yes, what sort?
- Do you want to create an environmental portrait showing your subject's lifestyle by shooting in his favourite room or her favourite place?
- Do you want to concentrate just on the person's face without any background distractions?

You should then consider what sort of lighting you wish to use. Do you want to:

- Shoot inside with window light for a soft romantic light?
- Use backlight with a reflector?
- Use spotlights for a more glamorous studio effect?

Having made those decisions, you then have to really look at your subject closely, probably for the first time. Consider the proportions of the face:

- Does the sitter have a double chin? Is he balding?
- Does she have a long nose?

By choosing the right angle, lighting and pose, you can help flatter your subject considerably. For example, it is usually more flattering if your subject turns their head towards you rather than shooting them straight on.

Finally, and most importantly, it is all up to the atmosphere that you create. The mood of your subject is mostly a reflection of your own feelings at the time of the session. If you can create a relaxed atmosphere, your sitter will look relaxed.

Fisherman

I enjoy taking portraits of people I meet on my travels, particularly those who typify the place and its style.

It was late afternoon when I took this picture on Sanibel Island, Florida. People were fishing off the pier and I asked this guy if he'd caught anything, so he showed me.

I used a wide-angle setting as I wished to distort the perspective to exaggerate the size of the fish (see Lenses and Depth of Focus, page 17). The inherent depth of focus of the wide-angle lens and the bright light has meant both the fish and the fisherman are sharp.

- Shot on 200 ISO film with the zoom at 32mm.

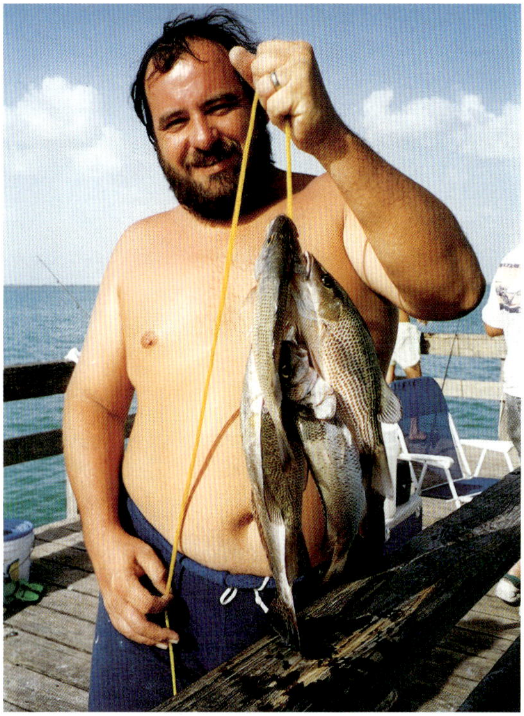

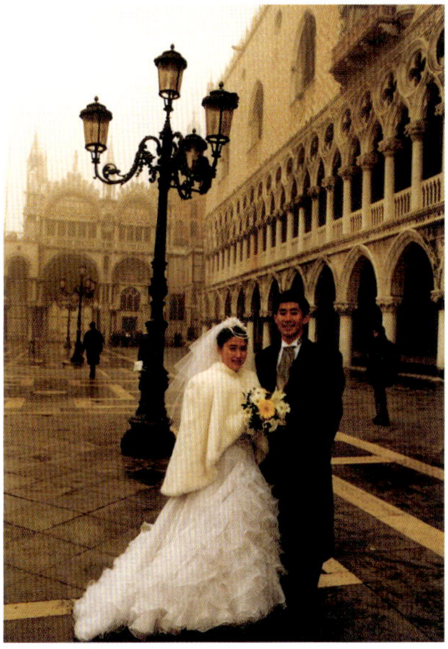

Venetian wedding

These Japanese tourists were married in Venice. I just happened to be passing by and I asked if I could take their portrait. This picture symbolizes for me the romance of Venice. I used a 35mm lens with a 81D filter over the lens, which has given a romantic sepia look to the colour (see Using Filters page 62).

- Shot on 1000 ISO film with the zoom at 32mm.

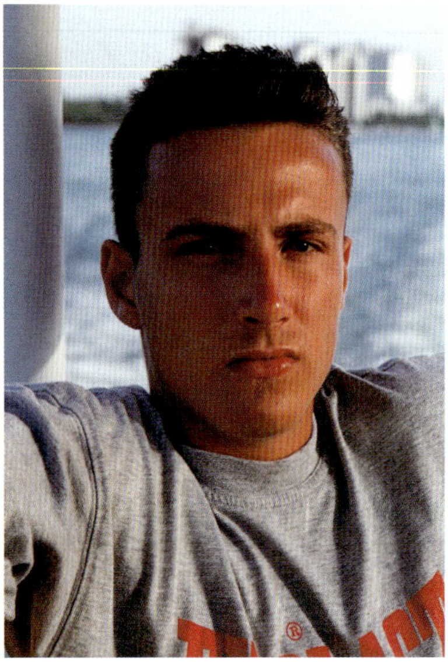

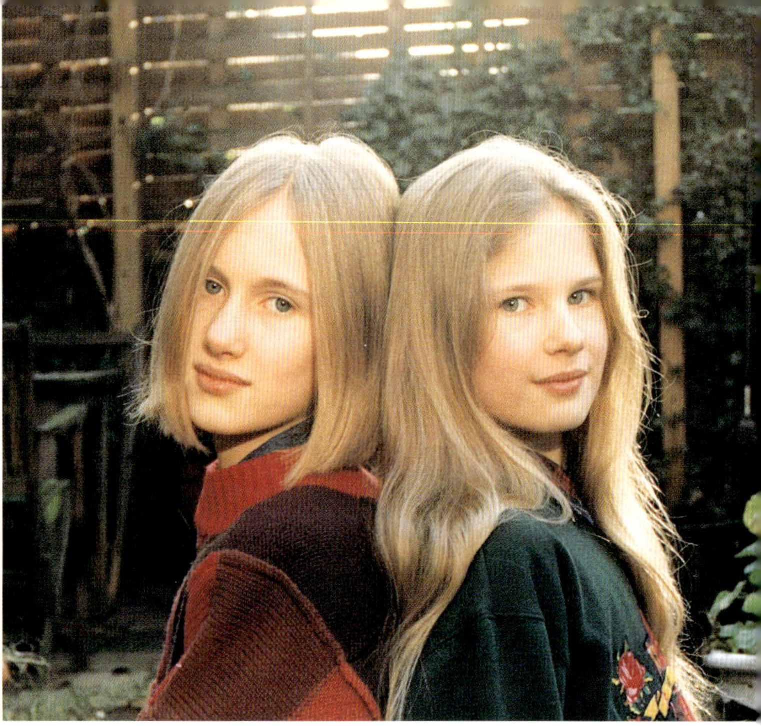

Nick

In this portrait of my eldest son, Nick, I wanted to concentrate on his face without the distractions of a sharp background. The narrow depth of focus available with the telephoto lens was therefore ideal. This type of portrait is the opposite to the environmental portrait which takes in everything. If you made a close-up portrait like this on a wide-angle lens, the face would be distorted, whereas this is a typical telephoto portrait because there is no distortion.

• Shot on 200 ISO film with the zoom at 105mm.

Two girls

The backlighting from the sun created a halo of light around the girls' heads which I then bounced back as a fill-in light using a gold reflector. A reflector gives a similar lighting effect to fill-in flash but has the advantage that you can actually see the effect you are going to get before taking the picture. Note that the gold of the reflector has given beautiful warm skin tones.

• Shot on 400 ISO film with the zoom at 70mm.

Fruit and vegetable market

I took this photograph of the fruit and vegetable market in Venice using a wide-angle lens. It shows how useful this type of lens can be when taking environmental portraits as it allowed me to show the man, with his typically Venetian features, at work. This is another portrait that brings back memories – this time of Italy's wonderful food.

• Shot on 400 ISO film with the zoom at 32mm.

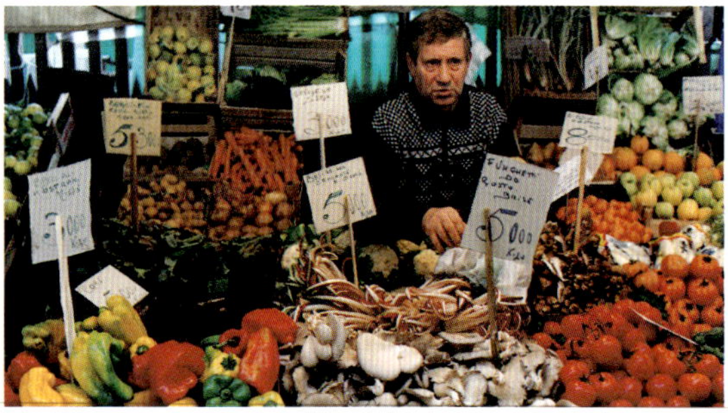

Fly fisherman

I met this gentleman fly fishing on a Snowdonian lake. It was a dull overcast day, which is ideal for portraits as it gives a soft descriptive light. I was attracted to the shape of his hands and face as he tied a new fly. The zoom allowed me to take this reportage portrait without being right on top of my subject.

• Shot on 400 ISO film with the zoom at 85mm.

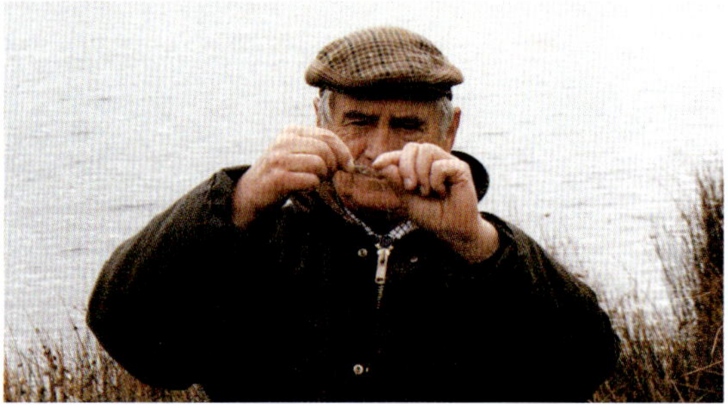

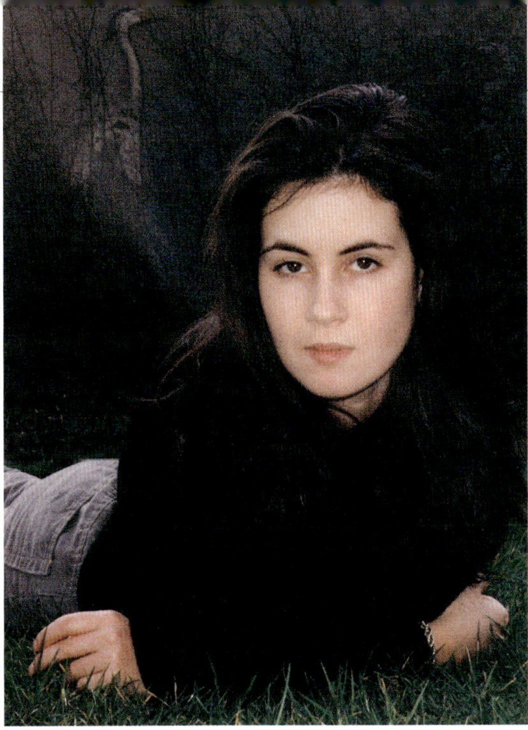

Girl with bird

The combination of daylight flash and fast film in this picture has produced a soft, gentle image. The backlight has picked out the girl's hair and the fast film has reproduced the stork mural in the background which I didn't expect to register as it looked so dark to the eye. The resulting image is rather surreal. Note that when you use daylight flash in daylight you do not get red-eye.

Try fast film on your portraits. The results can be soft and romantic.

- Shot on 1600 ISO film with the zoom at 70mm.

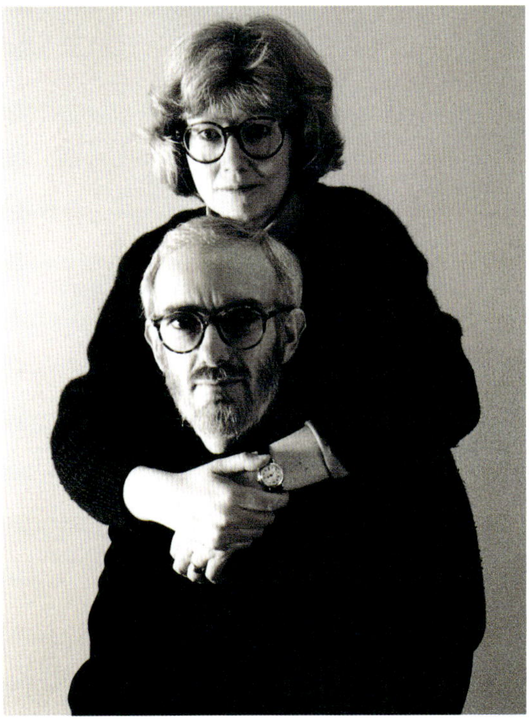

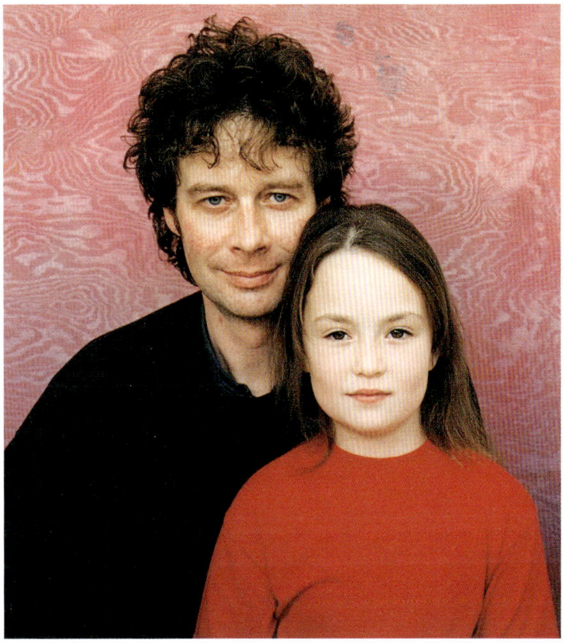

Father and daughter

I shot this picture of a friend and his daughter in my conservatory using window light which was coming from behind the camera. The plain colours of their tops combine well together and work with the background, and, more importantly, they do not detract from the faces. You have to be wary of highly patterned clothes when taking portraits as they can dominate the picture.

- Shot on 400 ISO film with the zoom at 70mm.

Man and woman

Compact cameras are not generally associated with studio photography such as this shot of a fellow photographer and his wife, but used alongside a couple of basic lighting techniques they can be very effective.

Because both my subjects wear glasses, I had to light them from the side to prevent unwanted reflections. I used an old spotlight to create the necessary side lighting and placed a white reflector on the other side to hold some detail in the shadows (see Artificial Light, page 68). We chose black tops and a grey paper background.

I find black-and-white portraits very satisfying: they have a certain strength and authority.

- Shot on 1600 ISO film with the zoom at 80mm.

Family group

I wanted to take this family portrait in the subjects' own home. By having Henry at the top and the children turning in towards their mother, we made a circular composition which allowed them to be a unit inside the busy space of the room. I find with family portraits that it helps to find something, such as the giant armchair here, to build the composition around.

Take time to make your composition first, before you start shooting. I used the available light in the room plus a mirror back flood on the balcony.

• Shot on 1600 ISO film with the zoom at 35mm.

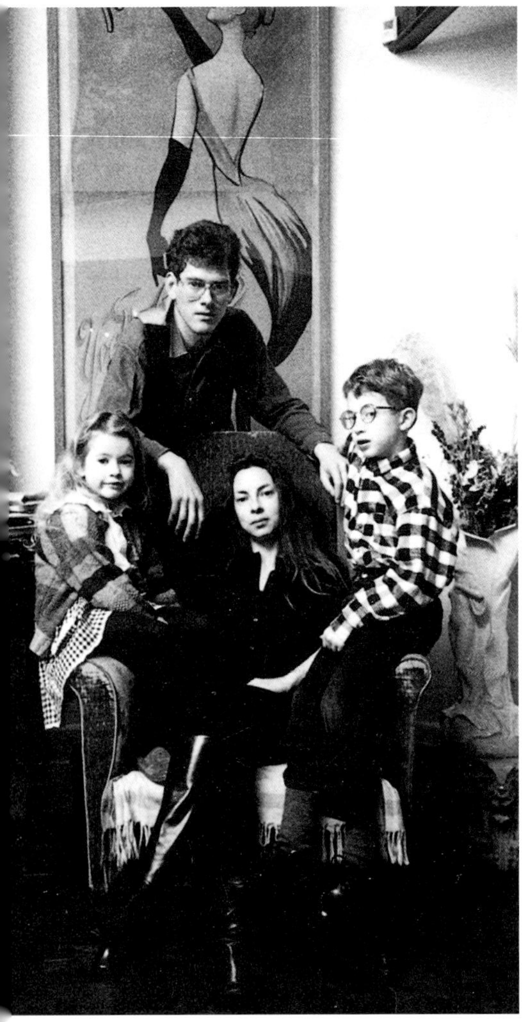

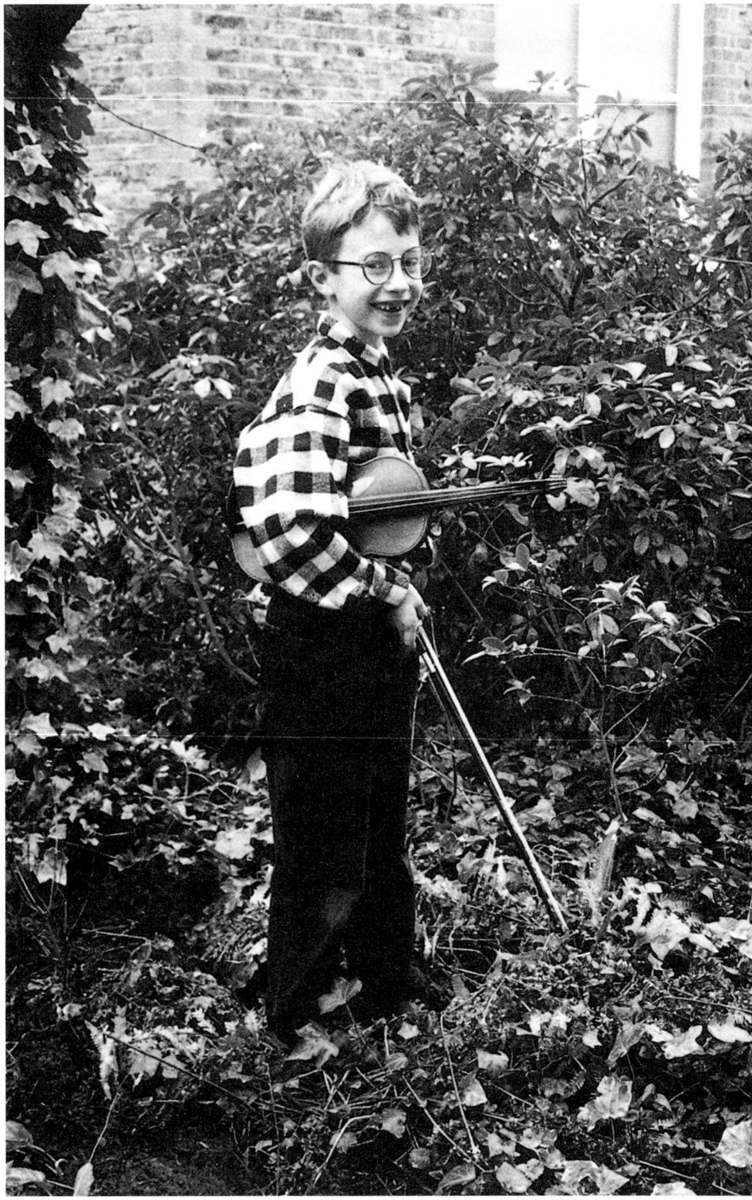

Violinist

Nathan was rather amused by the fact that I wanted him to stand in the middle of the garden for his portrait, so it wasn't a problem to get him to smile. Remember that the mood and expression your subject displays is very much down to you and you have to decide whether a jolly or serious tone is more appropriate.

• Shot on 1600 ISO film with the zoom at 50mm.

Note: All these black and white portraits were printed on an automatic colour printing machine (see Developing and Printing, page 74 and Black and White, page 122).

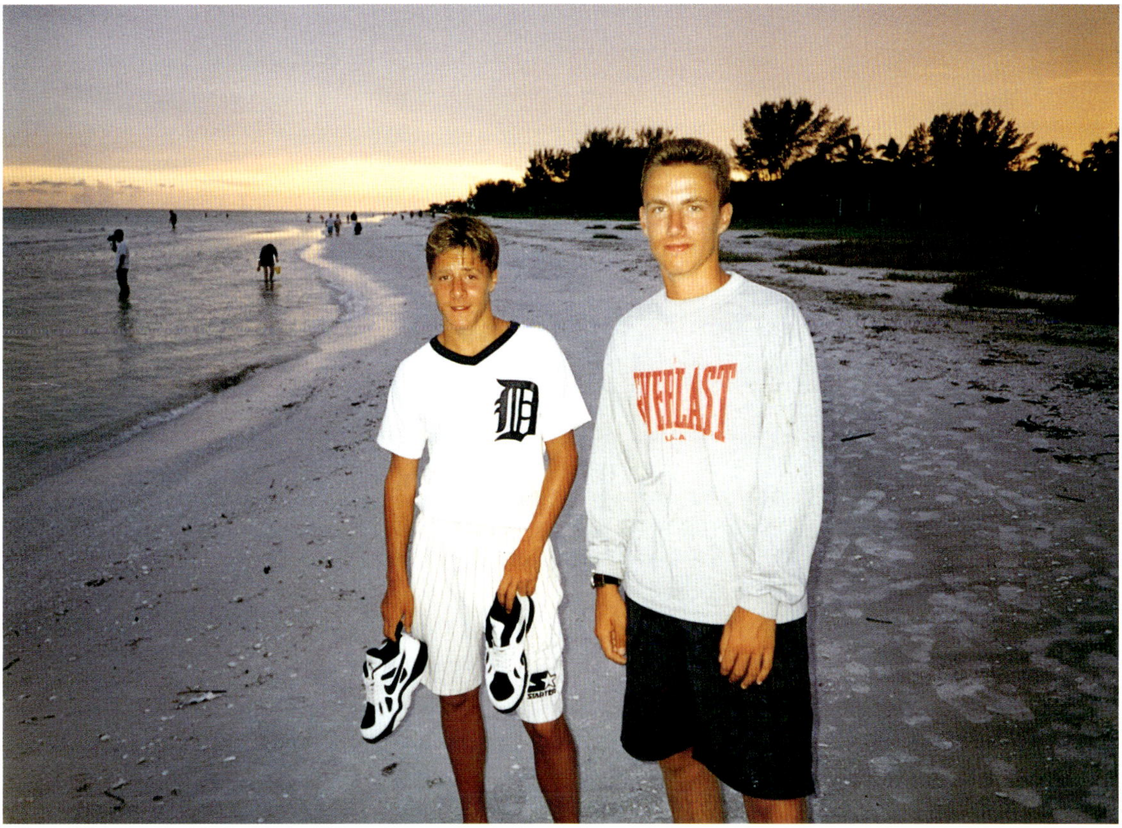

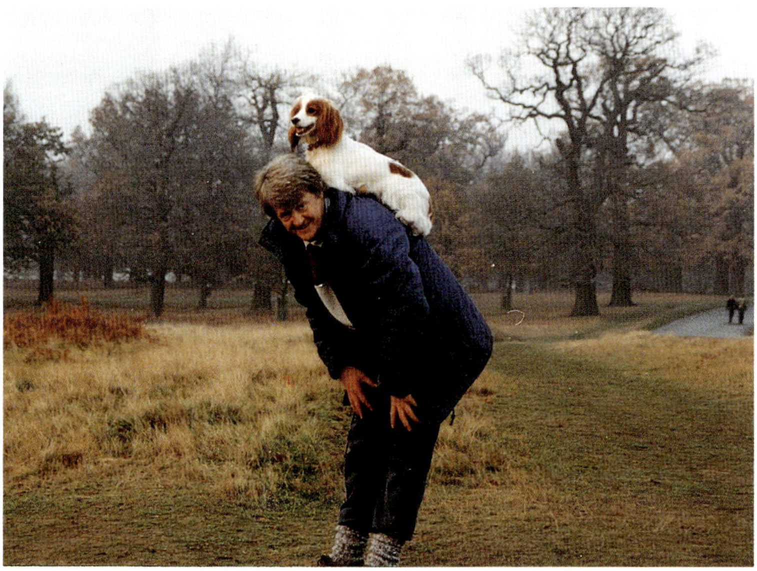

Nick and Matt

A family snapshot can be the most memorable portrait of all. I took this shot when I was out on a late afternoon walk and met my sons, Nick and Matt. It is on such occasions that the built-in flash on a compact comes into its own – capturing moments that would not be possible otherwise. I used the slow sync. mode flash and it has balanced the dusk light (it was much darker in reality) with the faces perfectly. Keep your compact with you at all times so that you don't miss opportunities such as this.

• Shot on 400 ISO film with the zoom at 35mm.

Man and his dog

My niece Joanne shot this crazy portrait of my dog, Bessie, and me in Richmond Park. I had bent down to pat another dog and Bessie, who is frightened of her other canine friends, had climbed onto my shoulders. This is a fun picture to keep and only possible because Joanne had her compact on hand. Keep taking the snapshots, they are as valid as any of Rembrandt's portraits.

CHAPTER THIRTEEN

Children

The fascination I have with child photography began with the birth of my first son, Nicholas. I photographed him and Michelle soon after his birth and for the next ten to twelve years I took pictures of him, and later of my younger son Matt, at least every week as a hobby, quite separate from my professional photography assignments. The fact that my sons and their friends became used to seeing me with a camera meant that they ignored me most of the time and continued with whatever they were doing, oblivious to the fact that I may have been taking pictures of them at the time.

Photography became a part of our family's routine life, and the camera was as familiar as the television or the telephone. Many of the pictures that I shot during this period remain as some of my favourite images. The development of the modern compact camera has made taking pictures of children much easier than it was ten years ago because it is so quick and easy to use, and can take photographs under almost any conditions.

When photographing children, the best advice I can give is to keep your camera nearby and loaded with film. Children have the greatest of talents for performing the most photogenic acts just as you've packed the camera away – so don't – keep it handy at all times. Fast film, 400 or 1600 ISO, is ideal for taking pictures of children because it enables you to shoot without the distraction of flash. Try, also, getting down to their level rather than always looking down at them from yours.

If you wish to take formal portraits, remember that young children can get bored quite quickly, so you'll need to talk to them and keep them amused while taking the photographs. They are real people, just smaller, so you don't have to communicate in baby-talk, and if the child doesn't feel like sitting for the picture on the day you planned, forget it. If you make a big fuss and create a lot of tension, you will undoubtedly jeopardize any future sittings. But if on the other hand you keep everything relaxed and don't make the child feel guilty for not wanting to be in the picture, he or she will probably cooperate on another occasion.

It also helps to plan your session before the child arrives. Make sure the background is set up and the camera loaded and ready, then you can concentrate on creating a relaxed atmosphere.

If the weather conditions are good, you can quite easily take formal portraits outside by using a painted board as a background, as a bright overcast day, for example, provides a very flattering light for portraiture.

Photographing children can be one of the most rewarding hobbies and the pictures will be appreciated by the family for generations. Just make sure it is an enjoyable experience for you and the children too.

Mother and newborn baby

I took this portrait just two minutes after my son was born. I had popped a little compact in my pocket loaded with a fast black and white film as I was not sure whether the hospital or my nerves would allow a picture; or indeed if Michelle would feel up to it. I obviously did take the picture and we have always felt grateful that I had the camera with me.

Compacts have made pictures like this possible. There are many great pictures of children and the family that you can capture with a compact simply because you have it to hand whereas, it would be impossible to carry around a heavy camera bag plus lenses the whole time.

- Shot on 1600 ISO film with the zoom at 32mm.

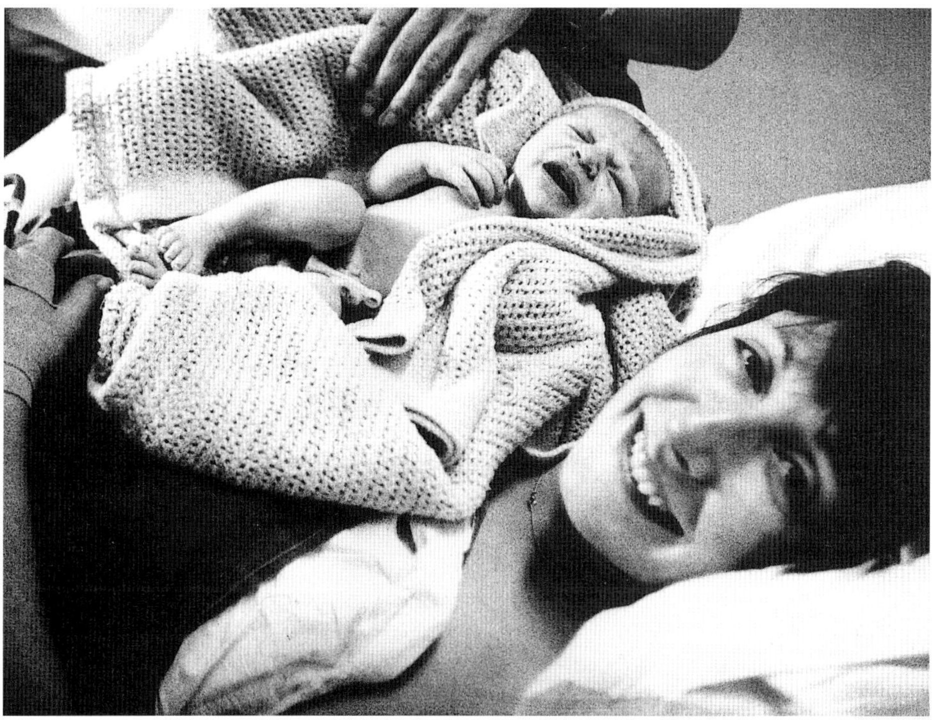

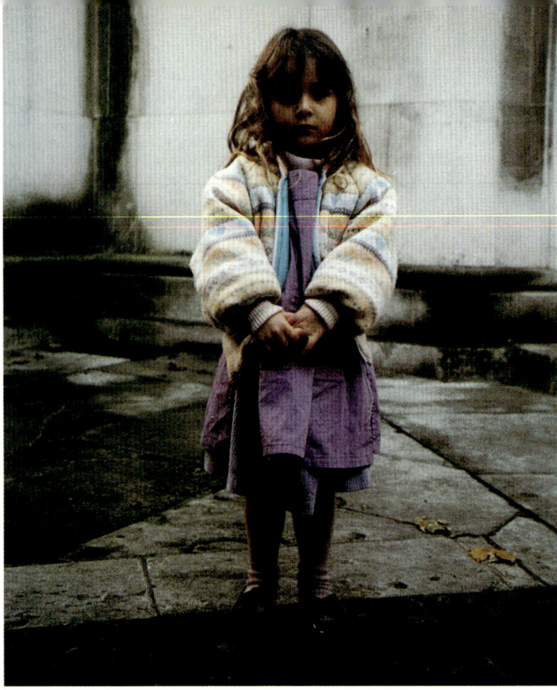

Girl in a purple dress

I took this picture at a nursery school. It was a cold and extremely dull winter's day so I used a fast film to avoid the flash going off. The colours and muted quality of the light have bestowed a rather melancholy mood to the portrait. Dull light like this creates a beautiful atmosphere. I crouched down so I was at the child's level, rather than looking down at her.

• Shot on 1000 ISO film with the zoom at 70mm.

Boy with yellow hat

Adults tend to put pressure on children to look the way they want them to look. It is often this pressure and the determination on the photographer's part to make the child smile that destroys a potentially good picture session. My advice is to let them be the way they want to be. This little guy was very serious, but perfectly happy for me to take his picture. If I had tried to make him smile and tidy up his clothes, he would have been off – quite right too!

• Shot on 400 ISO film with the zoom at 70mm.

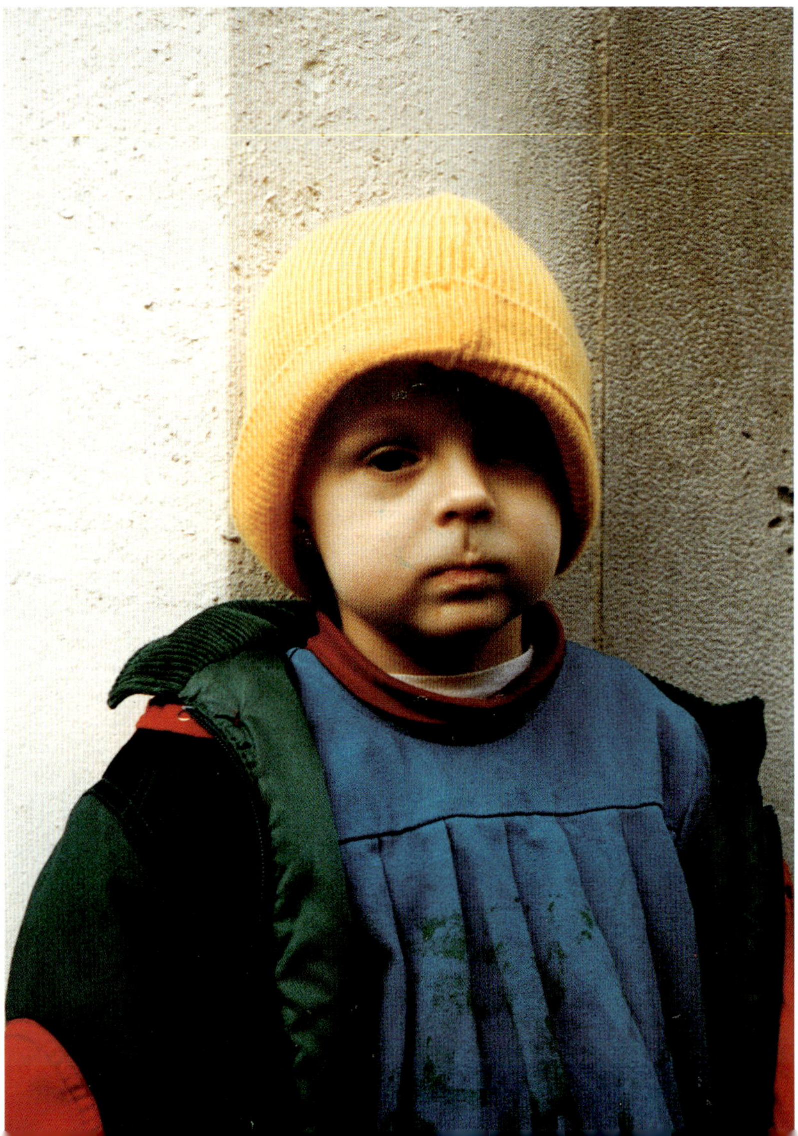

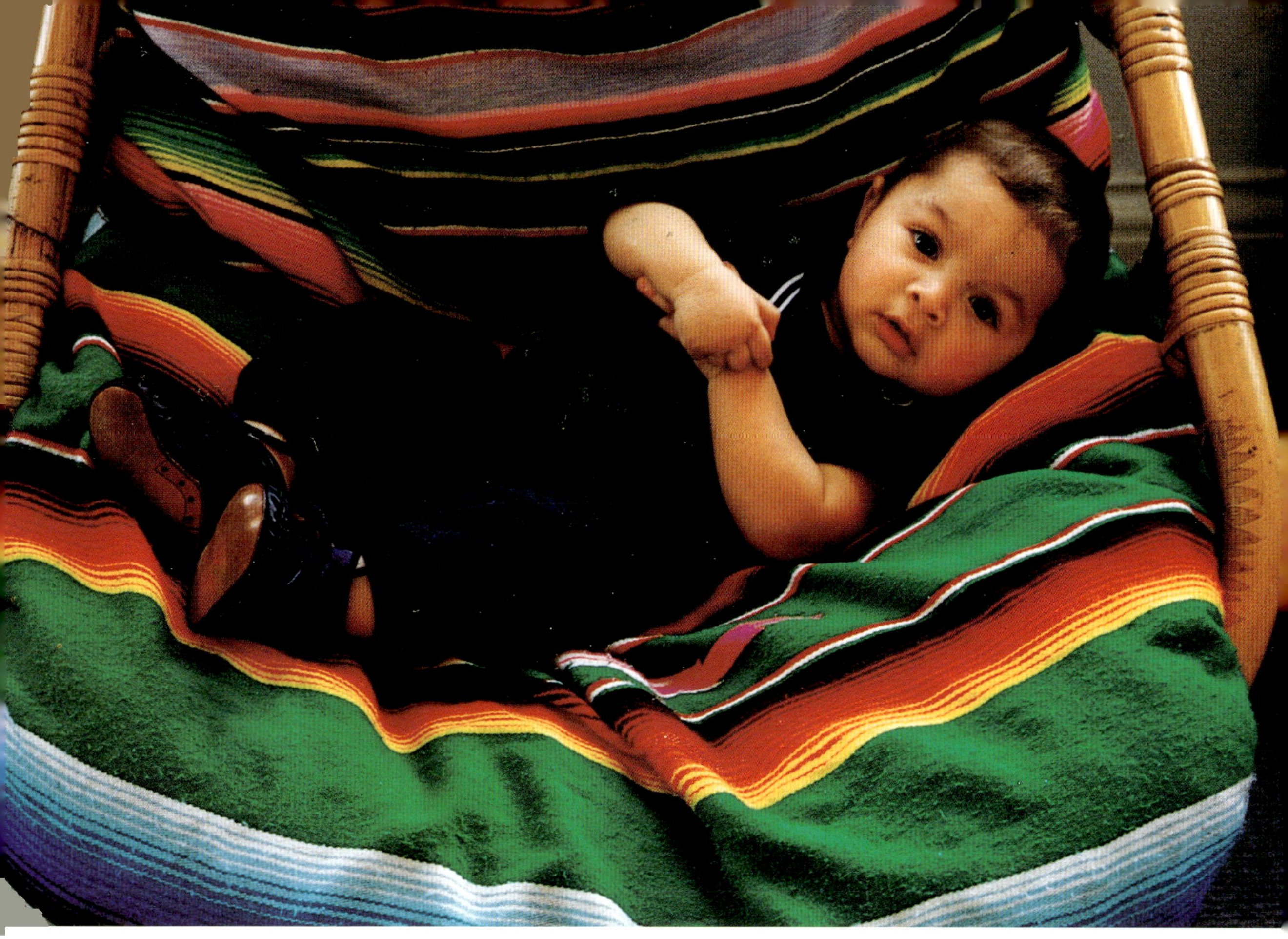

Baby against a multi-coloured background

Babies are tricky to photograph before they reach the sitting-up stage. You'll need someone to help you, firstly for safety reasons, to prevent the baby from falling, and secondly to wipe off any dribbles and to make the appropriate noises to attract their attention towards the camera.

Find a comfortable and attractive background to lie the baby on: this could be a bed or, as I have done here, a chair. If you are by yourself you should not photograph your baby anywhere other than on the floor or in a carrycot for safety reasons. If possible move as near to a window as possible as you need plenty of light and a fast film (400 or 1000 ISO) so that you can avoid harsh flash light. There was a window by the chair and I used the room light too, which helped to warm up the skin tones and fill in the shadows (see Flash, page 26). This little chap was very curious about me and the camera and as he had just eaten was quite relaxed, so it was easy to attract his attention for a few minutes. The session could have ended very abruptly, however.

• Shot on 400 ISO film with the zoom at 35mm.

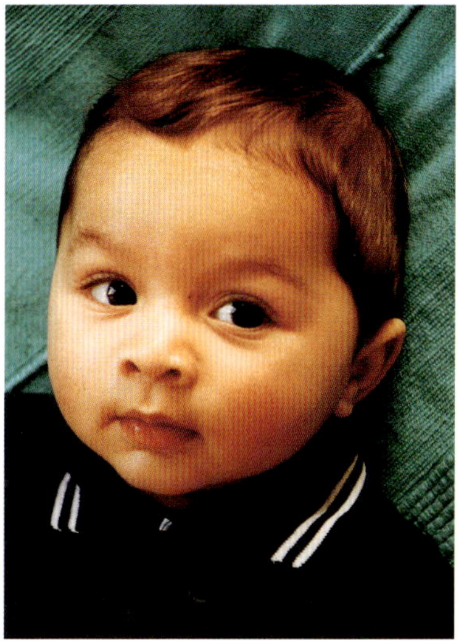

When I zoomed in to take a close-up portrait of the same baby, I found that the stripes of the blanket distracted attention from his face. I therefore placed a turquoise cushion under his head which worked much better.

Be careful with your framing when working this close – check your close-up framing lines in the viewfinder (see How It Works, page 18). Remember too that you need to shoot quite a number of pictures when photographing a baby. I shot fifteen frames of this close-up portrait and only three were successful – he moved in six, dribbled in three and closed his eyes for another three. But the ones which worked were well worth it.

• Shot on 400 ISO film with the zoom set at 80mm.

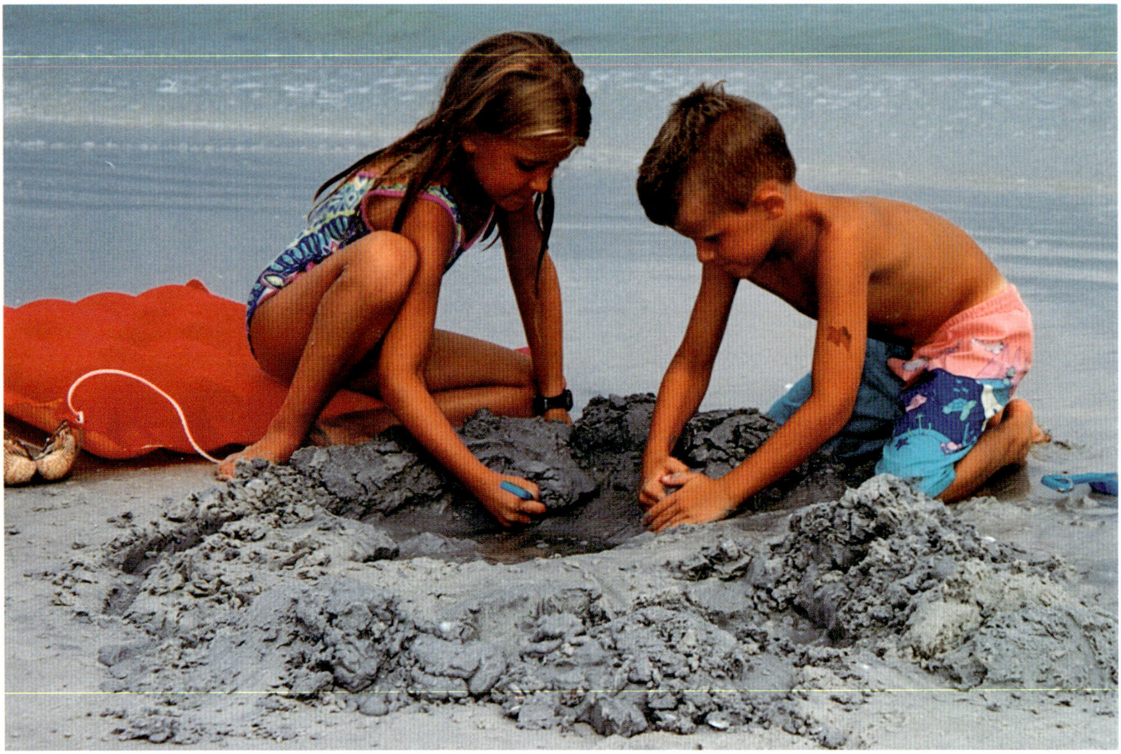

Sandcastles

When photographing the 'world of the child', be unobtrusive and patient, don't rush in and bang away taking pictures. If you stay a while and allow the children to get used to your presence, they will soon forget about your camera and remain absorbed in their own activities. If you want to set up an 'action' shot then organize an activity that you know they'll enjoy, wait for them to get involved and then start taking photographs.

I saw these two children playing on the beach and asked their parents, who were nearby, if I could photograph them. The children looked up and said 'hello' and then went straight back to digging in the sand. I used the zoom lens so that I could keep my distance and not inhibit their concentration. I was attracted to the circular shape their bodies made around their excavation, which gave the scene a private feeling while the late afternoon sun gave a warm glow to their skin.

• Shot on 200 ISO film with the zoom at 85mm.

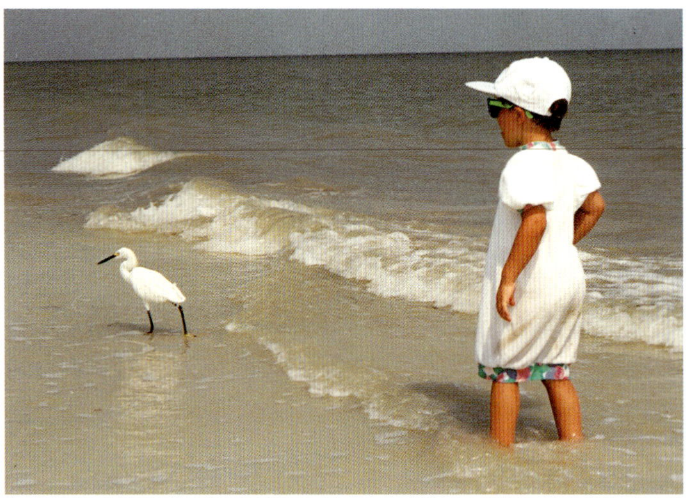

Girl and bird

The bird was stalking a fish and the girl was stalking the bird. The little girl didn't even know that I had taken the picture. The bird was aware of the fish, the girl and the photographer.

• Shot on 200 ISO film with the zoom at 50mm.

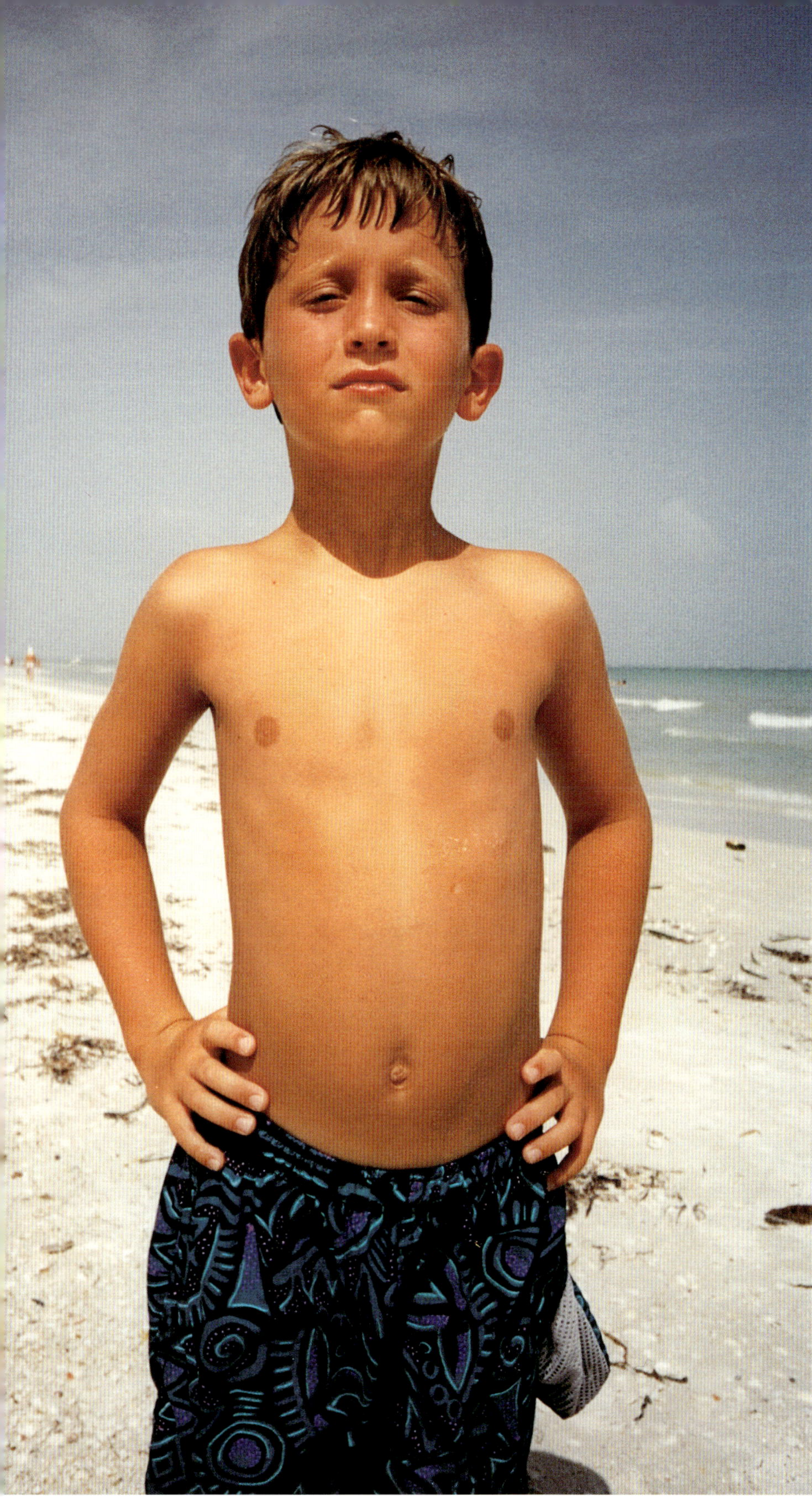

Beach boy

This little boy loved being photographed. I shot this portrait on a 28mm lens from a kneeling position. Because I was below his eye level he was able to look down at the camera, which has added to the sense of pride he is displaying. Most pictures of children are shot from an adult eye level, looking down at the child. I like to shoot from their eye level as the resulting pictures have much more impact – and dignity. The use of a wide-angle lens has also captured the boy's holiday environment.

• Shot on 200 ISO film with the zoom at 28mm.

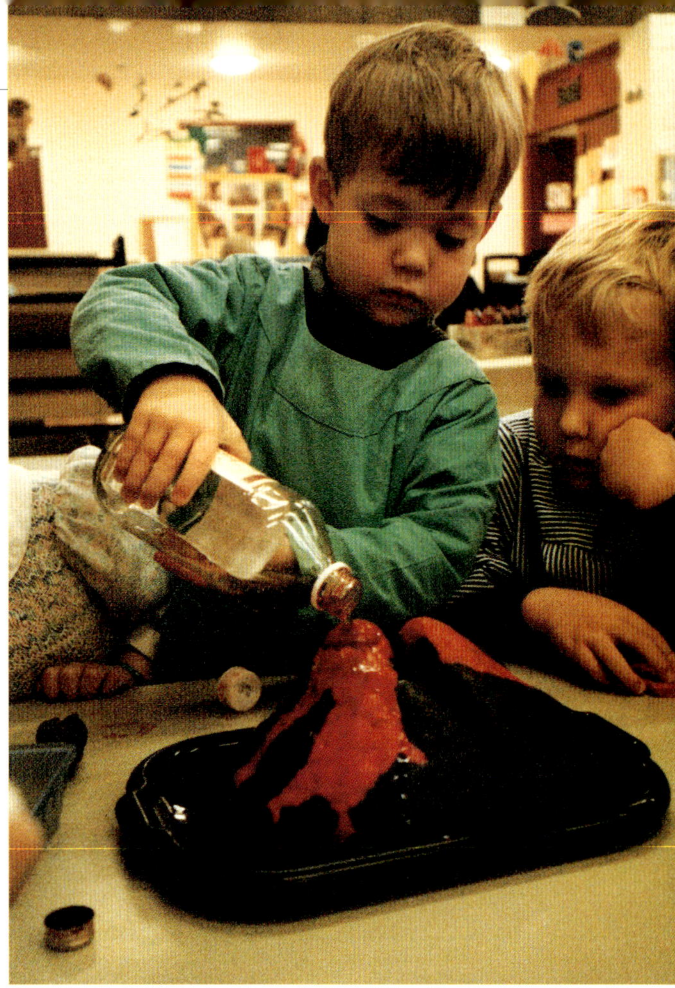

Children at work

In spite of the fact that the camera was right in front of them, these little lads were so involved in making a 'volcano' that they didn't notice I was taking pictures. I had been in the room for about an hour before I attempted this shot so they were used to my presence. I used a very fast film so the flash wouldn't go off in the low light conditions. The resulting print is very grainy (see Film, page 38), but I would never have achieved such a candid shot if I had been using flash.

- Shot on 3200 ISO film with the zoom at 40mm.

School photograph

The Iverna Gardens Nursery School all lined up for a group photograph. I use a tripod when taking group shots of children, because I can take my face away from behind the camera and entertain the children. Group shots like this are hard work because you need to throw yourself into the session and take on the role of the child entertainer for a while to keep their attention.

- Shot on 1000 ISO film with the zoom at 50mm.

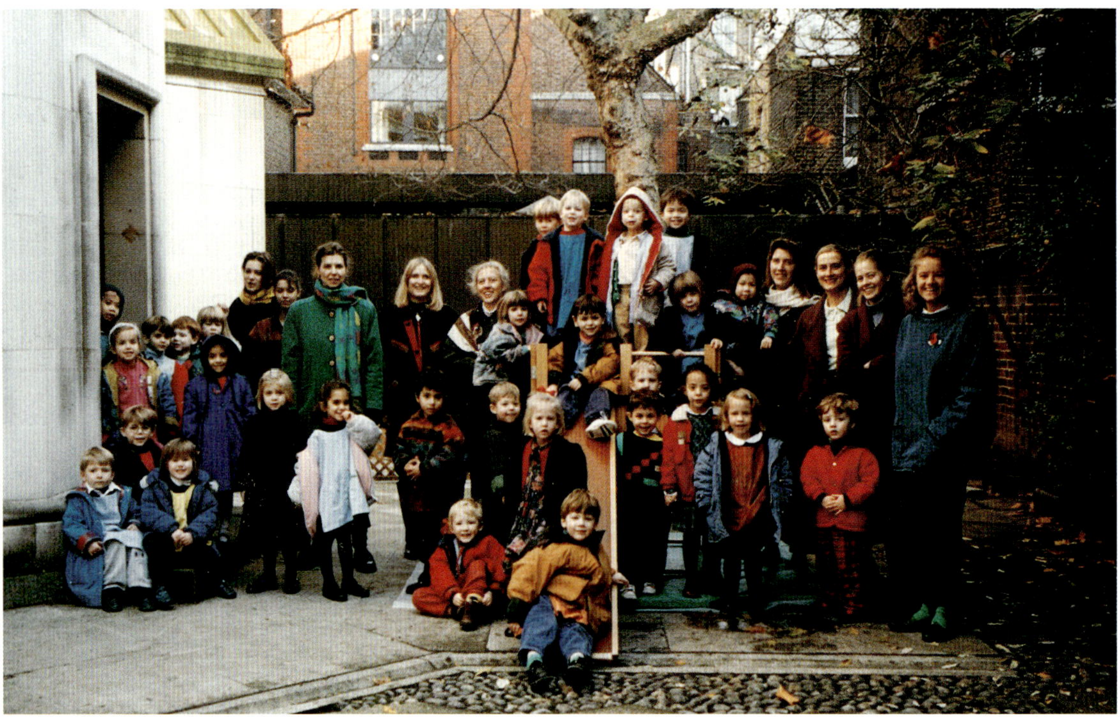

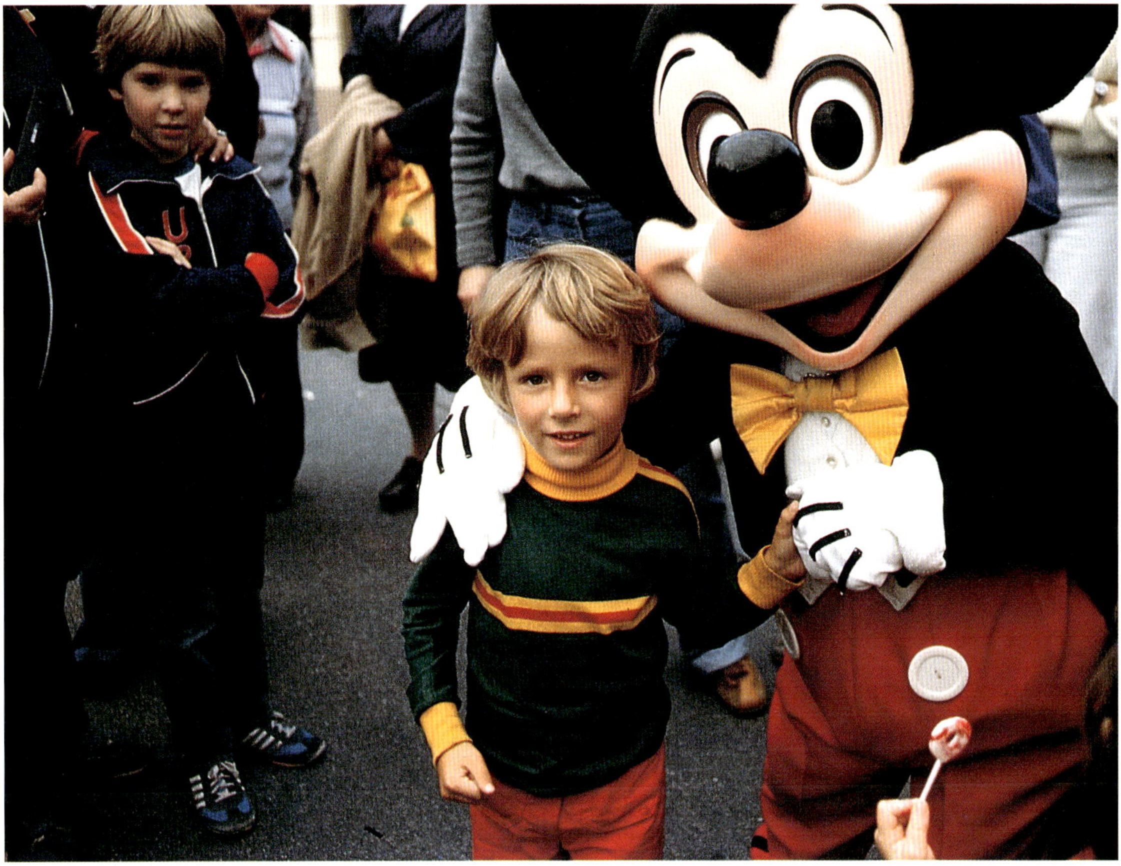

Disneyland

This is the ideal situation for using a fixed-focal-length compact. I visualized the picture, pulled the camera out of my pocket, shot the picture and the camera was back in my pocket within a few seconds. Concentrate on filling the frame with your subject.

• Shot on 400 ISO film with a 35mm fixed-focal-length camera.

Girl in red

This quite formal portrait was shot in my conservatory using the daylight from the windows. I have several painted boards I use as backgrounds and chose the pink one to tone with the little girl's T-shirt.

As with most portrait sessions, the atmosphere was a little strained at first, until we got used to each other. I used a tripod so that I could talk more freely without my head being stuck behind the camera. As the atmosphere became more relaxed, she began to smile more easily. I really like this picture – the smile reveals the little gap in her teeth.

• Shot on 400 ISO film with the zoom at 70mm

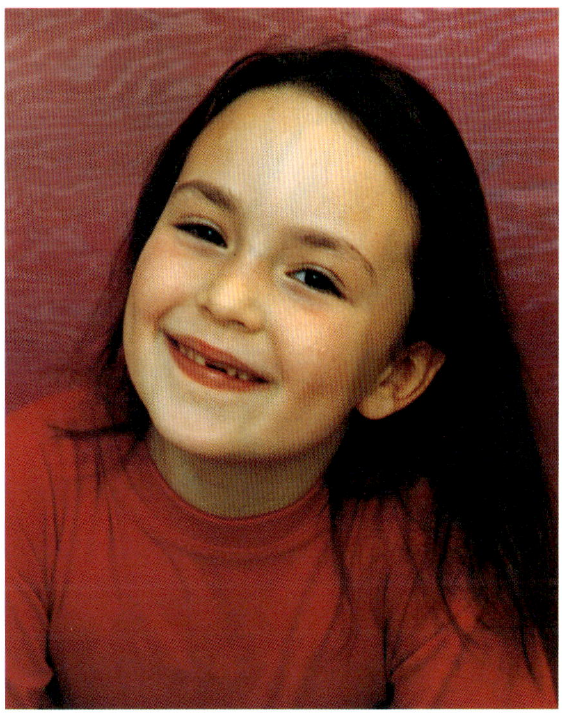

CHAPTER FOURTEEN

Animals

Patience, as the old saying goes, is a virtue. When applied to animal photography it is more than a virtue, it is an essential. Most of the animals we photograph fall into three categories: the family pet; zoo or safari park animals; wildlife we come across on our travels.

The major problem I have when photographing animals, particularly the family pet, is that old enemy, red-eye. The red-eye reduction facility built in to many modern compact cameras has little effect (see Flash, page 26), mainly because dogs and cats (and most other animals) have large dark eyes that reflect the flash like mirrors. The only way to avoid this is to prevent them looking at the camera when shooting inside or, best of all, try to photograph your pets outside. On the positive side, however, flash does give a wonderful shine to an animal's coat. As with children, the best advice I can give is to keep your camera handy and loaded to catch the cutest moments. Your inside knowledge of the animal is obviously a great help. For example, when is the dog most relaxed? After he's had a walk and something to eat? To avoid the flash going off use a fast film (400 ISO or 1000 ISO). Keep backgrounds simple and, as with children, try to involve the animal in a favourite pastime so that they he isn't distracted by your presence. It's important too to be realistic – you will need to take plenty of film to get a few great pictures – but they sure are worth it.

Fortunately, zoos have improved over recent years: the animal habitats are better and there are many more bar-free areas from which to view and photograph the animals – especially the dangerous ones. It is worthwhile phoning the zoo prior to your visit to find out the feeding times, if you are keen to obtain natural shots.

If you do have to photograph through bars, use the focus lock (see page 18) to prevent the auto focusing facility trying to focus on the bars in the foreground instead of the animal. If you are able to get close to the bars – between about 2.5 and 15cm (1–6in) – you will find that on the telephoto setting the depth of focus is so narrow that, when focused on the animals, the bars will be so out of focus that they will hardly register. If you are allowed, place the lens through the bars. Remember though that on a compact the viewfinder and the lens have different viewpoints; you can mistakenly be viewing through the bars while the lens (which is taking the picture, of course) is obstructed by a bar (see Problem Solving, page 81).

If you are trying to photograph through glass using flash, place the camera right on the glass but shoot at an angle, so that the flash goes through the glass and does not bounce back into the lens. Drape a coat over yourself and the camera (except for the lens of course) to prevent any unwanted reflections.

When photographing birds and animals in the wild (and I am assuming that all my readers are sensible, safety-conscious people) you need a great deal of patience. You have to be prepared to go to the animal's or bird's natural habitat and to wait patiently for them to appear.

I will not pretend that animal photography is easy on a compact camera as you have a limited range with the zoom and size of lens aperture. But it is possible to produce very satisfying pictures if you use a softly, softly approach.

Spaniel

This is a portrait of our family dog, Bessie. I made several pictures of her looking at the camera, but the red-eye (accentuated by her large eyes) looked awful. In this picture, however, she is looking away from the camera and the flash has emphasized her glossy coat. I sat her on a sofa and worked close from a low angle to get as much impact and as few background distractions as possible. She had just eaten her dinner so was quite relaxed. I also had my son next to me to keep her amused, so she didn't try to come forward and lick the camera.

As a general rule, it is better to avoid red-eye by taking photographs of pets outside. Use the flash on the anytime or fill-in setting (depending on the model of your camera), because it gives a shine to the animal's coat and, in daylight, there is no danger of red-eye.

• Shot on 400 ISO film with the zoom at 70mm.

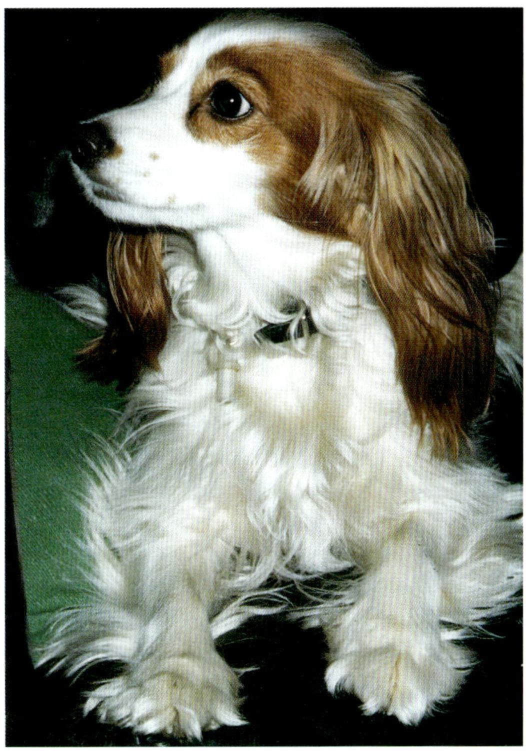

White swan

I walk the dogs regularly in Richmond Park and I have taken many pictures of the swans on my SLR Nikon cameras, but never produced such a good result as this taken on my little compact. I set the flash on the anytime mode and the camera has perfectly balanced the contrast in light between foreground and background.

Because the flash light is of such a short duration, it produces very sharp images and picks out incredible detail such as the swan's feathers. But you need to take the photograph when the bird is stationary, or almost, otherwise you will produce a double image.

I spent about one hour and shot a 36-exposure roll of film of the swans as I wanted to capture this classic shot of a swan spreading its wings. When photographing animals and birds, patience and some knowledge of animal behaviour is helpful plus a bag full of old bread!

• Shot on 200 ISO film with the zoom at 105mm.

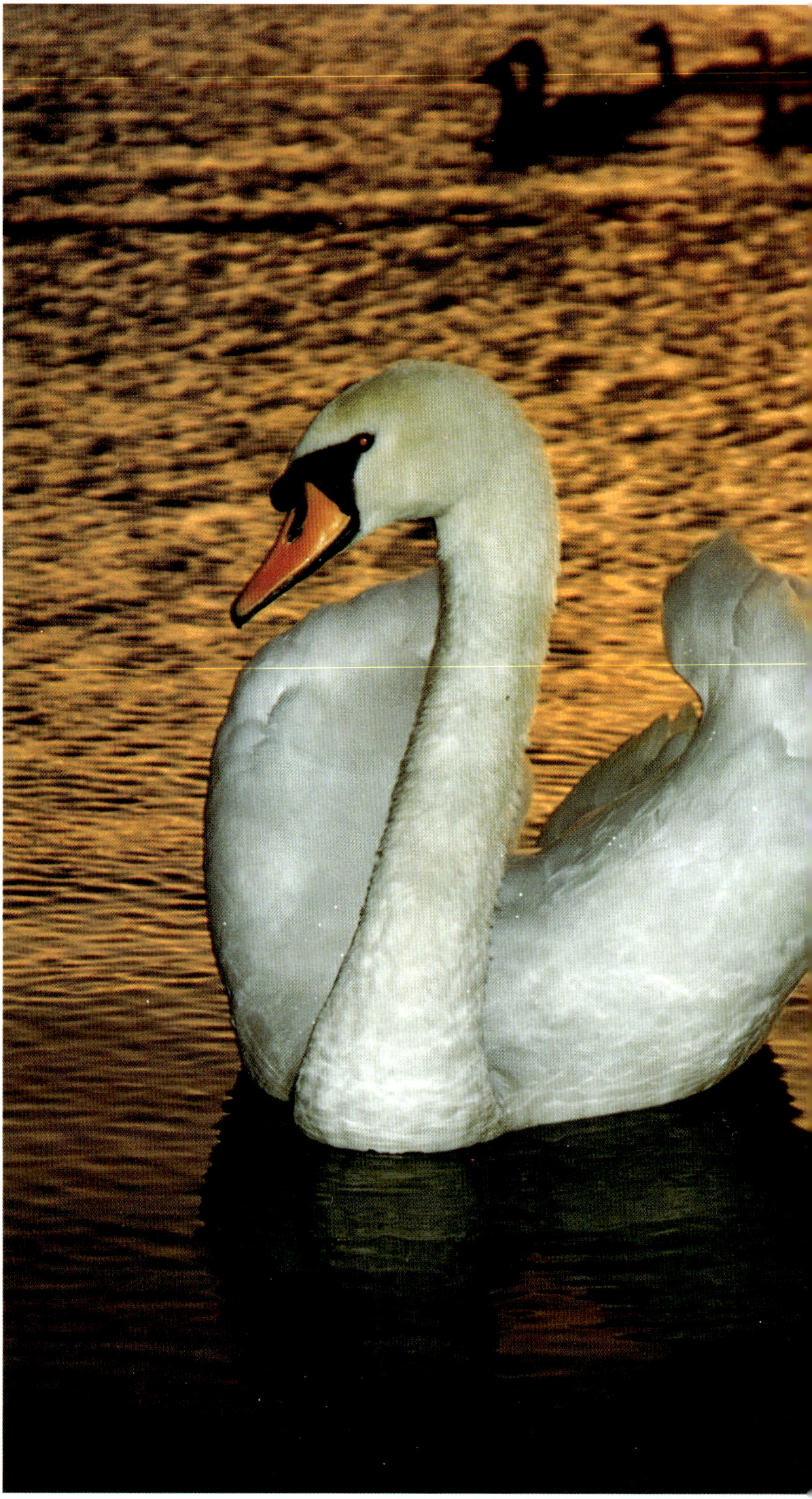

Beach birds

These rather eccentric-looking birds walk up and down the beach on Sanibel Island in Florida searching for shellfish. The first few times I tried to photograph them, they flew away, so I approached a group of them and quietly sat down in the shallows for about twenty minutes. They eventually became accustomed to my presence and their natural curiosity drew them towards me. They were perfectly happy for me to photograph them from this stationary position, but flew off whenever I tried to move closer.

With all wildlife photography, it is important to keep as still as possible to avoid frightening your subject. Because compact cameras do not have the long telephoto lenses normally associated with wildlife photography, it helps to choose animals with a natural curiosity in the hope that they will approach you.

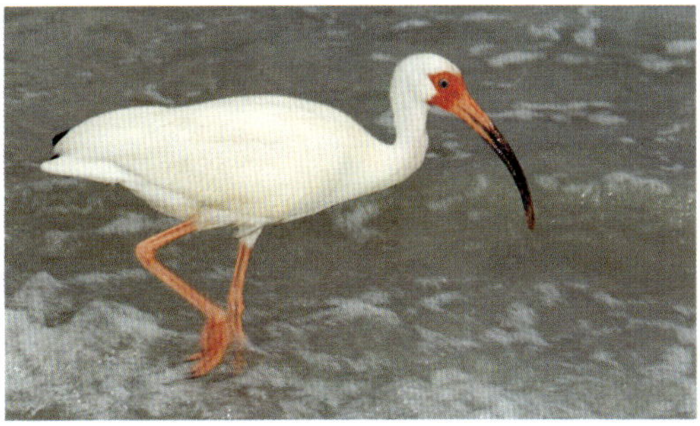

Note Fill-in flash has been used here also, which has thrown highlights onto the beak and brightened the image. There is a very slight double image because of the birds' movement, but I find that quite acceptable.

• Shot on 200 ISO film with the zoom at 85mm.

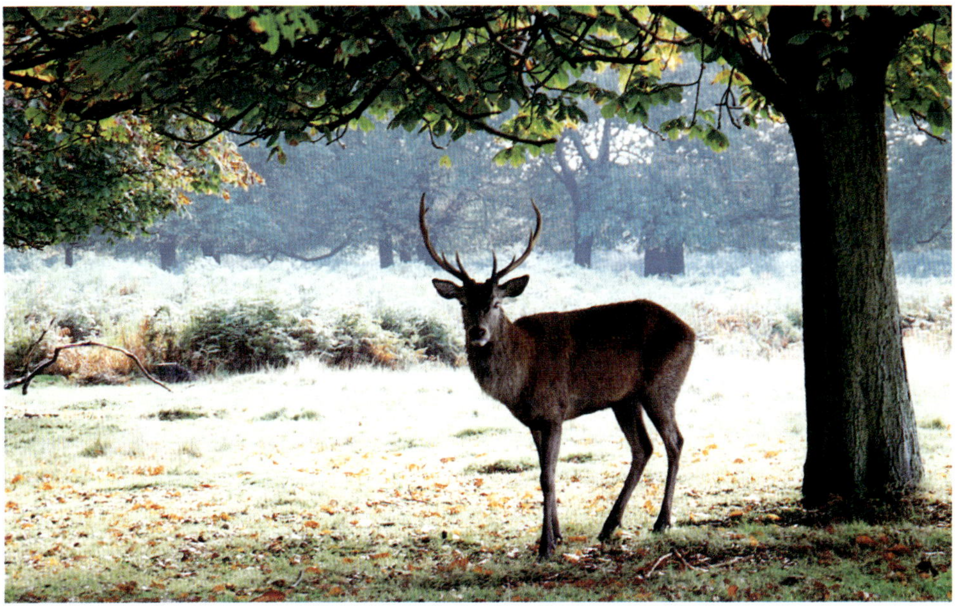

Deer

I photographed this deer in Richmond Park. Although the deer are used to people, they are nevertheless shy animals and are difficult to approach. The lack of a really long telephoto lens means that, unless you are very fortunate, you are unlikely to be able to fill the frame with the wild animal, so you need to use your compositional talents to make attractive pictures of animals in their habitat.

In the wild, animals are more active and most likely to be visible early in the morning and late afternoon when the light is low. Fast film (400–1600 ISO) will give you the best chance of success under these conditions.

• Shot on 1000 ISO film with the zoom at 115mm.

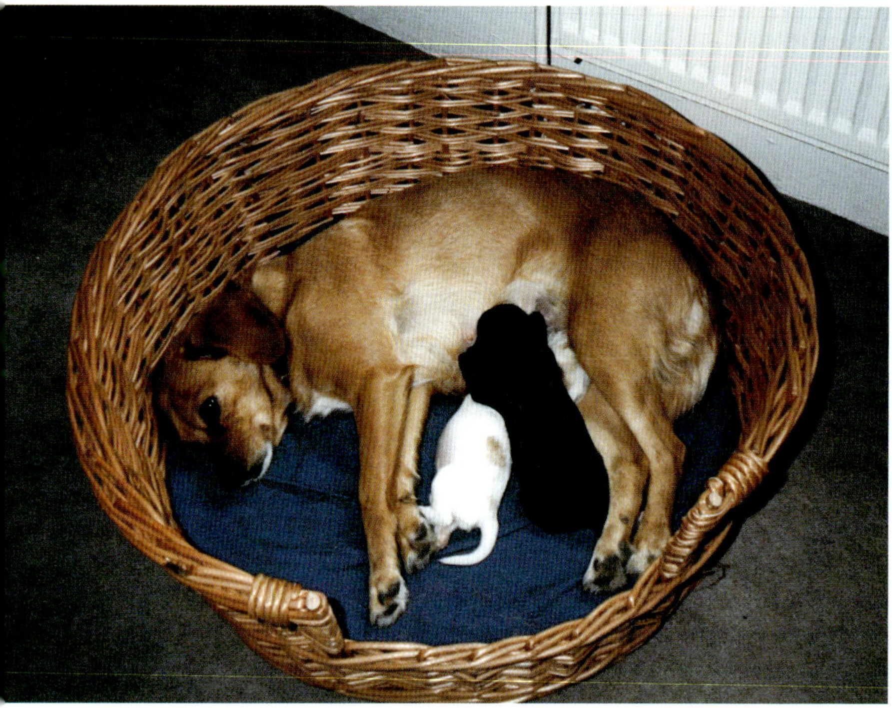

Puppies

A snapshot of our dog Sophie feeding her pups using auto flash. Remember, keep the compact close by and loaded so that you don't miss those wonderful moments.

• Shot on 400 ISO film with the zoom at 50mm.

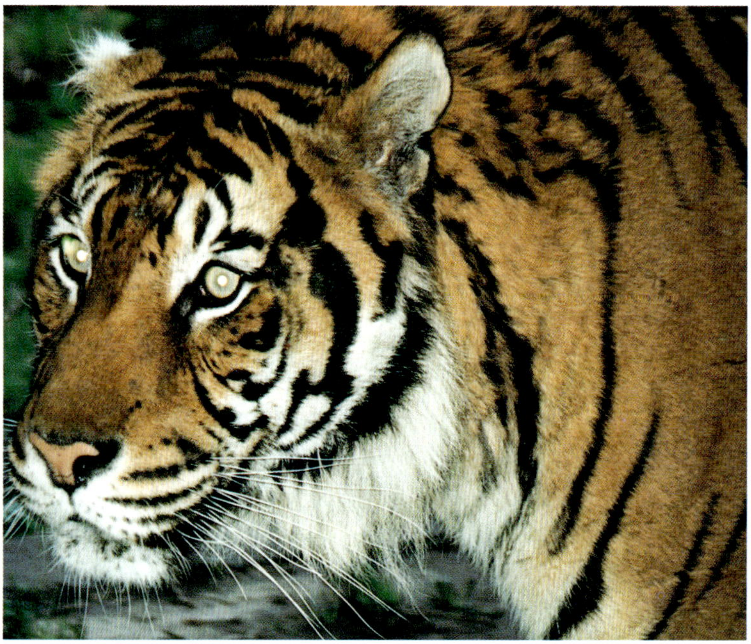

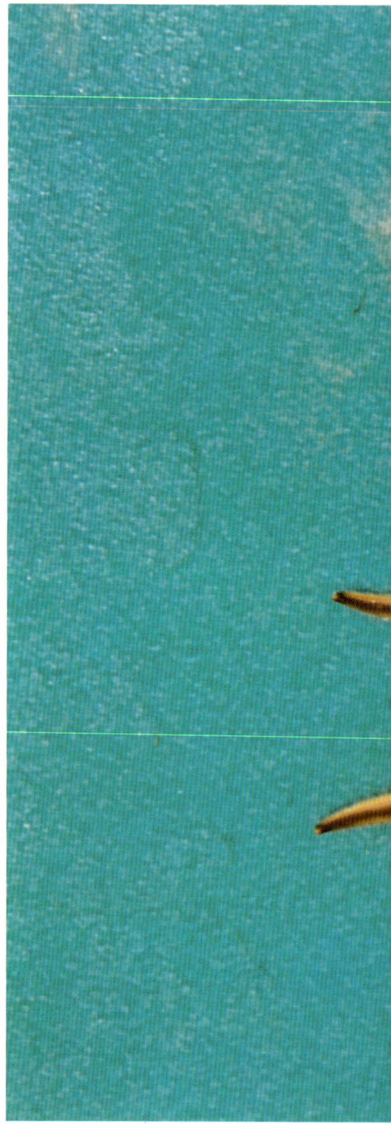

Tiger

This Sumatran tiger was pacing up and down behind the glass at London Zoo. Because the flash was at an angle of about 45 degrees to the glass, the flash has penetrated the glass without any reflection. The flash (on auto) has produced a very sharp image. You can produce some very strong animal portraits in zoos because you can get close to the animals.

• This was shot on 1000 ISO film with the zoom at 70mm.

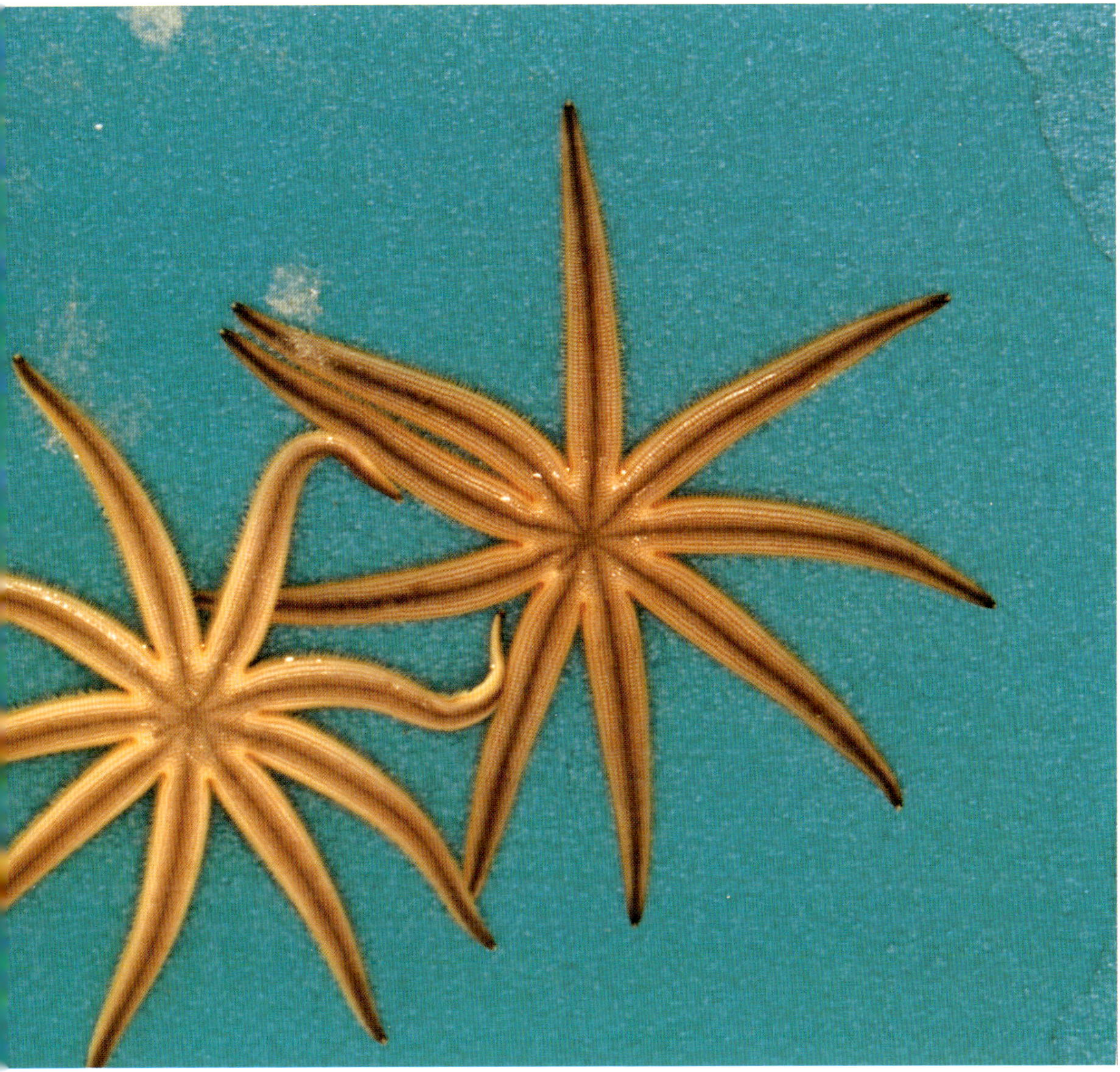

Starfish

I saw these starfish on a wet surf board. Unfortunately, many of the shots I took were out of focus as it is difficult when working close-up, to know if you are too near to the subject. To avoid this problem, I find it helpful to cut a piece of string the length of the minimum distance of the close-up setting on the camera, in this case 1 metre (3 feet). I then stretch it between the lens and the subject so that I can be sure that the pictures I take will be in focus and that I am taking full advantage of the camera's close-up or 'micro' facility. However, this minimum distance varies greatly between cameras, so check your instruction book to find the correct distance for your particular camera.

It is also important to check that you are composing within the close-up framing lines for your camera (see How It Works, page 18).

• Shot on 200 ISO film with the lens on the close-up setting.

CHAPTER FIFTEEN

Landscapes

When people show me their holiday prints and discuss which pictures worked out well and which ones were disappointing, the theme that most often disappoints is the landscapes: all those wonderful views that just didn't come out on the print the way they had looked to the eye.

When we survey a scene our eye darts around picking up all the most attractive features and then reassembles them in the brain's visual memory bank as a perfect landscape picture. Unfortunately, the camera can't do that – it's stuck with whatever we choose to point it at and all too often the feeling of depth and perspective that our eye picked out in the original scene is lost when transferred to our two-dimensional print. One of the main problems is that we try to include too much.

When I look at my favourite classic landscapes by photographers such as Ansel Adams, I am surprised how simple the images are, and yet, in my mind's eye, I see them as grand descriptions of the place. Really good landscape photographs are in fact carefully selected symbols which transmit the essential elements of a scene and pass on the emotion the photographer felt for it. A good landscape photographer will select a dominant feature or a focal point that will hold and arrest the viewer's attention.

The temptation when using a zoom compact is to use the wide-angle setting to 'get it all in', where in fact the tele end of the zoom can be the ideal means to isolate that essential dominant feature. A foreground that leads the eye towards the focal point and a harmonious background makes a classic composition for landscape photography. Sometimes a landscape that features a very strong pattern, for example, paddy fields, can work very well too.

In landscape more than any other area of photography (apart perhaps from architecture, see page 110), light is the magic ingredient. It transforms a scene according to the season, time of day and weather.

Early morning and late afternoon have traditionally been considered the best times of day for photographing landscapes as the early morning or late afternoon sunlight can give a scene more contrast and form (see Light, page 54). But as you can see from the photographs on the following pages, the weather conditions are also critical and a landscape captured during a change in light conditions can often produce the most dramatic of results.

The compact camera is particularly good for photographing landscapes because it enables you to produce high-quality pictures without having to carry masses of equipment with you. However, because the light conditions are often low in the early morning or late afternoon, a light tripod is very useful because your camera will be selecting a slow shutter speed.

In addition, I always carry a small compass with me so that I can assess the lighting possibilities. For example, if I am in a beautiful place in dull light, I look at the compass to ascertain where the sun rises and sets in relation to my proposed picture. I can then plan ahead and return at the best time to photograph the scene.

The best advice I can give when photographing landscapes is not to let your disappointments put you off. It takes time to learn to read different lighting conditions and how to select successful compositions, but you will improve quickly and start producing landscape photographs from those lovely views. Another important piece of advice is to be patient.

Note: if you are cold or wet or hungry, warm clothing and a pack of sandwiches plus a Thermos of coffee are just as important pieces of equipment as the tripod.

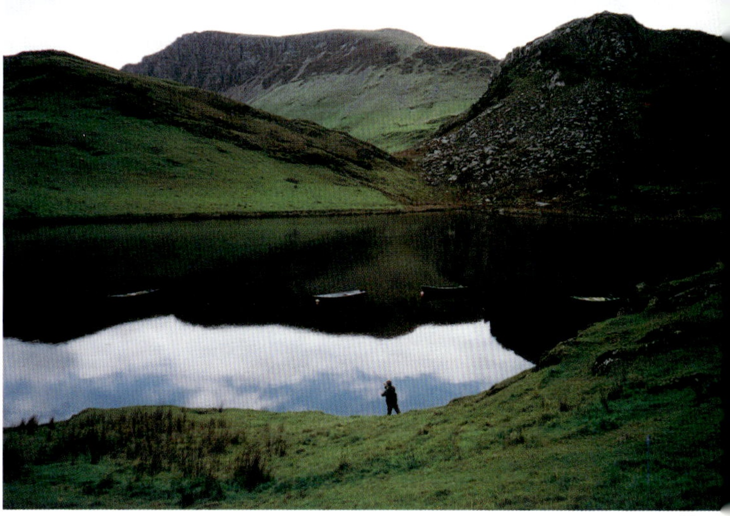

Fisherman

I spotted this little lake in the Snowdonia region of Wales from the road early one morning. On closer inspection, I saw the fly fisherman and made a half-mile walk around the lake so that I could use him as my focal point. The picture would have held little interest without the fisherman as not only does he give a focal point but he also acts as a measure of scale. To take this photograph I sat down, cross-legged and supported the camera with elbows on my knees.

• Shot on 400 ISO film with a 28mm fixed-focal-length camera.

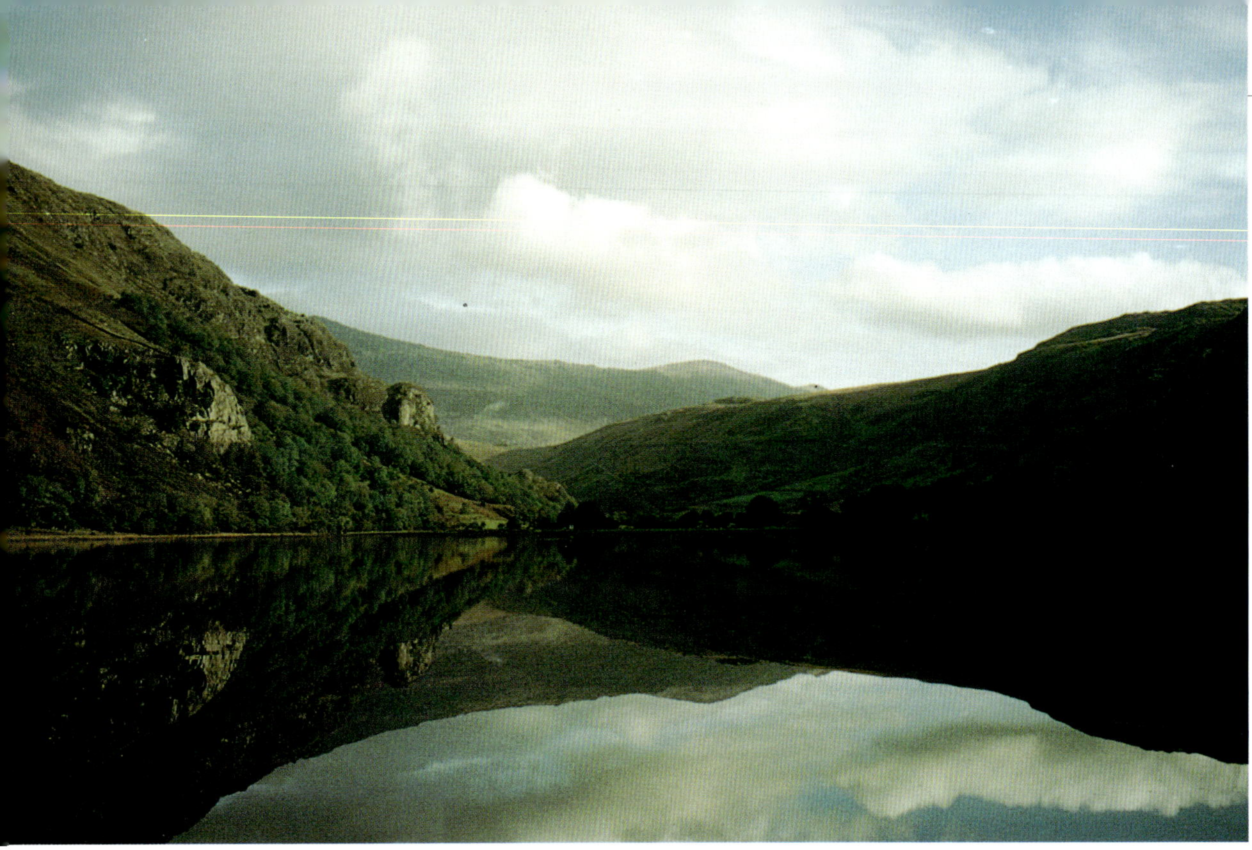

Reflections

This is a picture which has no real focal point, but is effective because of the strong pattern created by the hills and their reflections. The picture was taken in the late afternoon when the sun has warmed up the colours. I had driven past this spot several times but the wind had been blowing. This was the only time that the wind had dropped sufficiently to reveal the reflections.

- Shot on 400 ISO film with a 35mm fixed-focal-length camera.

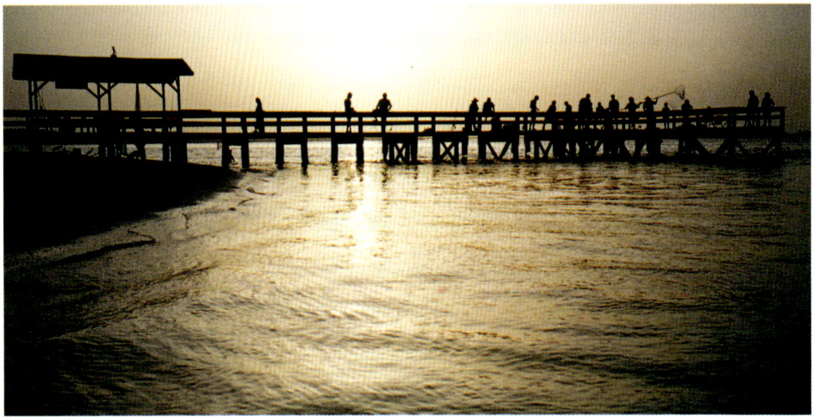

Florida jetty

This is more strictly a seascape but the same principles apply. Shot at sunset, I was attracted to the different shaped silhouettes of the fishermen along the jetty. Of course, the colours of a sunset are hard to resist but you need that extra interest to make a really good picture. I walked out into the sea to obtain this composition.

- Shot on 200 ISO film with a 28mm fixed-focal-length camera.

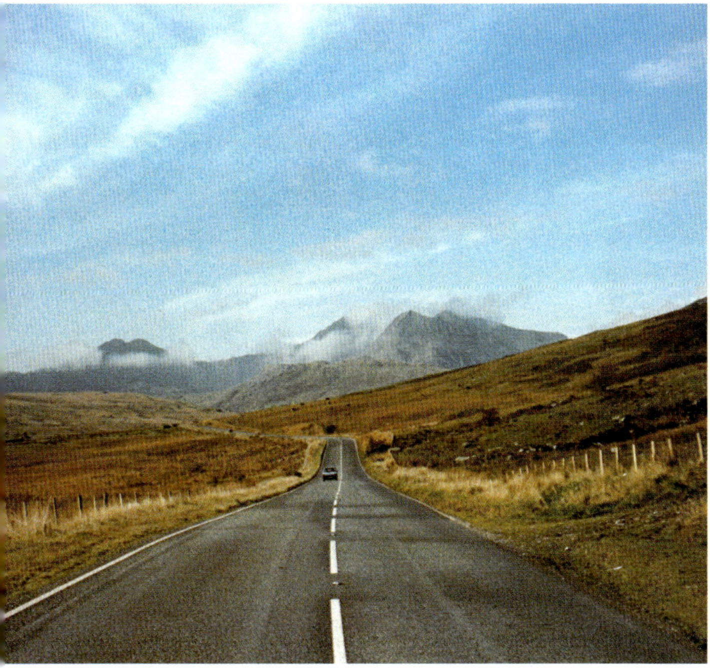

The road

I took this photograph in the late morning, about 11.30 am, on a fine sunny day. The result is a very accurate colour rendering of the Welsh moors. I waited for a car to come along as my focal point. The same view (below) was shot five hours later – this time from the side of the road instead of the centre. The weather conditions had changed dramatically, providing a complete change in the lighting conditions. A heavy rainstorm had just cleared and the sun had burst through a hole in the clouds over the mountains.

These two pictures show how different lighting conditions can dramatically change the appearance of a landscape and how, by using a telephoto instead of a wide-angle lens, you can completely change the perspective and emphasis of the picture.

• The first picture was shot on 400 ISO film with the zoom at 32mm and the second with the zoom at 85mm.

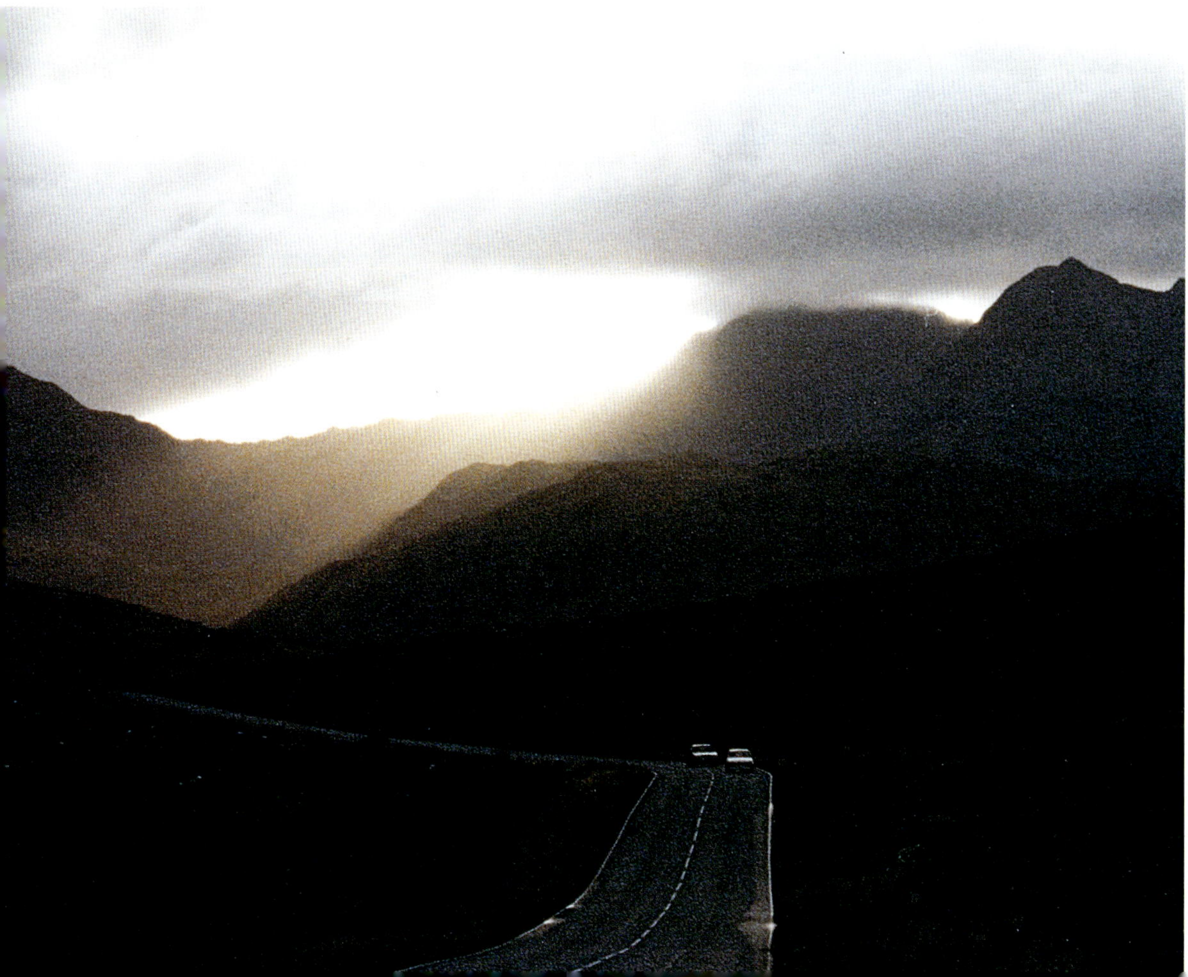

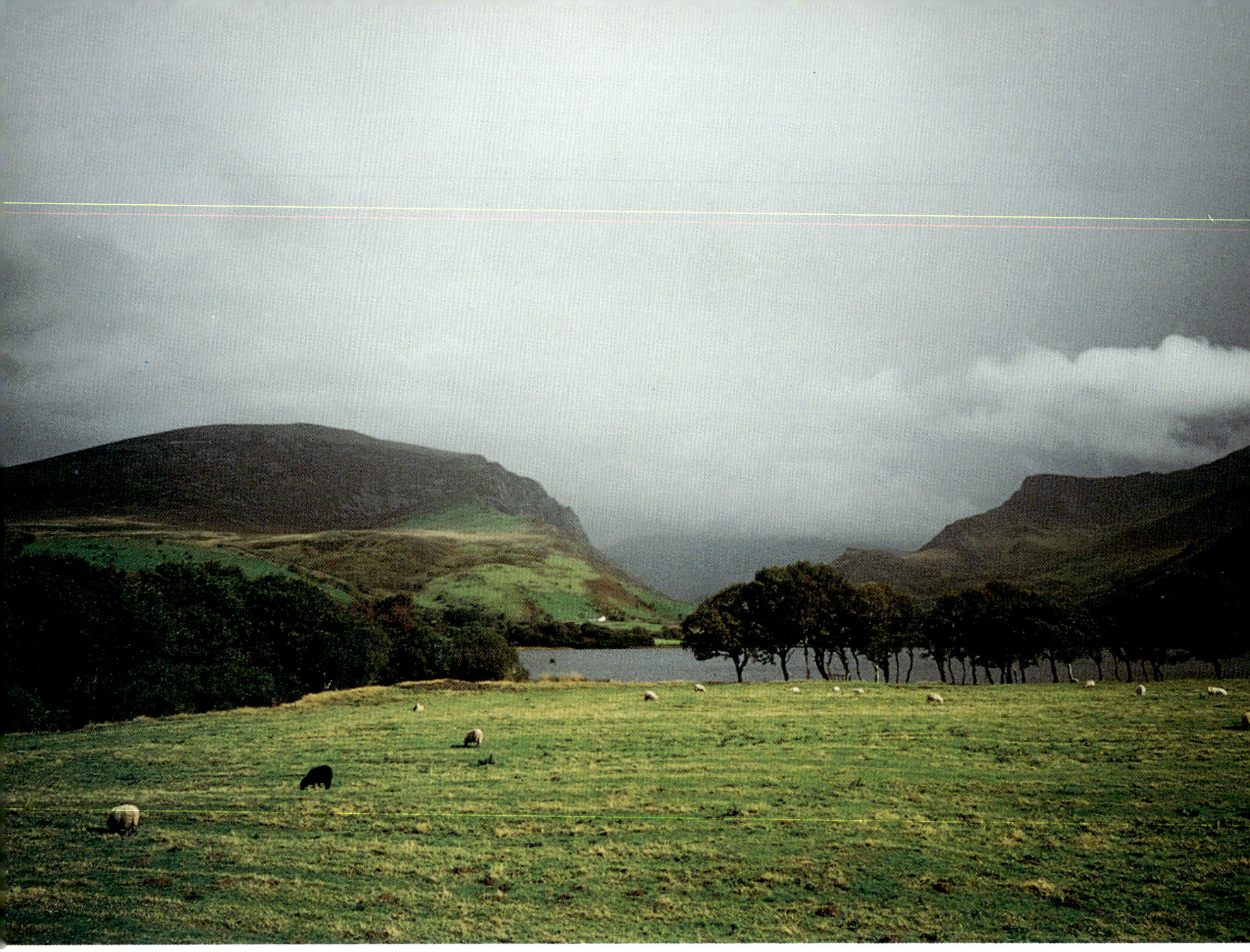

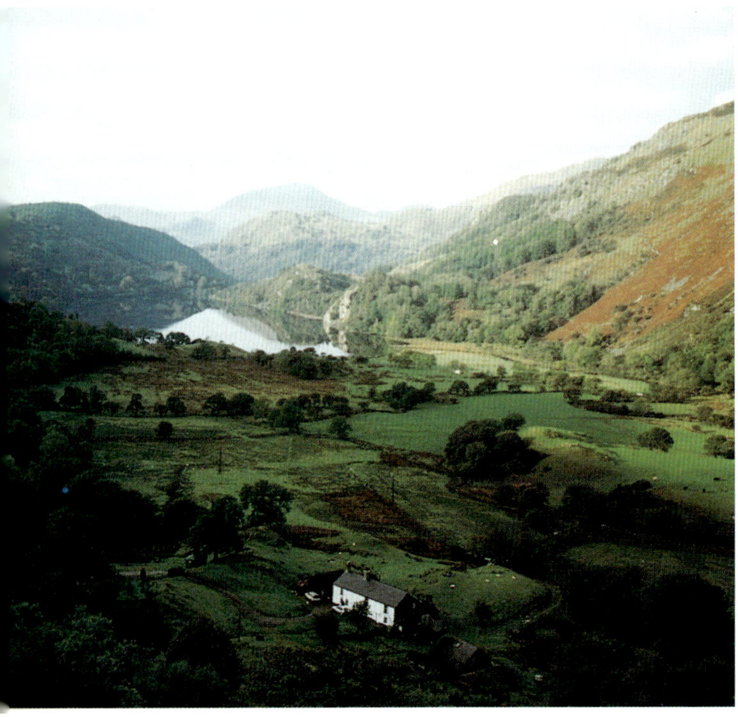

Sheep and hills

This landscape was taken on a very hot stormy day broken up by the sun bursting through every hour or so between the showers. This is the sort of day when personally I don't feel much inclined to take pictures, but if you can be patient and brave you will be rewarded by some fine light for landscapes. The sun has lit the foreground field and highlighted the farmhouse, my focal point, leaving me with a background of dramatic storm clouds.

- Shot on 200 ISO film with the zoom at 40mm.

Welsh valley farm

This picture of a farm in a Welsh valley breaks all the traditional rules of composition. There are two focal points, the farmhouse and the lake. However, it works as a whole because the farmhouse in the foreground leads the eye to the lake, and I just get that feeling of what a lovely place it must be to live in. I shot this picture early in the morning at about 8.30 am and I used the zoom to cut out several distracting features.

- Shot on 400 ISO film with the zoom at 70mm.

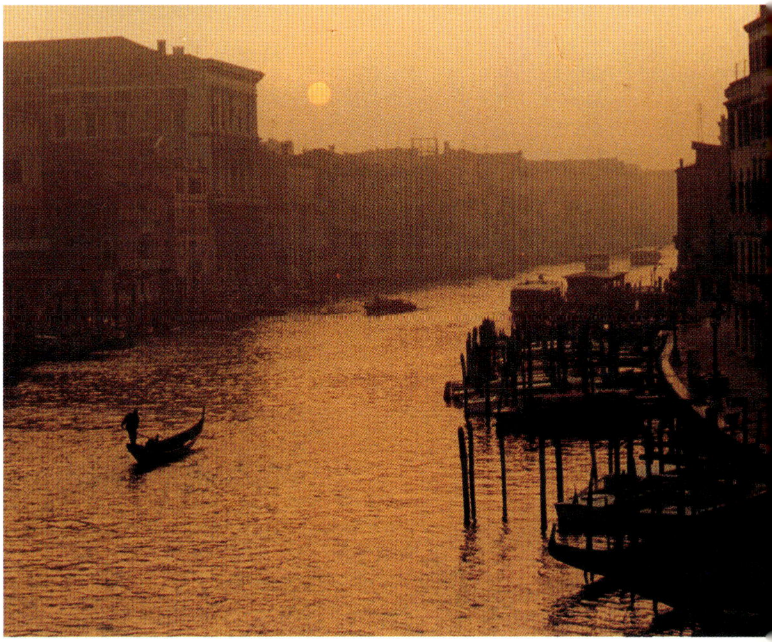

Grand Canal, Venice

I have included city scapes with landscapes because they require the same approach. When I arrive in a new city, I think it is a good idea to buy a good set of postcards which will show you the most famous and picturesque places. You can then go and photograph your own postcards – but more beautifully, of course.

It was from an old postcard that I knew the sun would set over the Grand Canal and that the best camera position would be from the Rialto Bridge. I arrived forty-five minutes before the sunset, which is essential – nothing is worse than trying to 'chase' a sunset through city traffic.

I have always loved the Caneletto paintings of the Grand Canal and, in homage to this great master, I chose an ultra fast film to obtain a grainy and painterly feel to the photograph. I stuck a 81D filter on the lens with Blu-Tack (see Filters, page 62) to increase the colour and supported the camera on my camera bag, which I sat on the bridge. However, I did not have a focal point so I waited for a gondola to appear to 'make' my picture. The zoom setting for this picture was about 70mm, although I shot about twenty exposures on a variety of settings from 32mm to 105mm.

- Shot on 1600 ISO film with the zoom at 70mm.

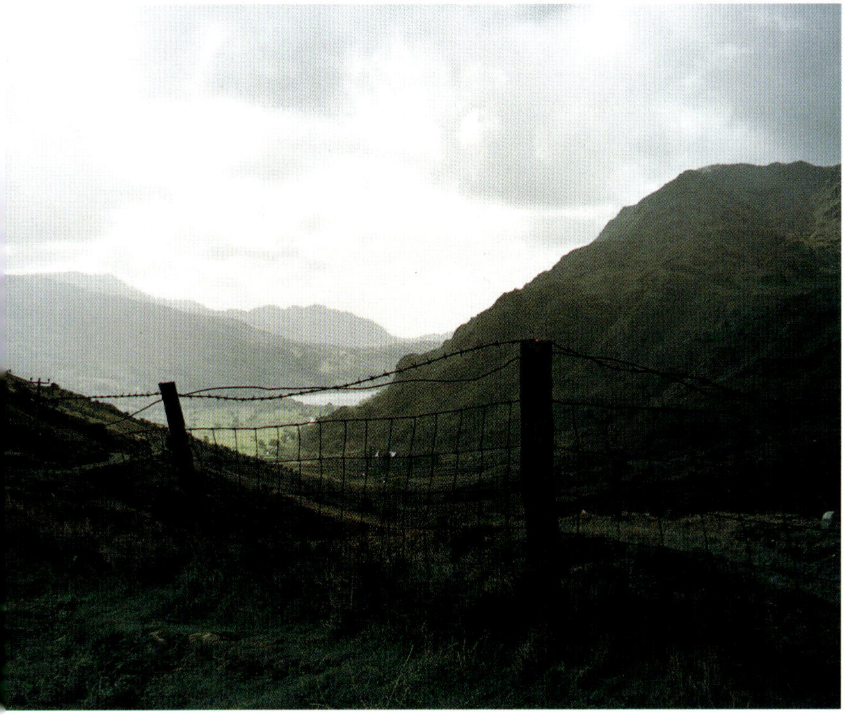

The fence

This is a picture of contrasts and I was attracted to it because it has an emotional quality that I like. The ugly manmade fence was silhouetted against the romantic hills and echoed the movements of the hills. The eye is drawn towards the lake, which served as a focal point for the picture. In fact, I climbed over this fence to photograph the farmhouse opposite. This too was photographed early in the morning at 8 am.

The success of this picture shows that it is always worth looking out for the unusual – not just the traditionally beautiful scenes.

- Shot on 400 ISO film with the zoom at 40mm.

CHAPTER SIXTEEN

Architecture

Lighting is the single most important consideration when photographing buildings. It is not unusual, for example, for a professional photographer to spend days investigating how the light affects a building at different times of the day. It is only after such an examination that he will actually photograph the building in what he considers to be the most flattering light and from the best angle.

Unfortunately, most of us do not have this amount of time to spend photographing a building and our architectural photography will probably be limited to shots of famous buildings taken while on holiday. All too often, you may also find that on the day you choose to visit a special building the sun is in the wrong place or it is pouring with rain. I made a four-day trip to Venice to take some photographs for this book, only to find that St Mark's Cathedral and Tower were covered in scaffolding; in addition, the sun didn't shine for three days.

However, if you do go on a city holiday you would do well to follow the professional's method of working. I'm not suggesting you spend days examining a building but if you could at least spend twenty minutes it would help. Use fifteen minutes to make a reconnaissance of the site: try to assess the lighting conditions, the best angle from which to take the building and, if it is packed with tourists, try to pick a time when there are less people around. Use your remaining five minutes to take the picture. You may find it helpful to carry a compass with you so that you can assess in which direction the light will be and when.

As a general rule, strong crosslight is considered to be the best light for photographing buildings as it brings out their texture and form. This type of light usually occurs in the middle of the morning or afternoon.

Camera angles and perspective are also important when taking architectural shots. If you wish to photograph a tall building, it can be difficult to get far enough away to capture the whole building without holding the camera at an angle. You can create some very dramatic results doing this, but the verticals will be distorted. It is must better to use the zoom lens from a greater distance, if possible, as this will enable you to hold the camera straight and prevent distortion. As with landscapes, it is often a good idea to include something in the photograph which will give an idea of the building's scale.

I hope the following tips and advice will help you to produce better photographs of your favourite buildings.

Art Deco façade

This is the façade of one of Miami Beach's famous Art Deco buildings. I took this picture in the middle of the morning, at 10.30am – the ideal time for photographing buildings. The light was glancing across the front of the hotel bringing out the textures and intricate design motifs. This picture was shot on extremely slow (25 ISO) film in order to produce the ultimate detail and colour saturation. This speed of film is ideal if you want to produce a high-contrast, very sharp print (see Film, page 36), but, unless the lighting conditions are extremely bright, as in Miami, you will need a tripod to cope with the slow shutter speeds. I photographed the building from across the street to get the best angle.

• Shot on 25 ISO film with the zoom at 60mm.

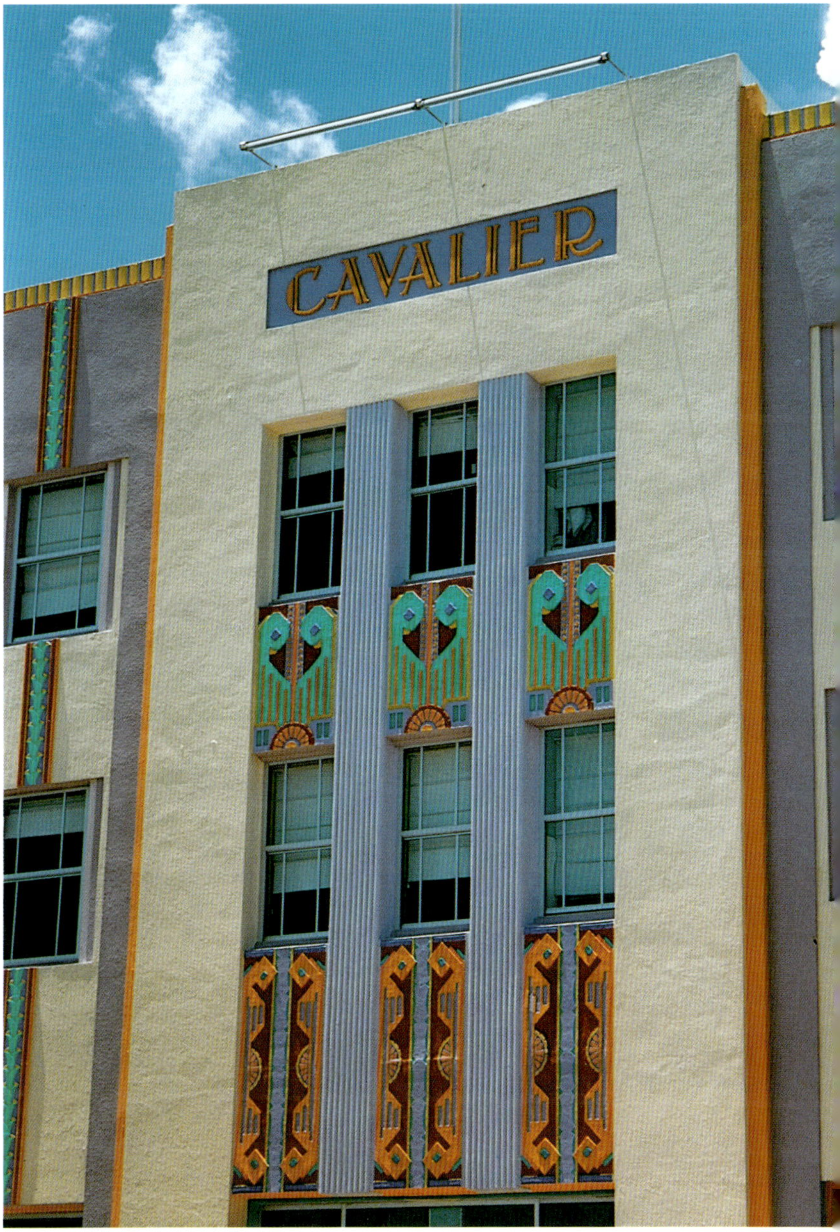

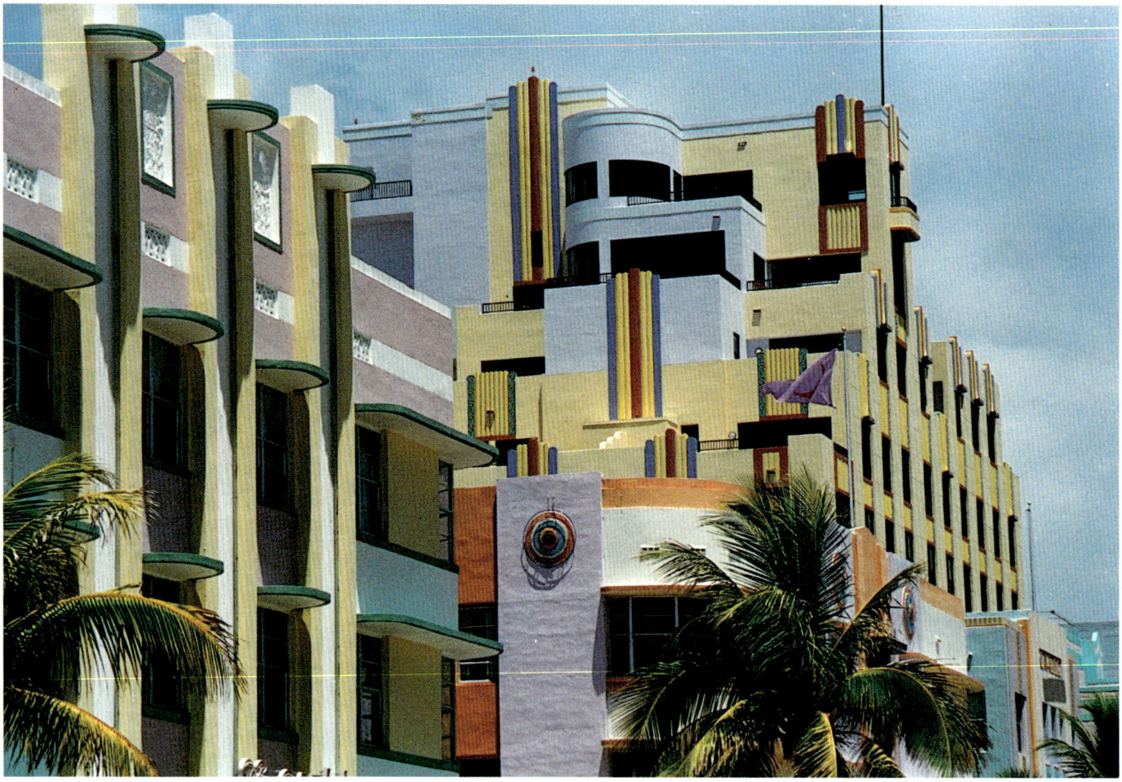

Miami beach style

I shot this picture in an attempt to show the great variety of Art Deco buildings, to convey a sense of the place and the particular Miami Beach style. I wanted to get as much of the buildings in as possible but wanted to avoid the distortion that you get with a wide-angle lens when the verticals appear to be falling away from you. I therefore moved back and was able to hold the camera straight (rather than at an angle) to the buildings. I used the zoom at 115mm and although there was no distortion, the zoom lens has compressed the composition, making the buildings appear closer together than they really are.

• Shot on 100 ISO film with the zoom at 115mm.

Big Ben

The early morning light highlighted the gold leaf on the clock tower very effectively. To capture this, I used the zoom to go in tightly on Big Ben with the foreground shapes acting as a frame. It is a very simple composition but effective because I was bold in my use of the zoom and framed tightly on the subject I wished to emphasize. Zoom lenses are great because they allow you to frame very accurately.

• Shot on 100 ISO film with the zoom at 85mm.

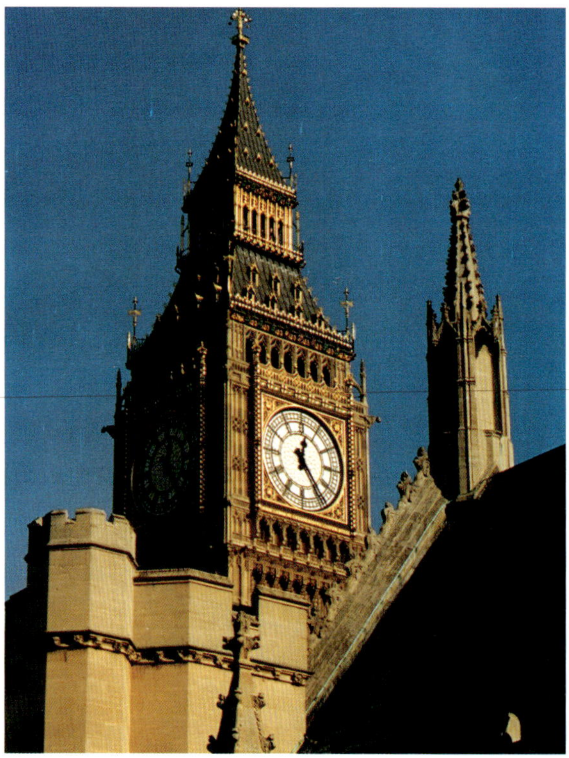

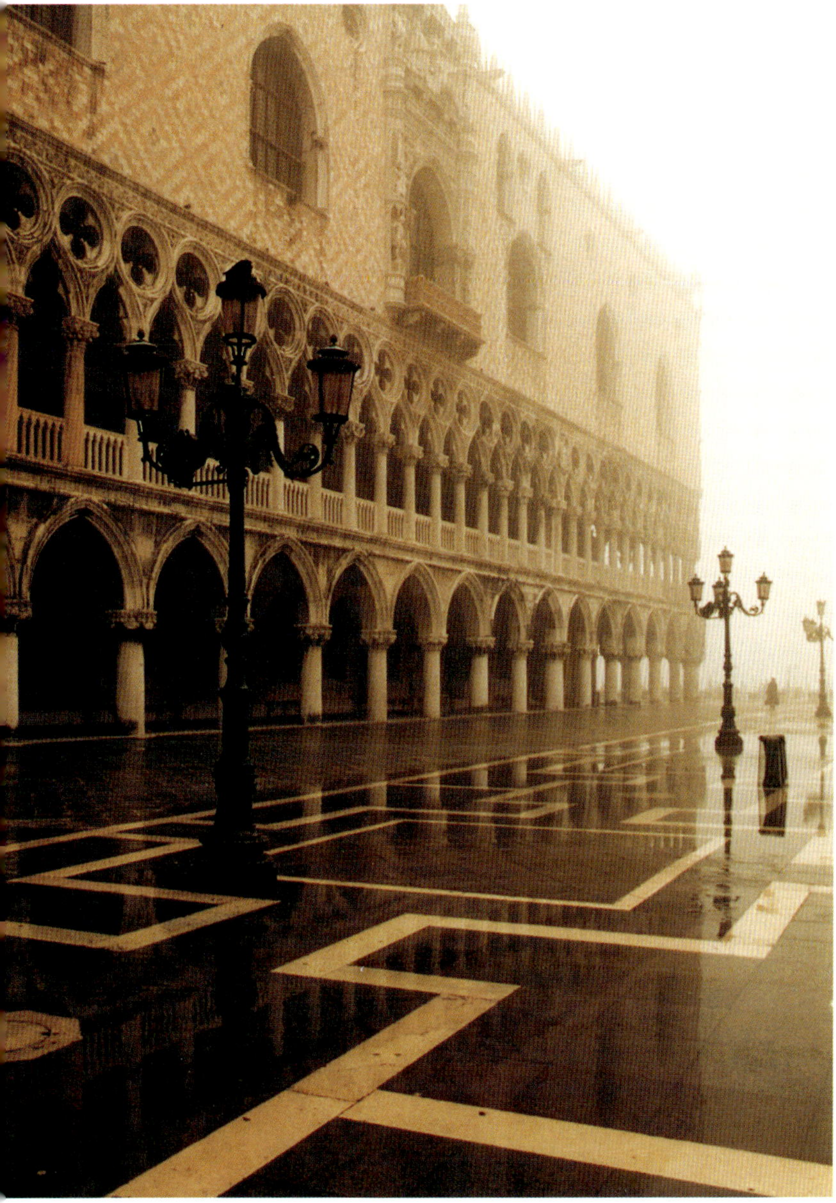

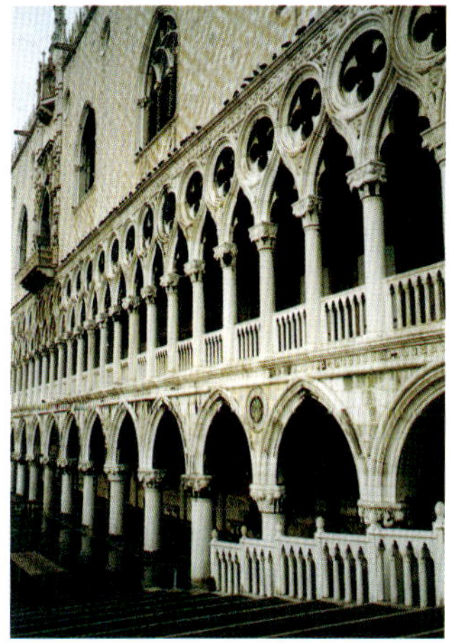

The Duke's Palace, Venice

When I visited Venice, St Mark's was surrounded by scaffolding and it was overcast for most of the time.

Despite the adverse circumstances, I was not deterred and searched around for an interesting shot. I was struck by the arches of the Duke's Palace as the overcast light seemed to enhance their beauty. In fact, because there was no light behind the columns of the arches, they stood out dramatically against the dark background. From my camera angle on the steps, I was also able to keep the camera vertical and so not distort the symmetry of the façade.

• Shot on 400 ISO film with the zoom at 35mm.

The Duke's Palace in the mist

This shot of the Duke's Palace was taken the morning after the one above right. The piazza had flooded during the night as it often does in the autumn and it was foggy. I decided to use the pattern of the paving stones and the reflections as part of my composition. I stuck an 81D filter on the front of the lens to add to the atmosphere by creating a warm light. In late afternoon sunlight, the Palace does in fact look that colour. I was far enough away from the building to hold the camera straight rather than at an angle, so the verticals of the building appear straight. By choosing sections of a building rather than the whole and trying something different, you can turn most things, even dull light and scaffolding, to your advantage.

• Shot on 1000 ISO film with the zoom at 32mm.

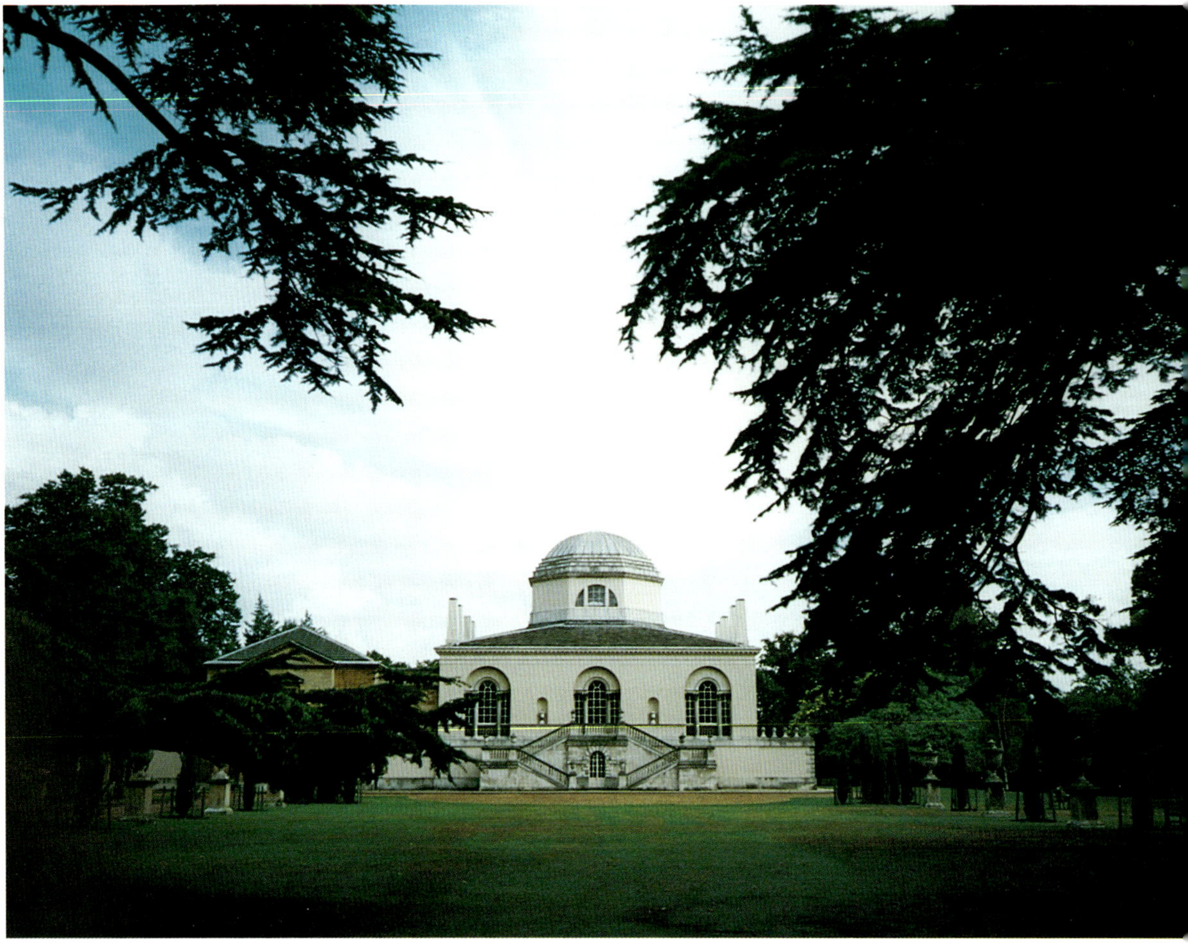

Chiswick House

The gardens and the great trees create a very important visual impact to this view of the north side of Chiswick House, London (above). The scale produced here by framing the villa inside the dark shape of the trees using the 32mm end of the zoom is very different to the scale of the second photograph (right) showing the west side of the house with the zoom at 85mm. Without the trees as a frame and with the inclusion of two people on the seat, the house appears much bigger than it does in the first photograph.
Note also how the house differs in colour due to the fact that the first shot was taken at 10 am and the second just before sunset. Both pictures were shot on 200 ISO film.

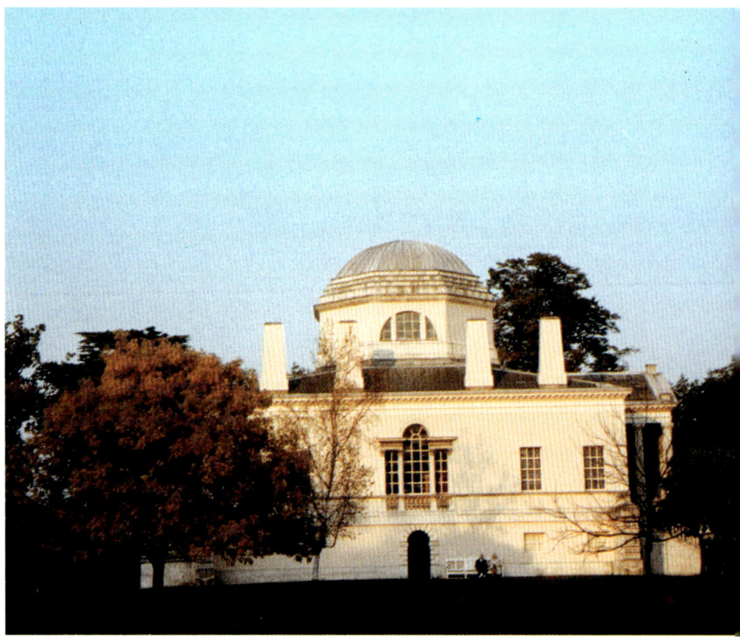

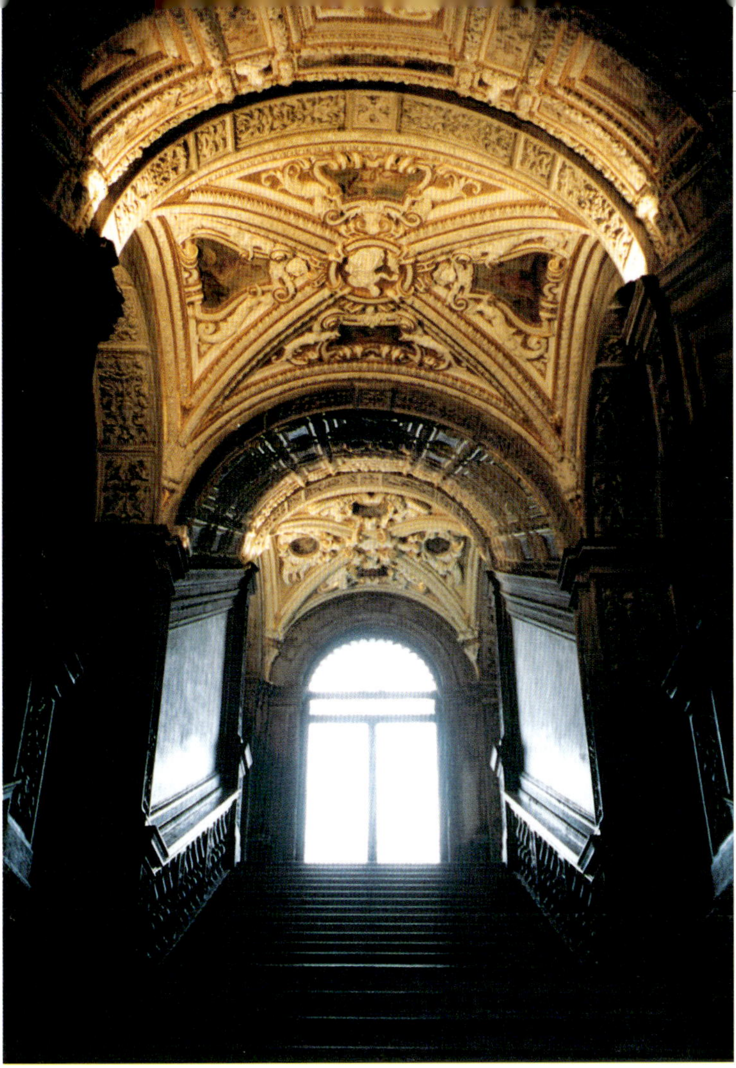

Venice interior

I shot this interior in Venice using a monopod to steady the camera. I set the exposure compensation facility to +1 because the strong light from the window would have caused the camera's meter to underexpose the picture. Where you have interior shots with windows always add extra exposure. If you do not have an exposure compensation facility, use the backlight control.

• Shot on 400 ISO film with the zoom at 28mm.

St Mark's Cathedral

By using the same zoom technique on St Mark's Cathedral as I did when shooting Big Ben (see page 112), I was able to isolate the fresco and the extraordinarily ornate sculptures surrounding it. The zoom allows us to concentrate on the individual features of a great building like this that we wouldn't really be able to see with the naked eye.

• Shot on 400 ISO film with the zoom at 105mm

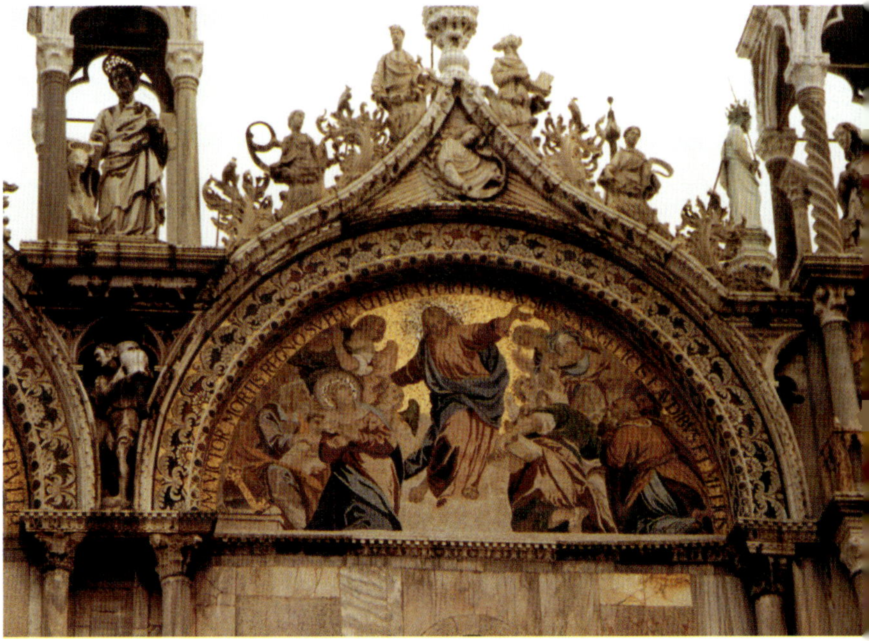

CHAPTER SEVENTEEN

Still Life

Still life is the theme that allows the photographer more control over the subject than any others as you make all the decisions – what props to include and type of background to use; the nature of the composition; the type of lighting; the camera angle; the lens setting (if using a zoom) and the speed of the film.

When assembling a still life, I find it best to choose one object and gradually build up the composition by adding others one by one, being aware at all times of the relationships between the colour and shape of each new object. Equally important to the overall effect is the type of background you choose. Decide whether you want a neutral colour or if you want a colour that blends or contrasts with the still life.

When you have the still life organized, set your camera on a tripod, then choose the best angle and zoom setting. In still life, you want the maximum depth of focus to ensure everything is sharp so the viewer can admire all the fine detail and textures of the objects. It is worth remembering, therefore, that a wide-angle setting gives you more depth of focus and also allows you to 'look into' the picture. I suggest that you set up your first still life picture in the garden or by a big window to allow plenty of daylight through to give you the maximum depth of field. If you are using soft, low lights, which can produce beautiful results, make sure you use a fast or ultra-fast film (400 or 1000 ISO film) to obtain the necessary depth of focus.

Be careful when framing your still life that the focusing brackets are not centred on an object in the background; otherwise the foreground may be out of focus. Line up the focusing brackets on an object in the centre, or ideally one third of the way into the picture to capture maximum depth of focus.

The closer the lens is to the still life the shallower will be the depth of focus, so it's best to start off with still lifes of generous proportions so that you can shoot from about 2 metres (6 feet) away. Finally, don't forget to turn off the auto flash which will otherwise destroy the daylight.

If there is not enough daylight available you may wish to use artificial light, so try the simple lighting set ups illustrated in Artificial Light, page 66.

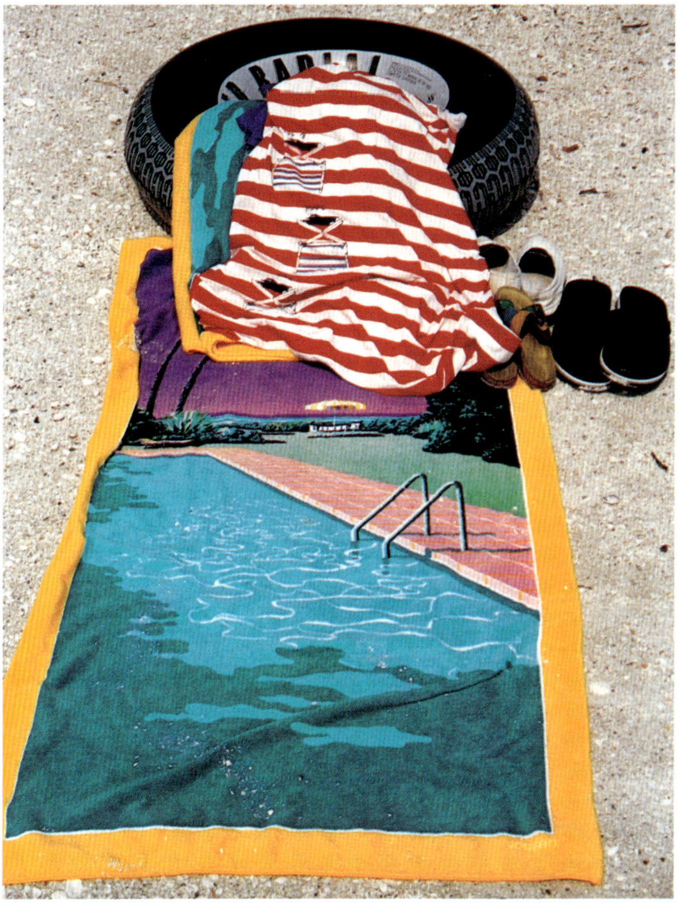

Sanibel beach scene

I became fascinated by the beautiful still-life pictures that people created every day along the beach in Sanibel Island. The 'beachy' objects were all brightly coloured and I had never noticed before how carefully people organize their possessions before they go for a walk or swim.

I particularly like this picture because the towel creates a picture within a picture. I shot this using a fixed-focal-length compact. The wide-angle lens has added an interesting perspective to the picture. Improve your ability to see still-life pictures around you by making a series of still lifes based on a theme that interests you. I find this approach really focuses the mind.

• Shot on 100 ISO film with a 28mm lens.

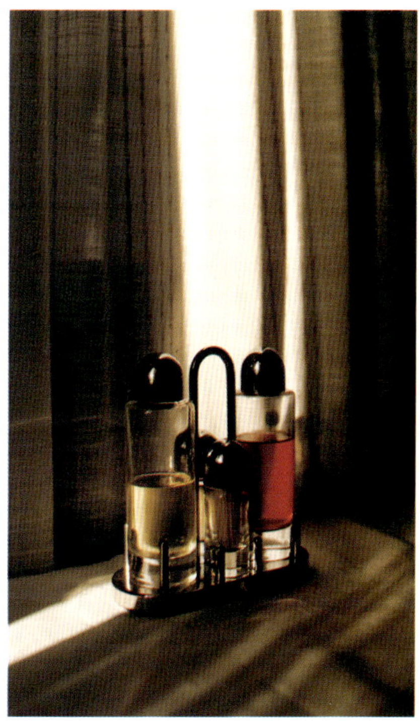

Oil and Vinegar

Although I found this a pleasing object, it was the backlight coming through the slit in the curtain that created the interesting colours and attracted me to take the picture. It is the perfect light for photographing glassware and liquids as it gives the correct exposure for the translucent liquids, but underexposes the solid objects. I used a monopod to steady the camera because of the slow shutter (about 1/8 sec). It is very often the quality of the light falling on a still-life that interests the photographer, so make sure you turn off the auto flash otherwise the picture will be ruined.

• Shot on 200 ISO film with the zoom at 35mm.

Sea horse

I had made several previous attempts to photograph one of these wonderful sea horses (below) that decorate the bows of gondolas in Venice. This one worked because the background is sympathetic to, without detracting from, the sea horse. When you photograph single objects like this, make sure the background is not too busy for the subject. The red that can be seen reflected in the horse comes from the red velvet cushions in the gondola.

• Shot on 400 ISO film with the zoom at 115mm.

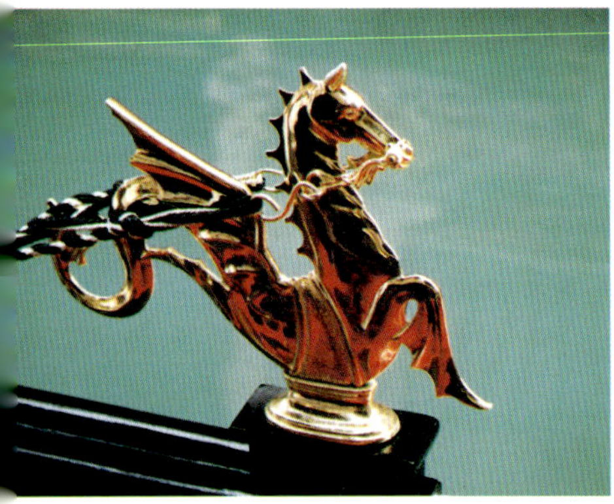

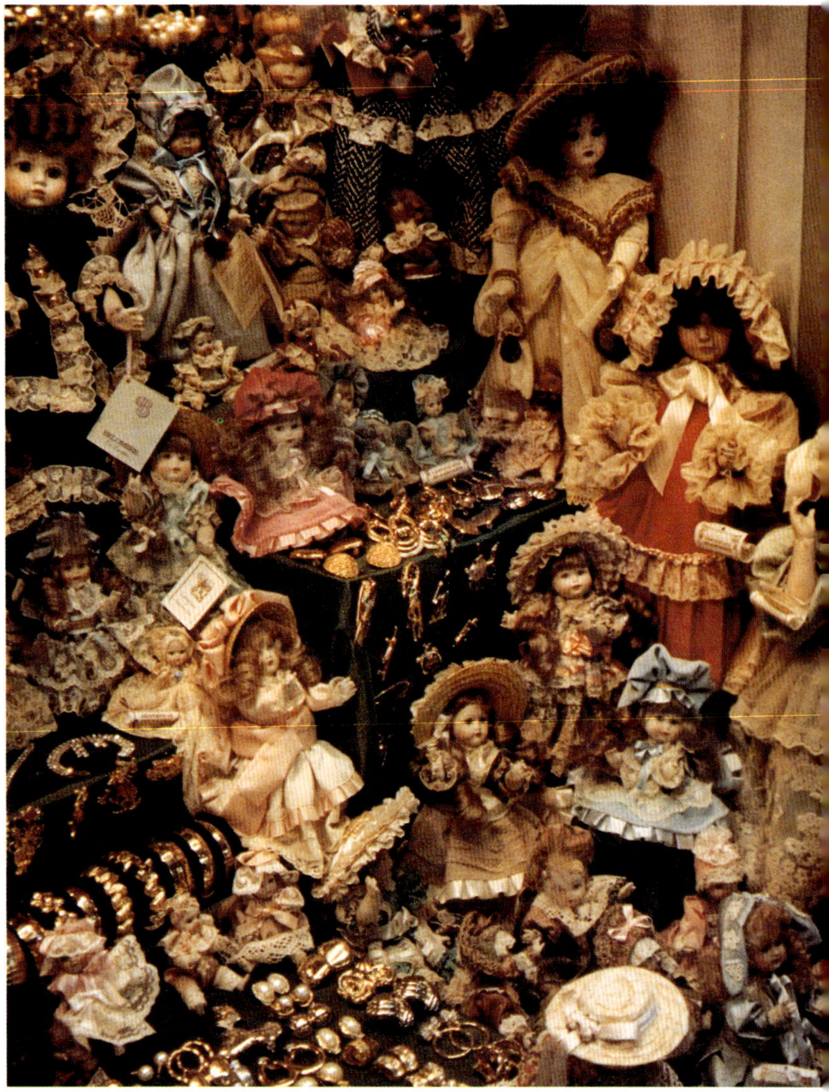

Useful items for making still lifes

- Large boards for attaching backgrounds
- Suitable background materials such as wrapping papers and old fabrics
- Baking foil for reflecting light
- Blu Tack, pegs or tape to attach things to backgrounds
- Large make-up brush for dusting away bits and pieces
- Scissors and pen knife
- Lighter fuel for taking fingerprints off glass and china
- Pastels or spray paints for colouring your own backgrounds
- Found objects such as autumn leaves, cones, shells and pebbles

Venetian dolls

My still-life theme in Venice was shop windows. The problem with this subject was the reflections, so I shot at night with fast film to avoid the problem. The window lighting produced a warm-coloured print.

If you don't like this colour, you can filter the warm colour out (see Using Filters, page 62) but in this case, I found the sepia look of the colour sympathetic with the Victorian style dolls. You could also ask the film processors to try to correct the colour balance.

• Shot on 1000 ISO film with the zoom at 60mm.

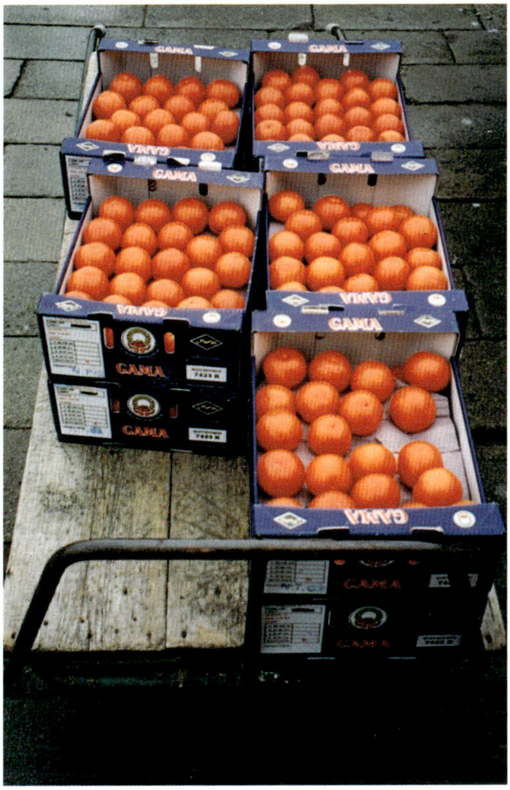

Tomatoes

Markets are a rich source for still-life pictures. I have used this photograph to illustrate how bright colours stand out in low light conditions. I shot these tomatoes on a wet dull day, which would traditionally have been thought too miserable for still-life photography. But if you choose bright colours, such as reds and yellows, and find a dark background to shoot them against, you can produce very effective results. I used a monopod to support the camera to avoid camera shake.

- Shot on 400 ISO film using the zoom at 32mm.

Silver and gold masks

On holiday, I like looking for objects that to me characterize the place, such as this Venetian mask sculpture. The sculpture was actually hidden half-way under a veranda which accounts for the beautiful crosslight. The light was low and as I had no means of supporting the camera, I held my breath and gently squeezed off the shutter. I also took a shot with flash, but this ruined the existing light and lit the shiny gold and silver surface too harshly. It is worth trying to capture a picture in low light conditions even if the camera indicates there is insufficient light, as you may still get an acceptable print.

- Shot on 400 ISO film using the zoom at 35mm.

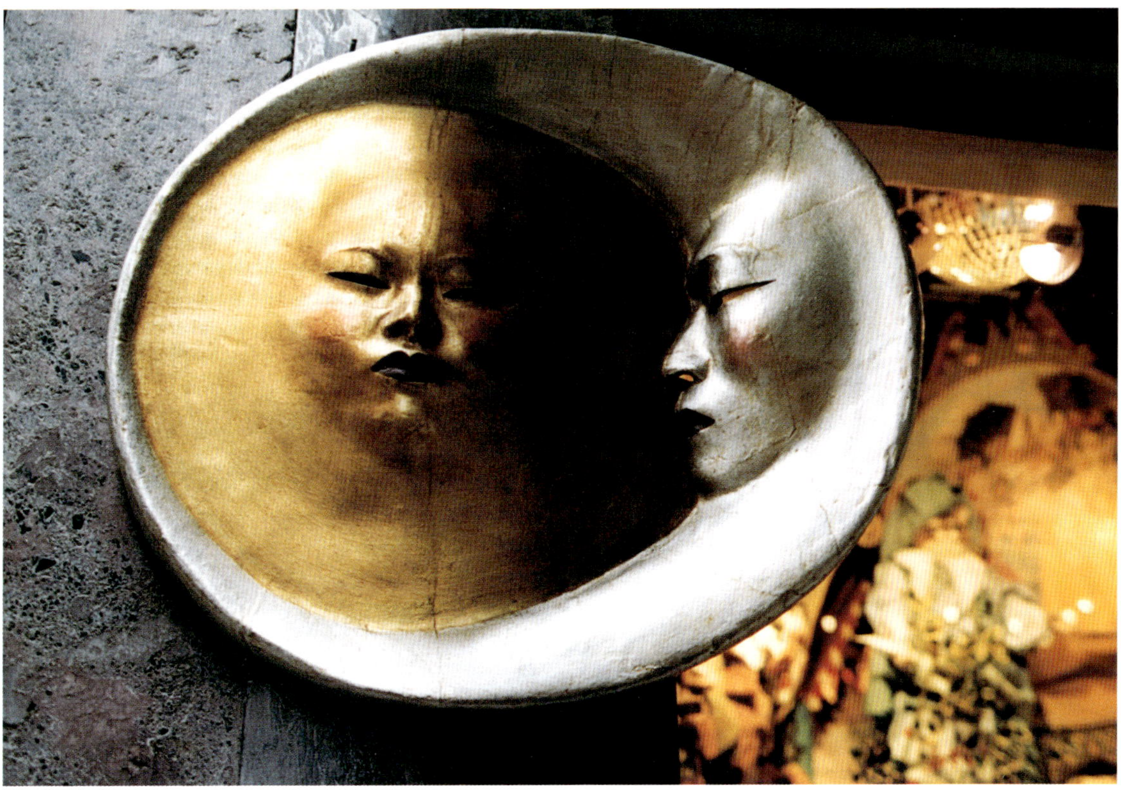

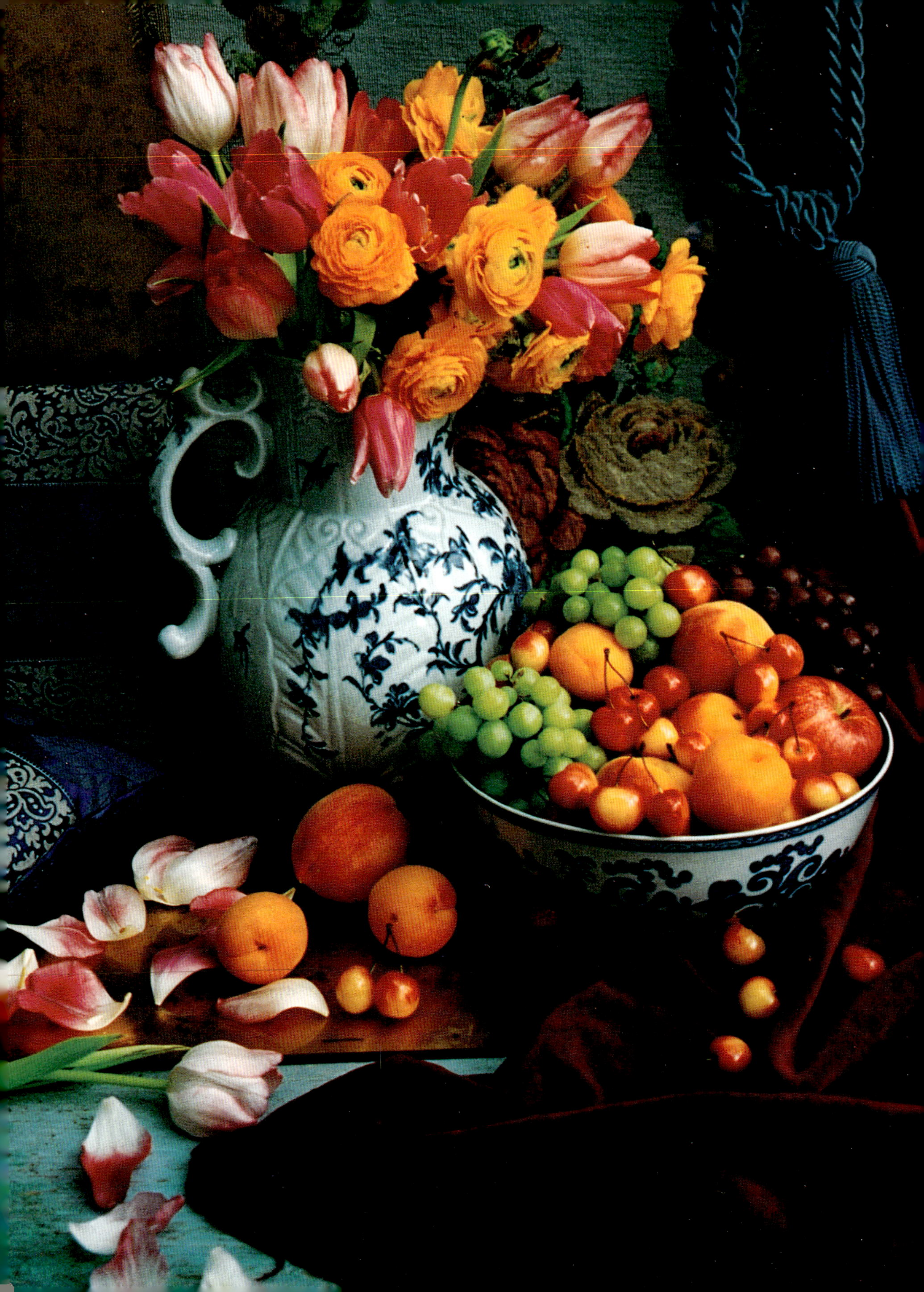

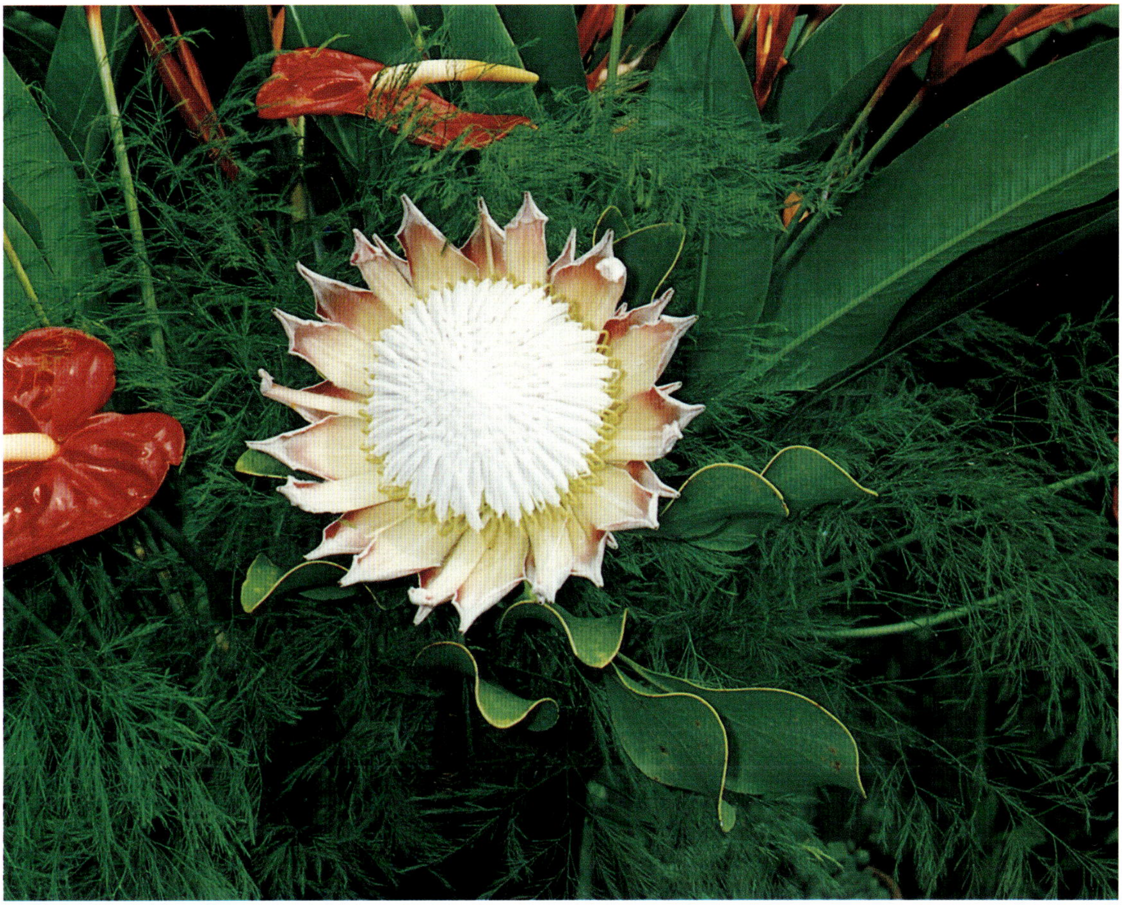

Antique jug and fruit bowl

Setting up your own still-life pictures can be very enjoyable. Try to work out before you arrange the objects the feeling you wish to convey. I had decided to go for a rich antique feel.

The starting point for this still life was the antique jug and fruit bowl, which of course suggested fruits and flowers as the main props. I chose colours that would complement each other and flow down through the picture.

I had positioned the objects on a table next to a large window to give a good crosslight. I then placed a big board behind the arranged objects and experimented with different background fabrics and colour combinations until I found the right one to go with the still life. Finally, I placed a few pieces of fruit and some petals on the table to link the whole thing together.

Experiment with different types of film. Very fast film is grainy and would give the picture a soft 'painterly' quality.

• Shot on 200 ISO film with the zoom at 35mm.

Flowers

The built-in flash on the compact is ideal for this type of picture. It produces a very descriptive, almost shadowless picture, which means you can shoot in bright or dull light and negates the effect of the nature photographer's worst enemy, wind. A sudden gust can move the subject matter at the critical moment to give an out-of-focus image. Flash solves this problem because it freezes movement and holds the subject, in this case the flowers, sharp. It is best to photograph in low light conditions when using flash because in bright light there is a danger of a double image if it is windy. For high definition and saturated colours use a 100 or 200 ISO film.

• Shot on 100 ISO film with the zoom on the close-up setting.

CHAPTER EIGHTEEN

Black and White

Black and White photography has undergone a great revival recently and, although it is not the photographic form normally associated with compacts, there is absolutely no reason why you can't take successful black and white pictures using one – so have a go. The most important skill required is the ability to visualize colours as tones of black and white and this only comes with time and experience. A good way of learning about this process is to turn the colour control button on your television so that the picture appears in black and white. Keep going back and forth between the two so that you can see what density of tone all the colours become.

Some black and white films can be processed in exactly the same way as colour films, which means you can get your black and white film processed through your usual High Street developers. You could take it to a specialist black and white processors, but this can be quite expensive. If you enjoy taking black and white pictures, there is no doubt that the real joy comes from developing and printing your own films as this is what gives you creative control over the final print.

I have been developing and printing my own black and white films for over thirty years and I have never lost the thrill of watching the image appear on the paper immersed in the developer.

Fortunately, home developing and printing has been made simpler and less expensive with the development of resin-coated multi-grade printing papers. Only one box of paper is needed instead of three or four and print washing takes two minutes instead of thirty. The equipment required is available at reasonable prices and the chemicals no longer pollute the whole house for days after printing.

To go into the techniques of developing and printing would take more space than this book allows and in my book *The Art of Black and White Photography* I have examined it in depth. If you are interested and wish to learn more about dark-room technique, there are many good evening classes which deal with this topic.

You can also print colour negatives as black and white prints, which can be fun as well as instructive in showing how colours convert to shades of grey. Kodak produce a paper especially for this purpose called Panalure II. They also make an extremely fast black and white film called TMAX 3200, which is capable (with the appropriate development) of working at a speed of 12,800 ISO. This means you can take photographs without flash in very low light conditions. Although there is no risk of red-eye when using black and white film (for obvious reasons) you can achieve flattering portraits with flash.

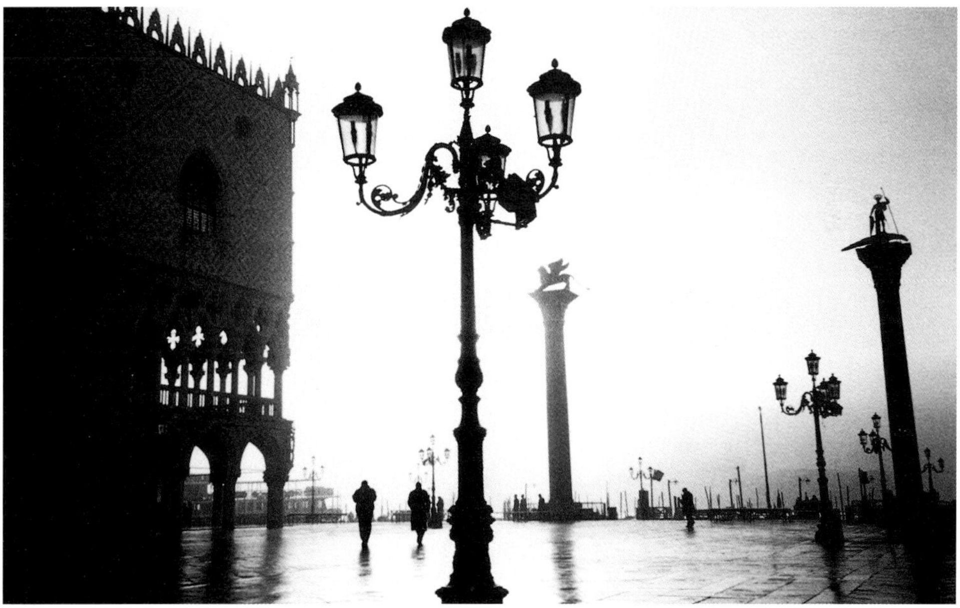

St Mark's Square, Venice

I took this picture early in the morning from St Mark's Square. The strong back lighting from the sun had silhouetted everything, making it a natural black and white picture. I was able to 'hide' the sun behind the lamp post.

It was easy to visualize this scene in black and white and it was just a matter of choosing a camera angle that produced a strong composition.

• Shot on 400 ISO film with the zoom at 35mm. I processed the film myself but had the negative machine printed by a High Street developers.

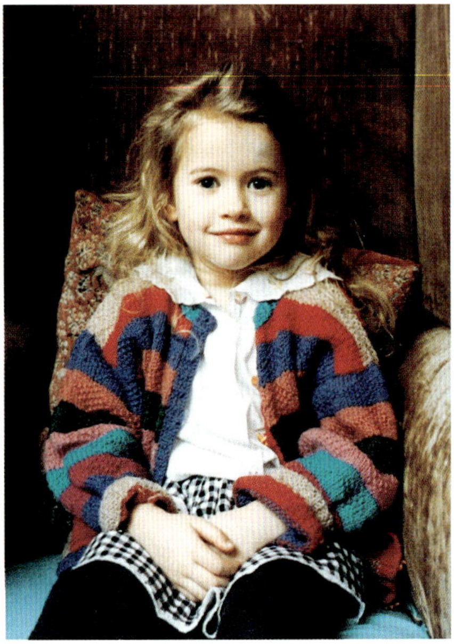

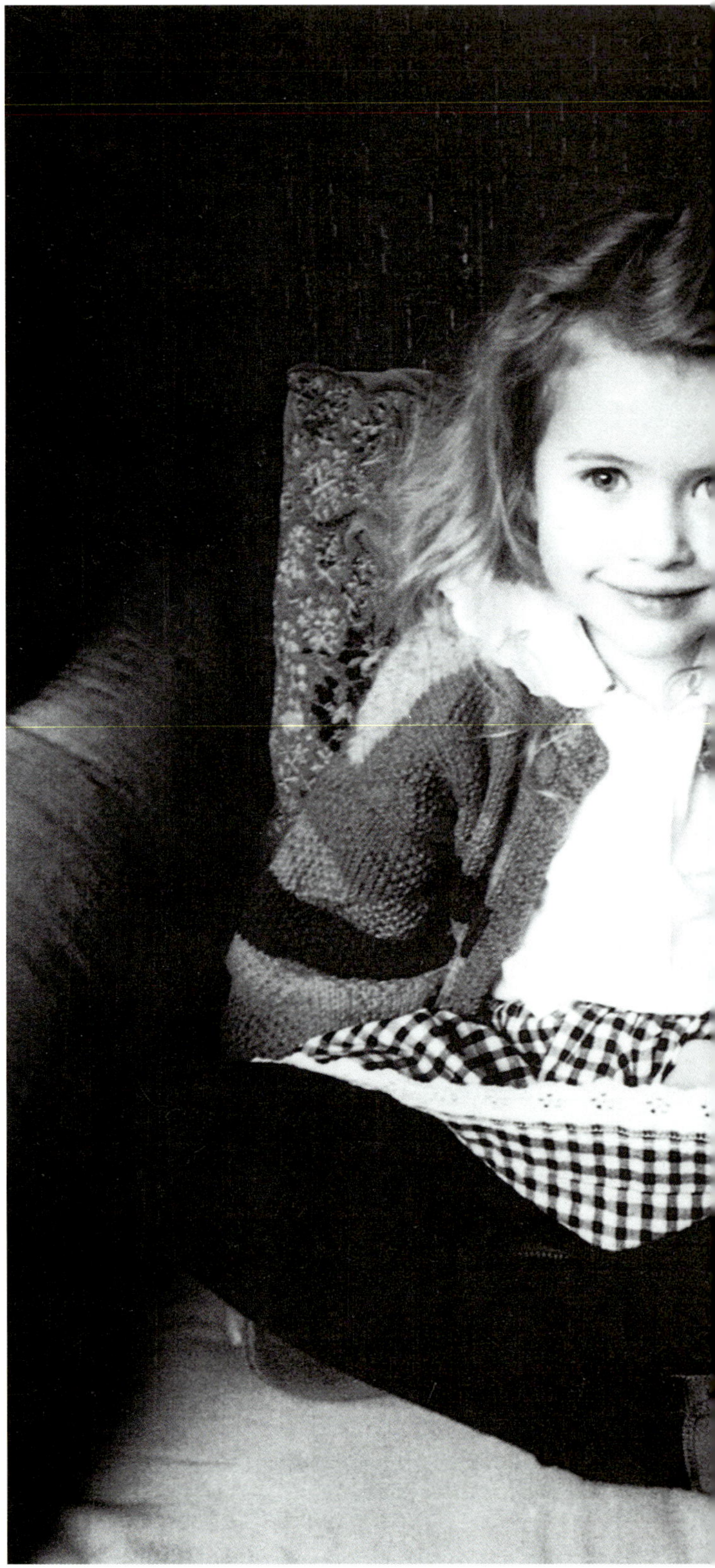

Roxanne

Roxanne shot in colour and black and white. Her cardigan possessed most colours of the rainbow so it is a good way of showing how different colours transpose into black and white. You may find it surprising that the neighbouring red-and-blue stripes convert to almost the same density of grey. When organizing a black and white portrait, I would recommend you choose clothes with less pattern than Roxanne is wearing because the pattern detracts from her lovely little face.

• Shot on 1000 ISO film with the zoom at 45mm.

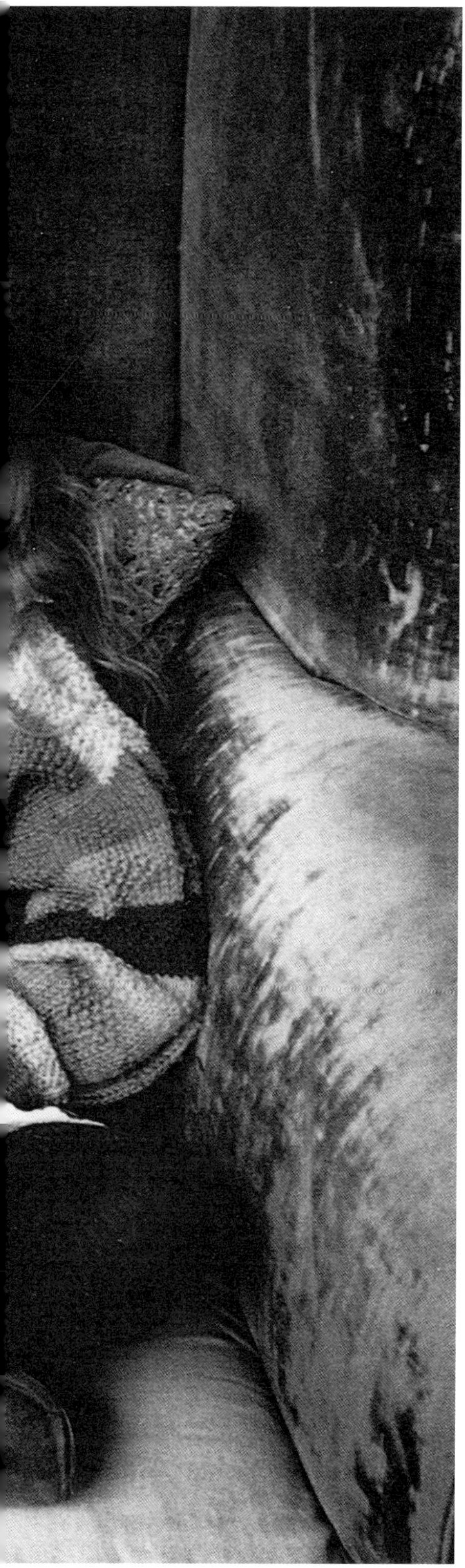

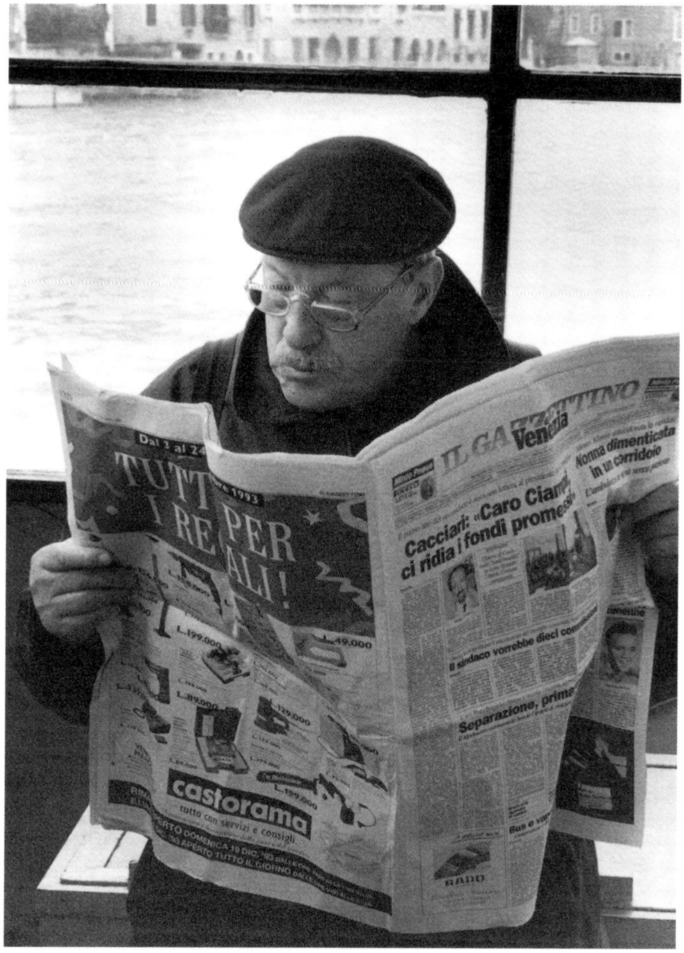

Man wearing beret

A fellow commuter on Venetian public transport. I was attracted to take this picture in black and white by the strong division of tones and its composition: the man's head was framed both by the frame of the window he was sat in front of and by the newspaper he was holding.

- Shot on 3200 ISO film with the zoom at 60mm.

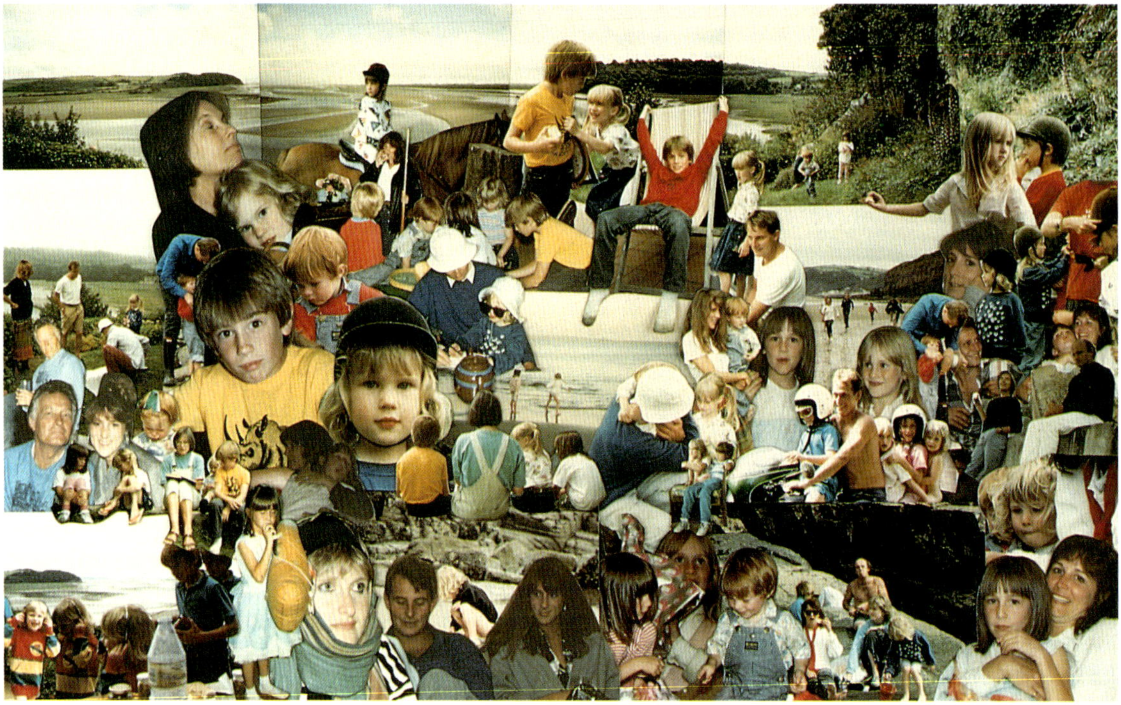

Having taken all your pictures, don't just let the prints gather dust in the back of the drawer. Why not make a collage of them like the one above, which was made by a friend of mine? Take a couple of rolls of film of a specific event such as a wedding or other family celebration and cut up the pictures to create a collage of the day's happenings. Framed it would make a wonderful present.

Acknowledgements

I would like to thank the following people:
Michelle Wu for styling my manuscript - correcting the spelling as she went along; Fiona MacIntyre for her enthusiasm for the project; Cindy Richards, my editor, whose contribution improved my book greatly; Denise Bates for her support; Michelle Garrett for assisting me in editing the pictures; Graeme Harris for encouraging me to undertake this project in the first place; Jerry Goldie for his design and everybody who allowed me to photograph them for the book.

Finally, thank you to Peter and Michelle of West 8 colour laboratory for doing an excellent job on all the processing and printing - machine and hand (tel: 081 968 5606).

For ambitious readers photographic competitions such as Ballantine's Finest International Photography Award are an excellent challenge. For an entry form contact Ballantine's Finest International Photography Award, 26 Fitzroy Square, London WlP 6BT.

Index